THE FATHERS
OF THE CHURCH

A NEW TRANSLATION

VOLUME 86

THE FATHERS OF THE CHURCH

A NEW TRANSLATION

EDITORIAL BOARD

SAINT AUGUSTINE

FOUR ANTI-PELAGIAN WRITINGS:
ON NATURE AND GRACE
ON THE PROCEEDINGS OF PELAGIUS
ON THE PREDESTINATION OF THE SAINTS
ON THE GIFT OF PERSEVERANCE

Translated by

JOHN A. MOURANT
The Pennsylvania State University
University Park, Pennsylvania

and

WILLIAM J. COLLINGE
Mount Saint Mary's College
Emmitsburg, Maryland

With Introductions and Notes by
WILLIAM J. COLLINGE

THE CATHOLIC UNIVERSITY OF AMERICA PRESS
Washington, D.C.

The paper used in this publication meets the minimum re-
quirements of American National Standards for Information
Science—Permanence of Paper for Printed Library materials,
ANSI z39.48-1984.
∞

LIBRARY OF CONGRESS CATALOGING-IN-PUBLICATION DATA
Augustine, Saint, Bishop of Hippo.
    [Selections. English, 1992]
    Four anti-Pelagian writings / Saint Augustine ; translated
by John A. Mourant and William J. Collinge ; with introductions and notes by William J. Collinge.
        p. cm.—(The Fathers of the church ; v. 86)
    Translations from Latin.
    Includes bibliographical references and indexes.
    Contents: On nature and grace—On the proceedings of
Pelagius—On the predestination of the saints—On the gift
of perseverance.
    1. Pelagianism—Controversial literature—Early works to
1800. I. Mourant, John A. (John Arthur), 1903– . II. Collinge, William J., 1947– . III. Title. IV. Series.
BR65.A52E6   1992
273'.5—dc20
91-2972
ISBN 0-8132-0086-5
ISBN 0-8132-1306-1 (pbk)
ISBN-13: 978-0-8132-1306-4 (pbk)

CONTENTS

Preface   vii

Abbreviations   xi

Select Bibliography   xv

On Nature and Grace
   Introduction   3
      Appendix: St. Augustine, *Retractationes* 2.68   21
   On Nature and Grace   22

On the Proceedings of Pelagius
   Introduction   93
      Appendix: St. Augustine, *Retractationes* 2.73   109
   On the Proceedings of Pelagius   111

On the Predestination of the Saints and *On the Gift
of Perseverance*
   Introduction   181
      Appendix: The Letters of Prosper and Hilary
      (*Epp.* 225 and 226)   200
   On the Predestination of the Saints   218
   On the Gift of Perseverance   271

General Index   341

Index of Holy Scripture   347

PREFACE

This volume brings together writings from early and late stages of Augustine's involvement in the Pelagian controversy. The first two books included here date from 415–16 and constitute two of Augustine's most extensive treatments of the actual words of Pelagius. In *On Nature and Grace (De natura et gratia)*, Augustine rebuts the work of Pelagius, *De natura*, which he says first convinced him of the dangers of Pelagius' teaching. In *On the Proceedings of Pelagius (De gestis Pelagii)*, he examines Pelagius' testimony at the Synod of Diospolis in Palestine in 415, in order to minimize, and even turn against Pelagius, the synod's verdict that Pelagius was orthodox. In *On the Predestination of the Saints (De praedestinatione sanctorum)* and *On the Gift of Perseverance (De dono perseverantiae)*, probably written in 428, near the end of Augustine's life, Augustine's opponents are, he admits, not really Pelagians at all. Labeled "Semi-Pelagians" in the sixteenth century, they were monks of Provence, led by John Cassian, who were disturbed by the more extreme consequences of the theology of grace and predestination that Augustine had worked out in his controversy with the Pelagians. Since Augustine's reply to these opponents continues and extends the lines of thought of those of his writings that were directed against Pelagius and his associates, we have seen fit to title this volume, *Four Anti-Pelagian Writings*.

These writings, taken together, afford an occasion to examine both the continuity in Augustine's theology of grace and the developments in it which have been pointed out in recent scholarship and to which we make reference in the introductions to the works in this volume. They also afford insight into the fifth-century status of many theological questions which are still alive today, such as the extent of the damage done to hu-

man nature by sin, the theology of original sin, the effects of
baptism, and the true meaning and scope of God's salvific will.

Our translation is deliberately quite literal. This has the un-
fortunate effect of introducing non-inclusive language into the
English which is not present in the Latin, that is, the use of
"man" for *homo* (indeterminate in Latin as to the gender of its
referent) and the use of the masculine pronoun for indeterminate third singular pronominal reference, normally accomplished by verb endings in Latin. The periphrasis commonly
used in English nowadays to avoid non-inclusive language,
such as pluralization of singular expressions, the use of "he or
she," and the use of "human person" for "man," would, we felt,
be excessively unfaithful to the wording of the Latin text and
lend itself to misinterpretation. But our choice is not an entirely
happy solution to the problem, we realize.

In quoting the Bible, we have sought to be faithful to the text
as Augustine quotes it. We have based our quotations on the
Douai translation of the Latin Vulgate, adapting for deviations
from the Vulgate in Augustine's quotations (he usually quotes
from an Old Latin version) and at times updating the language
of the translation. The edition used is *The Holy Bible* (Baltimore:
John Murphy, 1914).

A word is in order about the nature of the collaboration between the translators of this volume. John Mourant produced
the first draft of all the translations in this volume (except those
of *Letter* 225 and *Letter* 226, which are adapted from the translation of Sister Wilfrid Parsons in Volume 32 of the FOTC). William Collinge thoroughly revised the translations, wrote this
preface, the introductions, and all notes except for references
to Augustine's sources, and compiled the bibliography and in-
dices.

We would like to extend special thanks to Professor Thomas
F. Magner, emeritus of the Pennsylvania State University, who
first arranged for this collaboration and has assisted us
throughout the project. We would also like to thank Dr. Robert
J. Wickenheiser, President of Mount Saint Mary's College, for
President's Pride summer grants to William Collinge in 1987
and 1990 for work on this volume; Professor Robert D. Sider

of Dickinson College, for assistance with the revision of the translations; Professor J. Patout Burns of Washington University, for advice on the introductions; Professor William E. O'Toole of Mount Saint Mary's College, for assistance with the preparation of the final manuscript; and the staff of the Phillips Library at Mount Saint Mary's College, especially Lisa Davis, for help in locating and supplying often recondite research sources.

ABBREVIATIONS

Classical and Patristic Works

Ad Simpl.	Augustine, *Ad Simplicianum de diversis quaestionibus*
Apol.	Orosius, *Liber apologeticus*
C. coll.	Prosper, *Contra collatorem* (Against Cassian)
C. duas epp. Pel.	Augustine, *Contra duas epistolas Pelagianorum*
C. Iul.	Augustine, *Contra Iulianum*
C. Iul. op. impf.	Augustine, *Contra secundum Iuliani responsionem opus imperfectum*
Coll.	Cassian, *Collationes* (Conferences)
Conf.	Augustine, *Confessiones*
Comm. in Ezech.	Jerome, *Commentarii in Hiezechielem*
De bapt. parv.	Augustine, *De baptismo parvulorum*
De corr. et gr.	Augustine, *De correptione et gratia*
De dom. or.	Cyprian, *De dominica oratione*
De dono pers.	Augustine, *De dono perseverantiae*
De Gen. ad litt.	Augustine, *De Genesi ad litteram*
De gest. Pel.	Augustine, *De gestis Pelagii*
De grat. Chr.	Augustine, *De gratia Christi*
De grat. et lib. arb.	Augustine, *De gratia et libero arbitrio*
De haer.	Augustine, *De haeresibus*
De lib. arb.	Augustine, *De libero arbitrio*
De mor. eccl.	Augustine, *De moribus ecclesiae catholicae*
De nat. et gr.	Augustine, *De natura et gratia*
De ord.	Augustine, *De ordine*
De pecc. mer.	Augustine, *De peccatorum meritis et remissione*
De pecc. or.	Augustine, *De peccato originali*
De perf. iust. hom.	Augustine, *De perfectione iustitiae hominis*
De praed. sanct.	Augustine, *De praedestinatione sanctorum*
De princ.	Origen, *De principiis*

De sp. et litt.	Augustine, *De spiritu et littera*
De Trin.	Augustine, *De Trinitate*
Dial. c. Pel.	Jerome, *Dialogus contra Pelagianos*
Ep., Epp.	*Epistola, Epistolae* (Letters)
Exp. ev. sec. Luc.	Ambrose, *Expositio evangelii secundum Lucam*
In Ier.	Jerome, *In Hieremiam*
Nat. Hist.	Pliny, *Naturalis Historia*
Propp. ex Ep. ad Rom.	Augustine, *Expositio quarundam propositionum ex Epistola ad Romanos*
Retr.	Augustine, *Retractationes*

Other Abbreviations

ACW	Ancient Christian Writers. New York/Mahwah, NJ: Paulist, 1946– .
ANF	A Select Library of the Ante-Nicene Fathers of the Christian Church. New York, 1885–87. Grand Rapids: Eerdmans, Reprint 1969.
AS	*Augustinian Studies*. Villanova, PA.
BA	Bibliothèque augustinienne. *Oeuvres de saint Augustin.* Paris: Desclée de Brouwer, 1936– .
BAC	Biblioteca de Autores Cristianos. Madrid, 1946– .
CCSL	Corpus Christianorum Series Latina. Turnhout: Brepols, 1954– .
CSEL	Corpus Scriptorum Ecclesiasticorum Latinorum. Vienna, 1866– .
DB	McKenzie, John L., S.J. *Dictionary of the Bible.* New York: Macmillan, 1965.
DTC	Dictionnaire de théologie catholique. Paris, 1930–50.
FOTC	The Fathers of the Church. Washington, DC: The Catholic University of America Press, 1947– .
Gk	Greek
Hb	Hebrew
JRS	*Journal of Roman Studies*
JTS	*Journal of Theological Studies*
LCC	The Library of Christian Classics. Philadelphia: Westminster, 1953–66.
LXX	Septuagint
NAB	*The New American Bible*
NDT	Komonchak, Joseph A., Mary Collins, and Dermot A. Lane, eds. *The New Dictionary of Theology.* Wilmington, DE: Michael Glazier, 1987.

NJBC	Brown, Raymond E., S.S., Joseph A. Fitzmyer, S.J., and Roland E. Murphy, O.Carm., eds. *The New Jerome Biblical Commentary*. Englewood Cliffs, NJ: Prentice Hall, 1990.
NPNF	A Select Library of the Nicene and Post-Nicene Fathers of the Christian Church. New York and Buffalo, 1886–1900. Reprint 1956.
PG	Migne, J.-P., ed. *Patrologiae Cursus Completus: Series Graeca*. Paris, 1857–66.
PL	Migne, J.-P., ed. *Patrologiae Cursus Completus: Series Latina*. Paris, 1844–65.
PLS	Hamman, Adalbertus, ed. *Patrologiae Cursus Completus: Series Latina, Supplementum*. Paris, 1958–60.
REAug	*Revue des études augustiniennes*. Paris.
RSV	Revised Standard Version
ST	St. Thomas Aquinas, *Summa Theologiae*
TD	Rahner, Karl, and Herbert Vorgrimler. *Theological Dictionary*. New York: Herder and Herder, 1965.
Vg	Vulgate

SELECT BIBLIOGRAPHY

This bibliography includes all sources cited in the introductions to the works contained in this volume. It includes most works cited in the notes to the translations, except some cited on specialized issues. Citations in the introductions and notes are in abbreviated form. Translations are cited only if consulted; for texts and translations of the works translated in this volume, see the conclusions of the introductions to those works.

Patristic Sources: Texts and Translations

Ambrose. *De fuga saeculi.* CSEL 32.2.

———. *Expositio evangelii secundum Lucam.* CSEL 32.4.

Augustine. *Ad Orosium contra Priscillianistas et Origenistas.* PL 42.

———. *Ad Simplicianum de diversis quaestionibus.* CCSL, 44. *To Simplician—On Various Questions* [Book I only]. Tr. John H. S. Burleigh. LCC 6.

———. *Confessiones.* BA 13–14. *Confessions.* Tr. Albert C. Outler. LCC 7.

———. *Contra duas epistolas Pelagianorum.* CSEL 60. *Against Two Letters of the Pelagians.* Tr. Robert E. Wallis. NPNF 5.

———. *Contra Iulianum.* PL 44.

———. *Contra secundum responsionem Iuliani opus imperfectum.* PL 45.

———. *De correptione et gratia.* PL 44. *On Rebuke and Grace.* Tr. Robert E. Wallis. NPNF 5.

———. *De Genesi ad litteram.* CSEL 28. *The Literal Meaning of Genesis.* Tr. John Hammond Taylor, S.J. ACW 41–42.

———. *De gratia Christi et de peccato originali.* CSEL 42. *On the Grace of Christ and Original Sin.* Tr. Peter Holmes. NPNF 5.

———. *De gratia et libero arbitrio.* PL 44. *On Grace and Free Will.* Tr. Robert P. Russell, O.S.A. FOTC 59.

———. *De haeresibus.* PL 42.

———. *De libero arbitrio.* CSEL 74. *The Free Choice of the Will.* Tr. Robert P. Russell, O.S.A. FOTC 59.

———. *De moribus ecclesiae catholicae.* PL 32.

———. *De ordine.* CSEL 63. *Divine Providence and the Problem of Evil.* Tr. Robert P. Russell, O.S.A. FOTC 5.

———. *De peccatorum meritis et remissione et de baptismo parvulorum.*

CSEL 60. *On the Merits and Remission of Sins, and on the Baptism of Infants.* Tr. Peter Holmes. NPNF 5.

————. *De perfectione iustitiae hominis.* CSEL 42. *On Man's Perfection in Righteousness.* Tr. Peter Holmes. NPNF 5.

————. *De spiritu et littera.* CSEL 60. *The Spirit and the Letter.* Tr. John Burnaby. LCC 8.

————. *De Trinitate.* CCSL 50–50A. *On the Trinity.* Tr. Arthur West Haddan. NPNF 3.

————. *Enchiridion.* CCSL 46. *Enchiridion.* Tr. Albert C. Outler. LCC 7

————. *Epistolae.* CSEL 34, 44, 57, 58, 88. *The Letters of Saint Augustine.* Tr. Sister Wilfrid Parsons. FOTC 12, 18, 20, 30, 32. Tr. Robert B. Eno, S.S. FOTC 81.

————. *Expositio quarundam propositionum ex epistola ad Romanos.* PL 35.

————. *Quaestionum in Heptateuchum.* CSEL 28.

————. *Retractationes.* CSEL 36. *The Retractations.* Tr. Sister Mary Inez Bogan, R.S.M. FOTC 60.

Concilia Africae A. 345-A. 525. CCSL 149.

Cyprian. *Ad Quirinum (Testimoniorum libri III).* CSEL 3.1.

————. *De dominica oratione.* CSEL 3.1.

————. *De mortalitate.* CSEL 3.1.

Hilary of Poitiers. *Commentarius in evangelium Matthaei.* CSEL 65.

————. *Tractatus super Psalmos.* CSEL 22.

Jerome. *Adversus Iovinianum.* PL 23.

————. *Commentarii in Hiezechielem.* CCSL 75.

————. *Commentariorum in Matheum libri IV.* CCSL 77.

————. *Dialogus contra Pelagianos.* PL 23. *The Dialogue against the Pelagians.* Tr. John N. Hritzu. FOTC 53.

————. *Epistolae.* CSEL 54–56.

————. *In Hieremiam.* CCSL 74.

John Cassian. *Collationes.* CSEL 13. *The Conferences of John Cassian.* Tr. Edgar C. S. Gibson. NPNF second series, 11.

Lactantius. *Divinae institutiones.* CSEL 19.

Marius Mercator. *Commonitorium super nomine Caelestii.* PL 48.

————. *Liber subnotationum in verba Iuliani.* PL 48.

Orosius. *Commonitorium de errore Priscillianistarum et Origenistarum.* PL 31.

————. *Historiarum adversum paganos libri VII.* CSEL 5. *The Seven Books of History against the Pagans.* Tr. Roy J. Deferrari. FOTC 50.

————. *Liber apologeticus.* CSEL 5.

Pelagius. *Expositiones XIII epistularum Pauli.* Text: Alexander Souter, *Pelagius' Expositions of Thirteen Epistles of St Paul.* Cambridge: Cambridge University Press, 1922, 1926, 1931.

Prosper of Aquitaine. *Chronicon.* PL 51.

————. *De gratia et libero arbitro contra collatorem (Contra collatorem).* PL

51. *On Grace and Free Will against Cassian the Lecturer.* Tr. P. De Letter. ACW 32.

————. *Epistola ad Rufinum.* PL 51. *Letter to Rufinus.* Tr. P. De Letter. ACW 32.

————. *Pro Augustino responsiones ad excerpta Genuensium.* PL 51. *Answer to the Extracts of the Genoese.* Tr. P. De Letter. ACW 32.

Zosimus. *Epistolae.* PL 20.

Modern Sources

Amann, E. "Semi-Pélagiens," DTC 14. 1795–1850.

Anglin, W. S. *Free Will and the Christian Faith.* Oxford, 1990.

Bohlin, Torgny. *Die Theologie des Pelagius und ihre Genesis.* Uppsala: A.-B. Lundequistska, 1957.

Bonner, Gerald. *Augustine and Modern Research on Pelagianism.* The Saint Augustine Lecture 1970 ("Augustine and Pelagianism in the Light of Modern Research"). Villanova, PA: Villanova University Press, 1972.

————. "Les origines africaines de la doctrine augustinienne sur la chute et le péché originel." *Augustinus* (Madrid) 12 (1967) 97–116. Reprinted with original pagination in Bonner, *God's Decree and Man's Destiny.* London: Variorum Reprints, 1987.

————. *St Augustine of Hippo: Life and Controversies.* Philadelphia: Westminster, 1963.

Brown, Peter. *Augustine of Hippo.* Berkeley: University of California Press, 1967.

————. "The Patrons of Pelagius." *Religion and Society in the Age of St Augustine.* London: Faber and Faber, 1972. Pp. 208–26.

————. "Pelagius and his Supporters." *Religion and Society in the Age of St Augustine.* Pp. 183–207.

Burns, J. Patout. "Confessing the Glory of God." In *The Linguistic Turn and Contemporary Theology.* Ed. George Kilcourse. Pp. 133–43. The Catholic Theological Society of America, 1987.

————. *The Development of Augustine's Doctrine of Operative Grace.* Paris: Études Augustiniennes, 1980.

————. "The Interpretation of Romans in the Pelagian Controversy." AS 10 (1979) 43–54.

Chadwick, Owen. "Euladius of Arles." JTS 46 (1945) 200–05.

————. *John Cassian.* 2d ed. Cambridge: Cambridge University Press, 1968.

Chéné, Jean, and Jacques Pintard. *Aux moines d'Adrumète et de Provence.* BA 24. Paris: Desclée de Brouwer, 1962. (Contains text, translation, and notes to *De grat. et lib. arb., De corr. et gr., De praed. sanct., De dono pers.,* and *Epp.* 214–216A, 225–226.)

Collinge, William J. "Christian Community and Christian Understanding: Developments in Augustine's Thought." In *Raising the*

Torch of Good News: Catholic Authority and Dialogue with the World. Ed. Bernard P. Prusak. Pp. 25–40. The Annual Publication of the College Theology Society, Volume 32 (1986). Lanham, MD: The University Press of America, 1988.

Courcelle, Pierre. *Les Confessions de Saint Augustin dans la tradition littéraire*. Paris: Études Augustiniennes, 1963.

Duval, Yves-Marie. "Pélage est-il le censeur inconnu de l'*Adversus Iovinianum* à Rome en 393 ou Du 'Portrait-Robot' de l'hérétique chez S. Jerome." *Revue d'histoire ecclésiastique* 75 (1980) 525–57.

———. La date du *De Natura* de Pélage. REAug 36 (1990) 257–83.

Evans, Robert F. *Four Letters of Pelagius*. New York: Seabury, 1968.

———.. "Pelagius, Fastidius, and the Pseudo-Augustinian *De vita christiana*." JTS, n.s. 13 (1962) 72–98.

———. *Pelagius: Inquiries and Reappraisals*. New York: Seabury, 1968.

———. "Pelagius' Veracity at the Synod of Diospolis." In *Studies in Medieval Culture*. Ed. John R. Sommerfeldt. Pp. 21–30. Kalamazoo: Western Michigan University, 1964.

Ferguson, John. *Pelagius: A Historical and Theological Study*. Cambridge: W. Heffer and Sons, 1956.

Griffe, Elie. *La Gaule chrétienne a l'epoque romaine*. Volume 2, *L'église des Gaules au Ve siecle*. Rev. ed. Paris: Letouzey et Ane, 1966.

Haight, Roger, S.J. *The Experience and Language of Grace*. New York: Paulist, 1979.

Hanson, R. P. C. *Saint Patrick: His Origins and Career*. New York: Oxford University Press, 1968.

Jungmann, Joseph A., S.J. *The Mass of the Roman Rite: Its Origins and Development*. Tr. Francis A. Brunner, C.SS.R. 2 volumes. New York: Benziger Brothers, 1951, 1955.

Kelly, J. N. D. *Jerome: His Life, Writings, and Controversies*. New York: Harper and Row, 1975.

Kondoleon, Theodore J. "Augustine and the Problem of Divine Foreknowledge and Free Will." AS 18 (1987) 165–87.

Lesousky, Sister Mary Alphonsine, O.S.U. *The* De dono perseverantiae *of Saint Augustine*. The Catholic University of America Patristic Studies 91. Washington, D.C.: The Catholic University of America Press, 1956.

Morris, J. R. "Pelagian Literature." JTS, n.s. 16 (1965) 26–60.

Myres, J. N. L. "Pelagius and the End of Roman Rule in Britain." JRS 50 (1960) 21–36.

Pagels, Elaine H. *Adam, Eve, and the Serpent*. New York: Random House, 1988.

Pelikan, Jaroslav. "An Augustinian Dilemma: Augustine's Doctrine of Grace versus Augustine's Doctrine of the Church?" AS 18 (1987) 1–29.

———. *The Christian Tradition: A History of the Development of Doctrine*.

Volume. 1, *The Emergence of the Catholic Tradition* (100–600). Chicago: University of Chicago Press, 1971. Volume 4, *Reformation of Church and Dogma* (1300–1700). Chicago: University of Chicago Press, 1983.

Plinval, Georges de. *Pélage: ses écrits, sa vie et sa reforme.* Lausanne: Payot, 1943.

———— and Jeanne de La Tullaye. *La Crise Pélagienne* I. BA 21. Paris: Desclée de Brouwer, 1966. (Contains texts, with introduction, translation, and notes, of *De Nat. et gr., De gest. Pel.*, and two other works.)

Quasten, Johannes. Patrology. Volume 2, *The Ante-Nicene Literature after Irenaeus.* Westminster, MD: The Newman Press, 1953. Volume 3, *The Golden Age of Greek Patristic Literature from the Council of Nicaea to the Council of Chalcedon.* Westminster, MD: Newman Press, 1960. Volume 4, *The Golden Age of Latin Patristic Literature from the Council of Nicaea to the Council of Chalcedon.* Ed. by Angelo di Berardino. Tr. by Placid Solari. Westminster, MD: Christian Classics, 1986. (Quasten contributed only an introduction to this volume, which was written by eight authors. The section on Augustine is by Agostino Trapè [pp. 342–462]; that on Pelagius is by Vittorino Grossi [pp. 465–486].)

Rees, B. R. *Pelagius: A Reluctant Heretic.* Woodbridge, Suffolk: The Boydell Press, 1988.

Sage, Athanase. "*Voluntas praeparatur a Deo.*" REAug 10 (1964) 1–20.

TeSelle, Eugene. *Augustine the Theologian.* New York: Herder and Herder, 1970.

————. "Rufinus the Syrian, Caelestius, Pelagius: Explorations in the Pre-History of the Pelagian Controversy." AS 3 (1972) 61–95.

Valero, Juan B. *Las bases antropologicas de Pelagio en su tratado de las Expositiones.* Madrid: Universidad Pontificia Comillas de Madrid, 1980.

Van der Meer, F. *Augustine the Bishop: Religion and Society at the Dawn of the Middle Ages.* Tr. Brian Battershaw and G. R. Lamb. New York: Harper Torchbooks, 1965.

Wermelinger, Otto. *Röm und Pelagius: Die theologische Position der römischen Bischöfe im pelagianischen Streit in den Jähren 411–432.* Päpste und Papsttum, volume 7. Stuttgart: Anton Hiersemann, 1975.

ON NATURE AND GRACE

INTRODUCTION

On Nature and Grace (De natura et gratia) represents, in Augustine's own account, a turning point in his attitude toward Pelagius. Writing, together with Alypius, to Paulinus of Nola in 417, he speaks of Pelagius as follows:

> The love we have for him now is different from the love we had for him formerly; then we loved him as one who seemed to be of the true faith, whereas we now love him in order that, by the mercy of God, he may be set free from those antagonistic views which he is said to hold against the grace of God. It was not easy to believe this about him, when the rumor began to be circulated some time ago—for rumor is usually a liar—but what brought it home to us and made us believe it was a certain book of his which aims to set forth theories intended to destroy and remove from faithful hearts any belief in the grace of God bestowed on the human race through the one Mediator of God and men, Christ Jesus.[1]

(2) This book was the *De natura (On Nature)* of Pelagius. It had been sent to him by Timasius and James, whom he describes as "young men of very good birth, well-versed in the liberal arts," who, at the urging of Pelagius, "gave up their worldly prospects . . . and devoted themselves to the service of God."[2]

(3) To see Pelagius as a figure who could inspire such young men as Timasius and James to an ascetic life is a more promising starting point for understanding him than is his image, de-

---

1. *Ep.* 186.1, tr. Sr. Wilfrid Parsons, FOTC 30.
2. *Ep.* 179.2. Augustine also speaks of Timasius and James, in more or less the same terms, in *Ep.* 177.6 and *De gest. Pel.* 23.47. The article by Yves-Marie Duval, "La date du *De Natura* de Pélage," REAug 36 (1990) 257–83, came to my attention only as the volume was in galleys. This article presents a strong case for a date of ca. 406 for *De natura,* rather than the conventional date of 414 accepted here, and also challenges some positions assumed on related issues in this volume. In light of this article, I have made slight revisions in the text and notes, but I have not been able to give it the full consideration it merits.

veloped in later polemics, as a heresiarch. For "Pelagianism," as it comes later to be called, is first and foremost not a doctrine about grace and human nature but an ascetic and reforming movement, whose aim was to call Christians back to a life of gospel perfection. This introduction will trace the origin of the Pelagian movement and the controversy surrounding it up to 414, the commonly accepted date of the *De natura*. The subsequent course of the Pelagian controversy, as it relates to the later works included in this volume, will be traced in the Introductions to those works.

Pelagius

(4) "Perhaps most of the controversial issues exercising the Western Church in the latter two decades of the fourth and the first two decades of the fifth centuries were related to one large question: the nature of Christian perfection."[3] It was an issue which preoccupied Augustine in his earliest years as a Christian, as seen in the intellectual program set out in his Cassiciacum dialogues,[4] and which, although in a different form each time, stood at the center of his three great controversies—with the Manichaeans, the Donatists, and the Pelagians.[5]

(5) The issue became prominent against the background of the Christian empire in the late fourth century. The political and moral corruption of the state, the scandalous behavior of Christian clergy, and the half-Christian, half-pagan practices of many ordinary Christians are well documented in Christian writers of the period. To be a Christian was no longer a heroic act of social defiance but in many cases a consequence of conformity or desire for advancement.[6] "The conventional 'good man' of pagan Rome had become the conventional 'good Christian'."[7] In an attempt to recover an earlier ideal of "heroic spirituality" in such a climate, many Christians undertook mo-

---

3. Evans, *Pelagius*, 28–29.   4. See *De ord.* 2.8.25–9.26.
5. Some of the developments in Augustine's thought on this question are traced in Collinge, "Christian Community and Christian Understanding."
6. On the condition of the Church, see Ferguson, *Pelagius*, 18–22.
7. Brown, *Augustine of Hippo*, 346.

nastic life, either in solitude in desert areas or in urban communities, such as those Augustine describes in *De moribus ecclesiae catholicae*.[8]

(6) Ascetic ideals were by no means confined to the monasteries, but were also influential in such circles as the Christian Roman aristocracy, exemplified by the devout women Melania the younger, Demetrias the virgin, and her grandmother Proba. Late fourth century Rome was "a world where cultivated Christian laymen exercised more influence than at any time previously."[9] There were monastic communities at Rome[10], and a flourishing party of Manichaeans,[11] but these Christians were determined to remain firmly orthodox, and felt bound to retain something of their position in the social and political world.[12] In this environment, Jerome flourished briefly as a "guru"[13] in the 380s, and into this environment, some time in the 380s or 390s, came Pelagius.

(7) "Pelagius remains, after all our seeking, a somewhat shadowy figure."[14] He was, in all likelihood, from Britain,[15] and was probably born in the early 350s. Was he a monk? "This apparently simple and insignificant question has sharply divided scholars."[16] Augustine, in *De gest. Pel.*, refers to him as a "monk" and quotes the synod of Diospolis as doing the same;[17] likewise, Marius Mercator calls him a "monk."[18] Jerome, in his Letter 50, to Domnio, dated 393–94, attacks a certain "monk," who had criticized his treatise, *Adversus Jovinianum*, and many, though

8. *De mor. eccl.* 33.70–73.   9. Brown, *Augustine of Hippo*, 341.
10. *De mor. eccl.* 33.70.   11. *Conf.* 5.10.18.
12. On the social background of early Pelagianism, see Brown, "Pelagius and his Supporters," and "The Patrons of Pelagius." The argument put forward by J. H. Myres ("Pelagius and the End of Roman Rule in Britain") and J. R. Morris ("Pelagian Literature"), that Pelagianism is to be understood not only as a religious movement but also as a social movement (reflecting especially the situation of Roman Britain) protesting against the oppressive conditions of the late Empire, has not in general found favor among scholars. See Rees, *Pelagius*, 111–14.
13. Rees, *Pelagius*, 19.
14. Bonner, *Augustine and Pelagianism*, 31.
15. Many contemporary sources speak of him as a Briton; these are marshalled in Ferguson, *Pelagius*, 39–40.
16. Hanson, *Saint Patrick*, 144.   17. *De gest. Pel.* 14.36, 19.43.
18. *Liber subnotationum in verba Iuliani*, praef., 2.

not all, modern authorities have identified this figure with Pelagius.[19] On the other hand, *De lege divina*, generally regarded as an authentic work of Pelagius,[20] seems to disclaim the title: "I want you to be a Christian, not to be called a monk, and to possess the virtue of your proper praise rather than an alien name, which is vainly attached by the Latins to those living in society, although by the Greeks it is legitimately applied to those living in solitude."[21] Pelagius was not in holy orders; both Zosimus and Orosius refer to him as a layman *(laicus)*.[22] We may reasonably follow Hanson's judgment: "It seems entirely probable that, while Pelagius joined no monastic community, he did adopt a monastic or ascetic kind of regimen in his own life, at a time when in the West the distinction between this kind of individual, unorganized monasticism and fully developed coenobitic monasticism had not yet become fully defined."[23] Despite some aspersions in the later polemics of Jerome and Orosius, Pelagius' character seems to have been beyond reproach. He was a friend of Paulinus of Nola, and Augustine speaks of his "great reputation,"[24] elsewhere calling him "so worthy a man and so good a Christian."[25] Even here in *De nat. et gr.*, he prefers to see Pelagius' errors as the result of an excess of zeal (1.1).

(8) Pelagius' zeal was directed in the service of Christian asceticism, and especially in defense of the idea that Christian perfection was possible—indeed, it was for this that human nature was created—if only sufficient effort were made. While Pelagianism has at times been presented as a sort of humanism, in contrast to the position of Augustine, it is important to recognize the movement's "icy puritanism," to use a term from Peter

19. Thus de Plinval, *Pélage*, 50–55; Evans, *Pelagius*, 31–37; Rees, *Pelagius*, 4–5; arguing against this identification is Y.-M. Duval, "Pélage est-il le censeur inconnu de l'*Adversus Iovinianum* à Rome en 393?"
20. See the list in Quasten, *Patrology* 4, 469–70.
21. PL 30. 115: *Ego te Christianum esse volo, non monachum dici, et virtutem propriae laudis possidere magis quam nomen alienum, quod frustra a Latinis in turba commorantibus imponitur cum a Graecis solitarie viventibus legitime deputetur.*
22. Zosimus. *Ep.* 3.3 (PL 20. 657); Orosius, *Apol.* 4. 5 (CSEL 5. 607, 609).
23. Hanson, *Saint Patrick*, 145.   24. *De gest Pel.* 22.46.
25. *De pecc. mer.* 3.3.6.

Brown.[26] Thus, *De gest. Pel.* quotes Pelagius: "On the day of judgment no mercy will be shown to the wicked and the sinners, but they will be consumed in the eternal fires."[27] Pelagius must be understood as primarily a moralist, a religious teacher calling for a reform of Christians' lives according to a more demanding standard than that which he perceived to be prevalent, and not as a speculative theologian. Nevertheless, his moral teaching drew on (and perhaps also issued into) a distinctive and fairly well articulated theological anthropology.

(9) The attempt to reconstruct Pelagius' theology faces several obstacles at the outset. One is that, while we possess a fair amount of the writings of Pelagius and his sympathizers, it was their enemies who first attempted a theological synthesis of their ideas. Pelagianism as an *-ism*, Peter Brown reminds us, came into existence in the mind of Augustine.[28] A second is that this synthesis drew on the writings of a number of different figures. Pelagius' personal reputation, as well as his writings, put him at the head of what could legitimately seem a movement, and the word *Pelagiani* begins to be used in 415 by Jerome, followed not long after by Augustine. But the ideas of the main figures in this movement, such men as Rufinus the Syrian, Caelestius, the Sicilian Anonymous, and Julian of Eclanum, as well as of Pelagius himself, while they clearly belong to a "family" and overlap to a great degree, do not in all respects coincide.[29] In the work of disentangling the authentic teaching of Pelagius from that of his associates and followers, as well as from implications perceived in it by his enemies but not drawn out by Pelagius, Robert F. Evans has taken the lead, and his account will in the main be followed here.[30]

(10) Pelagius always wished to be orthodox, "to think in and with the Catholic Church."[31] As such, his writings contain polemical references to a variety of recognized heresies. However, he primarily opposed Manichaeism. Manichaeism was strong in Rome in the late fourth century, as noted above, and

26. Quoted in Bonner, *Augustine and Pelagianism,* 14.
27. *De gest. Pel.* 3.9.   28. Brown, *Augustine of Hippo,* 345.
29. Rees, *Pelagius,* 89.   30. Evans, *Pelagius,* 90–121.
31. Evans, *Pelagius,* 92.

in Pelagius' view, as in the view Augustine came to take, its doctrine of the two wills gave humans an excuse for wrongdoing, implanting in us a "necessity" of sinning. Against this position, Pelagius insists always and everywhere on human responsibility for our own sins.[32]

(11) For Pelagius, the dignity of humans resides in our freedom. This power of free choice is ours by nature, but in creating us with it, God set us apart from the necessity which governs the rest of created nature. By the use of reason, we are able to discern the law of nature within, "which directs man reliably to action in conformity to his own nature, which in turn is action in conformity to the will of God."[33] In our freedom, we retain the power to choose to obey this law or to disobey it. This unique status affords us the "possibility of not sinning," which is the main subject of *De nat. et gr.* It is not our own doing, but implanted in our nature by God, and as such it is "grace."[34]

(12) Pelagius does not confine the use of the term "grace" to this capacity of our nature, but also uses it in reference to the law of Moses and, especially, to the work of Christ. In both of these it is a question not of God's creation of our nature but of God's actions to restore our nature. Why, and in what sense, is that nature in need of restoration? The cause of the damage is, of course, sin, but Pelagius opposes any idea of an original sin transmitted through procreation. Such a doctrine would come too close to the Manichaean notion of a necessary component of sin in our nature, and would, in addition, seem to imply an adherence of sin in the body, not the soul, since Pelagius rejects any traducianist conception of the origin of the soul. Moreover, it is not possible, in his view, to hold someone guilty of a sin that is not his own action. Instead, the damage done by Adam's sin was that it established a model for human disobedience to God, so that subsequent sin is in imitation of Adam. This imitation, compounded over time, builds up a nearly inescapable "habit" or custom of sinning.[35] Although there were some sinless men between Adam and Moses,[36] by and large humans became

---

32. Bonner, *St Augustine*, 317.
33. Evans, *Pelagius*, 93.
34. *De nat. et gr.* 45.53 and 51.59.
35. Evans, *Pelagius*, 100–01.
36. *De nat. et gr.* 36.42.

oblivious of the law of their own nature. God therefore gave the law of Moses as a "file": "By constant application of its abrasive injunctions the rust of ignorance was to be done away and man's newly polished nature was to stand out again in its pristine brilliance."[37]

(13) But in time not even the law was able to free people from their habit of sinning. Once again, although some people were able to live sinless lives during the "time of the law", in most, the capacity of not sinning, which is inextricable from human nature, was untapped. It became, in most people, "a resource which their present condition places beyond their grasp."[38]

(14) It is this condition which is overcome by the "grace of Christ." The work of Christ, for Pelagius, is threefold. First, his sacrificial death on our behalf releases us from the condemnation that we have incurred on the basis of sins already committed. Second and third, Christ undoes the effects of the long-ingrained habit of sin in two ways: by his teaching, revealing what the law of God is, and by his example, showing and inspiring Christians to live by it.

(15) Evans thus summarizes the meaning of "grace" for Pelagius under five headings: (1) that original endowment with rational will by which men have the capacity to be without sin; (2) the law of Moses; (3) the forgiveness of sins in virtue of the redemptive death of Christ; (4) the example of Christ; (5) the teaching of Christ, conceived both as "law" and more generally as teaching concerning the things proper to man's nature and salvation.[39] "Pelagius," he concludes, "has no doctrine of grace other than this."

(16) Baptism, then, is the sacrament whereby the Christian, by an act of faith, appropriates the forgiveness from past sins that is made available by Christ's death. Pelagius insists on the importance of the consent of the believer's will; for grace to impose itself without that consent would violate the nature of the will.[40] Despite this, Pelagius upholds the importance of infant baptism,[41] in seeming disregard of the fact that he has de-

---

37. Evans, *Pelagius*, 99.
38. Evans, *Pelagius*, 103.
39. Evans, *Pelagius*, 111.
40. Evans, *Pelagius*, 114.
41. See, *inter alia*, the text preserved at Augustine, *De pecc. or.* 19.21.

prived it of any intelligible rationale. Thereafter, "The whole of Christian life . . . is one in which Christians avail themselves of the grace of teaching and example; always exercising that freedom of choice which has been made effectual by grace, they obey the precepts of the gospel and so merit the rewards of the final kingdom of heaven."[42]

Augustine and the Pelagian Controversy: Early Stages

(17) In his extant writing, Pelagius' theology is best worked out in a series of commentaries on the Pauline letters,[43] written, according to de Plinval, around 397–98. At the same time, another author was rethinking his theological anthropology by means of an intensive rereading of Paul. This was Augustine, as priest and newly ordained bishop at Hippo. In his earliest writings as a Christian, he was concerned to emphasize human free will, to stress human responsibility for sin, against Manichaean claims of an alien sinful substance within. Influenced by neo-Platonic writings, he proposed an ascent of soul through study and disciplined life, whereby one could in this life attain a contemplative state of continual inward tranquillity. But now his thought was taking on a different cast. There were several converging reasons for this: a disappointment with his own failure to make spiritual progress (eloquently captured in Peter Brown's chapter, "The Lost Future"[44]); a need, as an ecclesiastic, to come to terms with the character of the Christians who filled his church on Sundays, a far different group from the contemplative communities at Cassiciacum and Thagaste when he was a new convert; a reading of Ambrosiaster's commentaries on Paul and Tyconius' *Book of Rules*.[45]

(18) Writing in 397 to Simplicianus, Bishop of Milan, who as priest had played an influential role in Augustine's conversion, about the interpretation of the Epistle to the Romans, Au-

42. Evans, *Pelagius*, 119.   43. For text, see Souter.
44. Brown, *Augustine of Hippo*, 146–57.
45. TeSelle, *Augustine the Theologian*, 156–182. On Ambrosiaster, see note to *De nat. et gr.* 5.5 below.

gustine arrives at a statement of the theory of grace and human free will which he carries with him, only slightly modified, into the Pelagian controversy. Salvation is only possible through faith. And this faith is grace, given *gratis*, not in view of past good works or foreseen future ones. Without this grace, we lack the strength to do the good that we recognize we ought to do. "Unless the mercy of God in calling precedes, no one can even believe, and so begin to be justified and to receive power to do good works. So grace comes before all merits."[46] Why then are some given this gift and others not? All human beings are in fact deserving of punishment due to the sin of Adam, all are a "mass of sin."[47] By an act of mercy, however, God chooses to save some from this mass, to make them "vessels of honor" (Rom 9.21). To these, God gives a calling that is exactly suited to their circumstances and dispositions. This is the idea of the "congruous call", the *vocatio congrua*. The response of those given such a call is free, because it proceeds from the uncoerced human will, but foreknown by God to be positive. "He calls the man on whom he has mercy in the way he knows will suit him, so that he will not refuse the call."[48]

(19) This theory of grace and freedom plays an important role in the *Confessions*, begun around the time of the writing of the responses to Simplicianus. The theme of the "congruous call" in particular can be seen not only in Augustine's description of his own calling, but also in his vignettes of the lives of Alypius and Monica.[49] And it was the *Confessions* that provoked the first recorded clash between Pelagius and Augustine.

(20) Reflecting on his own inability to avoid sin, even after years as a Christian, Augustine commits himself to God's mercy: *Da quod iubes et iube quod vis,* "Give what you command, and command what you will."[50] Pelagius, hearing these words

46. *Ad Simpl.* 1.2.7, tr. John Burnaby, LCC, 6. 391.
47. *Ad Simpl.* 1.2.18. On the use of the term *massa*, see note to *De nat. et gr.* 5.5 below.
48. *Ad Simpl.* 1.2.13. See TeSelle, *Augustine the Theologian,* 177–81; Burns, *The Development of Augustine's Doctrine of Operative Grace,* 37–44.
49. Burns, *The Development of Augustine's Doctrine of Operative Grace,* 45–50.
50. *Conf.* 10.29.40, 10.31.45, 10.37.60.

quoted at Rome by a bishop,[51] perhaps around 405, "was not able to bear them" and attacked them "with considerable emotion."[52]

(21) Perhaps the controversy would have remained a private affair among theologians if the Goths under Alaric did not begin to threaten Rome, culminating in its sack on August 24, 410. But the ensuing turmoil produced an exodus of prominent Romans. One of these was Pelagius, who in 409 left Italy for Sicily, accompanied by a disciple, Caelestius, who had been trained as a lawyer. In 410, they landed at Hippo, but Augustine was out of town. They shortly went on to Carthage, where Augustine saw Pelagius several times at the Conference of 411[53] but did not speak with him. Pelagius soon went on to Palestine, but Caelestius remained in Carthage, "full of evangelical zeal and freed from [Pelagius'] moderating influence."[54] It appears also that Caelestius was impressed, in a way in which Pelagius was not, by the arguments of Rufinus the Syrian against the transmission of original sin.[55] He made some impact upon Christian circles at Carthage[56] and in time sought ordination,[57] but was accused of heresy by Paulinus of Milan, the biographer of St. Ambrose. At a synod in the late autumn of 411, he was accused of teaching six propositions: (1) That Adam was created mortal, and whether he had sinned or not, he would have been going to die. (2) That the sin of Adam injured only himself and not the human race. (3) That infants at the time of

---

51. Courcelle, *Les Confessions dans la tradition littéraire*, 580, argues that this bishop was Paulinus of Nola. Duval, "La date du *De Natura*" 283, favors Evodius of Uzalis.

52. *De dono pers.* 20.53.

53. Convoked by Count Marcellinus on behalf of the Emperor, to settle the controversy between the Catholics and the Donatists. The source for this story is *De gest. Pel.* 22.46.

54. Ferguson, *Pelagius*, 50.

55. On Rufinus the Syrian, see Bonner, *Augustine and Pelagianism*, 19–29, and Eugene TeSelle, "Rufinus the Syrian." This Rufinus arrived at Rome in 399 and wrote a *Liber de fide* not long afterward. Marius Mercator accused him of being the founder of Pelagianism. His attack on the idea of the transmission of original sin arose in the context of his opposition to traducianism as a theory of the origin of the soul. He is not to be confused with Rufinus of Aquileia, translator of Origen and opponent of Jerome.

56. *De gest. Pel.* 35.62.   57. Augustine, *Ep.* 157.3.22.

birth are in the same condition in which Adam was before his transgression. (4) That the race of man as a whole does not die through the death or transgression of Adam, nor does the race of man as a whole rise again through the resurrection of Christ. (5) That the Law leads people to the kingdom of heaven in the same way as does the Gospel. (6) That even before the coming of Christ there were men without sin.[58] Caelestius did not abjure these propositions, but rather, citing the authority of Rufinus the Syrian, held that these were permissible theological opinions. The synod did not agree, and excommunicated him.

(22) Thus it was on the issue of original sin and infant baptism that the Pelagian movement first encountered ecclesiastical difficulty. This was a question of little importance to Pelagius, and, in fact, the first of the propositions charged against Caelestius contradicts the opinion of Pelagius—and indeed also that of Rufinus the Syrian.[59] It is also worth noting, against those who would see the theology of original sin as Augustine's personal brainchild,[60] that, although Augustine was not present at this synod, a basically "Augustinian" view of original sin was put forward on behalf of the North African Church by Aurelius, Bishop of Carthage, and also espoused by Paulinus, from the Church of Milan.[61]

58. These six charges are listed in two sources: Marius Mercator, *Commonitorium super nomine Caelestii*, and, in a different order, Augustine, *De gest. Pel.* 11.23, recounting how these charges were brought against Pelagius at the Synod of Diospolis. Part of the official record of the synod at Carthage can be found in Augustine, *De pecc. or.* 2.3–4.3, from which it can be inferred that neither Mercator nor *De gest. Pel.* preserves the charges *verbatim* and that Mercator preserves the original order. The two versions are compared in Wermelinger, *Röm und Pelagius*, 11. In translating, I have followed the wording in *De pecc. or.* for charges 2 and 3, and the wording in Mercator for the other charges, except at the end of number 6, where (Wermelinger says under Jerome's influence) Mercator introduces the term *impeccabiles*. A comparison with the translation of *De gest. Pel.* below will show how close Augustine's wording is to Mercator's: the differences often are not reflected in the English at all.

59. Bonner, *Augustine and Pelagianism*, 29.

60. This seems to be the view of Pagels in *Adam, Eve, and the Serpent.*

61. Bonner, "Les origines africaines de la doctrine augustinienne sur la chute et le péché originel," 101: "Il est clair que la doctrine énoncée par Aurelius de Carthage au commencement même de la controverse pélagienne est, en effet, la doctrine dite augustinienne du péché originel, et que la même doc-

(23) Not long afterward, Augustine began opposing the views of Caelestius in "sermons and conversations,"[62] and, in response to a letter from Count Marcellinus, in 412 he produced what he came to regard as the first of his anti-Pelagian writings, *De peccatorum meritis et remissione et de baptismo parvulorum*. The first two books of this work do not mention Pelagius, but in a letter appended as a third book, he notes, "Within the last few days, I have read some writings by Pelagius—a holy man, as I am told, who has made no small progress in the Christian life—containing some very brief notes on the epistles of the Apostle Paul,"[63] and therein he found several arguments against the doctrine of original sin. He proceeds in this letter to refute them, noting that Pelagius does not put them forward as his own. Marcellinus observed in reply that he was troubled by Augustine's assertion that a human being could live without sin, with the help of God's grace, although only Christ had actually done so. Responding in turn, Augustine wrote the treatise, *De spiritu et littera*, arguing that no one could achieve perfection through obedience to the Law of God by means of free will alone. "The letter kills" in that the Law gives awareness of God's commandments but not the strength to carry them out; "the Spirit gives life" by writing the Law on the heart and lifting up the will to God. Although some teachings of Pelagius are probably criticized in this work, Augustine does not mention him directly. In 413, Augustine wrote to Pelagius, speaking of him in flattering terms—a letter which, when Pelagius produced it in his defense at Diospolis, Augustine had to scramble to explain away.[64] Also in 413, at the request of Aurelius, Augustine preached a sermon at Carthage, drawing on the au-

---

trine est maintenue par Paulin de Milan." This whole article provides excellent background to the Augustinian theory of original sin in general and to the synod of 411 in particular.

62. *Retractationes* 2.59.1. The *Retractationes* (for the title of which I propose the translation, *Reconsiderations*) will be cited in this volume according to the numbering system used in the edition by Pius Knöll in CSEL 36. This numbering is also used in the translation by Sister Mary Inez Bogan in FOTC 60.

63. *De pecc. mer.* 3.1.1.

64. *Ep.* 146; see *De gest. Pel.* 26.51–29.53.

thority of Cyprian in defense of the baptism of infants in order to free them from the effects of Adam's sin.[65] Finally, in 414, Augustine replied to a letter from a certain Hilary,[66] writing from Sicily and asking for a response to certain theses being taught by some Christians at Syracuse:

> That a man can be without sin and easily keep the commandments of God, if he wishes; that an infant who dies unbaptized cannot justly perish, since it is born without sin; that a rich man who remains in his riches cannot enter the kingdom of God, unless he has sold all his possessions, nor does it benefit him at all if perhaps he has fulfilled the commandments by means of his wealth; that one ought not to swear oaths at all; and concerning the Church, which is, as it is written, "without spot or wrinkle,"[67] whether that is [as some of them say] this one, in which we now gather, or that, for which we hope.[68]

The first, fourth, and fifth of these propositions are taught by Pelagius; the third goes well beyond anything he is known to have said, but was asserted by the author of the Pelagian treatise, *De divitiis*, whom Bonner has labeled the Sicilian Anonymous.[69]

(24) So, before the arrival of the *De natura* in 415, Augustine was already well enmeshed in the Pelagian controversy, but as yet he had not attacked Pelagius by name, treating him personally with respect and treating his arguments with circumspection. Even *De nat. et gr.* does not mention Pelagius' name (although it is introduced for the sake of clarity into our translation). But, as Augustine states in the passage quoted at the beginning of this introduction, it was the reading of *De natura*, to which he responds here, which fully alerted him to the dangers of the heresy of Pelagius. What was it about *De natura*

---

65. *Sermo* 294; see *De gest. Pel.* 11.25.
66. Not the Hilary who is later one of the addressees of *De praed sanct.* and *De dono pers.*
67. Eph 5.27.
68. Among Augustine's letters, *Ep.* 156; Augustine's lengthy reply is *Ep.* 157. Versions of the first three charges were brought up against Pelagius, with specific mention of Augustine's name, at the Synod of Diospolis. See *De gest. Pel.* 11.24.
69. Bonner, *Augustine and Pelagianism*, 6, 39.

which hardened Augustine's stance? Evans says bluntly, "In the work *On Nature* there appears to be no doctrine *to which Augustine seriously objects* which was not also present in Pelagius' commentary on Paul."[70] Perhaps Augustine became more sensitive to the overall thrust of Pelagius' teachings by seeing them expressed in fairly succinct form. Or perhaps, as Evans argues, what Augustine reacts to is the way in which Pelagius musters quotations from various Catholic authorities in apparent support of the orthodoxy of his teaching—in particular, Pelagius' use of a quotation from an early work of Augustine himself.[71] At any rate, with this work the lines of the conflict are firmly drawn. Before considering exactly what those lines were, however, we need to trace the progress of Pelagius between his departure from Carthage and the writing of *De natura*.

Pelagius in Palestine

(25) Pelagius had sailed from Carthage to Palestine, where he was welcomed among "the amazing group of Latin *émigrés* settled in Jerusalem," whose penchant for contention "threatened to turn the Holy Places into a theological bear-garden."[72] Here Pelagius found favor with Bishop John of Jerusalem and, perhaps not without connection, aroused the enmity (or rearoused it, if the identification with Pelagius of the "monk" criticized in the Letter to Domnio can be sustained) of the cantankerous Jerome, who had resided in the Holy Land since 386. Perhaps the controversy flared when both Jerome and Pelagius were asked to write letters of advice to the virgin Demetrias. It appears that Pelagius was reviving some old charges made against Jerome in earlier controversies over Jovinian and Origen.[73] In any event, Ctesiphon, probably a wealthy, lay supporter of Pelagius,[74] wrote to Jerome in a conciliatory manner

---

70. Evans, *Pelagius*, 82.
71. *De nat. et gr.* 67.80 considers Pelagius' use of a portion of *De lib. arb.* 3.18.50.
72. Brown, *Augustine of Hippo*, 356.
73. On the conflict between Jerome and Pelagius, see Evans, *Pelagius*, 6–25.
74. Kelly, *Jerome*, 314.

on Pelagius' behalf, whereupon Jerome responded in a lengthy polemic, *Ep.* 133, followed not long afterward by the *Dialogue against the Pelagians.*[75]

(26) Jerome was not particularly interested in the controversy over infant baptism. What exercised him was Pelagius' teaching on the possibility of living without sin, which he regarded as a revival of the Stoic doctrine of *apatheia*, freedom from passion or disturbance, a notion which he had criticized previously in Origen and Evagrius of Pontus. This he saw as, in a sense, equating the human being with God, ascribing to the human being a possibility of attaining a perfection which is possessed only by God.[76] He also charged Pelagius with teaching the Stoic doctrine of the equality of all sins, in that Pelagius held that all God's commandments were equally binding on Christians.[77]

(27) Pelagius' response to these charges is found in two works, both preserved chiefly in fragments quoted by Augustine: *De libero arbitrio* (ca. 417), which Augustine rebuts in *De gratia Christi* (418), and *De natura*. The former work was explicitly in the form of a dialogue with Jerome, while the latter, says Evans, bears some marks of having been written in dialogue form.[78] In these works, Pelagius shows that he has recognized that the fundamental issue between them is Jerome's claim that "Sin is an inescapable, unavoidable aspect of corporeal existence in this life. It is for this reason that Pelagius' two treatises are so largely taken up with issues related to the doctrine of creation and to the capacity for sinlessness defined in terms of man's created nature."[79] The grace of Christ, so important for Augustine, receives relatively little attention in these works, because it is not the issue in the conflict with Jerome.

75. For *Ep.* 133, see CSEL 56. 241–60. For the *Dial. c. Pel.,* see PL 23. 495–590 and the translation by John N. Hritzu, FOTC 57. 230–378.
76. *Ep.* 133.8, 10. Augustine explicitly dissociates himself from this view of Jerome's in *De nat. et gr.* 33.37.
77. Evans, *Pelagius*, 23.
78. Evans, *Pelagius*, 24, cites the passages quoted in *De nat. et gr.* 7.8 and 54.63. In contrast to Evans' view, see Duval, "La date du *De Natura*". On *De libro arbitrio*, see below, p. 99.
79. Evans, *Pelagius*, 25.

Synopsis

(28) 1.1–7.7 form an introduction. Augustine ascribes Pelagius' errors to an excessive zeal against those who blame human
nature, not free will, for sin. He quotes Pelagius to the effect
that human nature, apart from faith in Christ, has the power
to obey God's law (2.2). To this he opposes a short summary of
his own theology of sin and grace: that the nature which we
inherit from Adam is gravely impaired, such that we cannot do
good without the grace of faith, received in baptism (3.3–5.5).

(29) In 7.8–18.20 Pelagius distinguishes the possibility of living free from sin, which is what he wants to talk about, from
the actuality of a sinless life. Blame, he says, attaches to sins only
if they could have been avoided, only if the agent could have
done otherwise (7.8). Augustine counters that an unbaptized
infant lacks even the ability to do otherwise, yet is condemned
nonetheless (8.9). He contends that, if anyone can be justified
apart from faith in Christ, then the cross is pointless. Pelagius
argues that, if his opponent contends that a sinless life is possible only through grace, then the central point is conceded: a
sinless life is possible (10.11). But what Pelagius calls "grace"
appears, according to Augustine, to be simply the created
power of human nature (11.12). The discussion proceeds into
various passages of Scripture which appear to affirm, or to
deny, that a sinless life is possible; particular attention is paid
to James 3.8: "But the tongue no man can tame."

(30) From 19.21 to 34.39 the central questions concern the
nature of sin and its effects upon human nature. This section
is loosely structured, whether because of a loose structure in
Pelagius' book or because of Augustine's selectivity in responding to it. Pelagius wants to dispute the claim that sin has
changed and weakened our nature. His first line of argument
is that sin, not being a substance, cannot exercise causal force
on human nature (19.21). Augustine's reply is governed by the
image of sickness, which, though not a substance, certainly
harms the body. Corresponding to this, Augustine frequently
invokes the image of Christ the Physician (e.g., 23.25). He insists on the distinction between the power of human nature as

created and that of human nature as damaged by sin (e.g., 21.23, 34.39). Pelagius objects to the idea that the punishment of sin could be more sin (22.24). Augustine, relying on Romans 1, defends the appropriateness of a punishment which consists in the withdrawal of the "light of truth" whereby sin could have been avoided and faults Pelagius for ignoring the grace of Christ, whereby it can be avoided still (23.25). Pelagius seems willing to call on grace only for the forgiveness of past sins, not for help against the possibility of future sins (26.29, as also 18.20). Pelagius attacks the idea that sin is necessary in order to prevent further sin (27.30). Augustine replies that the point is not that sin directly prevents sin, but that it furnishes the occasion for humans to realize that that power in which they might be tempted to take pride is not their own but God's (28.32). Pride is uniquely harmful, he notes, because it tends to overtake us in our *good* deeds.

(31) In 35.40–40.47 the discussion now turns to the question of whether the Bible contains examples of people without sin. Pelagius offers a long list, including the Virgin Mary (36.42). Augustine exempts Mary from consideration (36.42) and argues that the others were not without sin, citing Scripture passages to the effect that all have sinned.

(32) In 41.48–51.59 Pelagius admits that the question of the *fact* of human sinlessness is not as important as the question of its possibility, and Augustine counters that even this is not the real issue. The issue is the *ground* of this possibility: our nature, or the grace of Christ (42.49, 44.51). Again, Pelagius objects to the charge that he denies God's grace (44.52), but again he situates that grace in God's creation of human nature, with its "inseparable" (50.58) possibility of not sinning—something which depends on God, not on us (48.56). Again, Augustine insists that the question is about the powers of our nature as it actually exists, corrupted by sin, lacking the power our nature had in its integrity and needing to cry out to its Physician (49.57).

(33) In 52.60–59.69 Pelagius argues that the Pauline passages about the contrariety of the flesh to the spirit apply to the unbaptized, not the baptized. Augustine notes that this under-

mines the claim which Pelagius makes for the powers of human nature, which the unbaptized possess equally with the baptized. He then proceeds to examine relevant Pauline texts and show that in them the Apostle is speaking of baptized Christians, who still suffer from the infirmities of corrupted human nature and who pray daily for the grace to overcome them (53.62).

(34) In 60.70–67.81 Pelagius advances texts from various Catholic writers—Lactantius, Hilary, Ambrose, John Chrysostom, Xystus the bishop of Rome (whom Pelagius mistakenly identifies as the author of the *Sentences of Sextus*), Jerome, and Augustine himself in his early work, *De lib. arb.*—to defend the possibility of a sinless life. Augustine begins by insisting that the question is not that of the possibility of sinlessness but of its cause. None of the other writers, Augustine argues, can be understood to disagree with the position that a sinless life is possible, if at all, only through the grace of Christ, and his own present position is perfectly compatible with that which is expressed in his earlier work.

(35) In 68.82–70.84 Pelagius concludes his book with an exhortation to obedience to God's commandments as found in the Scriptures. Augustine concurs with the exhortation, only insisting that there must be added an exhortation to pray for the grace which alone makes such obedience possible.

Texts and Translations

(36) This translation is based on the critical text of C. F. Urba and J. Zycha in CSEL 60 (Vienna, 1913) 233–299, as reproduced with slight emendations in BA 21: *La Crise Pélagienne I*, edited by Georges de Plinval and Jeanne de La Tullaye (Paris, 1966). Places where BA differs from CSEL are indicated in notes; the translation in almost all cases follows BA. The 1690 Benedictine edition is reprinted in PL 44. 247–90.

(37) In preparing this translation, we have consulted the French translation by Jeanne de La Tullaye in the BA volume and the earlier English translation by Peter Holmes originally published at Edinburgh in 1872 and reprinted in NPNF 5 (New York, 1887) 121–151. The NPNF volume mentions another

English translation by Woods and Johnston (London, 1887). There is a German translation (with text) by A. Maxsein in *Sankt Augustinus—Der Lehrer der Gnade I* (Würzburg, 1971) and a Spanish translation (with text) by V. Campagna in BAC 50 (Madrid, 1956) 820–941.

APPENDIX: *RETRACTATIONES* 2.68

On Nature and Grace, one book:

At that time there came into my hands a certain book of Pelagius, in which with as much argument as possible he defends the nature of man against the grace of God, by which the wicked man is justified and by which we are Christians. The book in which I replied to him, defending grace not as opposed to nature but as that through which nature is liberated and governed, I therefore called *On Nature and Grace.*

In that book [64.77], I defended certain words, which Pelagius quoted as the words of Xystus the Roman bishop and martyr, as if they were in fact the words of that same Xystus, for that is what I thought. But afterwards I read that they were the words of Sextus the philosopher, not Xystus the Christian.

This book begins as follows: "The book which you have sent."

ON NATURE AND GRACE

Introduction

HE BOOK which you have sent to me, dearly beloved sons Timasius and James,[1] I have read through somewhat rapidly—having set aside for a little while the books which I was reading—but with considerable attention. I saw [in this book] a man inflamed with a very ardent zeal against those who, although they ought, when they sin, to censure the human will, try instead to accuse the nature of human beings and thus to excuse themselves. He has flared up excessively against this plague, which even writers of secular literature have strongly reproved, exclaiming: "The human race wrongly brings a complaint against its own nature."[2] With all the strength of his intellectual talents, your author also has piled up support for precisely this judgment. I fear, nevertheless, that he will instead give support to those "who have a zeal for God, but not according to knowledge; for they, not knowing the justice of God, and seeking to establish their own, have not submitted themselves to the justice of God."[3] The Apostle makes clear the meaning of "the justice of God" in this passage by adding immediately, "For the end of the law is Christ, to justice for everyone who believes."[4] Therefore, whoever understands that the justice[5] of God lies not in the precept of the

1. The book is the *De natura* of Pelagius. On Timasius and James (Jacobus), see the Introduction.
2. Sallust, *Bellum Iugurthinum* 1.1.
3. Rom 10.2–3.   4. Rom 10.4.
5. *Iustitia* translates the Pauline δικαιοσύνη. In translating *iustitia* and its cognates into English, we have in general, in order to reflect similarities in words used by Augustine, used "justice" and its cognates, as opposed to the other common English translation, "righteousness." Neither alternative is wholly satisfactory. It should be kept in mind that the "justice of God" is God's saving power and will, while that of a human being is the condition of being

law, which incites fear, but in the help given by the grace of Christ—and it is to this grace alone that the fear of the law, as of a pedagogue,[6] leads—he understands why he is a Christian. "For if justice is through the law, then Christ died in vain."[7] However, if he did not die in vain, then only in him is the ungodly man justified, and to him who "believes in him who justifies the ungodly, his faith is attributed for his [CSEL 60.234] justification."[8] "For all have sinned and are deprived of the glory of God and are justified freely through his blood."[9] But those who do not believe that they belong to the "all" who "have sinned and are deprived of the glory of God," do not, of course, have any necessity to become Christians, for those who are healthy do not need a physician, but rather those who are ill.[10] For this reason Christ came to call, not the just, but sinners.[11]

2.(2) And thus the nature of the human race, born from the flesh of the one transgressor, ought, if it could be sufficient to itself to fulfill the law and to achieve justice, to be sure of its reward, that is, of eternal life, *even*[12] *if in some nation or in some past time faith in the blood of Christ was not known to it. For God is not unjust and would not deprive the just of their reward for justice, if the mystery of Christ's nature as both human and divine, which was manifest in the flesh, had not been proclaimed to them. For how could they believe what they had not heard? Or how could they hear without a preacher?*[13] *For "Faith is from hearing," as Scripture says, "and hearing by the word of Christ. But I say," says St. Paul, "Have they not heard? 'Their sound has gone forth into all the earth, and their words unto the ends of the whole world.' "*[14] *However, before all this has begun to be accomplished, before that preaching itself finally reaches the ends of the whole earth—for there still exist some people in remote places,*

---

delivered from sin and given a new life in God's Spirit (McKenzie, DB, s.v. "righteous").

6. Cf. Gal 3.24.   7. Gal 2.21.
8. Rom 4.5.
9. Rom 3.23–24. Gk and Vg read "grace" in place of "blood."
10. Matt 9.12.   11. Matt 9.13.
12. We follow the BA translation in taking the passage from "even if" to "resurrection of Christ" to be a long quotation from Pelagius' *De natura*. See the note by Georges de Plinval, BA 21. 600. [Ed. note: Writings of Pelagius quoted by Augustine are set in italics.]
13. Cf. Rom 10.14.   14. Rom 10.17–18; cf. Ps 18.5.

although it is said that they are few in number, to whom the gospel has not yet been preached—what should human nature do or what has it done, either before when it had not yet heard that salvation was to come to pass, or now if it has not learned that it was accomplished? What should it do except fulfill God's will by believing in him who made heaven and earth, and who created human nature itself (as it naturally perceives) and by living rightly, even though it has not been tinged with any faith in the passion and resurrection of Christ? If this could have been done or can be done, I also say what the Apostle said about the law: [235] "Christ died in vain."[15] For if he declared this regarding the law accepted by the one Jewish people, how much more truly may it be said concerning the law of nature which all mankind has received, "If justice is derived from [human] nature, then Christ died in vain." But if he did not die in vain, then human nature can in no way be justified and redeemed from the most righteous wrath of God, that is from punishment, unless through faith and the sacrament of the blood of Christ.

3.(3) In the beginning man's nature was created without any fault and without any sin; however, this human nature in which we are all born from Adam now requires a physician, because it is not healthy.[16] Indeed, all the good qualities which it has in its organization, life, senses, and understanding, it possesses from the most high God, its creator and shaper. On the other hand, the defect which darkens and weakens all those natural goods, so that there is a need for illumination and healing, is not derived from its blameless maker but from that original sin that was committed through free will. Consequently, that criminal nature draws upon itself the most righteous punishment. For, if we are now a new creation in Christ,[17] "we were," nevertheless, "children of wrath, even as the rest. But God, who is rich in mercy, because of the great love with which he loved

---

15. Gal 2.21.
16. Gerald Bonner, *St. Augustine of Hippo,* 325, says of this and the following chapter that they "virtually sum up Augustine's thought on the subject of Grace and afford an admirable summary of his doctrine."
17. Cf. 1 Cor 5.17.

us, even when we were dead through our offenses, has given us life together with Christ, by whose grace you have been saved."[18]

4.(4) This grace of Christ, then, without which neither children nor adults can be saved, is given gratuitously and not for our merits, and for this reason it is called "grace." "[They are] justified," says the Apostle, "freely by his blood."[19] Consequently, those who are not liberated through grace, either because they have not yet been able to hear, or because [236] they have not wished to obey, or also because, when on account of their age they were not capable of hearing, they did not receive the bath of regeneration,[20] which they could have received and by means of which they would have been saved, are justly condemned. For they are not without sin, either that which they contracted originally or that which they added through their own misconduct. "For all have sinned," either in Adam or in themselves, "and are deprived of the glory of God."[21]

5.(5) Consequently, the whole human mass[22] ought to be punished, and if the deserved punishment of damnation were rendered to all, beyond all doubt it would be justly rendered. This is why those who are liberated from it by grace are not called vessels of their own merits but "vessels of mercy."[23] But

---

18. Eph 2.3–5.   19. Rom 3.24.
20. Cf. Titus 3.5.   21. Rom 3.23.
22. *Massa:* 'mass', 'lump.' Here Augustine introduces what becomes his characteristic term in the anti-Pelagian writings for human solidarity in sin, deriving from the sin of Adam. The term is drawn from Rom 9.21: "Has not the potter power over the clay, of the same lump (*massa*), to make one a vessel unto honor and another unto dishonor?" Augustine first made use of *massa* in this sense as early as *De diversis quaestionibus ad Simplicianum* 1.2.19 (A.D. 397); in the anti-Pelagian writings he often speaks of humankind as *massa peccati, massa perditionis, massa damnati,* and similarly. In this use of *massa*, as in much else concerning the development of his theology of grace and original sin, Augustine is influenced by an unknown author who wrote commentaries on the Pauline *corpus* at Rome in the late fourth century. For this writer, Erasmus coined the name "Ambrosiaster," because his commentaries were transmitted among the writings of Ambrose. Augustine, however, does not speak of these commentaries as Ambrose's, but once cites them as the work of "Hilary" (*C. duas epp. Pel.* 4.4.7).
23. Rom 9.23.

whose mercy was it but his who sent Jesus Christ into this world to save sinners,[24] whom he foreknew, predestined, called, justified, and glorified?[25] Hence, who could be so advanced in foolish insanity as not to render ineffable thanks to the mercy of this God who liberates those whom he has wished, considering that one could not in any way reproach the justice of God in condemning all entirely?

6.(6) If we understand this according to Scripture, we are not obliged to dispute against the grace of Christ nor to try to show that human nature, in infancy, needs no physician because it is sound and, in adults, can be sufficient, if it wishes, to obtain justice for itself. These opinions indeed seem here to be expressed incisively, but in a "wisdom of speech,"[26] which makes void the cross of Christ. "For this is not wisdom descending from above."[27] I do not wish to quote the words that follow,[28] that we may not be thought to do injustice to our friends, whose most strong and quick minds we wish to see run in a straight, rather than a perverse, course.

7.(7) Therefore, however great is the zeal with which the author of this book which you have sent is inflamed against those who base a defense plea for their sins on the [237] infirmity of human nature, with equal and more ardent zeal must we be inflamed, so that the cross of Christ may not be made void.[29] But it is made void if it is said that one can arrive at justice and eternal life in any way besides its sacrament. And that is what is done in this book—I do not wish to say by someone who knows what he is doing, so that I may not judge that he who wrote it should not even be considered a Christian, but, as I tend to believe, by someone who writes in ignorance, though admittedly with great power. I only wish his powers were sound, and not the sort which madmen are accustomed to display.

24. Cf. 1 Tim 1.15.
25. Cf. Rom 8.29–30.
26. 1 Cor 1.17.
27. Jas 3.15.
28. "But earthly, sensual, devilish."
29. Cf. 1 Cor 1.17.

The Possibility of Living without Sin

(8) First of all Pelagius[30] makes this distinction: *It is one thing to ask whether something can be (which has to do only with its possibility) and another to ask whether it is.* No one doubts this distinction to be true, for if something is, it follows that it could have been, but it does not follow that what can be also is. For, given the fact that the Lord raised Lazarus,[31] it is evident that he was able to do so. But since he did not, in fact, raise Judas, are we to say, "He was not able to"? Certainly, he was able—but he was not willing. For if he had been willing, he could have done this too by the same power. For the Son gives life to whomever he wills.[32] Observe, however, where he is going with this obvious and evident distinction and what he endeavors to establish from it. *We are treating,* he says, *only of possibility, from which, unless something certain has been established, we would regard it as very serious and out of proper order to pass on to something else.* He considers this idea from many different aspects and at great length, so that no one would think that he was investigating anything else than the possibility of not committing sin. The following is one of the many arguments which Pelagius uses in treating this subject: *Once more I repeat: I say that it is possible for a man to be without sin. And what do you say? That it is impossible for a man to be without sin?* But I do not say, he adds, *that there is a man without sin, nor do you say that there is not a man without sin. We are disputing about what is possible and impossible, not about what is and is not.* Next he notes that a number of the passages of Scripture which are usually invoked against them do not bear upon the question in dispute, namely, whether or [238] not a man can be without sin: "For there is no man free from pollution,"[33] and, "There is no man that does not sin,"[34] and, "There is no just man on the earth,"[35] and, "There is no one that does good."[36] *These and other similar texts,* he says, *apply to non-existence, not to impossibility.*

---

30. As he explains in *De gest. Pel.* 23.47 Augustine does not mention Pelagius by name in *De nat. et gr.* For the sake of clarity, however, we have introduced it into the translation.

31. Cf. John 11.43–44.   32. Cf. John 5.21.
33. Job 14.4 (LXX).   34. 1 Kgs 8.46.
35. Eccl 7.21.   36. Ps 13.3.

*By examples of this kind it is shown how some men were at a given time,
not that they could not have been something else. For this reason they
are justly found to be guilty. For if they were as they were because they
could not have been otherwise, then they are free from blame.*
   8.(9) Notice what he has said. I, however, for my part, say that
an infant born where it was not possible for him to be rescued
through the baptism of Christ, having been overtaken by
death, was thereby in such a state—that is, of having departed
without the "bath of regeneration"[37]—because he could not
have been otherwise. Therefore, our author would absolve him
and, contrary to the statement of the Lord,[38] would open to
him the kingdom of heaven. But the Apostle does not absolve
him when he says, "By one man sin entered into this world, and
by sin, death, and so death passed upon all men, in whom all
have sinned."[39] Justly, therefore, because of the condemnation
which runs through the whole mass of humanity, he is not admitted into the kingdom of heaven, even though he not only
was not a Christian but could not have been one.
   9.(10) But they say, *He is not damned, because "All have sinned
in Adam" is said, not because of sin contracted in the origin of one's
birth, but rather because of imitation of him.* If, therefore, it may be
said that Adam is the author of all the sins which followed his
own, since he was the first sinner among men, how then does it
happen that Abel is not placed at the head of the just, rather

   37. Cf. Titus 3.5.
   38. Cf. John 3.5: "Unless a man be born again, he cannot enter the kingdom
of God."
   39. Rom 5.12. Augustine's text here reads: *Per unum hominem peccatum in-
travit in mundum et per peccatum mors et ita in omnes homines pertransiit, in quo omnes
peccaverunt.* This text provides the primary scriptural basis for Augustine's doctrine that all humankind, as a "mass" (the term from Rom 9.21, used above
in 5.5 and discussed in a note there, and used again here), s..ıned in Adam.
Augustine, preceded by Ambrosiaster, understands *in quo* to refer to Adam,
"*in whom* all have sinned," but the Greek will not bear this sense; *in quo omnes
peccaverunt* renders ἐφ' ᾧ πάντες ἥμαρτον, "*inasmuch as* all sinned" (NAB). For
the interpretation of *in quo* as referring to Adam to be correct, the Greek would
have to read ἐν ᾧ. (Vg renders *in quo* and Douai translates according to Augustine's interpretation.) See Bonner, *St Augustine of Hippo*, 372–74, and "Augustine on Romans 5, 12," *Studia Patristica* 5.2 (1965) 242–47; Stanislas Lyon-
net, "Le péché originel et l'exégèse de Rom. 5, 12–14," *Recherches de Science
Réligieuse* 44 (1956) 63–84; NJBC 845–46.

than Christ, because Abel was the first just man? But I do not speak of an infant. Consider instead the case of a young man, or of an old man, who died in a place where he could not have heard the name of Christ. Could he, or could he not, have become just by his own nature and [239] free will? If they say he could have, then see what amounts to rendering the cross of Christ void:[40] to contend that without it anyone can be justified by the law of nature and the choice of his will. Let us also say here: "Then Christ died in vain."[41] For this is something which everyone could do, even if Christ had not died. And if they were unjust, it would be because they wished to be, and not because they could not be just. If, however, one could not be justified in any way without the grace of Christ, let Pelagius absolve him, if he dares, in accordance with his statement that, *If he was as he was because he could not have been otherwise, then he was free from blame.*

10.(11) But, as though another person were saying it, he objects and declares: [A sinless life] *can indeed be, but through the grace of God, you will say.* Then, by way of a reply, he adds: *I am grateful for your indulgence, because you are now not only content not to oppose or merely to assent to my proposition, which previously you attacked, but actually do not shrink from supporting it. For to assert that something can indeed be, but through this or that, is this not the same thing as not only to admit that it could be but also to show how and in what sense it could be? For no one gives greater support to the possibility of any thing than someone who even grants one of its qualities, for the quality cannot exist apart from the thing.* Then Pelagius raises another objection to his position: *But, you will say, you appear to deny here the grace of God, since you do not mention it.* Then he answers: *Do I deny* [grace], *who in admitting the fact* [of a sinless life] *also acknowledge that that through which it can be accomplished is necessary? Or is it you, who in denying it undoubtedly also deny whatever may be the means to accomplish it?* He has already forgotten that he is replying to someone who does not deny the possibility of a sinless life and whose objection he had just put forward in these words: *It can indeed be, but through the grace of God.* [240]

40. Cf. 1 Cor 1.17.   41. Gal 2.21.

How then does that person deny that possibility, defended with great effort by his opponent, when he admits to that opponent, "It can indeed be, but through the grace of God"? However, if after having been dismissed as now acknowledging the important thing, he still contends against those who deny that it is possible for a man to be without sin—what is this to us? Let him contend against whomever he pleases, so long as he admits, which cannot be denied without the most villainous impiety, that without the grace of God a man cannot be without sin. Therefore he says, *Whether they recognize this to be through grace, or through help or through mercy or through whatever it is through which a man can be without sin, everyone admits the thing itself.*

11.(12) When I read these words, I confess to you, dear ones, that I was suddenly filled with joy, because the author did not deny the grace of God, through which alone a man can be justified. It is such a denial that I detest and dread above all else in controversies of this sort. But in continuing to read further, I began to be suspicious, at first because of some of the comparisons he presented. For he writes, *Now if I were to say that a man can dispute, a bird can fly, a rabbit can run, and I were not also to mention the means by which these acts can be accomplished, namely, the tongue, the wings, and the feet, then have I denied the conditions of these activities, when I have recognized the activities themselves?* It certainly seems as if he has mentioned things which are effective by nature, for these members, namely the tongue, the wings, and the feet, have been created for natures of a particular kind. Nor has he proposed anything that we would want to understand to be of grace, without which no human being is justified, for there the question concerns the healing rather than the formation of natures. From here on I began to read with misgivings and soon discovered that my suspicions were not unwarranted.

12.(13) Before I come to that, consider what he has said. When he treated the question of the difference of sins and raised as an objection to his position the allegation made by some persons, that some sins are light by their frequency, their constant occurrence making it difficult to avoid them all, he denied that *it was proper that they should be liable to correction even as light offenses, if they cannot be entirely avoided.* [241] Certainly, he has not noticed those texts of the New Testament in which we have learned that the purpose of the law in its accusation of us is that, on account of transgressions, people take refuge in the grace of the merciful Lord, like a pedagogue, keeping them under custody unto that faith, which was to be later revealed,[42] whence their transgressions might be forgiven and with the help of the same grace might not be committed again. For the way belongs to those who are making progress, although those who have progressed well are called "perfect travellers." But that is the supreme perfection, to which nothing can be added, when the goal toward which they aim begins to be possessed.

13.(14) Now certainly the question that is proposed to him,[43] *Are you yourself without sin?* is not in fact relevant to the inquiry at hand. Yet when Pelagius says, *It is owing rather to his own negligence that he is not without sin,* that is well put. But then he should see fit to pray to the Lord that this perverse negligence not rule over him—as one man prayed to the Lord when he said, "Direct my ways according to thy word and let not iniquity have dominion over me"[44]—so that, trusting in his diligence, as if it were in strength of his own, he should not fail to arrive at true justice, either here or in the next life, where beyond doubt we should hope and desire it will be complete.

14.(15) And the objection that some have raised to him,[45] *Nowhere is it written, in so many words, that a man can be without sin,* Pelagius refutes easily, *because it is not a question here of the precise words in which any statement is made.* Yet perhaps it is not without reason that, although several times in Scripture it is found that men are said to be without reproach, no one is found who is said without sin except him alone of whom it is openly said, "him, who knew no sin."[46] [242] In the passage regarding holy priests we read, "He was tempted in all things according to our likeness, without sin,"[47] tempted, that is, in that flesh which,

---

42. Gal 3.23–24.   43. Reading *ei* with BA (CSEL: *eis*).
44. Ps 118.133 (Augustine's text reads *itinera*, 'ways', where Vg reads *gressus*, 'steps').
45. See note 43.   46. 2 Cor 5.21.
47. Heb 4.15.

although it was not sinful flesh, possessed the likeness of sinful flesh, which "likeness" it would not have possessed, were not all other human flesh sinful flesh. Now, how we should understand the statement, "Anyone who is born of God does not sin and cannot sin, for his seed remains in him,"[48] considering that the Apostle John himself, as if he had not been born of God or was addressing those who had not yet been born of God, clearly has set forth, "If we say that we have no sin, we deceive ourselves, and the truth is not in us,"[49] I have taken pains to explain as best I could in the books on this subject which I wrote to Marcellinus.[50] And as to those words, "He cannot sin," when taken by Pelagius as if to say, "He ought not to sin," this assertion does not seem to me to be blameworthy. For who could be so foolish as to say that sin ought to be committed, when actually sin is sin precisely because it should not be committed?

15.(16) To be sure, that which the Apostle James says, "But the tongue no man can tame,"[51] does not appear to me to yield the interpretation that Pelagius wants to put upon it: *This is stated as a reproach, as if one were to say, 'Is no man therefore capable of controlling his tongue?' As though rebuking and saying, 'You can tame the wild beasts, can you not tame your tongue?' As if it were easier to tame the tongue than to tame wild beasts.* I do not believe that is the meaning of this passage. For if the Apostle had wished for this to be understood as referring to the ease of taming the tongue, he would have gone on to make the comparison with the wild animals. But he simply adds, "[The tongue is] an unquiet evil, full of deadly poison,"[52] a poison certainly more harmful than that of beasts and serpents, for the one kills the body, [243] but the other the soul: "For the mouth that lies, kills the soul."[53] Saint James did not put forward this statement, or wish it to be put forward, in the sense that it would be easier to tame the tongue than to tame wild beasts. Rather, he was intent on showing what a great evil a man's tongue can be, so great that it cannot be tamed by any man, though even beasts are

48. 1 John 3.9.   49. 1 John 1.8.
50. *De pecc. mer.* 2.7.9–8.10 (written ca. 412).
51. Jas 3.8.   52. Jas 3.8.
53. Wis 1.11.

tamed by men. Nor did he say this in order that through negligence we might tolerate in ourselves the tyranny of such an evil, but in order that we might ask for the help of divine grace to tame our tongue. For he does not say, "No one can tame the tongue," but "no man," so that, when it is tamed, we may admit that it was done by the mercy of God, the assistance of God, the grace of God. Therefore, let the soul try to control the tongue, and, while it tries, let it ask for assistance; and let the tongue pray that it be controlled by the gift of him who said to his disciples, "For it is not you that speak, but the Spirit of your Father that speaks in you."[54] So by this precept we are admonished to make the attempt and, failing in our own strength, to pray for the assistance of God.

16.(17) Accordingly, after emphasizing the evils of the tongue, saying among other things, "My brothers, these things ought not so to be,"[55] the Apostle at once, upon completing the remarks which arose from this subject, counsels by what help those things which he says ought not to happen would not happen: "Who is a wise man and endowed with knowledge among you? Let him show, by a good way of life, his work in the meekness of wisdom. But if you have a bitter zeal and there be contentions in your hearts, glory not, and be not liars against the truth. For this is not wisdom descending from above, but earthly, sensual, devilish. For where envy and contention is, there is inconstancy and every evil work. But the [244] wisdom that is from above first indeed is chaste, then peaceable, modest, easy to be persuaded, consenting to the good, full of mercy and good fruits, without judging, without dissimulation."[56] This is the wisdom that tames the tongue, descending from above, not springing from a human heart. Would anyone dare to take it away from the grace of God and with overweening vanity place it in the power of man? Why therefore do we pray to receive it, if it is from man that it is to be had? Or should one object to this prayer in order not to detract from the freedom of the will, which because of its natural ability is sufficient unto

54. Matt 10.20.   55. Jas 3.10.
56. Jas 3.13–17.

itself to carry out all the precepts of justice? If so, let him object to the Apostle James himself, when in these words he admonishes us: "If any of you is in need of wisdom, let him ask of God, who gives to all abundantly and does not upbraid, and it shall be given to him. But let him ask in faith, nothing wavering."[57] This is the faith toward which the commandments impel us, so that what the law commands, faith accomplishes. For through the tongue, which no man, but only the wisdom which descends from above, can tame, "In many things we all offend."[58] And the same apostle did not say this in any different sense than that in which he states, "But the tongue no man can tame."

17.(18) Nor will anyone raise in objection to them, in support of the impossibility of not sinning, that passage which says, "The wisdom of the flesh is an enemy to God, for it is not subject to the law of God, neither can it be. And they who are in the flesh cannot please God."[59] The Apostle refers to the wisdom of the flesh, not the wisdom which comes from above, and [245] clearly by "in the flesh" he is designating, not those who have not yet left the body, but those who live according to the flesh. But what I am waiting to hear from our author, if I could, is whether those who live according to the spirit and who on this account, even while still living here, are in some sense not living in the flesh, are living according to the spirit by the grace of God or, on the contrary, are sufficient unto themselves because of the power of their nature given at their creation and of their own will. For the fulfillment of the law is nothing other than charity,[60] and "The charity of God is poured forth in our hearts," not by ourselves, but "by the Holy Spirit who is given to us."[61]

(19) Pelagius also treats of the sins of ignorance and declares, *A man should be vigilant not to be ignorant, and thus ignorance is blameworthy, for it is through his negligence that a man is ignorant of that which he should have known if he had applied diligence,* while he prefers to dispute all things rather than to pray and say, "Give

57. Jas 1.5–6.
58. Jas 3.2.
59. Rom 8.7–8.
60. Cf. Rom 12.10.
61. Rom 5.5.

me understanding, and I will learn thy commandments."[62] For it is one thing not to have taken care to know (and even these sins of negligence were apparently expiated by certain sacrifices of the law[63]), but it is another thing to wish to understand and fail, and to act contrary to the law because of not understanding what it intended to have been done. Accordingly, we are exhorted to ask wisdom of God, "who gives to all abundantly,"[64] at least to all who ask in such a way and to such an extent as so great a gift ought to be sought.

18.(20) Pelagius declares, *Nevertheless, sins which have been committed must be divinely expiated, and because of them it is necessary to address our prayers to the Lord,* so that we may obtain a pardon for them, *because that which has been done,* as even he admits, *cannot be undone by the power of nature,* which he praises so highly, *and the will of man.* Because of this necessity, therefore, it remains the case that one must pray to be forgiven. Yet that a man must obtain help in order not to sin, he has never said, and I do not read it here. His silence here is truly astonishing, considering that the Lord's prayer requires that we pray both that we may be forgiven our debts and that we may not [246] be brought into temptation,[65] the first of these seeking that our past offenses be forgiven, the second that future offenses be avoided. Indeed, this cannot be accomplished without the cooperation of our will; nevertheless, our will alone is not enough. Hence, the prayer which is offered up to the Lord for this purpose is neither superfluous nor offensive. For what can be more foolish than to pray to do what you already have it in your power[66] to do?

The Nature and Effects of Sin

19.(21) Now consider—which is most central to our subject—how Pelagius tries to present human nature as if it were entirely without fault and how, against the clearest evidence of God's Scriptures, he prefers that "wisdom of speech" by which

62. Ps 118.73.   63. Cf. Lev 4.2–3.
64. Jas 1.5.   65. Cf. Matt 6.12–13.
66. Correcting CSEL: *postestate* to *potestate.*

the cross of Christ is made void.[67] But certainly it will not be made void, rather this "wisdom" will be overturned. When we have shown this, perhaps the mercy of God will intervene, so that Pelagius may regret that he ever said these things. *First,* he says, *we must dispute the view which maintains that our nature has been weakened and changed through sin. I think, therefore, that before all else we must inquire what sin is. Is it some substance, or is it a name wholly lacking substance, by which is expressed neither a thing, nor an existence, nor some kind of body, but the action of doing something evil?* Then he adds, *I believe it is the latter, and if it is,* he says, *how could that which lacks substance have weakened or changed human nature?* Observe, I beseech you, how he endeavors in his ignorance to distort the most salutary words of our health-giving Scriptures: "I said, O Lord, be merciful to me; heal my soul, for I have sinned against thee."[68] But what is healed if nothing is wounded, nothing injured, nothing weakened and corrupted? But if there is something to be healed, whence came the injury? You hear the Psalmist confessing—what need is there for discussion? "Heal my soul," he says. Ask him how the soul, which he prays to be healed, became injured, and listen to what follows: "For I have sinned against thee." Let our author question him, let him ask of him what he thinks ought to be asked and [247] say, "Oh you who cry, 'Heal my soul, for I have sinned against thee,' tell me, what is sin? Is it some substance, or is it a name lacking all substance, by which is expressed neither a thing nor an existence nor some kind of body, but merely the action of doing something evil?" The Psalmist replies, "It is just as you say: sin is not some substance, but only the act of doing something evil is expressed by this name." Then Pelagius objects, "Then why do you cry out, 'Heal my soul, for I have sinned against thee'? How could that which lacks substance have injured your soul?" Then would not his respondent, exhausted by the anguish of his wound, briefly, so that he may not be diverted from prayer by the discussion, answer, "Leave me, I beg of you! Instead discuss the issue, if you can, with him who said, 'They that are in health need not a physician, but they

67. Cf. 1 Cor 1.17.   68. Ps. 40.5.

that are ill. .... I am not come to call the just, but sinners,'[69] where clearly he calls the just 'healthy,' while he calls sinners 'ill.' "

20.(22) Do you not perceive where this discussion is leading and what outcome it is reaching toward? It is that it will be thought to be said completely in vain, "And you will call his name Jesus. For he shall save his people from their sins."[70] For how can he bring about salvation where there is no sickness? For the sins from which the gospel says the people of Christ have to be saved are not substances and hence, according to our author, are not capable of injuring. O my brother, it is good for you to remember that you are a Christian! Perhaps it would be sufficient to believe these words, but, since you wish to continue the discussion, there is no reason not to do so, indeed it may do some good, provided the strongest faith precede, and we do not suppose that human nature cannot be corrupted by sin, but rather, believing with the divine Scriptures that it is corrupted by sin, we inquire how this could have come about. Since we have already learned that sin is not a substance, let us consider [248] (omitting other things) whether abstinence from food is also not a substance. One indeed abstains *from* a substance, since food is a substance. But to abstain from food is not a substance—yet nevertheless if we abstain entirely from food, the substance of our body languishes and is so impaired by frailty of health, so exhausted of strength, and so weakened and broken with weariness, that even if it were able in some way to continue to live, it would barely be capable of being restored to the use of that food, by abstaining from which it became corrupted. Likewise, sin is not a substance, but God is a substance, the supreme substance, the only true nourishment of the rational creature. Listen to how the Psalmist expresses what it is to withdraw from him by disobedience and to be unable through weakness even to receive that in which one truly ought to rejoice: "My heart is withered and beaten like grass, because I forgot to eat my bread."[71]

69. Matt 9.12–13. 70. Matt 1.21.
71. Ps 101.5.

21.(23) But observe how Pelagius with superficially plausible arguments continues to oppose the truth of Holy Scripture. The Lord Jesus, who is called Jesus because "He shall save his people from their sins"[72]—the Lord Jesus therefore declares, "They that are in health need not a physician, but they that are ill. . . . For I am come not to call the just but sinners."[73] In accordance with this, the Apostle also says, "A faithful saying and worthy of all acceptance, that Christ Jesus came into the world to save sinners."[74] However, Pelagius, contrary to this "faithful saying and worthy of all acceptance," says, *This sickness should not have been contracted by sins, lest the punishment of sin should come to this: that more sins are committed.* So great a physician is sought as a help even for infants, and yet Pelagius asks, *What do you seek? Those for whom you seek a physician are in good health. And not even the first man was condemned to death for such a reason, for he did not sin afterwards.* It is as though he had heard something of his perfection in justice afterwards, aside from what the Church commends: that Adam himself had been [249] liberated by the mercy of Christ our Lord. *His descendants also,* he says, *not only are not weaker than he, but have actually fulfilled more commandments, since he neglected to obey even the one.* He who saves his people from their sins[75] sees these descendants to be born in such a state (in which Adam certainly was not created) that they not only are not capable of obeying precepts of which they are altogether unaware, but are scarcely capable of taking the breast when they are hungry, yet nevertheless, he wishes to save by his grace even these, in the bosom of Mother Church. But men oppose him and, as if they had a deeper insight into the creature than does God, who made it, declare, with a statement that is not sound, that such infants are sound.

22.(24) *Punishment,* declares Pelagius, *is the very matter of sin, if the sinner is weakened to the point that he commits more sins.* Pelagius does not consider how worthily the light of truth abandons the transgressor of the law. When thus abandoned, a man becomes blinded and necessarily offends all the more. By falling

72. Matt 1.21.
74. 1 Tim 1.15.

73. Matt 9.12–13.
75. I.e., Jesus; cf. Matt 1.21.

he is injured and thus injured does not arise sufficiently to hear the voice of the law, which admonishes him to ask for the grace of the savior. Is not punishment to be theirs of whom the Apostle says, "Because when they knew God, they have not glorified him as God, or given thanks, but became vain in their thoughts, and their foolish heart was darkened"?[76] Surely, that darkening of the heart was already a penalty and punishment, and by that penalty, that is by the blinding of the heart because of the abandonment by the light of wisdom, they fell into more and serious sins. "For professing themselves to be wise, they became fools."[77] This is a serious punishment, if anyone understands it, and from that punishment see to where they have gone on: "And they changed," says the Apostle, "the glory of the incorruptible God into the likeness of the image of a corruptible man, and of birds, and of four-footed beasts, and of creeping things."[78] All this they did because of the punishment of their sin, by which [250] "their foolish heart was darkened."[79] And because of these things, since although they were punishments they were nonetheless also themselves sins, the Apostle goes on to say, "Wherefore God gave them up to the desires of their heart, unto uncleanness."[80] Behold how much more severely God condemned them, giving them up to the desires of their heart, unto uncleanness. Observe also what they do because of this punishment: They "dishonor," says the Apostle, "their own bodies among themselves."[81] And that this is punishment of iniquity, as well as being itself iniquity, the Apostle sets forth very clearly in his statement: "Who changed the truth of God into a lie, and worshipped and served the creature rather than the creator, who is blessed forever. Amen. For this cause God delivered them up to shameful affections."[82] Behold how often God inflicts punishment, and how from such punishment more numerous and severe sins arise: "For their women have changed their natural relations into relations which are against nature. And in like manner the men also, leaving their natural

76. Rom 1.21.   77. Rom 1.22.
78. Rom 1.23.   79. Rom 1.21.
80. Rom 1.24.   81. Rom 1.24.
82. Rom 1.25–26.

relations with women, have burned in their lusts one towards
another, men with men, bringing about degradation."[83] And
in order to show that these sins were also the punishment for
other sins, he also adds, "and receiving in themselves the recompense which was due to their error."[84] Observe how often
God punishes and the very punishment engenders and gives
rise to other sins. Consider further: "And as they cared not
to have God in their knowledge, God delivered them up to a
reprobate [251] mind, to do those things which are not proper,
being filled with all iniquity, with deviousness, malice, avarice,
full of envy, murder, contention, deceit, malignity, whisperers,
detractors, hateful to God, contumelious, proud, haughty, in-
ventors of evil things, disobedient to parents, foolish, dissolute,
without affection, without mercy."[85] And now let this man
come along and say, "Sin should not have been punished in
such a way that the sinner, through his punishment, should
commit more sins."

23.(25) Perhaps Pelagius may reply that God does not compel men to do these evil deeds, but only that he abandons those
who deserve being abandoned. This is most true if this is what
he says. For, as I have already said, what can those who have
been deprived of the light of justice and thereby plunged into
darkness produce except all those works of darkness which I
have noted, until it is said to them, and they obey the command,
"Rise, you that sleep, and arise from the dead, and Christ shall
enlighten you"?[86] The truth declares that they are dead, as in
the passage, "Let the dead bury their dead."[87] The truth declares dead those whom our author says cannot have been
wounded nor corrupted by sin, because, as he has apparently
discovered, sin is not a substance! No one has said that man was
so made that he could indeed move from justice to sin, and yet
could not return from sin to justice; however, to descend into
sin, that free will, through which man corrupted himself, was
sufficient, whereas to return to justice he needed a physician,
since he was sick, he needed a giver of life, since he was dead.

83. Rom 1.26–27.   84. Rom 1.27.
85. Rom 1.28–31. Augustine's text differs somewhat from Vg.
86. Eph 5.14.   87. Matt 8.22.

Concerning this grace, Pelagius says nothing at all, as if the sinner could cure himself through his own free will, since by this alone he corrupted himself. We do not [252] say to him that the death of the body contributes to sin, because it is only its punishment (for no one sins through the death of his body); rather it is the death of the soul—when it is abandoned by its life, which is its God—which contributes to sin. Thus abandoned, it necessarily accomplishes only dead works, until through the grace of Christ it is brought back to life. Far be it from us to say that hunger and thirst and other bodily troubles produce the necessity of sin. When tested by such troubles, the life of the just shines out more vividly, and in surmounting such troubles, it achieves a greater glory—but assisted by the grace of God, assisted by the spirit of God, assisted by the mercy of God, not exalting itself through a proud will, but earning fortitude through humble confession. For it has learned to say to God, "For you are my patience."[88] Regarding this grace, this aid, this mercy, without which we cannot live properly, Pelagius for some reason has absolutely nothing to say. Indeed, on the contrary, defending nature as if it were sufficient to itself, provided only that the will be present, for the attainment of righteousness, he quite openly opposes the grace of Christ, by which we are justified. Why, on the other hand, once the guilt of sin is absolved through grace, for the exercise of faith, the death of the body remains, although it has come from sin, I have already explained to the best of my ability in those books which I wrote to Marcellinus of blessed memory.[89]

24.(26) Regarding the statement of Pelagius that *the Lord, though he was without sin, was able to die*—his birth also was the work of his mercy and not the requirement of his nature. He died by virtue of this same power, and this is the price which he paid to deliver us from death. And this their argument attempts to nullify, for they defend human nature in such a way as to say that free will might not need such ransom in order to be delivered from the power of darkness and of him who has the power of death unto the kingdom of Christ our Lord. And

88. Ps 70.5.   89. *De pecc. mer.* 2.30.49–34.56.

yet when the Lord approached his passion, he cried out, "For the prince of this world comes, and in me he finds nothing"[90]— finds nothing indeed of sin, by which he who has the power of death [253] might bring him under his rule, in order to destroy him. "But," he added, "that all may know, that I do the will of my Father, arise, let us go hence,"[91] that is, I die, not through the necessity of sin, but through a will of obedience.

(27) Pelagius asserts, *No evil is the cause of anything good,* as though punishment were a good since because of it many have been reformed. Thus, there are evils which are beneficial, by the wonderful mercy of God. For has he experienced anything good, who said, "You turned your face from me, and I became troubled"?[92] Certainly not. And yet this very trouble was in some way a remedy for him against pride. For in the time of his prosperity he had said, "I shall never be moved,"[93] and attributed to himself what he had received from the Lord. For what did he have that he had not received?[94] For this reason it became necessary to reveal to him the source of what he had received, so that what he had lost in his pride he might receive in humility. Thus he says, " 'Lord, in your favor you gave strength to my beauty.'[95] In that abundance of mine, I said to myself, 'I shall never be moved,'[96] but this abundance came to me from you and not from me. Then at last 'You turned your face from me, and I became troubled.' "[97]

25.(28) The proud mind[98] has no liking for this, but God is great enough to persuade it of what he himself knows. For we are more inclined to be thinking of what we will say in response to those who argue against our errors than to acknowledge how much better off we would be if we were free from error. Therefore, we ought to answer such adversaries not by discussions but by prayers for themselves and for ourselves as well. For we do not say to them, what Pelagius opposed to himself, *Sin was necessary, so that there might be a cause for God's mercy.* Would that

---

90. John 14.30.   91. John 14.31.
92. Ps 29.8.   93. Ps 29.7.
94. Cf. 1 Cor 4.7.   95. Ps 29.8.
96. Ps 29.7.   97. Ps 29.8.
98. Reading *animus,* with PL and BA; CSEL: *amicus.*

there had never been misery to make such mercy necessary! Rather, we say that the iniquity of sin is the greater the more easily man, as yet unencumbered by any infirmity, might have avoided sin. [254] A most just punishment has followed, so that he received a recompense in himself corresponding to his sin, namely, losing somehow the obedience of a body which had been set under him, when it was obedience above all that he, set under his Lord, had despised.[99] Therefore, if we are now born with this same law of sin, which in our members fights against the law of the mind,[100] we should neither murmur against God, nor dispute this most evident fact, but should rather, because of our punishment, seek and implore the mercy of God.

26.(29) Observe very carefully how Pelagius says, *No doubt God applies his mercy to this function, if at some time it should become necessary, because after sin man requires this kind of help, not because God wished that there should be a cause for such a need.* Do you not see how he says that the mercy of God is necessary, not in order that we should not sin, but because we have sinned? Then he adds, *In a similar manner, it is the duty of a physician to be ready to heal a man who is now wounded; however, he ought not to wish that a man who is sound should be wounded.* If this comparison has application to the subject we are discussing, certainly it cannot be that human nature is wounded by sin, since sin is not a substance! Thus, for example, just as he who is crippled by an injury is treated so that, his past injury healed, his future steps may be normal, in like fashion the heavenly physician heals our ills, not only so that they no longer exist, but so that we may ever after be able to walk upright, something which, even when healthy, we could not really do except by his assistance. For a human physician, when he has cured a man, in order that he be sustained by bodily elements and nourishment, so that his health be restored and persist through suitable aid, commends him to God, who bestows such assistance on all who live in the flesh, and whose are all those things which the physician has applied during the course of treatment. For the physician does

99. See *De civitate Dei* 14.15–16.   100. Cf. Rom 7.23.

not cure anyone by means of things which he has himself created, but out of the resources of him who has created all things which are needed for both the healthy and the sick. But God himself, when, through the "one mediator of God and men, the man Christ Jesus,"[101] [255] he spiritually heals a sick person or raises a dead one, that is, justifies the ungodly,[102] and when he has restored him to perfect health, that is, to perfect life and justice, does not forsake him (if he is not forsaken [by him]), so that he may always live in piety and justice. For just as the bodily eye, even when completely unimpaired, can distinguish nothing unless aided by the brightness of light, so also a man, even if he is most fully justified, cannot live rightly, unless he is divinely assisted by the eternal light of justice. Thus God heals us not only so that he may eradicate the sins that we have committed, but also in order that he may enable us to avoid further sin.

27.(30) No doubt Pelagius is ingenious in discussing, reviewing, and, as it seems to him, rebutting and refuting, a statement made in opposition to his party, that *It was necessary for man, in order to take away all occasion for pride and boasting, that he should not be able to exist without sin. It is completely absurd and foolish*, he thinks, *that there should have been sin so that sin should not be, since pride itself is, of course, a sin.* This is as though a wound did not involve pain, and an operation did not produce pain, so that pain might be taken away by pain. If we did not know this from experience, but heard about it in some part of the world, where such things had never occurred, then no doubt we might deride this, perhaps using the very words of Pelagius and saying, "It is completely absurd that pain should have been necessary in order that the pain of a wound should not be."

(31) *But God,* they say, *can heal all things.* God does indeed act in order to heal all things, but he acts on his own judgment and does not take his method of curing from the one who is sick. Without doubt, God wished to give his Apostle great strength, and yet he said to him, "Power is made perfect in infirmity."[103] Nor did he remove from this Apostle, who often begged him

101. 1 Tim 2.5.   102. Cf. Rom 4.5.
103. 2 Cor 12.9.

to do so, that thorn in the flesh, whatever it was, which he told was given to him so that he should not become unduly exalted by the greatness of the revelation.[104] For all other vices flourish only in evil deeds; pride alone is to be guarded against even in things that are rightly done. Hence they are warned, so that attributing to their own power the gifts of God and thereby glorifying themselves, [256] they may not perish with a greater loss than if they had done no good at all, to whom it is said, "With fear and trembling work out your salvation. For it is God who works in you, both to will and to accomplish, according to his good will."[105] Why then with fear and trembling, and not rather with security, if it is God who works? It can only be because of our will, for, since without it we can do nothing good, the idea quickly insinuates itself in the human soul to attribute to itself exclusively all the good that it has accomplished and to say in its prosperity, "I shall never be moved."[106] That is why God, who in his good will had added strength to our beauty, turns his face away for a little while, so that the man who had boasted becomes troubled,[107] for that swollen pride can only be cured through sorrows.

28.(32) Therefore it is not said to a man, "It is necessary to sin, so that you may sin no more," but rather it is said to him, "God abandons you for a short time, that you may know that that in which you take pride is not your own but his, and learn not to be proud." For what kind of account was that of the Apostle?[108] Is it not so remarkable that, unless it had been stated by the Apostle, who spoke so truly that no one would dare to contradict him, it would have been incredible?[109] For who among the faithful does not know that the first incentive to sin came from Satan, and that he is the first author of all sins? And yet some are "delivered up to Satan, that they may learn not to blaspheme."[110] How does it happen then that the work of Satan is prevented by the work of Satan? These and similar questions

104. Cf. 2 Cor 12.7–8.   105. Phil 2.12–13.
106. Ps 29.7.   107. Cf. Ps 29.8.
108. The episode from 2 Cor 12.7–9 recounted in the preceding chapter.
109. Reading *non sit* with PL and BA; CSEL: *sit.*
110. 1 Tim 1.20.

one ought to examine, so that they may not seem to him to be
too subtle, for although they sound quite subtle, when they are
discussed they are found to be straightforward. Also, what
must we say to the comparisons Pelagius uses, by which he
rather suggests the answers that should be given to him? He
asks, "What more shall I say than that we may believe that fires
are quenched by fires, if we may believe that sins are cured by
sins?" But what if no one can put out fires by fires, yet, as I have
shown, pains can be cured by pains? Furthermore, one can in-
vestigate and observe that poisons can be eliminated by poisons. [257] And if he also notices that sometimes the heat of a
fever can be broken by the heat of certain remedies, perhaps
also he will admit that fires may be extinguished by fires.

29.(33) *How*, Pelagius asks, *shall we distinguish pride itself from
sin?* Why does he raise this question, since it is obvious that
pride itself is a sin? *To sin*, he says, *is to be proud, just as much as to
be proud is to sin. For just ask what any sin is, and see whether you can
discover a sin that does not fall into the category of pride.* Analyzing
this point further he endeavors to prove it as follows: *All sin*, he
says, *is, if I am not mistaken, contempt for God, and all contempt for
God is pride. For what is more proud than to have contempt for God?
Hence, all sin is also pride, just as Scripture says, "Pride is the beginning of all sin."*[111] Let him examine with care, and he will discover that in the law considerable distinction is made between
the sin of pride and other sins. For many sins are committed
through pride, but not all things that are done wrongly are
done in pride—certainly not those done by the ignorant, or the
infirm, nor ordinarily by those who weep and sorrow. And a
certain pride, although it is itself a great sin, exists by itself apart
from other sins, in such a way that, as I have said above,[112] usually indeed it steals upon and overtakes, not our sins but, all the
more rapidly, our good actions themselves. But it is most truly
said, in a sense different from that in which Pelagius understands it, "Pride is the beginning of all sin,"[113] for the reason
that it was this sin that overthrew the devil, from whom arose

111. Sir 10.15.   112. Above, 27.31.
113. Sir 10.15.

the origin of sin, and who, through subsequent envy, over-turned the man who was standing in the justice from which he had fallen. For the serpent, seeking a way to enter, clearly sought the door of pride, when he declared, "You shall be as gods."[114] That is why it is written, "Pride is the beginning of all sin," and "The beginning of the pride of man is to fall away from God."[115]

30.(34) [258] What does Pelagius mean in the following passage? *Next, how can a man be answerable to God for the guilt of a sin which he knows is not his own? For if it is necessary, it is not his own. Or if it is his own, it is voluntary; and if it is voluntary, it can be avoided.* We answer, Beyond all doubt it is his own, but the fault through which it was committed has not yet been completely healed. And the fact that it grows in us happens because we did not correctly use the good health with which we were endowed. From this fault man, who is now becoming increasingly ill, through weakness or blindness commits more sins. He ought to pray that he may be healed and that from then on he may enjoy a life of perpetual good health, not becoming proud, as if a man could be healed by the very same power by which he became corrupted.

31.(35) And indeed I would have said these things in such a way as to confess my ignorance of the profound judgment of God—why he does not cure at once this pride which, in good actions, easily insinuates itself into the human soul. It is for this cure that pious souls supplicate him with tears and great sighs, imploring him to extend a hand to them in their efforts, in order to conquer this pride and in some way beat it down and crush it. For when a man has rejoiced that he has overcome pride in some good work, from this very joy he raises his head and says, "Behold I live, why do you triumph? Indeed, I live because you triumph." Perhaps he delights prematurely in that triumph over pride, as if it were already conquered, when in fact its last shadow will be absorbed in the light of noon, the noon that is promised by Scripture in the verse, "And he will bring forth your justice as the light, and your judgment as the

114. Gen 3.5.   115. Sir 10.15,14.

noonday,"[116] if it is done as written in the preceding words, "Commit your way to the Lord, and trust in him, and he will do it"[117]—not, as some think, because they do it themselves. For when he said, "and he will do it," evidently he had no one else in mind than those who declare, "We do it," that is, we ourselves justify ourselves. We do in fact work, but when [259] we work, we cooperate with God who works, for his mercy comes before us.[118] It comes before us, however, that we may be healed, as it also will follow, so that being healed we may gain strength. It comes before us so that we may be called, and it will follow, so that we may be glorified. It comes before us so that we may lead pious lives; it will follow so that we may always live with him, for without him we can do nothing.[119] For Scripture says both, "He is my God, his mercy shall come before me,"[120] and, "Your mercy will follow me all the days of my life."[121] Therefore, let us reveal to him our way through confession, rather than praise it by defending it. For if it is not his way but ours, then surely it is not the right way. Let us reveal it to him by our confession, for it is not hidden from him, even if we try to conceal it. For "it is good to confess to the Lord."[122]

32.(36) Thus, he will give us what pleases him, if whatever in us displeases him also displeases us. As Scripture says, he will turn aside our ways from his way,[123] and make his way our own, for he extends this favor to those who believe in him and trust in him that he will do it.[124] For this is the way of justice, ignored by those who "have a zeal for God, but not according to knowledge, and who, seeking to establish their own justice, have not submitted themselves to the justice of God. For the end of the law is Christ, unto justice for everyone that believes,"[125] Christ who said, "I am the way."[126] Yet even those who have already begun to walk in his way are fearful of the voice of God, fearful that they may praise themselves for walking in his way by their

116. Ps 36.6.
118. Cf. Ps 58.11.
120. Ps 58.11.
122. Ps 91.2.
124. Cf. Ps 36.5.
126. John 14.6.

117. Ps 36.5.
119. John 15.5.
121. Ps 22.6.
123. Cf. Ps 43.19.
125. Rom 10.2–4.

own strength. This is why the Apostle has said to them, "With fear and trembling work out your salvation. For it is God who works in you, both to will and to accomplish, according to his good will."[127] For the same reason [260] the psalm says to them, "Serve the Lord in fear, and rejoice unto him with trembling. Embrace discipline, so that at some time the Lord may not be angry, and you perish from the just way, when his wrath shall be enkindled in a short time upon you."[128] He does not say, "So that at some time the Lord may not be angry and not show you the way of justice," or, "not lead you into the way of justice," but even when they are walking in that way, he could instill fear into them in saying, "that you may not perish from the just way." How could this be if not from pride, which, as I have said so many times and must keep saying often, has to be guarded against even in things which are rightly done, that is, in the way of justice itself, so that a man, regarding what is of God as his own, may not lose what is of God and be reduced to what is his own? Therefore, let us follow the concluding words of that psalm, "Blessed are all they that trust in him,"[129] so that he himself acts and shows us his own way, he to whom it is said, "Show us, O Lord, your mercy;"[130] may he himself grant salvation, so that we can walk in his way, he to whom it is said, "And grant us your salvation;"[131] may he himself guide us in this way, he to whom it is said, "Guide me, O Lord, in your way, and I will walk in your truth;"[132] may he himself direct us to that promised happiness, wheresoever his way leads, he to whom it is said, "There also shall your hand lead me, and your right hand shall guide me;"[133] may he himself there feed those who sit down with Abraham, Isaac, and Jacob, he of whom it is said, "He will make them sit down to eat and will pass by and minister to them."[134] In recalling these words we do not take away the freedom of the will, but rather we preach the grace of God. For to whom are these words helpful, except to the one who uses his own will, but uses it humbly, not priding himself in the

127. Phil 2.12–13.
128. Ps 2.11–13.
129. Ps 2.13.
130. Ps 84.8.
131. Ps 84.8.
132. Ps 85.11.
133. Ps 138.10.
134. Luke 12.37.

strength of his will, as if it alone were sufficient to achieve justice?

33.(37) But far be it from us to say to him as he says certain persons have said against him, *Man is placed on an equal level with God if he is said to be without sin.*[135] [261] As if indeed an angel who is without sin is placed on an equal level with God. I, in fact, think that even when there will be established in us a justice so great that nothing at all can be added to it, the creature will still never become equal with the creator. However, if others believe that our progress will be so great that we shall be changed into the substance of God, and thus become altogether what he is,[136] they ought to consider how they support this opinion—for my part, I confess that I am not convinced.

34.(38) I am very favorably disposed to the author of this book when, against those who say, *What you say appears to be reasonable, but it is arrogant to declare that a man can be without sin,* he replies that, if it is true, it ought not to be regarded as at all arrogant to say so. For he adds with much clarity and truth, *On what side must humility be placed? On the side of falsehood, no doubt, if you maintain that arrogance is to be placed on the side of truth.* Hence he concludes, and concludes correctly, that humility should be placed on the side of truth rather than of falsehood. From which it follows that he who said, "If we say that we have no sin, we deceive ourselves, and the truth is not in us,"[137] must without the least doubt be considered to have spoken the truth, and that he should not be considered to have spoken falsely for the sake of humility. Why, therefore, did he add, "and the truth is not in us," when it might have been quite sufficient to say, "we deceive ourselves," if not that he was aware that some could

135. Cf. Jerome, *Ep.* 133.8.
136. Augustine here distances himself from charges made by Jerome (*Ep.* 133.3 and *Dial. c. Pel.* 2.14,17) and Orosius (*Apol.* 16–18) which ascribe to Pelagius a doctrine which equates human sinlessness with that of God, and thus leads to an extreme form (which Jerome labels "Pythagorean" and which he sees in Evagrius of Pontus and the *Sentences of Sextus* [see below 64.77 and note]) of the doctrine of deification (θέωσις, θεωποίησις) found in more nuanced terms in Athanasius and other Greek patristic writings. For Augustine's own understanding of deification, see Gerald Bonner, "Augustine's Concept of Deification," *JTS*, n.s. 37 (1986) 369–86.
137. 1 John 1.8.

suppose that he had said, "we deceive ourselves," as if to mean that even the person who praises himself for a truly good act is exalting himself in pride. Hence, by adding "the truth is not in us," he shows very clearly—as Pelagius quite rightly admits—that it is in no way true "if we say that we have no sin," lest humility, placed on the side of falsehood, lose the reward of truth.

(39) Beyond this, however, when he thinks that he is serving the cause of God by defending nature, he forgets that in declaring this nature to be sound he rejects the mercy of the physician. But the same person who created him is also [262] his savior. Therefore, we should not so praise the creator that we are compelled to say, or rather convicted of saying, that there is no need for the savior. Therefore let us honor man's nature with fitting praises, and let us attribute these praises to the glory of the creator; but let us not be grateful to him for having created us in such a way that we are ungrateful to him for having healed us. Let us not attribute our defects of which we are healed to the action of God, but rather to the will of man and to his just punishment. Nevertheless, we must admit that it was in our power that they should not have come about, just as we confess that their cure depends upon his mercy more than upon our own power. However, Pelagius reduces this mercy and healing aid of the savior to the fact that he forgives the transgressions of the past, not that he will help us to avoid sins in the future. Here he is most dangerously mistaken, for, however unknowingly, he hinders us from being careful, and from praying that we "enter not into temptation,"[138] since he maintains that it is entirely within our power that it should not happen to us.

Scriptural Examples of Sinlessness?

35.(40) Pelagius observes with sound judgment, *The examples of certain persons, of whom we read in Scripture as having sinned, have not been written to encourage the despair of not sinning and to*

138. Mark 14.38.

seem somehow to offer us security in committing sin, but rather that
we might learn either the humility of repentance or recognize
that even in such falls salvation ought not to be despaired of.
For there are some who, when they have fallen into sin, perish
more completely from despair and not only neglect the remedy
of repentance, but, gratifying their depraved and shameful desires, become the slaves of lusts and evil passions, as if they
would lose something if they failed to accomplish what they
were driven to by their lusts, whereas a sure condemnation already awaits them. Against this deadly and very dangerous
sickness the remembrance of those sins into which even just
and holy men have fallen has some force.

(41) But Pelagius seems to ask very acutely, *How should we
believe these holy men have left this life: In a state of sin, or without
sin?* [263] If the response were, "in a state of sin," then it would
be supposed that damnation followed them, which is impious
to believe. If, however, it is said that they departed this life
"without sin," this would show that at least at the approach of
death a man had been without sin in this life. Although he is
quite perspicacious, Pelagius does not give sufficient attention
to the fact that even just persons ask with good reason in their
prayer, "Forgive us our debts, as we also forgive our debtors,"[139] and that the Lord Christ, in explaining this prayer in
his teaching, most truly added, "But if you will forgive men
their offenses, your heavenly Father will forgive you your offenses."[140] Through our forgiveness, which is a sort of daily
incense of the spirit offered to God on the altar of the heart—
the heart which we are bidden to lift up[141]—we are enabled,
even if we do not live here without sin, to die without sin, when
time and again God's forgiveness erases those sins which time
and again, through ignorance or weakness, we commit.

36.(42) Pelagius then recounts those who are said not only to
have lived without sin, but to have lived justly: Abel, Enoch,
Melchizedek, Abraham, Isaac, Jacob, Joseph, Joshua the son of

139. Matt 6.12.   140. Matt 6.14.
141. In the dialogue which precedes the Preface at the Mass. See below, note
to *De dono pers.* 13.33.

Nun, Phineas, Samuel, Nathan, Elijah, Elisha, Micaiah, Daniel, Hananiah, Azariah, Mishael, Ezekiel, Mordecai, Simeon, Joseph to whom the Virgin Mary was espoused, and John. He also adds the women: Deborah, Hannah the mother of Samuel, Judith, Esther, the other Hannah, daughter of Phanuel, Elizabeth, and she who was the mother of our Lord and savior, *who,* he says, *we are obliged out of piety to confess was without sin.* Therefore, I make an exception of the Blessed Virgin Mary,[142] in whose case, out of respect for the Lord, [264] I wish to raise no

142. The text of this sentence reads: *Excepta itaque sancta virgine Maria, de qua propter honorem domini nullam prorsus, cum de peccati agitur, haberi volo quaestionem—unde enim scimus quid ei plus gratiae conlatum fuerit ad vincendum omni ex parte peccatum, quae concipere ac parere meruit, quem constat nullum habuisse peccatum?* In medieval and later times, this was often cited as a proof-text to establish that Augustine taught the doctrine of the immaculate conception of Mary (see Pelikan, *The Christian Tradition* 4.45). Pelikan himself reads it in this sense in "An Augustinian Dilemma: Augustine's Doctrine of Grace versus Augustine's Doctrine of the Church," AS 18 (1987) 14. Against this interpretation is Augustine's frequent insistence on the universality of original sin, transmitted through the concupiscence attendant upon the process of conception via sexual intercourse—an evil from which Jesus alone was excepted, owing to his virginal conception. Augustine's references to Mary in this connection are ambiguous here and also in *C. Iul. op. impf.* 4.122: "We do not deliver Mary to the devil by the condition of her birth, but for this reason, that this very condition is resolved *(solvitur)* by the grace of rebirth" (PL 45. 1418). Clearer, however, are *C. Iul.* 5.15.52: "And thus it appears that the concupiscence through which Christ did not wish to be conceived has propagated evil in the human race, for the body of Mary, though it came from this, nevertheless did not transmit it into the body which she did not conceive from this" (PL 44. 813), and *De Gen. ad litt.* 10.18.32: "And what more undefiled than the womb of the Virgin, whose flesh, although it came from procreation tainted by sin, nevertheless did not conceive from that source?" (tr. John Hammond Taylor, S.J., ACW 42.120). Does the passage at hand affirm, if not Mary's freedom from original sin, at least her freedom from personal or actual sin? "It is not so much that he declares her personal sinlessness, as that he absolutely refuses to discuss the matter *propter honorem domini,* for the honour of the Lord" (Bonner, *St Augustine,* 328). In part, the interpretation of this passage hinges on whether it is construed as a question, as in CSEL and BA, or as a declarative statement, as in NPNF (perhaps following a textual variant, cited in PL but not CSEL, which reads *inde enim scimus* rather than *unde enim scimus*). On this passage and the questions it raises, see the note in BA 21. 609–11, and the literature cited there; Michael O'Carroll, *Theotokos: A Theological Encyclopedia of the Blessed Virgin Mary* (Wilmington, DE: Michael Glazier, rev. ed. 1983), s.v., "Augustine," and "Immaculate Conception"; and Athanase Sage, "Saint Augustin et l'Immaculée Conception," RÉAug 11 (1965) 305–06.

question at all when the discussion concerns sins—for whence
do we know what an abundance of grace for entirely overcom-
ing sin was conferred on her who had the merit to conceive
and bear him who undoubtedly was without sin?[143] The Virgin
Mary therefore excepted, if we were to bring together all these
saints, men and women, while they lived here and ask them
whether they were without sin, what can we suppose would be
their answer? I ask you, would it be what Pelagius says or what
the Apostle John says? However excellent might have been
their sanctity in this life, if they had been able to be questioned
about it, they would have declared with one voice, "If we say
that we have no sin, we deceive ourselves, and the truth is not
in us."[144] Or would they have been responding to this with more
humility than truth? But Pelagius has already, and correctly,
decided "not to place the praise of humility on the side of falsehood." Consequently, if they spoke the truth in their answer,
they were sinners, and because they humbly confessed it, the
truth would be in them; but if in their answer they lied, they
were no less sinners, for the truth would not be in them.

37.(43) Pelagius remarks, *Perhaps some will ask, How could
Scripture possibly have mentioned the sins of all of these?* Those who
would ask that would speak the truth. Nor do I see that he has
anywhere given a sound answer to them, although I see that he
was not willing to be silent. Observe, I beg of you, his reply: *This
question,* he says, *might justly be asked about those of whom Scripture
mentions neither good deeds nor bad, but, regarding those whose justice
it mentions, it would undoubtedly also have mentioned their sins, if it
had perceived that they had sinned in any way.* Let him say, then,
that their great faith did not have to do with justice, they who
made up "the multitudes that went before and that followed"
the ass on which the Lord rode, when, even among enemies,
who murmuring asked why they were doing this, they shouted,
"Hosanna to the son of David. Blessed is he who comes in the
name of the Lord."[145] Let him therefore dare tell us, if he can,
that [265] there was no one in all that vast crowd who had any

143. Cf. 1 John 3.5.   144. 1 John 1.8.
145. Matt 21.9.

sin at all. If it is most absurd to say this, why has not Scripture mentioned any of their sins, when it took care to mention the great good of their faith?

(44) But perhaps even Pelagius observed this and for that reason went on to say: *Let us admit that in other times, because of the large crowd* [of people who existed], *Scripture passed over the task of narrating the sins of everyone. However, in the very beginning of the world, when there were only four people, how do we explain,* he asks, *why it did not choose to mention the sins of all? Could it have been because of the great number of people who did not yet exist, or because it preserved the memory only of those who had sinned, and could not preserve the memory of him who had not indeed sinned?* He makes additional comments in order to explain more fully and clearly his thought: *Certainly,* he says, *it is written that first in time only four persons existed: Adam and Eve, and Cain and Abel born from them. Eve sinned—Scripture tells us that. Adam also sinned—the same Scripture makes this clear—and in like manner it also testifies that Cain sinned. And not only does it mention their sins, it also tells the nature of their sins. If Abel also had sinned, Scripture undoubtedly would have said so, but it has not said so; therefore he did not sin, but on the contrary it shows him to have been just. Therefore let us believe what we read and let us consider it wicked to add that which we do not read.*

38.(45) In saying this Pelagius pays too little attention to what he himself had said not long before: *By the time a multitude of the human race had sprung up, it was possible that because of the large crowd Scripture passed over the task of narrating the sins of everyone.* For, if he had been sufficiently attentive to this, he would have discovered that even in the case of one man there exists such a crowd and multitude of lesser sins that it would have been impossible, or if possible not desirable, to write them all down. Those were written down for which due measure called, and by which the reader could be instructed through a few examples in the practice of many of the necessary virtues. For even when the number of human beings was still small, [266] Scripture has not mentioned how many and who they were, that is, how many sons and daughters Adam and Eve had and what names they gave them. Because of this omission, some commentators, taking too little note of the fact that Scripture passes

silently over many things, have thought that Cain cohabited
with his own mother and thus produced by her the children
that are mentioned,[146] believing that the sons of Adam had no
sisters, because Scripture had not at that point mentioned
them, although later in recapitulation it implies what had previously been omitted, that Adam "begot sons and daughters,"[147] without saying anything of the time of their birth, nor
their number, nor their names. Similarly, it was unnecessary to
state whether Abel, even though he was deservedly called
just,[148] ever indulged in too much laughter, or ever got carried
away in jesting, or ever looked upon something with excessive
desire, or ever picked too much fruit, or suffered indigestion
from overeating, or if during prayers he thought of something
which caused his attention to wander. How many times must
these and many similar faults have crept stealthily into his
mind? Are they not perhaps the same sins that in a general
way the Apostle admonishes us to guard against and to refrain
from, when he says, "Let not sin reign in your mortal body, so
as to obey the lusts thereof"?[149] We must engage in a constant,
daily struggle that we not obey these desires that are forbidden
or at least improper. For from this sort of fault it comes about
that the eye is turned or turned away, where it ought not to
look, and if this fault grows strong and prevails, even bodily
adultery is carried out, which is committed in the heart as much
more quickly as thought is quicker than action and has nothing
to hinder or delay it. Those who have in great measure curbed
this sin, that is, this appetite of a corrupt affection, so as not
to obey its desires, "nor yield their members as instruments of
iniquity"[150] to it, have indeed deserved to be called "just," and
this by the help of the grace of [267] God. In fact, because sin
often stole over them in very small matters, and sometimes
when they were taken off guard, they were both just and at
the same time not without sin. Finally, if in Abel, the just man,
divine charity, by which alone whoever is just is truly just, could
and should have increased, then whatsoever degree it fell short

146. Cf. Gen 4.17.   147. Gen 5.4.
148. Cf. Matt 23.35.   149. Rom 6.12.
150. Rom 6.13.

was due to sin.[151] And who does not fall short, up to that time when he arrives at that strength of God, in which all men's weakness is absorbed?

39.(46) Clearly it is an important statement with which Pelagius concluded this passage when he said, *Therefore let us believe what we read and let us consider it wicked to add that which we do not read, and let it suffice for all instances to have said this once.* For my part, on the contrary, I say that we ought not to believe everything that we read—as the Apostle says, "Read all things; hold fast to what is good"[152]—and that it is not wicked to add something which we have not read. For we can add something in good faith which we have experienced as witnesses even though we may not have read it. Perhaps Pelagius will reply, "When I said that, I was concerned with Holy Scripture." Oh, would that he were unwilling to add anything, I do not say *other than* what he reads in Scripture, but *contrary to* what he reads there. Let him faithfully and obediently listen to what it says: "By one man sin entered into the world, and by sin death; and so death passed upon all men, in whom all have sinned,"[153] and let him not weaken the grace of so great a physician in refusing to admit that human nature has been corrupted. How I wish that he would read as a Christian should, that apart from that of Jesus Christ,"there is no [other] name under heaven, . . . whereby we must be saved,"[154] and not defend the power of human nature to the point of believing that a man can be saved by free will alone even without that name.

40.(47) But perhaps Pelagius thinks that the name of Christ is necessary so that we may learn by his gospel how we ought to live [268], but not so that by his grace we may also be helped to lead good lives. At least, this consideration should lead him to admit that there are wretched shadows in the human soul, which knows how to tame a lion, but not how to live. But are a free will and the natural law sufficient for us to know this? This is the "wisdom of speech" by which "the cross of Christ is made

---

151. Cf. *De sp. et litt.* 36.65; *De perf. iust. hom.* 6.15.
152. 1 Thess 5.21. Vg reads, "Test [*probate*] all things. . . ."
153. Rom 5.12.   154. Acts 4.12.

void."[155] But he said, "I will destroy the wisdom of the wise,"[156] because that cross cannot be made void, and straightway is overthrown that "wisdom" through the "foolishness of preaching," by which those who believe are healed.[157] For if the natural power through free will is sufficient for us not only to know how we ought to live, but actually to live well, "then Christ died in vain,"[158] "then is the scandal of the cross made void."[159] Why may I not also cry out here? Yes, I will cry out and reproach them with the sorrow of a Christian: "You are made void of Christ, you who are justified in" nature; "you are fallen from grace."[160] Ignorant of the justice of God, you are seeking to establish your own justice and you have not submitted to the justice of God.[161] For even as Christ is the end of the law, so also is he the savior of corrupted human nature, to justice for all who believe.[162]

The Possibility of Not Sinning: Nature or Grace?

41.(48) But what did he put forward on his own part to be said by those against whom the Apostle says, "For all have sinned"?[163] He replied, *It is evident that the Apostle was speaking of his contemporaries, that is the Jews and the Gentiles.* But the passage that I have quoted, "By [269] one man sin entered into this world, and by sin death, and so death passed upon all men, in whom all have sinned,"[164] clearly includes the generations of antiquity, and the more recent past, and ourselves and our posterity. Pelagius also cites this passage when he would show that when "all" is used, we ought not always to understand all without exception. He quotes, "As by the offense of one, unto all men to condemnation, so also by the justice of one, unto all men to justification of life,"[165] and contends, *It is evident that not*

---

155. Cf. 1 Cor 1.17.
157. 1 Cor 1.21.
159. Gal 5.11.
160. Gal 5.4. Augustine adapts Paul's text by inserting "nature" in place of "the law."
161. Cf. Rom 10.3.
163. Rom 3.23.
165. Rom 5.18.

156. 1 Cor 1.19, citing Isa 29.14.
158. Gal 2.21.

162. Cf. Rom 10.4.
164. Rom 5.12.

all are sanctified through the justice of Christ, but only those who were willing to obey him and who have been purified by the cleansing of his baptism. However, with this quotation he does not clearly establish what he would like to demonstrate. For, just as it is said, "By the offense of one, unto all men to condemnation," in such a sense that no one is omitted, so also in the corresponding statement, "By the justice of one, unto all men to justification of life," no one is excepted, not because all believe in him and are cleansed through his baptism, but because no one is justified unless he believes in him and is cleansed by his baptism. Therefore, the term, "all," is said, so that it is not believed that anyone is capable of being saved by any other means than through Christ himself. Thus, when one teacher of literature is appointed in a city, we say quite correctly, "He teaches literature to all," not because everyone who lives in the city learns literature, but because no one learns it unless he is taught by him. Similarly, no one is justified unless Christ has justified him.

42.(49) *All right,* declares Pelagius, *suppose I grant that the Apostle teaches us that all have been sinners. He declares what they have been, not that they could not have been otherwise. Wherefore,* he adds, *even if all men could be proved to be sinners, that would not in any way prejudice our position, since we insist not so much on what men are as on what they are able to be.* Here he is right when for once he admits that no man living is justified in the sight of God,[166] but contends that the problem does not lie there but in the possibility of not sinning—a problem about which we need not take issue with him. For I am not at all concerned to know whether in this life there existed, or exist, or can exist any persons who have had, [270] are having, or will have the love of God to such a degree of perfection that nothing can be added to it—for this is the most true, most complete, and most perfect justice. For I accept and contend that this can be done by the will of man assisted by the grace of God, and I ought not to contest too much when, where, and in whom it might happen. Nor do I argue about the possibility itself, since, once the will of man is

166. Ps 142.2.

healed and assisted, this possibility together with its actuality is present in the saints, when the love of God, as fully as our cleansed and healed nature can receive it, is poured forth in our hearts through the Holy Spirit who is given to us.[167] Therefore, God's cause is promoted in a better way—the cause which Pelagius says he promotes in defending our nature—when God is acknowledged as both our creator and our savior, than when, by defending the creature as if it were healthy and in full strength, the help of the savior is made worthless.

43.(50) Still, what he says here is true: *God, being as good as he is just, created man with sufficient ability to be without the evil of sin, if only man had been willing.* For who does not know that man was created sound and faultless, endowed with a free will and a free ability to live a just life? But now we are concerned with the man whom the thieves left half dead on the road, who, being torn and pierced with serious wounds, is not as capable of ascending to the heights of justice as he was able to descend therefrom, who, even though he is now present in the inn, is still undergoing treatment.[168] Accordingly, God does not command the impossible, but by his commandments he counsels to do what you can and to pray for his aid in that which you cannot do. Now let us see whence comes the possibility and the impossibility. Pelagius declares, *That which a man can do by his nature proceeds not from his will.* But I say, "without doubt a man is not just by his will if he can be by nature, but through a remedy he will be able to do that which, because of his defect, he is unable to do."

44.(51) But why should we linger on such general considerations? Let us go more deeply into the dispute which we have with our opponents, which rests entirely or almost entirely on one particular point. As Pelagius himself has said, [271] *The question at hand is not to determine whether there have been or now are any men in this life without sin, but whether there could have been or can be any.* But even if I were to admit that there were or are such men, I would still affirm that in no way could there have been or can there be such, unless justified by the grace of God

167. Cf. Rom 5.5.   168. Cf. Luke 10.30–35.

through our Lord Jesus Christ and him crucified.[169] Assuredly it is the same faith which healed the just people of old and which also heals us, that is faith in the mediator between God and men, the man Jesus Christ,[170] faith in his blood, faith in his cross, faith in his death and resurrection. Therefore, "having the same spirit of faith . . . , we also believe, for which cause we speak also."[171]

(52) But when Pelagius brings before himself this question, in which he appears to be so intolerable to Christian hearts, note his reply. For he says, *But that which disturbs many persons, you will say, is that you do not maintain that it is by the grace of God that a man can be without sin.* Definitely this is what disturbs us; this is what we object to. He touches the essential point. We bear all this with great distress, and it is because of the love we have toward others as well as toward themselves that we cannot endure to hear these things debated by Christians. Therefore, let us hear how he overcomes the objection that has been brought against him on this question: *O blindness of ignorance,* he declares, *O listlessness of an inexperienced mind, to suppose that I defend without recourse to the grace of God, that which, let him understand, should be attributed only to God.* Now if we did not know what follows, but had heard only these words, then we might think that we had been led to a false opinion of our opponents by a spreading rumor and by the testimony of some reputable witnesses among our brothers who vouched for it. For how could it have been said more briefly and truly that the possibility of not sinning, to whatever extent it exists or will exist in man, should only be attributed to God? This we also affirm; let us join hands.

45.(53) Shall we go on and listen to the rest? Certainly, we must listen to it, correct it, and guard against it. *But when it is said,* observes Pelagius, *that this very quality is altogether not of man's will but of nature, that is, of God, the author of nature,* [272] *is there any way that what is considered to belong to God particularly can be regarded as without the grace of God?* It begins to become apparent already what he is saying, but so that we may not,

169. Cf. Rom 7.25 and 1 Cor 2.2.   170. Cf. 1 Tim 2.5.
171. 2 Cor 4.13.

perhaps, be deceived, he sets out his position more fully and clearly. *In order that this may become more evident*, he says, *it is necessary to discuss it more fully. We affirm, then, that the possibility of anything lies not so much in the power of the human will as in the necessity of nature.* Then he proceeds to illustrate his statement by examples and comparisons. *For instance*, he says, *I can speak. That I can speak is not my own, but that I do speak is my own, that is, it is of my own will. And because that I do speak is my own, I can do both, that is, either speak or not speak. But because the fact that I can speak is not my own, that is, does not belong to my choice and will, it is necessary that I always be able to speak, and even if I wished that I could not speak, nevertheless I cannot become unable to speak, unless I were to remove that member by means of which I carry out the task of speaking.* Actually, many ways might be mentioned by means of which a man might, if he wished, deprive himself of the possibility of speaking, without removing the member by which we speak. For example, if anything were to happen whereby the voice itself were taken away, no one could speak, even though all members remained, for a man's voice is not a member. Again, the member may be somehow injured internally, without being taken away. However, let me not appear to quibble over a word and have it be said to me by way of rejoinder, that even to injure an organ is to lose it; for also we can so arrange it that by closing and sealing the mouth with a gag of some kind, we become quite incapable of opening it, nor is it in our power that it be opened, even though it was in our power that it be closed, while the integrity and health of our members yet remains.

46.(54) But what is that to us? Let us see what Pelagius adds next: *Whatever*, he declares, *is bound by natural necessity is not subject to the choice and deliberation of the will.* But there is some problem with this. For it is absurd to say that it does not belong to our will that we want to be happy, simply because, [273] by some good constraint in our nature, we are incapable of *not* wanting to be happy. Nor do we dare to say that God does not possess the will but the necessity to be just, because he cannot want to sin.

47.(55) Note the words which come next. *We may perceive*, says Pelagius, *that the same thing is true of hearing, smelling, and seeing, that to hear, to smell, and to see are within our power, while to be able to hear, to smell, and to see is not within our power but rests on a natural necessity.* Either I do not understand what he says, or he himself does not understand it. For how is the possibility of seeing not in our power, if the necessity of not seeing is in our power, since blindness is in our power, in that we can destroy, if we wish, the very power of seeing? Besides, how is it within our power to see whenever we will, since, even if the integrity of the nature of our body and our eyes is preserved, we cannot see even though we might wish to, either during the night when the lights on which we rely outside are removed, or if a person encloses us in some dark place? Similarly, if the possibility or the impossibility of hearing is not in our power, but is based on the necessity of nature, whereas actually to hear or not to hear arises from our own will, why does Pelagius not consider how many things we hear against our will, which penetrate our sense even when our ears are stopped up, as in the case of the scraping of a saw nearby or the grunting of a pig? Although, on the one hand, the stopping up of our ears shows that it is not in our power not to hear as long as our ears are open, on the other hand, such stopping up, which deprives us of our very sense of hearing, perhaps makes it the case that even the *possibility* of not hearing lies within our power. As to what he says regarding the sense of smell (at least if he paid a little attention to what he says): *It is not within our power to be able to smell or not to be able, but it is within our power,* that is, [274] in our free will, *to smell or not to smell* —well, if at some time we were placed in the midst of strong and disagreeable odors, if someone set us there with our hands bound, while the integrity and health of our members is completely preserved, we would wish not to smell but be altogether unable not to do so, since every time we had to draw a breath we would also inhale that odor which we did not wish to smell.

48.(56) Just as the comparisons used by Pelagius are false, so also is the matter which he wishes them to illustrate. Thus he continues: *In a like manner, we should understand the possibility of not sinning: it depends upon us not to sin, but the very possibility of not sinning does not depend upon us.* But even if he were speaking of sound and perfect human nature (which we do not yet possess, "For we are saved by hope. But hope that is seen is not hope. . . . But if we hope for that which we see not, we wait for it with patience"[172]), it would not be correct for him to say that not to sin depends solely upon us, although to sin would in fact depend on us. For even in this case there would be the help of God, and it would offer itself[173] to those who were willing, just as does light to those with healthy eyes, so that with its help they may see. But since Pelagius raises the question about our present life, where "The corruptible body is a load upon the soul, and the earthly habitation presses down upon the mind that muses upon many things,"[174] I am surprised that he has the nerve to think that without the healing assistance of our savior, it is within our power not to sin, and to contend that the ability not to sin belongs indeed to our nature, which is so evidently flawed that its failure to perceive this fact makes its flaw all the greater.

49.(57) *Because it depends upon us not to sin,* Pelagius says, *we are able to sin and not to sin.* What if someone else should say, "Because it depends upon us not to wish for unhappiness, we are able both to wish for it and not to wish for it"? And yet we absolutely cannot wish for it. For who could wish in any way to be unhappy, even if he wishes for something else which against his will would bring him unhappiness? Again, since it is within the power of God, much more than our own, not to sin, shall we dare to say that he is able both to sin and not to sin? Far be it from us to say that God could sin! For, contrary to the opinion of fools, [275] he does not become any less omnipotent, because he cannot die and "he cannot deny himself."[175] What then does Pelagius mean, and by what rules of rhetoric does he endeavor to persuade us of a point that he does not want to examine carefully? He adds still further, *Because indeed the possibility of not sinning does not depend upon us, even if we should want not to be able not to sin, we cannot not be able not to sin.* He has said this in a convoluted manner and for this reason somewhat obscurely.

172. Rom 8.24–25.
173. Reading *praeberet* with PL and BA; CSEL: *praebere*.
174. Wis 9.15.   175. 2 Tim 2.13.

But it is possible to put it more clearly as follows: because the possibility of not sinning does not depend upon us, then, whether we wish it or not, we are able not to sin. For he does not say, "Whether we wish it or not, we do not sin"—undoubtedly we do sin if we wish to. Nevertheless, whether we wish it or not, we have, he asserts, the possibility of not sinning, which he says is inherent in our nature. Yet it can reasonably be said of a man with healthy feet that whether he wish it or not he has the possibility of walking, but if they are broken, then even if he wishes, he does not have this possibility. Thus our nature is corrupted, of which it is written, "Why is earth and ashes proud?"[176] It is corrupted and it implores the physician: "Save me, O Lord,"[177] it cries; "Heal my soul,"[178] it cries. Why does Pelagius block these cries, and thus hinder the future health [of the soul] by defending it as a present possibility?

50.(58) Note also what he adds, by which he thinks his position is confirmed: *No will*, he declares, *can take away that which is demonstrated to be inseparably bound up with our nature.* Whence then that statement, "so that you do not the things that you would"?[179] Whence also this: "For I do not the good which I will; but the evil which I hate, that I do"?[180] Where is that possibility "which is demonstrated to be inseparably bound up with our nature"? Behold, men do not do the things that they would. And the question was concerned above all with not sinning, not with flying, for the subject was men and not birds. Behold, man does not do the good that he wills, but the evil that he does not will, that he does;[181] to will is present with him, but to accomplish that which is good is not [276] present.[182] Where is that possibility that "is demonstrated to be inseparably bound up with our nature"? For whoever the Apostle represents in saying "I", if he does not speak these things of himself personally, he certainly represents by himself a man. It is maintained, however, by Pelagius that our human nature actually possesses an inseparable possibility of not sinning at all. But the effect of

176. Sir 10.9.
177. Ps 11.2.
178. Ps 40.5.
179. Gal 5.17.
180. Rom 7.15.
181. Cf. Rom 7.19.
182. Cf. Rom 7.18.

these words, even when uttered by a man who is unaware of what he is saying—but this man is not unaware, who puts forward these things to be said to some listeners who are God-fearing but not on their guard—is to cause the grace of Christ to be of no effect, as if human nature were sufficient to itself for its own justification.

51.(59) Nevertheless, to deflect the indignation with which Christians protest for the sake of their own salvation and ask him, "Why do you affirm that man is able to avoid sin without the help of the grace of God?" Pelagius replies, *The very possibility of not sinning lies not so much in the power of the will as in the necessity of nature. Whatever is based in the necessity of nature undoubtedly belongs to the author of nature, that is, to God. How, therefore,* he asks, *can one judge it to be said that that is without the grace of God, which is shown to belong to God particularly?* Here his underlying position is made clear; there is no way in which it could be concealed. He attributes the possibility of not sinning to the grace of God, because God is the author of that nature with which, he declares, the possibility of not sinning is inseparably bound up. Therefore, when a man wills a thing, he does it;[183] and if he does not do it, it is because he does not will it. For when this inseparable possibility exists, there can be no infirmity of the will, or rather no combination of the presence of the will and the lack of accomplishment of the good. And if this is so, then how does it happen that it is declared, "For to will is present, but to accomplish that which is good is not present"?[184] For if the author of this book spoke of that human nature, such as it was in the beginning, created sound and without fault, then this statement would be acceptable in some sense, although to have the inseparable possibility [of not sinning], that is to say, a possibility which cannot be lost, should not be ascribed to that nature. [277] For that nature could be corrupted and require the help of a physician to heal the eyes of the blind and to restore the capacity of seeing, which had been lost through blindness, since I think a blind man would wish to see, but cannot—

183. Reading *facit* with PL and BA; CSEL: *faciat*.
184. Rom 7.18.

yet if he wishes and cannot, then the wish remains in him, but the possibility has been lost.

The Opposition of Flesh and Spirit

52.(60) Consider further what obstacles Pelagius tries to overcome, if he can, in order to introduce his position. He addresses to himself the following objection, saying, *But, you will say, according to the Apostle, the flesh is contrary to us.*[185] To this he replies, *How can it be that to any baptized person the flesh is contrary, since according to that same Apostle he is not considered to be in the flesh? For he says, "But you are not in the flesh."*[186] Let us grant for now that for the baptized the flesh cannot be contrary to them; whether this is true we shall see later. Now indeed, since he could not altogether forget that he is a Christian, however slightly he remembers it, he has retreated from his defense of nature. Where, then, is the "inseparable possibility"? Are those who are not yet baptized perhaps not included in human nature? Here Pelagius comes close to waking up, and if he is careful he can. *How can it be,* he asks, *that to any baptized person, the flesh is contrary?* Therefore the flesh can be contrary to those who are not baptized. Let him explain this somehow, since that nature which he has strongly defended also exists in them. In any case he concedes that in them at least it has been corrupted, even if now among the baptized the injured traveller has left his inn healthy, or is healthy while yet in that inn to which the compassionate Samaritan took him so that he might be healed.[187] Now if he will just concede that in the non-baptized the flesh is contrary, let him tell us what occurred to cause this, since both the flesh and the spirit alike are the work of one and the same creator and, since he is good, are beyond doubt good, excepting only that damage that has been inflicted by man's own will. That this defect in our nature may be healed, we need that same savior, by whom as creator our nature was brought forth. But if we confess that this savior and his remedy,

185. Cf. Gal 5.17.   186. Rom 8.9.
187. Cf. Luke 10.30–35.

by which the Word was made flesh to dwell among us,[188] are required by both great and small, by all, that is, from crying [278] infants to white-haired elders, then all controversy between us on this question will be resolved.

53.(61) Now let us see whether it is to be read that the flesh is contrary to baptized persons also. On this subject, I ask, to whom did the Apostle say, "For the flesh lusts against the spirit, and the spirit against the flesh, for these are contrary one to another, so that you do not the things that you would"?[189] I presume he wrote this to the Galatians, to whom he said, "He therefore who gives the Spirit to you and works miracles among you, does he do it by the works of the law, or by the hearing of the faith?"[190] Thus it appears that he speaks to Christians, to whom God has given his Spirit, and therefore to the baptized also. Hence, we see that even in the baptized the flesh is contrary, and that they lack that possibility, which, according to Pelagius, is inseparably bound up with our nature. Where, then, is the basis for his assertion, *How can it be that to any baptized person, the flesh is contrary?* However he may understand "flesh"—for in reality it is not human nature, which is good, but the carnal sins of the flesh that are designated in this passage by the word, "flesh"—note nonetheless that even in the baptized the flesh is contrary. And in what way contrary? That they do not do what they would. Notice that the will is present in man, but where is that "possibility" of nature? Let us admit that grace is necessary; let us cry out, "Unhappy man that I am, who shall deliver me from the body of this death?" And let us reply, "The grace of God, by Jesus Christ our Lord."[191]

(62) For when it is rightly asked of them, "Why do you say that without the help of the grace of God man is able to be without sin?" it is not there a question of that grace by which man was created, but of that by which he is saved through Jesus Christ our Lord. For the faithful say in prayer, "Bring us not into temptation, [279] but deliver us from evil."[192] But if this

---

188. Cf. John 1.14.   189. Gal 5.17.
190. Gal 3.5.   191. Rom 7.24–25.
192. Matt 6.13. For Matt 6.13a, Augustine prefers the wording, *Ne nos inferas in tentationem*, over the more common, *Ne nos inducas in tentationem* (as in Vg),

ON NATURE AND GRACE 69

possibility is in them, why do they pray? Or from what evil do they pray to be delivered, if not above all else "the body of this death," from which only "the grace of God by Jesus Christ our Lord" delivers them?[193] Certainly not from the substance of the body, which is good, but from the sins of the flesh, from which a man is not freed without the grace of the savior, not even when through the death of the body he departs from the body. In order that the Apostle might say this,[194] what did he say previously? "But I see another law in my members, fighting against the law of my mind and captivating me in the law of sin that is in my members."[195] Behold what damage has been inflicted upon human nature by the disobedience of the will! Let him be allowed to pray that he may be healed. Why must he presume so much about the "possibility of nature"? It is wounded, hurt, damaged, lost. It is in need of a true confession, not of a false defense. Let it seek then the grace of God, not that by which it was created, but that by which it is restored—that unique grace which Pelagius by his very silence proclaims to be unnecessary. If he had said absolutely nothing about the grace of God, and if he had not proposed to resolve this problem in order to remove opposition on the subject, one might have considered that he thought what is in fact true, but did not mention it, because one does not have to mention all one's opinions everywhere. But he raised the question of grace and responded to it with what he

accurately rendered by Douai as 'Lead us not into temptation.' According to D. de Bruyne, "The reading *ne nos inferas in tentationem* is not found in any manuscript nor in any other Father. Burkitt seems correct in seeing here a revision made by Augustine" ("Saint Augustin reviseur de la Bible," *Miscellanea Agostiniana* 2. 596, as quoted in Lesousky, 233). T. van Bavel, however, argues that *ne nos inferas* was the text used in the liturgy at Hippo: "Plutôt que d'y voir une correction personnelle d'Augustin, ce sera l'usage liturgique qui aura determiné son choix" (*"Inferas—Inducas:* A propos de Mtth. 6,13 dans les oeuvres de saint Augustin," *Revue Bénédictine* 69 [1959] 349). Augustine commented on these two variant translations as early as 393, in *De sermone Domini in monte* 2.9.30, and in *De dono pers.* 6.12 he expresses the view that *inferas* is an accurate rendering of the Greek εἰσηνέγκης, which in fact it is. Both the Lt and the Gk verbs could perhaps best be translated into English as "*Subject* us not" (as NAB renders the Gk), but we choose the translation, "*Bring* us not into temptation," as closer to the breadth of the meaning of *inferas*.

193. Rom 7.24–25.   194. That is, Rom 7.24–25.
195. Rom 7.23.

had in his heart. The question has been resolved, not in the way we wished, but according to the doubts we had concerning his meaning.

54.(63) Then, with many quotations from the Apostle, he endeavors to demonstrate something concerning which there is no controversy: *that what the Apostle often calls the "flesh," he wants to be understood to be not the substance but the works of the flesh.* What does this have to do with the subject? The sins of the flesh are contrary to the will of man; our nature is not at fault, but its defects require a physician. What does he mean when he asks, *Who made the spirit of man?* and answers himself, *God without a doubt?* Again he asks, *Who created the flesh?* And again he answers, *The same God, I believe.* And a third time he asks, *Is God, who created both, good?* [280] He replies, *No one doubts it.* Again he asks, *And are both good, since a good creator made them?* And to this he replies, *It must be admitted that they are.* Then he concludes, *If, therefore, the spirit is good and the flesh is good, since made by a good creator, how can it be that two good things should be contrary to one another?* I pass over remarking that his entire argument would be upset if one were to ask him, "Who made heat and cold?" To which, without a doubt, he would respond, "God." I will not press further my interrogation; let him determine whether heat and cold may be considered not to be good, or whether they do not appear to be contrary to one another. To this he might say, "These are not substances, but the qualities of substances." Yes, that is true, but still they are natural qualities and ones which without a doubt belong to the creation of God; substances indeed are not said to be contrary to one another in themselves, but rather through their qualities, as with water and fire. And what if this were also true of flesh and spirit? We do not declare this to be so, but we have set this forth in order to show that his argument does not reach its conclusion by a necessary inference. For even contrary elements may not be in mutual opposition, but instead may temper one another and produce a good equilibrium, for example, in the human body, dryness and moisture, cold and heat, in the proper balance of which bodily health consists. However, the fact that the flesh is contrary to the spirit, so that we do not do the things we would, is a defect, not a condition, of nature. Let the grace which heals it be sought, and let the dispute come to an end.

(64) Despite the argument of Pelagius, how can these two good elements, created by a good God, be contrary to one another in unbaptized persons? Or will Pelagius regret having made this statement, which he said because of some sentiment of Christian faith? For when he said, *How can it be that to any person already baptized, the flesh is contrary?* he indicated that in the case of unbaptized persons it is possible for the flesh to be contrary. Why did he add "already baptized," when, without adding these words, he could equally well have said, "How can it be that to any person the flesh is contrary?" and to demonstrate this, have appended that argument of his to the effect that both flesh and spirit are good, for they are created by a good God, and therefore [281] they cannot be contrary to one another. So if the unbaptized persons, for whom he clearly recognizes that the flesh is contrary, were to press him with questions and ask, "Who made the spirit for man?" Pelagius will reply, "God." Suppose they ask him again, "Who created the flesh?" He replies, "The same God, I believe." They ask a third time, "Is God, who created both, good?" And he replies, "No one doubts it." Finally, they put to him the one remaining question, "And are both good, since a good creator made them?" He will admit this. Then they will cut his throat with his own sword by drawing his conclusion and saying, "If therefore the spirit is good and the flesh is good, since made by a good creator, how can it be that two good things should be contrary to one another?" Perhaps he will reply here, "Pardon me, I should not have said that the flesh cannot be contrary to any baptized person, as if to imply that it is contrary to you unbaptized persons, but rather I ought to have said without any exception that the flesh is not contrary to anyone." See how he has boxed himself in, see what he says, who is unwilling to cry out with the Apostle, "Who shall deliver me from the body of this death? The grace of God, by Jesus Christ our Lord."[196] *But why,* Pelagius asks, *should I, who am already baptized in Christ, cry out in this*

196. Rom 7.24–25.

way? Let them cry out who have not yet received such a great benefit and whose cries the Apostle represents in himself, if indeed they go so far as to say this. But this defense of nature does not permit them to cry out in these words. For it is not as though there is nature in the baptized and no nature in the unbaptized. Or, if it is recognized that among the latter it is corrupted, so that it is not unreasonable for them to exclaim, "Unhappy man that I am, who shall deliver me from the body of this death?" then help arrives for the former also in what follows, "The grace of God, by Jesus Christ our Lord."[197] So let it be admitted at least that human nature at all times stands in need of Christ the physician.[198]

55.(65) So, I ask, where did our nature lose that freedom, which he desires to be given to him when he declares, "Who shall deliver me?"[199] [282] For the Apostle finds no fault with the substance of the flesh when he expresses the desire to be delivered "from the body of this death,"[200] since the nature of the body as well as that of the soul must be attributed to God as their good author, but rather the Apostle speaks of the defects of the body. For the death of the body separates us from the body, but the sins contracted from it adhere [to the soul], and a just punishment is due them, as that rich man found out in hell.[201] It was from these sins that he was unable to free himself, who said, "Who shall deliver me from the body of this death?"[202] But wherever it was that he lost this freedom, certainly the "possibility of nature" remains "inseparable." From the help of nature, he has the possibility; from his power of free choice, he has the will. Why then does he desire the sacrament of baptism? Is it because of past sins committed, so that they may at least be forgiven, since they cannot be undone? Release this man, let him cry out what he cried out before. For he desires not only that he be mercifully freed from punishment for past sins, but also that he might be strengthened and

---

197. Rom 7.24–25.
198. On this title, a favorite of Augustine, see Rudolph Arbesmann, "The Concept of 'Christus Medicus' in St. Augustine," *Traditio* 10 (1954) 1–28.

199. Rom 7.24.   200. Rom 7.24.
201. Cf. Luke 16.22–26.   202. Rom 7.24.

fortified so as not to sin in the future. For he is "delighted with the law of God, according to the inward man," but then he sees another law in his members fighting against the law of his mind;[203] he *sees* it is there, not *remembers* it was there. He is pressed by what is present, not recalling what is past. And he not only sees this law warring against him but even taking him captive in the law of sin, which *is*, not which *was*, in his members.[204] Thence comes his cry, "Unhappy man that I am, who shall deliver me from the body of this death?"[205] Let him pray, let him importune for the help of the most powerful physician. Why contradict this prayer? Why drown it out? Why should this unhappy person be restrained from asking for the mercy of Christ, and that too by Christians? For it is they who were walking with Christ who tried to prevent the blind man from begging, with loud outcries, for light.[206] But even in the midst of all the tumult of those who were opposing the blind man, Jesus heard him crying out. Whence the response to this person also: "The grace of God through Jesus Christ our Lord."[207]

(66) [283] Furthermore, even if we receive from these people the acknowledgement that unbaptized persons may beg for the help of the grace of the savior, this will certainly not be a minor point against the false defense of nature as if it were self-sufficient, and of the power of free will. For he is not sufficient to himself who says, "Unhappy man that I am, who shall deliver me?"[208] Nor can he be said to have full liberty, who still asks to be delivered.

56. Still, let us consider this question: Do those who are baptized accomplish the good which they would do, without any resistance from the concupiscence of the flesh? But what we would say on this subject, Pelagius himself brings forward in concluding this passage: *As we have remarked*, he says, *the passage in which these words occur, "The flesh lusts against the spirit,"*[209] *should be understood not of the substance, but of the works, of the flesh.* We also affirm that this is spoken, not of the substance of the flesh,

---

203. Rom 7.22–23.
205. Rom 7.24.
207. Rom 7.25.
209. Gal 5.17.

204. Rom 7.23.
206. Cf. Mark 10.46–52.
208. Rom 7.24.

but of its works, which proceed from carnal concupiscence, that is, of sin, which the Apostle admonishes us not to let reign in our mortal body, so as to obey its desires.[210]

57.(67) But even Pelagius ought to notice that it is to those already baptized that it was said, "The flesh lusts against the spirit, and the spirit against the flesh, . . . so that you do not the things that you would."[211] But, so as not to discourage them from this struggle and to seem through this statement to have given them latitude for sin, the Apostle adds, "But if you are led by the spirit, you are no longer under the law."[212] For someone is under the law who wishes to abstain from sin out of fear of the punishment which the law threatens, and not from any love of justice; he is not yet free nor separated from the will to sin. Actually, in his will he is guilty, for by it he would prefer, if it were possible, that what he fears would not exist, so that he might freely do what he secretly desires. Therefore he declares, "If you are led by the spirit, you are no longer under the law,"[213] under that law, of course, which inspires fear but does not give love. For this "charity of God is poured forth in our hearts" not by [284] the letter of the law, but "by the Holy Spirit, who is given to us."[214] This is the law of liberty, not of servitude, for it is above all the law of love, not of fear; concerning it the Apostle James also says, "But he that has looked into the perfect law of liberty."[215] Thus Paul too was no longer terrified by the law as of God as a slave, but was delighted with it according to the inner man, although he nonetheless saw another law in his members, fighting against the law of his mind.[216] Likewise he declares also, "If you are led by the spirit, you are no longer under the law."[217] Insofar as one is led by the spirit, he is not under the law, because insofar as he delights in the law of God, he lives not in fear of the law, "because fear has pain,"[218] and not delight.

58.(68) Consequently, if we think rightly, we ought to be

210. Cf. Rom 6.12.
211. Gal 5.17.
212. Gal 5.18.
213. Gal 5.18.
214. Rom 5.5.
215. Jas 1.25.
216. Cf. Rom 7.22–23.
217. Gal 5.18.
218. 1 John 4.18.

grateful for the healing of our members and to pray for further healing in order that we may enjoy absolutely complete health, to which nothing can be added, the perfect sweetness of God and full freedom. For we do not deny that human nature can be without sin, and we ought not in any way to deny that it can become perfect, since we admit that it can make progress, but only by "the grace of God, by Jesus Christ our Lord."[219] We say that by his aid it can become just and happy, he by whom it was created to be at all. Thus it is easy to refute the objection which Pelagius says some have made against him, "The devil is against us." To this objection we immediately reply with the same words that he has used, *Let us resist him, and he will flee.* "*Resist the devil,*" *says the blessed Apostle,* "*and he will flee from you.*"[220] *From this it can be noticed to what extent he can harm those whom he flees, and to understand what power he has, when he prevails only against those who do not resist him.* These words are also mine, for it cannot be said more truly. However, there is this difference between us and them, that, when the devil is to be resisted, we not only do not deny but actually proclaim that the help of God is to be implored, but they attribute so much power to the will, that they would exclude prayer from our religious duties. For it is above all [285] that we might resist the devil and that he might flee from us that we pray, "Bring us not into temptation."[221] And thus we have been put on our guard, just as soldiers are exhorted by their commander in the words, "Watch and pray that you enter not into temptation."[222]

59.(69) But Pelagius argues against those who say, "And who would not wish to be without sin, if that depended on the power of man?" He rightly declares, *By their very question they admit that this is not impossible, because many or even all desire it.* Only let him recognize how this is possible, and there will be peace. For it is "the grace of God, by Jesus Christ our Lord,"[223] the grace by which Pelagius has nowhere been willing to say we, when we pray, are helped, so as not to sin. If by chance he implicitly acknowledges this, he must forgive us for having suspected

219. Rom 7.25.   220. Jas 4.7.
221. Matt 6.13.   222. Mark 14.38.
223. Rom 7.25.

otherwise. In that case, it is he himself who is the cause of all the discredit which he suffers on this matter, for he is willing to acknowledge it and yet unwilling to confess or declare it. What would be the big problem with saying it, especially when he has undertaken to treat and to clarify this question, as if he had received objections on the part of opponents? Why did he choose on such occasions only to defend nature, and to assert that man was so created that he could have avoided sin if he had wished not to sin. And why does he state that, because human nature was created thus, that possibility, by which, if he had wished not to sin, he would not have sinned, belongs to the grace of God, and refuse to say anything concerning the fact that nature itself is either healed by "the grace of God, by Jesus Christ our Lord,"²²⁴ because it has been corrupted, or is helped because it is not sufficient to itself.

Is Freedom from Sin Possible in This Life? Texts from Various Authors

60.(70) Whether in this world there has ever been or could be anyone living so just a life as to be entirely without sin can be a subject of some discussion among true and pious Christians. Nevertheless, if anyone doubts that such a person surely can exist after this life, he lacks good sense. But, for my part, I do not wish to argue the point even as it concerns this life. For although it appears to me that one cannot understand otherwise the passage of Scripture which reads, "In thy sight no man living shall be justified,"²²⁵ and other similar passages, still I would that it were possible to show either that such testimonies could be understood more favorably, or that a complete and perfect justice, to which it would be impossible to add anything, [286] had in the past been realized in someone while he lived in this body, is presently being realized, and will be realized in the future. But even so, there are far more who, while not doubting it is necessary for them up to the last day of their life to say, "Forgive us our debts, as we also forgive our debtors,"²²⁶

224. Rom 7.25.   225. Ps 142.2.
226. Matt 6.12.

still confess that in Christ and his promises they have a true,
certain, and firm hope. At all events, there is no other way than
the helping grace of the savior, Christ crucified, and the gift of
his Spirit, by which any persons, whoever they be, can arrive at
absolute perfection, or by which anyone can attain the slightest
progress to true and holy justice—whoever denies this, I question whether he can be counted in the number of true Christians of any sort.

61.(71) Again, with respect to the citations he provides, not
indeed from canonical Scriptures, but from certain works of
Catholic writers, in his attempt to rebut those who say he is
alone in defending such opinions, these statements are so neu-
tral that they oppose neither our opinion nor his. Among them
he wished to insert some passages taken from my books, regarding me as someone who seemed worthy of being cited with
them. I ought not to be ungrateful for this, and I do not want,
I say in a quite friendly spirit, for him to be in error, since he
has conferred this honor upon me. As to the first quotation,
why do I need to examine it at length, since I do not find there
the name of the author, either because Pelagius did not give it,
or because perhaps through some error the copy which you
sent me did not contain it? Especially since I am free with respect to the writings of such authors [to use my own judg-
ment]—for it is only to the canonical Scriptures that I must give
my unqualified assent—[I admit that] one passage, which he
quotes from the works of this author, whose name I did not
find there, bothers me somewhat: "It was fitting for the Master
and Teacher of virtue to become most like man, so that by con-
quering sin he might show that man is able to conquer sin."[227]
In whatever sense this statement was made, let the author attend to [287] how it can be explained. For our part, we could
not possibly doubt that Christ had no sin in him to conquer,
Christ who was born in the likeness of sinful flesh, not in sinful
flesh itself. He cites another passage by the same author: "And

227. The quotation is from Lactantius, *Divine Institutes* 4.24 (CSEL 19. 373).
A work in seven books, written ca. 304–313, this is "the first systematic presen-
tation of the main Christian doctrines in the Latin language" (Quasten, *Patrology* 2, 398).

furthermore, by subduing the desires of the flesh, he would teach us that one sins not through necessity, but through intention and will."[228] As for myself, I understand "the desires of the flesh," unless these words are spoken of the illicit desires, to be such things as hunger, thirst, the need for rest, and other things of this nature. For it is through these, although they are in themselves faultless, that some men fall into sin. But this was absent from that savior, even though, as we learn from the testimony of the gospel, these affections were in him because of his likeness to sinful flesh.

62.(72) Pelagius quotes the following passage from the Blessed Hilary: "It is only when we are perfected in spirit and changed by immortality, which blessedness has been reserved only for the pure in heart, that we shall discover what is immortal in God."[229] How that which he said is contrary to what we have said, or in what way it is of any use to Pelagius, I cannot say, unless it is because it witnesses to the possibility of a man's being pure of heart. But who denies that? Only it is through "the grace of God, by Jesus Christ our Lord,"[230] not merely by the freedom of our will. He also quotes the following passage: "What books, then, had Job read in order to abstain from every evil work? For he worshipped God with a pure mind, unmixed with any vice, and such worship of God is the proper work of justice."[231] He tells us what Job [288] had done, but not that which Job had brought to perfection in this world, or what he either did or brought to perfection without the grace of the savior, whom he had prophesied. For he abstains from all evil acts who has sin in him and does not let it rule over him,[232] and who, whenever an evil thought insinuates itself in him, does not allow it to result in an actual deed. However, it is one thing not to have sin and another not to yield to its demands. It is one thing to obey the command, "Thou shalt not covet,"[233] and an-

---

228. Lactantius, *Divine Institutes* 4.25 (CSEL 19. 377).
229. Hilary of Poitiers (313–367), *Commentarius in Evangelium Matthaei* 4.7 (PL 9. 933).
230. Rom 7.25.
231. Hilary, *Tractatus in Iob*, fr. 2 (CSEL 65. 230).
232. Cf. Rom 6.12.   233. Exod 20.17.

other, by some attempt at abstinence, to bring it about that one at least follows what is also written, "Go not after your lusts,"[234] and yet to know that without the grace of the savior one can accomplish neither the one nor the other. To do justice in the true worship of God is to fight in an inward struggle with the inward evil of concupiscence, but to realize perfect justice is to have no adversary at all. For he who fights is always in danger, and sometimes he is wounded, even if he is not brought down. But he who has no enemy enjoys complete peace. And he is most truly said to be without sin, in whom no sin lives, and not he who, through abstaining from evil deeds, declares, "It is no more I that do it, but sin that dwells in me."[235]

(73) For even Job himself is not silent concerning his own sins, and certainly our friend is right in his judgment that humility can by no means be placed on the side of falsehood.[236] Therefore, whatever Job confesses, since he is a true worshipper of God, he undoubtedly confesses it sincerely. And Hilary himself, when he explains the verse of the psalm, in which it is written, "You have despised all them that fall off from your judgments,"[237] says, "For if God were to despise sinners, he would indeed despise everyone, for no one is without sin. But he despises those that fall away from him, who are called apostates."[238] Notice how he does not say that no one *was* without sin, [289] as if he were speaking of people of the past, but no one *is* without sin. On this point, as I have said, I have no quarrel. But if someone does not yield to the Apostle John, who does not himself say, "If we say that we *had* no sin," but, "If we say that we *have* no sin,"[239] how will he be ready to yield to Bishop Hilary? I raise my voice in the defense of the grace of Christ, without which no one is justified, as though the free will of our nature were sufficient. Indeed, it is Christ himself who raises his voice in defense of this; let us submit to him when he says, "Without me you can do nothing."[240]

63.(74) However, the holy Ambrose certainly, in the passage

234. Sir 18.30.   235. Rom 7.20.
236. See above, 34.38.   237. Ps 118.118.
238. Hilary, *Tractatus super Psalmos* 118.15.10 (CSEL 22. 493).
239. 1 John 1.8.   240. John 15.5.

which Pelagius mentions,[241] opposes those who say that a man cannot be without sin in this life. To support this position, he cites the case of Zechariah and Elizabeth, for they are said in the gospel to have walked in all the justifications of the law without blame.[242] But does he deny that this has been done through "the grace of God, by Jesus Christ our Lord"?[243] Undoubtedly, it was through a faith in him that the just lived, even before his passion. It is he who bestows the Holy Spirit, through whom love is poured forth in our hearts,[244] by which alone whoever is just is just. It is this Spirit that the bishop referred to when he specifically reminds us that he is to be obtained through prayers—for the will is insufficient without divine assistance—when in his hymn he says, "To our earnest prayers he grants the Holy Spirit to be gained."[245]

(75) I will also cite a passage from the same work of the blessed Ambrose from which Pelagius has quoted what he saw fit to quote: " 'It seemed good to me,'[246] he says. What he says seemed good to him cannot have seemed good to him alone. For it is not simply the human will to which it seemed good [290], but he likewise has found it good, 'Christ that speaks in me,'[247] who brings it about that that which is good can also seem good to us. For him upon whom he has mercy he also calls. Therefore, he who follows Christ can answer when asked why he wished to be a Christian, 'It seemed good to me.' When he says this, he does not deny that it also seemed good to God, for 'by God is prepared the will of man.'[248] For it is by the grace of God that God is honored by a saint."[249] This is what our author

241. Ambrose, *Exp. ev. sec. Luc.* 1.17 (CSEL 32. 4, 21) (written between 377 and 389).

242. Luke 1.6.   243. Rom 7.25.
244. Rom 5.5.
245. Ambrose, *Hymn.* 3.7–8:
                 Votisque praestat sedulis
                 sanctum mereri spiritum.
This hymn, which begins, "Iam surgit hora tertia," is found in PL 16. 1410.
246. Luke 1.3.   247. 2 Cor 13.3.
248. Prov 8.35 (LXX).
249. Ambrose, *Exp. ev. sec. Luc.* 1.10 (CSEL 32. 4, 17). Augustine also cites this text at *De dono pers.* 19.49, below.

must understand, if he is attracted by the words of Ambrose: that God prepares the will of man. Besides this there is no problem, or no great problem, as to who might have attained perfection and at what time, provided that no doubt is raised concerning whether the thing itself can occur without the grace of Christ. Then, how important it is that our author should observe one line from the statement that he quoted from Ambrose. For when he had said, "For since the Church has been assembled from among the nations, that is, from sinners, how can it be unpolluted when it is composed of such polluted material, unless it first be cleansed of sin by the grace of Christ, and secondly that it abstain from sins through its quality of not sinning?" he added a statement, which for obvious reasons our author has refused to quote. For Ambrose declares, "The Church was not immaculate from its origin, for that was impossible for human nature, but by the grace of God and its own quality, according to which it no longer sins, it becomes such that it appears to be immaculate."[250] Who does not understand the reason why our author has not added these words? This concerns the fact that even now in this world the Church can arrive at that most immaculate purity which all holy persons desire—a perfection which in the next world, without any admixture of evil men, and without any law of sin in it resisting the law of the mind,[251] will permit it to lead [291] an absolutely pure existence in divine eternity. Yet our author should consider well what, following the Scriptures, Bishop Ambrose has said, "The Church was not immaculate from its origin, for that was impossible for human nature."[252] By the phrase, "from its origin," he means of course from the time of our being born of Adam. For no doubt Adam himself was created immaculate. But in the case of those who are by nature the children of wrath,[253] deriving from him that which was corrupt in him, Ambrose has established that to be immaculate from its origin was impossible for human nature.

250. Ambrose, *Exp. ev. sec. Luc.* 1.17 (CSEL 32. 4, 21).
251. Cf. Rom 7.23.
252. Ambrose, *Exp. ev. sec. Luc.* 1.17 (CSEL 32. 4, 21).
253. Cf. Eph 2.3.

64.(76) *Also John, the bishop of Constantinople,* Pelagius says in citing him, *said that sin is not a substance, but an evil act*—who denies this?—*and that because it is not natural, therefore the law was promulgated against it, and that it comes from the freedom of the will.*[254] Again, who denies this? However, our present question does not concern our human nature as it is in this life; rather it concerns the grace of God, by which our nature is healed through Christ the physician, whom our nature would not need if it were well, our nature which Pelagius defends as if it were sound or as if, the free choice of the will being sufficient to it, it were able not to sin.

(77) Again, what Christian is ignorant of the truth which Pelagius quotes from the most blessed Xystus, bishop of the church of Rome and martyr of the Lord, who said, "God has allowed men the freedom of their will, so that by living in purity and without sin they may become like unto God."[255] But it belongs to free will to listen to him calling and to believe and to ask of him in whom one believes for help so that one may not sin. For when he says, "they may become like unto God," it is through God's love, "which is poured forth in our hearts," not by the possibility of nature nor by the free choice which is in us, but "by the Holy Spirit, who is given to us,"[256] that they will become like God. This same martyr also says, "A pure mind

254. From a lost treatise of St. John Chrysostom (344/54–407).
255. In *Retr.* 2.68, Augustine notes that the words which he had taken to be those of Xystus (or Sixtus), bishop of Rome (257–58) and martyr, "were really the words of Sextus the philosopher, not of Xystus the Christian." Henry Chadwick, in *The Sentences of Sextus: A Contribution to the History of Early Christian Ethics,* Texts and Studies, New Series, V (Cambridge: Cambridge University Press, 1959), argues that Sextus was a Christian. This opinion is followed by Evans, *Pelagius,* 44: "The 451 maxims, largely ethical in concern, have as their author a Christian sage active probably in the late second century and writing in Greek," who "drew upon a collection or collections of pagan maxims, for the most part neo-Pythagorean in provenance." Jerome argued (*Comm. in Ezech.* 6; *Ep.* 133.3; *In Ier.* 4.41.4) that Sextus was a pagan, "and it is undoubtedly on the basis of having read Jerome that Augustine in his late years makes the same assertion" (Evans, 46). The three sayings quoted here are numbered 36, 46, and 60, respectively, in Chadwick's edition. The Greek of number 36 reads, ἐξουσίαν πιστῷ ὁ θεὸς δίδωσι τὴν κατὰ θεόν· καθαρὰν οὖν δίδωσι καὶ ἀναμάρτητον: 'God gives to the man who has faith a liberty like unto his, therefore pure and free from fault.'
256. Rom 5.5.

is a holy temple for God, and the best altar to him is a heart that is clean and without sin." Who does not know that a pure heart is to be brought to this perfection while "the inward man is renewed day by day,"[257] but that this renewal is not accomplished without "the grace of God, by Jesus Christ our Lord"?[258] Again he says, "The man who is chaste and without sin has received from God the power to be a son of God." He meant this as an admonition that when anyone had become so chaste and without sin—there remains some question where and when this perfection might have been attained, a question well worth exploring among the pious, among whom nevertheless there is agreement, on the one hand, that this can be done, and, on the other hand, that it cannot be done except through "the mediator of God and men, the man Christ Jesus"[259]—nevertheless, as I began to say, Xystus prudently admonished that when any man attains such a high character and thus is rightly considered to be among the sons of God, such an achievement must not be considered to have been accomplished by his ability alone. This ability he has received through the grace of God, because he did not possess it in a nature that had become corrupted and depraved, as we read in the gospel, "But as many as received him, he gave them power to be made the sons of God,"[260] which indeed they were not by nature, nor would they have become at all unless by receiving him they also received that power through his grace. This is the power which is claimed for itself by the strength of that love which does not exist in us unless "by the Holy Spirit, who is given to us."[261]

65.(78) Pelagius[262] then quotes from a commentary by the venerable priest Jerome on the following passage from Scripture: "Blessed are the clean of heart, for they shall see God."[263] Jerome states, "Their conscience does not charge them with any sin," and he adds, "The pure God is perceived by a pure

257. 2 Cor 4.16.   258. Rom 7.25.
259. 1 Tim 2.5.   260. John 1.12.
261. Rom 5.5.
262. Pelagius now attempts to support his case with citations from the works of his great enemies, Jerome and Augustine.
263. Matt 5.8.

heart, for the temple of God cannot be defiled."[264] Such purity is to be brought about in us by endeavor, by labor, by prayer, and by having our prayers answered, so that we may be brought to that state of perfection in which we may be able to perceive God with a pure heart, by his grace, through Jesus Christ our Lord.[265] Again he quotes from the aforementioned preacher: [293] "God created us with a free will, and we are led by necessity neither to virtue nor to vice; otherwise, where there is necessity, there is no crown."[266] Who would not accept this? Who would not subscribe to this with all his heart? Who would rejoin that human nature was created otherwise? But in doing good there is no bond of necessity, for liberty belongs to love.

66.(79) Return to the statement of the Apostle, "The charity of God is poured forth in our hearts, by the Holy Spirit, who is given to us."[267] Given by whom, if not by him who "ascended on high, led captivity captive, and gave gifts to men"?[268] But since, because of the defects of our nature, not the constitution of our nature, there exists a certain necessity to sin, a man should listen, and so that this necessity should cease to exist, should learn to say to God, "Deliver me from my necessities."[269] For in such a prayer there is a struggle against the tempter, who fights against us because of this very necessity. And through this struggle, with the help of grace through our Lord Jesus Christ, not only will the evil necessity be removed but full liberty will be restored.

67.(80) Let us come to our own case. *Bishop Augustine also, says Pelagius, in his books,* On Free Choice of the Will, *writes this: "Whatever may be the cause which acts upon the will, if it is impossible to resist it, to submit to it is not sinful; if, however, it may be resisted, let it not be submitted to, and there will be no sin. By chance does this deceive the unwary man? Let him take care, therefore, not to be deceived. But what if the deception is so great that it is impossible to guard*

264. Jerome, *Commentariorum in Matheum libri IV*, 1.5.8 (CCSL 77. 25) (written ca. 398).
265. Cf. Rom 7.25.
266. Jerome, *Adversus Iovinianum* 2.3 (PL 23. 286) (written 390–91).
267. Rom 5.5.   268. Eph 4.8.
269. Ps 24.17.

against it? In that case there are no sins. For who sins in a matter where precaution is quite impossible? Sin, however, is committed; therefore precaution is possible."[270] I acknowledge that these are my words, but he in turn should see fit to acknowledge all that was said before. [294] For the discussion is about the grace of God, which comes to our aid as a remedy through the mediator, and not about the impossibility of justice. It is possible, it is clearly possible, to resist this cause [that acts upon the will], whatever it is. For in this situation we pray for help, saying, "Bring us not into temptation,"[271] and we would not ask for this help if we thought that it was absolutely impossible to resist. Sin can be guarded against, but only with the help of him who cannot be deceived. For this itself also pertains to guarding against sin, if we truly say, "Forgive us our debts, as we also forgive our debtors."[272] For there are two ways by which, even in the case of bodily sickness, evil can be guarded against: by taking care either to prevent its occurrence or, if it occurs, to obtain a quick cure. To prevent its occurrence, let us take care by saying, "Bring us not into temptation," and in order that we may be quickly cured, let us take care by praying, "Forgive us our debts." Whether the danger is menacing or already present within, it may therefore be guarded against.

(81) Moreover, so that my thought on this subject is perfectly clear, not merely to him but also to those who have not read my books, *On Free Choice of the Will,* and not having read them, may perhaps read this present work, I must quote a passage from those very books. If Pelagius had agreed with this statement and quoted it in his book, there would be no further controversy between us on this point.[273] For, immediately after my statement which he has quoted, I myself added and worked through as fully as I could the objection that might arise: "Nevertheless, certain actions are disapproved of, even when they

---

270. Augustine, *De libero arbitrio* (begun ca. 388 and completed ca. 395) 3.18.50.
271. Matt 6.13.   272. Matt 6.12.
273. Cf. *Retr.* 1.8.5 where Augustine also quotes from the remainder of *De lib. arb.* 3.18 in order to refute Pelagius' interpretation of the passage quoted here.

are done in ignorance, and are judged deserving of punishment, as we read in the inspired authorities."[274] After citing
some examples of these, I proceeded to speak of infirmity as
follows: "Some actions deserve disapproval even when done
from necessity, as when a man wishes to act rightly but cannot.
For whence else are these words, [295] 'For the good which I
will, I do not; but the evil which I hate, that I do?' "[275] Then,
after quoting other passages from the divine Scriptures in support of this opinion, I say, "But all these are statements of persons coming from that time of condemnation to death. For if
this is not man's punishment, but his nature, then these are not
sins." Then a little later I say this:

It remains, therefore, that this just punishment comes from man's
condemnation. Nor ought it to be wondered at, that either by ignorance man has no free choice of the will to select what is right to do, or
that because of the resistance of carnal habit, which through the force
of mortal transmission, has somehow become rooted in his nature, he
perceives what ought to be done and wills it but cannot accomplish it.
For it is a very just punishment of sin that someone should lose the
power of which he was unwilling to make good use, when he might
without any difficulty have done so had he willed. And indeed it is the
case that just as the one who, knowing what is right, does not do it,
loses the knowledge of what is right, so also the one who does not wish
to do what is right when he can loses the ability to do it when he wishes.
For in reality for every[276] sinful soul there are two punishments, ignorance and difficulty. From ignorance arises the shame of error; from
difficulty arises the affliction of anguish. But to accept the false as true,
so that one errs unwillingly, and to be unable, because of the resisting
and tormenting pain of carnal bondage, to abstain from acts of passion, are not the nature of man as he was created, but rather the punishment of man under condemnation. But whenever we speak of the
free will to do what is right, we mean that freedom in which man was
created.[277]

[296] To some men, who from this raise what seems to them to
be a just objection to the transmission and transfer of the de-

274. *De lib. arb.* 3.18.51.
275. *De lib. arb.* 3.18.51, citing Rom 7.15,19.
276. Reading *omni* with PL and BA; CSEL: *omnia*.
277. *De lib. arb.* 3.18.51–52.

fects of ignorance and difficulty from the first man to his posterity, my answer is this:

To them I say, it should be briefly responded, that they should be silent
and cease murmuring against God. Perhaps their complaint might
have been just, if no one among men had stood forth to vanquish error
and lust. But when indeed there is everywhere present one who in
many ways, through the created world which serves him as its master,
calls him who has turned away, instructs him who believes, comforts
him who hopes, encourages him who loves, assists him who endeavors,
hears him who prays, you are considered at fault not because you are
involuntarily ignorant, but because you do not seek that of which you
are ignorant, not because you do not bind up your wounded members,
but because you despise him who wishes to heal them.[278]

In this way I exhorted them, as best I could, nor did I render
empty the grace of God, without which the nature of man, now
darkened and wounded, can be neither enlightened nor
healed. On this issue turns the entire discussion with our opponents: that we do nothing to frustrate the grace of God, which
is in Christ Jesus our Lord, by a perverse defense of nature. In
reference to that nature I said, shortly after the passage just
quoted, "In fact, of nature itself we speak in one sense, the
proper sense, when we describe it as that human nature in
which man was first created faultless according to his kind, and,
in another sense, when we speak of that nature in which we are
born ignorant, mortal,[279] and subject to the flesh by reason of
our condemnation. It is in the latter sense that the Apostle says,
'We were by nature children of wrath, even as the rest.' "[280]

Conclusion

68.(82) [297] If, therefore, we wish, with Pelagius, *to arouse
and enkindle cold and sluggish souls, by Christian exhortations, to lead
good lives*, let us first exhort them to that faith whereby they may
become Christians and be subject to the name of him without

278. *De lib. arb.* 3.19.53.
279. Adding, with BA and PL, *et mortales*, omitted by CSEL.
280. *De lib. arb.* 3.19.54, citing Eph 2.3.

whom they cannot be saved. However, if they are already
Christians but neglect to live rightly, they must be chastised
with threats and aroused by the praises of rewards, but in such
a manner that we remember to urge them to pious prayers as
well as to good actions. Let us remember also to instruct them
in such soundness of doctrine that they will both give thanks,
from that time when they have begun to live rightly, because
they have done something without difficulty, and, whenever
they do experience some difficulty, endeavor to obtain facility
from the Lord by faithful and persevering prayers, and actions
stemming from mercy. For those who progress in this way,
where and when they attain the fullness of justice does not concern me greatly. But wherever and whenever they realize perfection, I maintain that it cannot be realized except by "the
grace of God, by Jesus Christ our Lord."[281] And, when they
have attained the clear knowledge that they have no sin, shall
they not say they have no sin, lest the truth be not in them,[282]
just as the truth is not in those who, although they have sin, yet
say they do not?

69.(83) Indeed, *the precepts are good,* as Pelagius says, if we use
them lawfully.[283] And in virtue of our strong conviction "that
the good and just God could not have prescribed impossibilit-
ies," we are admonished both what to do in easy things and
what to ask for in difficult ones. Indeed, all things are easy for
love, to which alone the burden of Christ is light,[284] or which
alone is itself the burden which is light. Thus it is said, "And his
commandments are not heavy,"[285] so that whoever finds them
heavy should consider that the inspired statement that they
"are not heavy" could only mean that there is a disposition of
heart to which they are not heavy, and should pray for that
disposition, which he lacks at present, in order to carry out what
is commanded. Concerning what is said [298] to Israel in Deuteronomy, if we interpret it with piety, with veneration, and in
a spiritual sense, this text has the same meaning, since, in fact,

281. Cf. Rom 7.25.   282. Cf. 1 John 1.8.
283. Cf. 1 Tim 1.8.   284. Cf. Matt 11.30.
285. 1 John 5.3.

after having quoted this passage, "The word is near you, even in your mouth, and in your heart"[286] (the text here adds, "in your hands,"[287] for in a spiritual sense there are hands in the heart), the Apostle continues, "This is the word of faith, which we preach."[288] Hence, whoever turns back, as it is commanded here, to the Lord his God, with all his heart and with all his soul,[289] will not find God's commandment "heavy." For how can it be heavy when it is the precept of love? For either a person does not love, and then it is burdensome, or he does love, and then it cannot be burdensome. And he loves if, as Israel is there enjoined, he has turned back to the Lord his God with all his heart and with all his soul. "A new commandment," says Christ, "I give unto you: that you love one another."[290] And, "For he that loves his neighbor has fulfilled the Law."[291] And again, "Love is the fullness of the law."[292] In the same sense is this statement also: "If they walk in good paths, they will indeed find the paths of justice easy."[293] Why therefore is it said, "For the sake of the words of your lips, I have kept hard ways,"[294] unless because both this and the preceding statement are true? The paths are hard for fear, easy for love.

70.(84) Thus the beginning of love is the beginning of justice; progress in charity is progress in justice; great charity is great justice; perfect charity is perfect justice; but it is "the charity from a pure heart, and a good conscience, and an unfeigned faith,"[295] which in this life is the greatest, when because of it life itself is contemned.[296] But I would be astonished to discover that it had no place to grow after it had left this mortal life. Yet wherever and whenever it becomes complete, in such a way that nothing can be added to it, it is certainly not "poured forth in [299] our hearts" by the powers of nature or the will that are

---

286. Deut 30.14.
287. Augustine here follows the LXX; see *Quaestiones in Heptateuchum* 54.
288. Rom 10.8.   289. Cf. Deut 30.2.
290. John 13.34.   291. Rom 13.8.
292. Rom 13.10.   293. Prov 2.20.
294. Ps 16.4.   295. 1 Tim 1.5.
296. Cf. John 15.13.

within us, but "by the Holy Spirit, who is given to us,"[297] who both helps our weakness and cooperates with our strength. For this is the very "grace of God, by Jesus Christ our Lord,"[298] to whom, with the Father and the Holy Spirit, belong eternity and goodness, for ever and ever. Amen.

297. Rom 5.5.   298. Rom 7.25.

ON THE PROCEEDINGS
OF PELAGIUS

INTRODUCTION

Orosius

As it turned out, it was Spain that linked Africa and Palestine in the Pelagian conflict. Orosius,[1] a Spanish priest, native of Braga, came to Augustine in 415 to consult with him about Origenism and Priscillianism, the latter of which especially was gaining prominence in Spain. For Augustine he wrote a brief work, *Commonitorium de errore Priscillianistarum et Origenistarum*, and to this Augustine replied in 415 with *Ad Orosium contra Priscillianistas et Origenistas*. Augustine describes him as "religious," "alert of mind, ready of speech, burning with eagerness."[2] Putting together what Augustine says with what he leaves unsaid, Bonner characterizes him thus: "In Orosius, a burning zeal for the Faith was united with a narrow and ungenerous nature, and the whole allied to an impetuous temperament, and a remarkable naivety, which was later to have full rein in his *History against the Pagans*."[3] This work, the main basis for Orosius' reputation, was written at Hippo at Augustine's behest in 417–18.

(2) But now, in 415, after his own response to Orosius' inquiries, Augustine recommended he travel to Palestine to study with Jerome and made him the bearer of two long letters to Jerome (*Epp.* 166 and 167), having to do with the Pelagian controversy. He settled in at Jerome's monastery in Bethlehem, but from there was called to testify at a synod at Jerusalem on July 28, 415. Bishop John of Jerusalem[4] wanted to inquire concerning the disputes involving Pelagius and Caelestius, and called on Orosius as a source of information about events in North Africa.[5]

1. His surname, Paul, is not attested before the sixth century.
2. *Ep.* 166.2.   3. Bonner, *St Augustine*, 332.
4. Bishop from 386 or 387 to 417.
5. Our main source for this synod is Orosius, *Apol.* 3–6.

(3) At the synod, Orosius, who spoke in Latin and had to make use of an interpreter, described the condemnation of Caelestius at Carthage in 411 and read to those assembled from Augustine's *Ep.* 157 to Hilary, against Pelagian ideas being spread about in Sicily. John summoned Pelagius and offered him a chance to reply to the charges made against him. Asked if he had taught the doctrines to which Augustine had responded, Pelagius answered, "And who is Augustine to me?" Orosius tells us the audience was shocked, but John asked Pelagius, "although a layman in an assembly of priests," to sit down and declared, "I am Augustine here." Orosius, not one to be overawed by a Greek bishop, retorted, "If you are going to assume Augustine's person, follow his faith!"[6] Orosius then declared that Pelagius had said to him, "A man can be without sin and easily keep the commandments of God, if he wishes."[7] Pelagius readily admitted he had said this and still said it. Orosius replied that it had been condemned at Carthage and attacked by Augustine and Jerome. John asked if Orosius and his associates wanted to act as Pelagius' accusers, while Orosius regarded the matter as already having been decided for the Church as a whole at Carthage. Pressed further on the question of a sinless life, Pelagius anathematized anyone who said this was possible without the grace of God.[8] This was enough to satisfy John, who thereupon challenged Orosius as to whether he denied that humans could avoid sin even with God's help. Orosius, to avoid complete defeat, urged that the issue, since it was a dispute among Latins, be referred to Pope Innocent at Rome, and this the synod agreed to do.

(4) John clearly had not heard Orosius with sympathy, and when Orosius presented himself on September 12 to assist the bishop in celebrating the feast of the dedication of the Church of the Resurrection, John denounced him as having declared that a man cannot be without sin even with the help of God.[9] It was to clear himself of this charge that Orosius wrote the *Liber apologeticus.*

6. *Apol.*4.
7. See *De gest. Pel.* 14.37–15.38 and 30.54.
8. *De gest. Pel.* 14.37, 30.54.   9. *Apol.* 7.

The Synod of Diospolis

(5) Gaul furnishes the next *dramatis personae*. The cause against Pelagius was taken up by two Gallic bishops, Heros and Lazarus, living in Palestine after having both been exiled from their sees for their support of the usurper, Constantine III.[10] Heros, a former disciple of Martin of Tours, was bishop of Arles from 408–11, while Lazarus was bishop of Aix during those same years. Lazarus had already drawn public attention some years earlier when he had unsuccessfully brought charges against bishop Briccius (or Brictius), the successor of Martin at Tours, and Pope Zosimus later expresses a view of him as nothing but a trouble-maker.[11]

(6) Working from Pelagius' *Book of Testimonies*, the propositions condemned at Carthage in 411, Augustine's Letter 157 to Hilary, and a lost work ascribed to Caelestius, they drew up a *libellus* of charges against Pelagius, which they presented to Bishop Eulogius of Caesarea, the primate of Palestine. Eulogius summoned thirteen other bishops, including John of Jerusalem, to meet with him in a synod at Diospolis, also known as Lydda (or Lod in the Old Testament and modern Israel), a town about twenty-five miles northeast of Jerusalem.

(7) The synod was convoked in mid-December of 415, with Pelagius present but Heros and Lazarus absent, owing, according to Augustine, to the illness of one of them.[12] Still, "the way in which they brought accusations against Pelagius, and failed to appear to press them, suggests that they were not acting on their own behalf, but were the mouthpieces of Jerome and Orosius."[13] At the synod, then, Pelagius, speaking through an interpreter,[14] "had the field to himself."[15]

(8) Since Augustine, in *De gestis Pelagii*, gives the *libellus* in full, as well as substantial portions of Pelagius' replies to the

---

10. For brief biographies of Heros and Lazarus, see Griffe, *La Gaule chrétienne* 2. 237–39 and 252–56. Our main sources for the history of Heros and Lazarus prior to 415 are Prosper of Aquitaine's *Chronicon* for the year 412 (PL 51. 590–91), on Heros, and letters 2–4 of Pope Zosimus (PL 20. 649–65).

11. Zosimus, *Ep.* 4.2. 12. *De gest. Pel.* 1.2, 35.62.
13. Ferguson, *Pelagius*, 86. 14. *De gest. Pel.* 1.2.
15. Bonner, *St Augustine*, 335.

charges, a detailed examination of the exchanges at Diospolis will be deferred to the part of this Introduction which offers a synopsis of *De gestis Pelagii*. Brown summarizes epigrammatically: "With a lack of scruple, common in men of high principles, [Pelagius] condemned his own disciple, Caelestius, and explained away the passages in his own works which had made him seem an *enfant terrible* in the West."[16] He was able to explain, to the synod's satisfaction—although not to Augustine's —the passages from the *Book of Testimonies* adduced against him, while (mendaciously?[17]) disclaiming authorship of several quotations brought forward in support of one charge. To a few of the propositions attributed to Caelestius or his followers, Pelagius gave explanations acceptable to the synod; the rest, including most of those which were most offensive to Augustine, he disavowed, anathematizing those who held them. The final verdict of the synod said simply, "Now that we have received satisfactory reply to the charges brought against Pelagius the monk, here present, and since he is also in agreement with the holy doctrines and anathematizes those things which are contrary to the faith of the Church, we recognize him to belong to the communion of the catholic Church."[18]

From the Synod of Diospolis to De gestis Pelagii

(9) Pelagius felt vindicated and sought to take advantage of the situation by seeing to it that his account of the proceedings was publicized far and wide. First, a letter, which Augustine reasonably surmised to be by Pelagius, was circulated, glorying in the verdict of the bishops, and in particular in their approval of the claim that "a man can be without sin and easily keep the commandments of God, if he wishes." This was a statement Pelagius made in his *Book of Testimonies;* the trouble was that, in the *libellus* against him, and in his successful defense of the proposition at Diospolis, the word *easily* nowhere appeared.[19] Second, by way of the deacon Charus, but without a letter of

16. Brown, *Augustine of Hippo*, 357.
17. See Evans, "Pelagius' Veracity at the Synod of Diospolis."
18. *De gest. Pel.* 20.44.   19. *De gest. Pel.* 30.54–55.

introduction, Pelagius sent Augustine a brief report (*chartula*) giving his own account of the synod, omitting (as Augustine later found out) his own anathemas, as well as those of the synod, of many of the propositions attributed to Caelestius.[20] (10) Meanwhile, Orosius returned to North Africa early in 416, bearing a brief letter from Jerome to Augustine (*Ep.* 172) and another letter, unfortunately now lost, from Heros and Lazarus. Soon after, Augustine received another letter from Jerome, brought by Lazarus and a third, brought by a priest, Innocentius.[21] Augustine replied in *Ep.* 19*, included in the collection of Augustine's letters discovered by Johannes Divjak and translated by Robert Eno in FOTC 81 (1989). In it he mentions that he has sent Jerome a copy of Pelagius' *De natura* as well as his own *De natura et gratia.* He also notes that he has written to Pelagius "something which, unless I am mistaken, he will receive with bad grace, though perhaps it will eventually serve for his salvation."[22] Again, regrettably, this has not survived, nor is there anywhere a mention of a reply by Pelagius. Augustine also speaks of having "written a long letter concerning him to the bishops Eulogius and John, and briefly to the holy priest Passerio."[23] As noted below, Augustine did not get the response he wanted from John.

(11) The letter from Heros and Lazarus which Orosius had brought was read before a provincial synod at Carthage in mid-416, and the synod decided to anathematize the opinions of Pelagius and Caelestius (allowing that Pelagius and Caelestius may have been converted from their errors) and to write to Innocent I of Rome to enlist the support of the Roman see for their action.[24] Shortly afterwards, the bishops of Numidia, including Augustine, wrote to Innocent in a similar vein.[25] Finally, Augustine, joined by Aurelius, Alypius, Evodius, and Possidius, wrote a longer letter to Innocent, describing and at-

---

20. *De gest. Pel.* 32.57–33.59.
21. *Ep.* 19*.1. The letters from Jerome (other than *Ep.* 172) have not survived.
22. *Ep.* 19*.4.
23. *Ep.* 19*.4. Passerio was associated with Orosius in his attack upon Pelagius before John at Jerusalem in July 415. See Orosius, *Apol.* 6 and 7.
24. Augustine, *Ep.* 175.　　25. Augustine, *Ep.* 176.

tacking the errors of Pelagius and asking that he be summoned to Rome for questioning, or at least be asked by way of a letter to denounce these errors. Along with this letter, the authors sent Innocent a copy of Pelagius' *De natura* and the *chartula* which had been sent to Augustine via Charus.[26]

(12) At around the same time, Augustine wrote to John of Jerusalem for a copy of the official proceedings of the Synod of Diospolis.[27] This was probably a second request,[28] and along with it Augustine enclosed a copy of *De natura,* noting that it contradicts what Pelagius was reported to have said at Diospolis about whether the Old Testament mentions people who lived sinless lives. *Ep.* 4*, from the Divjak collection, makes it clear that John did not honor Augustine's request for a copy of the proceedings. "John probably never responded to Augustine's request because he did not like Jerome and associated Augustine with him."[29] Instead, it was Cyril of Alexandria, to whom *Ep.* 4* is addressed, who sent the proceedings.

(13) Augustine thereupon set about writing *De gestis Pelagii.* It is difficult to determine the precise date of this treatise. *Ep.* 4*, which Eno dates to the summer of 417, speaks of *De gest. Pel.* as having been written some time previously—long enough for an argument to have broken out over Augustine's contention in it that not all sinners are punished in eternal flames.[30] *Ep.* 186, written to Paulinus of Nola after July 28, 417 (it speaks of Pope Innocent as dead), appears to allude to the arrival of the proceedings as recent.[31] But de Plinval argues that *De gest. Pel.* must predate the arrival of news of the condemnation of Pelagius by Pope Innocent, which occurred on January 27, 417, for Augustine would have made mention of this had he known of it.[32] Though commentators date this work anywhere from late 416 to early 418, I find de Plinval's argument persuasive and

26. Augustine, *Ep.* 177. The reference to Pelagius' *chartula* is in n. 15.
27. Augustine, *Ep.* 179.
28. *Ep.* 179.1. The letter mentioned in *Ep.* 19* may have been the first request.
29. Eno, 38.
30. *Ep.*4*.3–4; see *De gest. Pel.* 3.9–11.
31. *Ep.* 186.27.   32. BA 21. 423–24.

not obviously refuted by any data from the Divjak collection, and therefore propose for it a date of late 416–early 417.

Pelagius after Diospolis

(14) Presumably after circulating his account of the proceedings at Diospolis, Pelagius turned to the task of working out his theology of the relation between grace and free will and of the effects of Adam's sin. These had not previously been central topics for him, but it was now necessary to answer his critics. So, in four books, he produced a *Defense of Free Will* or *De libero arbitrio*. It has not survived, but Augustine preserves significant excerpts from it in *De gratia Christi et de peccato originali,* which he wrote in 418 in order to refute it. In it, Pelagius develops his well-known distinction between *posse, velle,* and *esse:* in every action, there is the ability to do it, the willing to do it, and the actual doing of it. The first pertains to our nature and is the gift of God; the second and third are our own.[33] Moreover, God's assistance helps humans to act rightly more easily.[34] It is easy to see how this would fail to satisfy Augustine that, in Pelagius' understanding, grace did not reduce to the capacity of our nature, plus the illumination provided by the law and the gospel. It is equally easy to see that Augustine would not be satisfied with Pelagius' explanation of how he could condemn Caelestius' proposition that "Adam's sin injured only himself and not the human race": Adam's sin did indeed harm all subsequent humans by the *example* it set.[35]

(15) But the climate was very different by the time Augustine came to refute this work in 418 from what it had been in 416, when Pelagius wrote it. In 416, Pelagius was at the height of his career. Vindicated, he felt, by a synod of fourteen bishops of the East, and enjoying the support of the venerable bishop of Jerusalem, he could take the offensive against his enemies. By the end of 416, things were already beginning to change. Late

33. *De grat. Chr.* 4.5.
34. *De grat. Chr.* 7.8. For an exposition of Pelagius' theology of grace, see the Introduction to *De nat. et gr.* in the present volume.
35. *De pecc. or.* 15.16.

in 416, perhaps in November, there was a violent attack on the monastery where Jerome lived in Bethlehem. Report had it that "a deacon was killed, that the buildings of the monastery were burned, and that only a well-fortified tower managed to protect Jerome himself."[36] While no evidence connects Pelagius himself with this attack, many held his followers responsible for it.

(16) Word of this reached Augustine while he was writing *De gest. Pel.*, and he added a brief postscript (35.66), making reference to it. With this, the portion of the Pelagian crisis touched upon in *De gest. Pel.* comes to an end. For the sake of completeness, however, there follows a brief summary of further events involving Pelagius.[37]

(17) On January 27, 417, Innocent issued his formal judgment on Pelagius and Caelestius in replies to the three letters of 416 from the African bishops.[38] In them he pronounces that Pelagius and Caelestius are "deprived of communion with the Church" until they should repudiate their errors.[39] Innocent acknowledges having received a report of the synod at Diospolis, but questions its authenticity, since it was not accompanied by any official attestation.[40] He thereby manages to avoid having to condemn the verdict of Diospolis, which would have brought about a serious strain in relations between the Latins and the Greeks. In *De natura*, however, he finds "many statements against the grace of God, many blasphemies; nothing that pleases, nothing that is not deeply displeasing, worthy of being condemned and trampled underfoot by all."[41]

(18) Very shortly afterward, Innocent received word of the assault on Jerome's monastery, where such well-born Roman ladies as Eustochium lived, and he responded vehemently in

---

36. *De gest. Pel.* 35.66.

37. For an exhaustive treatment of these events, see Wermelinger, *Röm und Pelagius*, 116–253. For briefer reviews, see Bonner, *St Augustine*, 339–46, Ferguson, *Pelagius*, 98–115, and de Plinval, *Pélage*, 303–355. Unless otherwise indicated, the present account is based on these sources.

38. That is, *Epp.* 175, 176, and 177 among the letters of Augustine.

39. *Ep.* 182.5,6.   40. *Ep.* 183.3.

41. *Ep.* 183.5.

support of Jerome and in castigation of John of Jerusalem.[42] John was dying, and Pelagius withdrew briefly from Jerusalem, but when John's successor Praylius proved favorably disposed, Pelagius returned and composed a *libellus fidei* for Innocent.[43]

(19) Innocent meanwhile had died and was succeeded by Zosimus, who, perhaps because he was a Greek, as his name would indicate, was initially much more sympathetic to the Pelagian party than Innocent had been. Caelestius, who had been expelled from Constantinople by Bishop Atticus, visited him and presented him with a *libellus fidei*, very similar to that of Pelagius but adding some distinctively Caelestian points about infant baptism.

(20) Zosimus called a synod and, after hearing Caelestius, deferred action on him, but "roundly condemned, suspended and excommunicated Heros and Lazarus, regarding them as mere trouble-makers."[44] He then took up the case of Pelagius, whose *libellus fidei* he had read, together with a letter of recommendation from Praylius, and pronounced him orthodox, communicating his decision to the African bishops together with reproof of them for their hastiness and with further denunciation of Heros and Lazarus.[45] It was around this time, before Zosimus' letters had arrived in Africa but after rumors of his disposition had circulated, that Augustine preached at Carthage the sermon which contained the famous words, "causa finita est"[46] (often misquoted, "Roma locuta est, causa finita est"), in the vain hope that in Rome's eyes the case would have been closed by Innocent's judgment. But the case was not closed in Pelagius' favor, either. Once they had received Zosimus' letters, the African bishops responded promptly with letters of their own to Zosimus. And there was opposition to Pelagius and Caelestius at Rome as well, perhaps led by Marius Mercator, while Caelestius and Julian of Eclanum took the lead for the other side. Eventually this strife resulted in a violent

42. See the letters of Innocent included among the letters of Jerome as *Ep.* 136 and 137.

43. Augustine, *De grat. Chr.* 30.32.

44. Ferguson, *Pelagius*, 104, drawing on Zosimus, *Ep.* 2.

45. Zosimus, *Ep.* 3.   46. *Sermo* 131.10.

attack upon Constantius, another leader of the anti-Caelestian party. Such disturbances, and probably also pressure from the African bishops, brought the conflict to the attention of the imperial government, which had recently been involved in the suppression of Donatism. Zosimus began to have second thoughts, and on March 21, 418, he wrote to the Africans both criticizing their attitude and backing away from any approval of Caelestius, holding that the case remained open.[47] On April 30, the emperor Honorius issued a rescript banishing Pelagius and Caelestius from Rome (Pelagius was not in fact in Rome at that time).

(21) On May 1, 418, a council of over 200 bishops met at Carthage and passed nine canons against Pelagianism.[48] The first three concerned original sin: that Adam would not have undergone bodily death had he not sinned, that infants must be baptized for the remission of original sin, and that unbaptized infants cannot be saved or enter into some intermediate state of happiness (i.e., limbo). The fourth through sixth condemn Pelagius' theory of grace, holding that it is more than the forgiveness of sins or illumination and that it does more than simply make it easier to do the good which we could already do by our own power. The seventh through ninth affirm that no one is completely free from sin and that all must pray for forgiveness.

(22) Around this time—but we do not exactly when, in relation to Honorius' rescript and the decision of Carthage—Zosimus summoned Caelestius to appear before him. "Caelestius saw what was in the air, and not merely failed to appear, but left the city itself."[49] Zosimus, apparently regarding this flight as an admission of guilt, issued a lengthy letter, now lost, known as the *Epistola Tractoria*, condemning Pelagius and Caelestius and affirming original sin, grace, and infant baptism, though perhaps not going so far as the Council of Carthage on the

---

47. Zosimus, *Ep.* 12 (PL 20. 675–78).
48. For text, see PL 56. 486–90, and CCSL 149. 69–73. Wermelinger, *Röm und Pelagius,* 169–196, provides a German translation and extensive commentary.
49. Ferguson, *Pelagius,* 112.

subject of the damnation of infants.[50] The letter was circulated widely, and in Italy subscription was enforced by the imperial authority; eighteen bishops, however, led by Julian of Eclanum, refused to sign and were deposed. Pelagius was condemned by a synod headed by Theodotus of Antioch and expelled from the holy places of Jerusalem. He left Palestine, quite possibly for Egypt, and we hear no more of him. Caelestius reappears twice more. In 423, according to Prosper,[51] he appealed to Celestinus, the bishop of Rome, for a fresh hearing, but was unsuccessful and was banished from Italy. In 429, he took refuge with Bishop Nestorius of Constantinople, who offered some sympathy, a fact which soon "was used against both of them,"[52] as in the dénouement of the Nestorian controversy, at the Council of Ephesus in 431, the names of Pelagius, Caelestius, and Julian were included among those condemned, although no specific doctrines were mentioned.

Synopsis

(23) Title and Preface (1): Augustine addresses the work to Bishop Aurelius of Carthage and announces that he will examine the *gesta* of the Synod in Palestine at which Pelagius was acquitted. *Gesta* here is usually synonymous with *acta*, that is, the official record of a meeting; however, it can also mean the meeting or procedure itself, as in the review of *De gest. Pel.* in the *Retr.* Our choice to translate *De gestis Pelagii* as *On the Proceedings of Pelagius*, not *On the Proceedings against Pelagius*, as it is sometimes rendered, preserves the ambiguity of *gesta*.[53] In *De pecc. or.*,[54] Augustine speaks of the present work as *De gestis Palestinis*, a somewhat more accurate title, but in the *Retr.*, he calls it *De gestis Pelagii*.[55]

(24) In 1.2–2.4 Augustine treats the first of six objections

50. Wermelinger, *Röm und Pelagius*, 209–18 and 283.
51. *C. coll.* 21.2.   52. Ferguson, *Pelagius*, 115.
53. TeSelle's rendering, *The Deeds of Pelagius* (*Augustine the Theologian*, 281), is in error.
54. *De pecc. or.* 14.15.
55. *Retr.* 2.73. CSEL, following one ms.: *De gestis Pelagi*.

raised against Pelagius from his lost *Book of Testimonies*.[56] The *libellus* first charges Pelagius with having said, "No one can be without sin except one who has acquired knowledge of the law." Pelagius replied that he had meant that by knowledge of the law one is assisted in avoiding sin but (denying the converse of his statement as if that were what his accusers took him to be saying) not altogether prevented from sinning. This the synod accepted. Augustine comments that Pelagius' statement ought to be taken to mean that knowledge of the law is a necessary, not a sufficient, condition for avoidance of sin, and he attacks the statement, thus understood, by counterexample.

(25) In 3.5–8 the second charge is that Pelagius had said, "All are ruled by their own will." Pelagius in reply explained that he meant to emphasize human responsibility for sins, although God assists human free will when it chooses the good. The synod found this acceptable. Augustine objects that Pelagius understates the assistance of God and that, in doing the good, people are "ruled" not by their own will but by God.

(26) In 3.9–11 the third objection is that Pelagius had said, "On the day of judgment no mercy will be shown to the wicked and the sinners, but they will be condemned in the eternal fires." Pelagius interprets his statement as having been spoken in opposition to the Origenist position that no one is ultimately damned (and thus as logically equivalent to the proposition that *some* sinners are damned), and with this construction the synod accepts it. Augustine construes it as asserting that *all* sinners will be damned and opposes it with something like an inchoate doctrine of purgatory.

(27) In 4.12 the fourth objection is that Pelagius had said, "Evil does not come into our thoughts." Pelagius said this was a statement not of fact but of what ought to be the case, and in this sense the synod approved it. Augustine notes that the *libellus* did in fact misquote Pelagius here and that in Pelagius' actual wording the statement is acceptable.

(28) In 5.13–15 it was next objected that Pelagius said, "The

56. See note to *De gest. Pel.* 1.2 below.

kingdom of heaven was promised even in the Old Testament."
Pelagius defended this statement, citing Daniel 7.18, and the
synod accepted it. Augustine agrees that the kingdom of
heaven is promised in the Scriptures called "Old Testament,"
but insists that it was not promised in the covenant (testament)
made with Israel on Mount Sinai, which he holds is the apparent referent of Pelagius' words.

(29) In 6.16–10.22 the sixth objection is that Pelagius said,
"A man can, if he wishes, be without sin;" the *libellus* supports
this with three quotations from other works alleged to be by
Pelagius. Pelagius replied, "We stated that a man can be without sin and keep the commandments of God, if he wishes, for
God has given him this possibility. On the other hand, we did
not say that anyone could be found who from infancy to old
age had never sinned, but that whoever has turned away from
sin, by his own labor and the grace of God could be without sin,
yet nevertheless would not be incapable of regression afterwards." He disavowed the other three quotations (although
modern opinion regards at least one of them as definitely his)
and anathematized "as fools" those who agreed with them. The
synod accepted this answer. Augustine notes that he had seen
a work, taken on good authority to be by Pelagius, which contained the quotations which Pelagius repudiated, but withholds
judgment, observing that spurious works had circulated under
his own name. He then addresses the principal statement Pelagius made in reply to the charge and argues, on the basis of *De
natura*, that for Pelagius the grace of God reduces to the natural
capacity for free choice and to the gift of knowledge of the law.
He also takes note of the discrepancy between what Pelagius
said in *De natura*[57] and what he said at Diospolis on the question
of whether anyone had in fact lived without sin.

(30) In 11.23–26 Augustine relates that next were raised in
objection the propositions of Caelestius that were condemned
at Carthage in 411, together with three from Augustine's *Ep.*
157 to Hilary in Sicily:

57. *De nat. et gr.* 36.42.

That Adam was created mortal, and, whether he had sinned or not, he would have been going to die. That the sin of Adam injured only himself and not the human race. That the law leads to the kingdom just as does the gospel. That before the coming of Christ there were men without sin. That newborn infants are in the same condition in which Adam was before his transgression. That the race of man as a whole does not die through the death or transgression of Adam, nor does the race of man as a whole rise again through the resurrection of Christ. That a man can, if he wishes, be without sin. That infants, even if they are unbaptized, have eternal life. That rich people, even if they are baptized, unless they renounce all they have, should not be credited with whatever good they may seem to have done, nor can they possess the kingdom of heaven.

Pelagius responded that he had already explained in what sense a man could be without sin, and that the statement, "Before the coming of Christ, there were men without sin," was correct in the sense that before Christ, "some people lived holy and just lives." All the other statements he disowned, and he "anathematize[d] those who hold or have ever held these opinions." The synod accepted Pelagius' responses, including his anathemas. Augustine emphasizes that, even if Pelagius himself was cleared, the most objectionable opinions of Caelestius had been condemned by the synod. As to the two points which Pelagius did not deny were his, Augustine notes how he had diluted their meaning. It is one thing, Augustine says, to live a holy and just life, quite another to be altogether without sin.

(31) In 12.27–28 Augustine discusses the next objection: that Pelagius had said, "The Church here is without spot or wrinkle," applying Ephesians 5.27 to the empirical Church, as the Donatists had done. Pelagius interpreted this as referring to the remission of sins in baptism, and in this sense the synod gave its approval, and so does Augustine, while rejecting any perfectionism about the lives of Christians between baptism and the kingdom.

(32) 13.29 treats the ninth objection, that Caelestius had said "that we do more than is commanded in the law and the gospel." Pelagius defended this statement, referring it to the prac-

tice of virginity, and the synod accepted this interpretation. Augustine holds that Caelestius meant that through free will we can do more than is commanded *in addition to* keeping all the commandments, and to this he takes exception.

(33) In 14.30–31 the following propositions from a lost work attributed to Caelestius were raised in objection:

The grace and assistance of God is not given for individual acts, but consists in the freedom of the will or in the law and doctrine. The grace of God is given according to our merits, for if God were to give it to sinners, he would seem to be unjust. And grace itself has been placed in my will, in accordance with whether I have been worthy or unworthy. For if we do all things through grace, then when we are overcome by sin, it is not we who are overcome, but God's grace, which wanted to help us in every way but could not. If, when we conquer sins, it is by the grace of God, then it is God who is at fault when we are conquered by sin, for either he was unable or unwilling to protect us altogether from sin.

Pelagius replied that he had never held such views and that he anathematized anyone who held them; of this condemnation the synod approved, and so does Augustine.

(34) In 14.32–17.41 the next objection is that Caelestius had said, "Each person can possess all virtues and graces," which statement was held to "eliminate the diversity of graces, which the Apostle teaches." Pelagius admitted having said this but went on, "We do not eliminate the diversity of graces, but we say that God gives all graces to him who has been worthy to receive them, just as he gave them to the Apostle Paul." The synod accepted this. Augustine, however, first argues that Paul possessed, not all graces, but all those enumerated in 1 Corinthians 12.28. Then at much greater length he responds to Pelagius' statment that graces are given "to him who has been worthy to receive them"; in his rebuttal, he makes extensive use of passages which indicate that this was not Paul's view of his own case. He also argues that this statement of Pelagius is incompatible with Pelagius' own previous anathema of those who hold that "The grace of God is given according to our merits."

(35) In 18.42–19.43 the twelfth objection takes more statements from the book alleged to be by Caelestius:

No one can be called the children of God except those who will in every way have been made free from sin. Forgetfulness and ignorance are not counted as sin, for they do not occur through the will, but through necessity. The will is not free if it needs the aid of God, since everyone possesses in his own will the power either to do something or not to do it. Our victory comes not from the help of God but from free will. If the soul cannot be without sin, then God is also subject to sin, since a part of him,[58] that is, the soul, is vulnerable to sin. Pardon is given to those who repent, not according to the grace and mercy of God, but according to their own merit and effort, who through repentance will have been worthy of mercy.

The synod proclaimed its rejection of these statements before even asking Pelagius for a reply, and in his reply Pelagius denied they were his, rejecting them "in accordance with the judgment of the holy Church" and anathematizing all those who oppose the doctrines of the Church.

(36) In 20.44–21.45 the synod pronounced its verdict that Pelagius was in agreement with the doctrines of the Church and belonged to the communion of the Church. Augustine emphasizes the point that, even though Pelagius was acquitted, the most objectionable doctrines of Pelagius and his followers were condemned.

(37) In 22.46–29.53, having concluded his commentary on the proceedings of the Synod of Diospolis, Augustine moves on to review his own involvement with Pelagius, from the time he first heard of his reputation up through the writing of *De natura et gratia*. He also reproduces and explains away his own *Ep.* 146 to Pelagius, which Pelagius had adduced in his defense.

(38) In 30.54–33.58 Augustine comments on the letter and brief report (*chartula*) which Pelagius circulated after his acquittal, and he points out several discrepancies between these documents and the official record.

(39) In 34.59–35.65 Augustine now reviews the whole affair of Pelagius, including the Synod of Diospolis, again arguing that the worst of the doctrines of Pelagius and Caelestius were repudiated by Pelagius and condemned by the bishops at Diospolis.

58. This was supported by reference to 2 Pet 1.4.

(40) In 35.66 Augustine adds a postscript concerning the raid on Jerome's monastery at Bethlehem.

Texts and Translations

(41) This translation is based on the critical text of C. F. Urba and J. Zycha in CSEL 42 (Vienna, 1902) 51–122, as reproduced with slight emendations in BA 21, edited by Georges de Plinval and Jeanne de La Tullaye (Paris: Desclée de Brouwer, 1966) 432–578. Places where BA differs from CSEL are indicated in notes; the translation normally follows BA. The 1690 Benedictine edition is reprinted in PL 44. 319–60.

(42) In preparing this translation, we have consulted the French translation by Jeanne de La Tullaye in BA 21 and the earlier English translation by Peter Holmes, NPNF 5 (New York: Charles Scribner's Sons, 1887) 183–212. There is a German translation by Berthold Altaner, with Latin text, in *Schriften gegen die Pelagianer*, Bd. II (Würzburg, 1964) 198–319; an Italian translation by Italo Volpe, together with Latin text and with introduction and notes by Agostino Trapè, in Sant' Agostino, *Natura e grazia II: Gli atti di Pelagio, La grazia di Cristo e il peccato originale, L'anima e sua origine* (Rome: Città Nuova Editrice, 1981); and a Spanish translation by P. Gregorio Erce Osaba (with text), BAC 79 (Madrid, 1952) 685–779.

APPENDIX: *RETRACTATIONES* 2.73

On the Proceedings of Pelagius, one book:

During the same time in the East, that is, in Palestinian Syria, Pelagius was brought before a tribunal of bishops by certain Catholic brothers. In the absence of those who had brought the accusation against him, for they could not be present on the day of the synod, he was heard by fourteen bishops. There, since he condemned the very teachings opposed to the grace of Christ which were read from the indictment against him, they pronounced him a Catholic. But when the proceedings of the same synod came into our hands, I wrote a book about them, so that, although it was as if he had been absolved, the judges would not be thought to have approved those teachings, for unless he had condemned them, he would in no way have escaped without condemnation by the bishops.

The book begins as follows: "After . . . into our hands."

ON THE PROCEEDINGS OF PELAGIUS

Preface

FTER THERE came into our hands, O holy father Aurelius, the ecclesiastical proceedings wherein the fourteen bishops[1] of the province of Palestine had proclaimed Pelagius to be a Catholic, my hesitation, which had been making me reluctant to furnish any more extensive and more forthright statement concerning the defense that Pelagius had made, came to an end. For I had already read the defense he had made in a paper[2] that he had sent to me, and, since I received no letter from him accompanying it, I was afraid that there might be some discrepancy between my statement and the ecclesiastical proceedings. Moreover, if perhaps Pelagius should say that he had not himself sent me that paper, which would have been difficult for me to refute, since there was only one [CSEL 42.52] witness, then I would instead appear guilty in the eyes of those who were sympathetic to him in his denial, either of a fraudulent falsification or, to put it more mildly, of an ill-considered credulity. Therefore, now when I examine in detail that to which the proceedings testify, it will become apparent,[3] as much as it is already apparent to me, whether he conducted his defense in the way described, and with all doubt removed your holiness and all who read this work will surely be able to judge both his defense and my present work more readily and more certainly.

1. According to Augustine in *Contra Iulianum* 1.5.19 and 1.17.32, the names of these bishops were Eulogius, John of Jerusalem, Ammonianus, Porphyrius, Eutonius, another Porphyrius, Fidus, Zoninus, Zoboennus, Nymphidius, Chromatius, Jovinus, Eleutherius, and Clematius.

2. *Chartula*. Augustine speaks of this paper at length below in 32.57-33.58. He also discusses it in *Epp.* 177.15, 179.7, and 19*.2.

3. Reading, with BA, *mihi visum est videbitur utrum;* CSEL: *mihi videbar utrum,* PL: *mihi videtur utrum.*

First Objection: Can One Be Sinless without Knowledge
of the Law?

(2) And so I offer first to the Lord my God, our guide and our protector, unutterable thanks, because I was not misled in my estimation of our holy brothers and fellow bishops who presided as judges in the case. For it was with some justification that they approved his answers, for they were not considering how in his writings he had stated the points which were brought against him, but only what he responded about them during the course of the interrogation at hand. For the judgement of an unsound faith is one thing, that of an imprudent language another. In brief, certain objections were raised against Pelagius in a written complaint brought by our holy brothers and fellow bishops in Gaul, Heros and Lazarus,[4] who, because of the serious illness of one of them (as we later found out from a credible source), were unable to be present. The first of these was that Pelagius wrote in one of his works, *No one can be without sin except one who has acquired a knowledge of the law.*[5] After this had been read, the synod asked, "Did you publish that, Pelagius?" And he answered, "I did indeed say that, but not in the sense in which they understood it. I did not say that one who has acquired a knowledge of the law cannot sin, but that through knowledge of the law one is assisted in not sinning, as it is written, [53] 'He gave them his law for help.' "[6] Having heard this, the synod declared, "The statements of Pelagius are not contrary to the Church." Plainly, his response is not con-

4. On Heros and Lazarus, see the Introduction to the present work.
5. This is taken from a lost work, which is referred to by several different titles: *Liber capitulorum (Book of Chapters)* in the present work (e.g., 3.7), *Liber testimoniorum (Book of Testimonies)* (Augustine, *C. duas epp. Pel.* 4.8.21), *Liber eclogarum (Book of Selections)* (Gennadius, *De viris illustribus* 43). According to Evans, this work "probably had no connected prose writing of Pelagius in it at all, but was composed of single assertions each followed by a series of biblical quotations to support it" ("Pelagius' Veracity," 22). Augustine tells us, in *C. duas epp. Pel.* 4.8.21, that Pelagius wrote it after the model of Cyprian's book of testimonies addressed to Quirinus. Although in *De gest. Pel.* this work is called the *Liber capitulorum*, we prefer to translate the title with the more descriptive, *Book of Testimonies*.
6. Isa 8.20 (LXX).

trary to the Church. But the extracts from his works have a different sense. But the bishops, Greek-speaking men who heard his words through an interpreter, were not concerned to dispel the ambiguity. They were taking into consideration only what Pelagius said was his meaning during the interrogation, not the terms in which this same opinion was said to have been expressed in his book.

(3) It is one thing to say that a man can be helped, through knowledge of the law, not to sin, and another to say that no one can be without sin, except one who has knowledge of the law. For we see, for example, that grain may be threshed without threshing sledges, although it helps to use them. Also, children can succeed in school without pedagogues, although the assistance of pedagogues is of some benefit to this end. Also, many people recover from illness without doctors, although the benefit of doctors is obvious. And men can live on other foods, without bread, although no one denies that they are much better off with the help of bread. And many other examples will easily occur to the reader, without further suggestions from us. From this we are reminded that there are two kinds of assistance. For there is one kind, without which that toward which they assist cannot be accomplished. For example, no one sails without a ship, no one speaks without a voice, no one walks without feet, no one sees without light, and so on for many other such examples—among which is also the fact that no one lives rightly without the grace of God. There is another kind of assistance, by which we are helped in such a way that, even if it was lacking, that which we sought could come about in another way, as those examples I cited above, a sledge for threshing grain, a pedagogue for guiding a child, [54] medicine prepared by human skill for the recovery of health, and other such examples. It is necessary then to inquire to which of these two classes belongs the knowledge of the law, that is to say, in which way it helps us to avoid sin. If its assistance is such that without it it is impossible that this end can be obtained, then not only was the answer of Pelagius before the tribunal true, but what he wrote in his book was also true. If, however, it is such that it indeed helps, if it is present, but it is nevertheless possible for that to-

ward which it helps to come about in another way, even if it is not present, then indeed the answer of Pelagius to the judges was still true, and not without reason the judgment that man is assisted by knowledge of the law not to sin found favor with the bishops. But then what he wrote in his book, that *there is no man without sin, except him who has acquired a knowledge of the law,*[7] is not true. The judges left this statement undiscussed, for they were ignorant of the Latin language and were satisfied with the deposition of him who pleaded his case before them, especially since there was no one present from the other side, who could compel the interpreter to explain clearly the statements from Pelagius' book and could show why our brothers were not needlessly disturbed. For very few people have a thorough knowledge of the law. On the contrary, the great majority of Christians who are scattered everywhere are ignorant of this law, which is so profound and complex, but their simple faith, their firm hope in God, and their sincere charity commend them to God, so that, endowed with such gifts by "the grace of God," they have confidence that they can be purified from their sins "by Jesus Christ our Lord."[8]

2.(4) If perhaps Pelagius were to say that he had spoken of precisely this knowledge of the law, without which a man cannot be free [55] from his sins, a knowledge which is transmitted through the teaching of the faith to neophytes and infants in Christ, a knowledge in which even those who are preparing for baptism are instructed, so that they may know the creed—in truth, this is not what is usually meant when someone is said to have a knowledge of the law, but rather, it is said of that knowledge according to which some are called experts in the law. Nevertheless, if these words, which are few in number but great in weight and which, according to the tradition of all the churches, are faithfully inculcated in all catechumens, are what Pelagius designates "knowledge of the law," and if it was of this knowledge that he said he had declared, *No one is without sin,*

7. The slight variations in the translation of this and other phrases from the indictment of Pelagius, at the various times Augustine quotes them, reflect slight variations in the form in which they are quoted.
8. Rom 7.25.

except one who has acquired a knowledge of the law, a knowledge which must be transmitted to believers before they come to that remission of their sins—even in this case, a great multitude of baptized infants would crowd around him, not disputing but crying, and call out, not in words but with the very truth of innocence, "What is it, what is it which you have written, *No one can be without sin, except one who has acquired a knowledge of the law?* For here we are, a large flock of lambs without sin, and yet we have no knowledge of the law!" Assuredly, the little ones with their silent voices would at least compel him to silence, or perhaps even to confess either that he was now chastened of his perverse error or that he indeed even before had held this opinion which he has now expressed in the ecclesiastical inquiry, but that he had not formulated his view with sufficient caution in words, so that his faith should be approved, but his book corrected. For it is the case, as it is written, "There is one that slips with the tongue, but not from his heart."[9] Now if he said or says this, who would not readily overlook those words which he had too carelessly and heedlessly put in writing, particularly since he declined to defend the opinion which [56] these words expressed, but declared that to be his view, of which the truth approves? We must suppose that this is also what the pious judges thought, at least if they could adequately understand that which had been carefully translated from the Latin of his work, just as they judged his reply, which was spoken in Greek and therefore readily intelligible to them, not to be contrary to the Church. But now let us consider other propositions.

Second Objection: "All Are Ruled by Their Own Will"

3.(5) The episcopal synod then went on to say, "Let another chapter be read." And it was read that in the same book Pelagius had declared, *All are ruled by their own will.* When this was read, Pelagius replied, "I said this because of free will, which God assists when it chooses the good; but the man who sins is

9. Sir 19.16.

himself at fault, since his will is free." Having heard this, the
bishops said, "Again, this statement is not contrary to the doctrine of the Church." For who would condemn or deny the
freedom of the will, when the assistance of God is proclaimed
along with it? Therefore, the reply which Pelagius gave was
rightly considered satisfactory by the bishops. But nevertheless, the opinion which he had set down in his book, *All are ruled
by their own will*, undoubtedly ought to have disturbed our
brothers, who had learned in what sense these men are accustomed to argue against the grace of God. For it is said, *All are
ruled by their own will*, as if God rules no one and Scripture says
in vain, "Save your people, O Lord, and bless your inheritance,
and rule them and exalt them forever,"[10] so that in fact they
remain, if they are ruled by their own will without God, "as
sheep not having a shepherd,"[11] which God forbid we should
say. For without a doubt to be *led* implies more compulsion than
to be *ruled.* For he who is ruled [57] also acts in some measure
and is ruled precisely in order that he should act rightly. But he
who is led can hardly be understood to do anything by himself.
Nevertheless, the grace of the Savior is so far superior to our
wills that the Apostle says without hesitation, "For whoever are
led by the Spirit of God, they are the sons of God."[12] And our
free will can do nothing better than to commit itself to him to
be led, who cannot act wrongly, and, when it has done this, not
to doubt that it was assisted to do it by him of whom it is said in
the psalm, "My God, his mercy shall go before me."[13]

(6) And in fact, in that book, where Pelagius wrote these
propositions, to the passage where he said, *All are ruled by their
own will, and each one is subjected to his own desire*, he adds some
testimony from the Scriptures, from which it should be clear
enough that no man should commit himself to himself for governance. For on this very subject it is written in the Wisdom of
Solomon, "I myself am a mortal man, like all others, and of the
race of him that was first made of the earth,"[14] and so on to the
end of the verses where we read, "For all men have one en-

10. Ps 27.9.   11. Mark 6.34.
12. Rom 8.14.   13. Ps 58.11.
14. Wis 7.1.

trance into life, and the like going out. Wherefore I wished, and understanding was given me, and I called upon God, and the spirit of wisdom came upon me."[15] Is it not clearer than light that Solomon, on considering the misery of human weakness, did not dare commit himself to himself for governance, but "wished, and understanding [sensus] was given" to him (of which the Apostle says, "But we have the mind [sensum] of the Lord"[16]) and "called," and "the spirit of wisdom came upon" him? And it is through this spirit, rather than through the strength of their own will, that they are ruled and "led" who "are the sons of God."[17]

(7) [58] For in that same Book of Testimonies,[18] in order to justify somehow his assertion that All are ruled by their own will, Pelagius has cited this passage from the psalm, "And he loved cursing, and it shall come unto him, and would not have blessing, and it shall be far from him."[19] But who does not know that this is a fault, not of nature, as God created it, but of the human will, which turned away from God? The fact is that, even if he had not loved cursing and had desired blessing, but if in this instance he denied that his will was helped by divine grace, in his ingratitude and impiety he would be abandoned to be ruled by himself, so that, deprived of divine guidance and brought to ruin, he would discover through punishment that he was incapable of being ruled by himself. Similarly, in another passage which Pelagius has quoted in the same chapter of the same book, "He has set water and fire before you; stretch forth your hand to what you desire. Before man is life and death, good and evil; that which he shall choose shall be given to him,"[20] it is evident that if he puts his hand to the fire, and if evil and death please him, then it is his human will that is responsible; on the contrary, if he loves the good and life, then not only does his will make this choice, but it is divinely assisted. For the eye is sufficient in itself for not seeing, that is to say in darkness, but for seeing it is not sufficient in its own light unless the assistance of a clear external light is made available to it. But far be it from

15. Wis 7.6–7.   16. 1 Cor 2.16.
17. Rom 8.14.   18. See note to 1.2 above.
19. Ps 108.18.   20. Sir 15.17–18.

us to say that those who "according to his purpose are called
. . ., whom he foreknew" and "predestined to be conformable
to the image of his Son,"[21] should be abandoned to their own
desire, so that they perish. For this is suffered by the "vessels of
wrath, fitted for destruction,"[22] and by their very perdition God
makes known "the riches of his glory on the vessels of his
mercy."[23] It is for this reason that after saying, [59] "My God,
his mercy shall come before me," the psalmist at once adds,
"God shall let me see over my enemies."[24] Therefore it happens
to them as is written, "Wherefore God gave them up to the
desires of their heart."[25] But this does not happen to the predestined, whom the Spirit of God rules, for not in vain is their
cry, "Give me not up, O Lord, from my desire, to the wicked,"[26]
since it is also against these same desires that they have prayed,
as is written, "Take away from me the greediness of the belly,
and let not the lusts of the flesh take hold of me."[27] God grants
this favor to those over whom he rules, but not to those who
think they are fit to rule themselves and who, in the stiff-necked
presumptuousness of their own will, disdain to have him as
their guide.

(8) This being so, how could the children of God, who knew
this and were happy to be ruled and led by the Spirit of God,
have been affected when they heard or read from the writings
of Pelagius, *All are ruled by their own will, and each one is subjected
to his own desire?* And yet when Pelagius was questioned by the
bishops, he was well aware that those words might create a bad
impression, and so he replied that "he had said this because of
free will," adding at once, "which God assists when it chooses
the good; but the man who sins is himself at fault, because his
will is free." Because he spoke thus, the pious judges approved
this opinion also, and they were not willing to ask or examine
how carelessly and in what sense these words had been used in
his book; they considered it sufficient that he had made this
confession regarding free will, that God helped it in choosing

21. Rom 8.28–29.   22. Rom 9.22.
23. Rom 9.22–23.   24. Ps 58.12.
25. Rom 1.24.   26. Ps 139.9.
27. Sir 23.6.

the good, but that the one who sins would himself be at fault, since his own will was sufficient to him for this. It is in this sense that God rules those that he assists [60] in choosing the good, and in turn they rule well whatever they rule, since they are themselves ruled by the good.

Third Objection: Eternal Punishment for All Sinners?

(9) Next, a statement was read which Pelagius had set forth in his book, *On the day of judgment no mercy will be shown to the wicked and the sinners, but they will be consumed in the eternal fires.*[28] This disturbed the brothers to the point where they thought they should raise an objection because it seemed to imply that all sinners were to suffer eternal punishment, not even excepting those who had Christ as a foundation, although on this foundation they built wood, hay, stubble.[29] Of these the Apostle writes, "If any man's work burn, he shall suffer loss, but he himself shall be saved, yet so as by fire."[30] However, when Pelagius had replied that he had spoken according to the gospel, where it is said regarding sinners, "And these shall go into everlasting punishment, but the just, into life everlasting,"[31] this statement in the gospel by our Lord could not in any way displease the Christian judges, for they did not know what the

---

28. Pelagius explains in the next paragraph that in this statement he intended to oppose Origen's idea of *apocatastasis*, at least as it was understood in the West following the circulation of Rufinus of Aquileia's translation of Origen's *On First Principles,* that ultimately all, including the devil and his angels, would be saved. Robert Eno (FOTC 81.39) adds, in reference to this statement, "There was also a growing belief among at least some that no baptized Christian or at least Catholic, no matter how evil a life he may have led, would ever be condemned to the flames for eternity." Augustine interprets this statement of Pelagius as putting forward a sort of perfectionism, which would lead either to presumption, if Christians were to believe they could be altogether without sin, or to despair, if they were to believe that any sin would suffice for their damnation. His position in regard to this statement of Pelagius is made much clearer in *Ep.* 4*. There, as here, Augustine cites 1 Cor 3.10–15, as speaking of a purificatory fire before the Last Judgment "either in this life or after death" (*Ep.* 4*.4). On the general topic of Augustine and purgatory, see J. Ntedika, *l'Evolution de la doctrine du purgatoire chez saint Augustin* (Paris: Etudes Augustiniennes, 1966).

29. Cf. 1 Cor 3.11–12.   30. 1 Cor 3.15.
31. Matt 25.46.

words taken from Pelagius' book contained which had disturbed our brothers, who were accustomed to hear his discussions and those of his followers. But with those absent who had brought up the petition against Pelagius to the holy bishop Eulogius, there was no one to press the point that he ought to differentiate, by some qualification, between those sinners who are to be saved by fire and those who are to suffer eternal punishment. Thus, if the judges understood why objection had been made to his statement, then he would have been justly blamed, if he had refused to make this distinction.

(10) To this statement Pelagius then added, "And anyone who believes differently is an Origenist." This the judges accepted, for actually it was that which the Church most justly detested in Origen. That is, that even those whom the Lord says are to be punished everlastingly and the devil himself [61] and his angels after a time, admittedly a long time, will be purged and delivered from their sins and reunited with the saints who reign with God in the society of blessedness. The synod therefore declared, "This statement is not contrary to the Church," not as put forward by Pelagius but rather as in the gospel, that such impious and sinful men as the gospel judges worthy of such punishment shall be consumed by eternal fires, and that anyone who says that their punishment, which the Lord has said is eternal, can come to an end, shares in the abominable opinion of Origen. But concerning those sinners of whom the Apostle says that after their work has been burned, they will be saved as if by fire,[32] since evidently no objection was raised against Pelagius with reference to them, the synod passed no judgment. Therefore, anyone who maintains that the impious and the sinners, whom the truth condemns to eternal punishment, can ever be liberated from it, is not inappropriately designated by Pelagius as an Origenist. On the contrary, anyone who considers that no sinner whatever deserves mercy in the judgment of God, may be given whatever name Pelagius wishes, provided that he understands that this error is not accepted in the truth of the Church. For there will be

32. Cf. 1 Cor 3.15.

"judgment without mercy to him that has not done mercy."[33]

(11) But how this judgment will be rendered is not easy to understand in Holy Scripture, for what will be accomplished in only one way is described in many ways. For in one place the Lord says that he will shut the door against those whom he does not admit into his kingdom, and when they cry out and say, "Open to us, ... We have eaten and drunk in your name,"[34] and the other things which it is written that they say, he will reply to them, "I know you not, . . . you workers of iniquity."[35] In another passage he says that he will order [65] all those who did not wish him to be their ruler to be brought into his presence and killed.[36] Elsewhere he says that he will come with his angels in his majesty, so that before him all the nations shall be gathered, and he will divide them and place some on his right, whom, after recounting their good works, he will take into eternal life, others on his left, and, charging them with barrenness of good works, he will condemn them to eternal fire.[37] In other passages, he orders that the wicked and slothful servant, who had neglected to invest his money,[38] as well as the man who was discovered at the wedding feast not dressed in a wedding garment, be bound hand and foot and thrown into the outer darkness.[39] Elsewhere, after having admitted the five wise virgins, he closes the door upon the five other foolish ones.[40] Such accounts, and whatever others there are which at the moment do not occur to me, speak of the future judgment, which indeed will be carried out, not over one, or five, but over a multitude of persons. For if it were merely the one case of the man who was cast into the darkness for not having the wedding garment, he would not have added immediately these words, "For many are called, but few are chosen,"[41] when it is evident that, though the one was cast out and condemned, there still remained many in the house. However, it would take us too long to discuss each of these passages adequately at present. Briefly,

33. Jas 3.13.
35. Luke 13.27.
37. Matt 25.33.
39. Cf. Matt 22.11–13.
41. Matt 22.14.

34. Luke 13.25–26.
36. Luke 19.27.
38. Cf. Luke 19.20–24.
40. Cf. Matt 25.10–12.

and without prejudice—as it is customary to say in monetary reckonings—to a more thorough discussion, I can say that there will be but one form of judgment, the nature of which is unknown to us (with this reservation: that the diversity of merits will be preserved in the assignment of rewards and punishments), which is symbolized in many ways in Holy Scripture. But for the question now under discussion, it is sufficient to point out that [63] if Pelagius had said without qualification that all sinners would be condemned to eternal fire and eternal punishment, then whoever approved this judgment would first have brought condemnation down upon himself, "For who can glorify himself and say he is pure from sin?"[42] But since Pelagius did not say either "all" or "certain" and made only an indefinite statement and responded that he had said this in accordance with the gospel, his opinion was indeed confirmed as true by the judgment of the bishops. But still, even after this judgment by the bishops, it is not improper to inquire whether Pelagius may not hold another opinion which has not yet become apparent.

Fourth Objection: "Evil Does Not Come into Our Thoughts"

4.(12) It was also objected that Pelagius had written in his book, *Evil does not come into our thoughts,* but he replied, "We did not say this in those terms; what we did say was that the Christian should take care not to have evil thoughts." The bishops, as was fitting, approved of this, for who can doubt that we ought not to think of evil? And in fact in his book it is more accurately read concerning *evil* that it *is not to be thought of,* which is usually understood in this sense,[43] that no one ought to think of evil. And if anyone denies this, does he say anything other than that evil is to be thought of? So, if this were true, it could not be said in praise of charity that it "thinks no

---

42. Prov 20.9 (LXX).
43. Reading, with BA, *ad "malum" accuratius ita legitur: "nec cogitandum" quod in hoc;* CSEL: *ad "malum" cautius ita legitur: "nec cogitandum" quod in hoc;* mss. and PL: *ad malum cuius ita legitur: "nec cogitandum" quod in hac.*

evil."[44] Still, that evil enters [64] the thoughts of the just and the pious is not so improper to assert, because ordinarily we designate it as "thought" even when something comes into the mind, although consent does not follow. However, the "thought" which involves sin, and which is rightly forbidden, does not occur without our consent. It therefore could have been the case that those men, who judged that this passage should be brought forward in objection, as if Pelagius had said, "Evil does not come into our thoughts," that is, that evil does not enter into the minds of the just and holy, were working from a faulty text. For this opinion is obviously absurd, for even when we condemn evils, we cannot express this condemnation in words unless we have thought about them. but, as we have said, that thought of evil is termed "culpable," which carries assent with it.

Fifth Objection: Continuity of Old and New Testaments?

5.(13) When, therefore, the judges had given their approval also to this reply of Pelagius, another passage in his book was read, *The kingdom of heaven was promised even in the Old Testament.* To this Pelagius replied, "This also can be demonstrated through the Scriptures, but the heretics[45] deny it, to the disparagement of the Old Testament. I, however, followed the authority of Scripture when I said this, for it is written in the prophet Daniel, 'And the saints shall receive the kingdom of the most high.' "[46] Having accepted his reply, the synod declared, "And this is not contrary to the faith of the Church."

(14) Could our brothers have been moved without reason by these words, so as to include them with the others brought as objections? Certainly not. For in fact the name, "Old Testament," is used in two different ways, one according to the authority of the divine Scriptures, the other according to the most common custom of speaking. For the Apostle Paul [65] says to

44. 1 Cor 13.5.
45. Pelagius probably has the Manichaeans in mind, though this position goes back to Marcion (d. ca. 160).
46. Dan 7.18.

the Galatians, "Tell me, you that desire to be under the law, have you not heard the law? For it is written that Abraham had two sons, the one by a bondswoman, and the other by a free-woman. These things are in allegory. For these are the two testaments, one engendering unto bondage, which is Hagar. For Sinai is a mountain in Arabia, which has affinity to that Jerusalem which now exists, for she is in bondage with her children. But that Jerusalem which is above, is free, which is our mother."[47] Therefore, since the Old Testament concerns bondage (whence again it is written, "Cast out the bondswoman and her son, for the son of the bondswoman shall not be heir with my son Isaac"[48]), but the kingdom of heaven concerns liberty, how could the kingdom of heaven have to do with the Old Testament? But because, as I have already said, we are also accustomed to speak in such a manner that we designate by the name, "Old Testament," all the Scriptures of the law and the prophets which were delivered prior to the incarnation of our Lord and accepted by canonical authority, what man, however slightly versed in ecclesiastical writings, does not know that the kingdom of heaven could be promised in these Scriptures, just as also was the New Testament, to which the kingdom of heaven belongs? In fact in the Old Testament it is very clearly stated, "Behold the days shall come, says the Lord, and I shall make a new covenant [testamentum] with the house of Israel and with the house of Jacob. Not according to the covenant I made with their fathers, in the day that I took them by the hand to lead them out of the land of Egypt."[49] For the latter was made on Mount Sinai. But then the prophet Daniel [66] did not yet exist, who said, "The saints shall receive the kingdom of the most high."[50] For by these words he prophesied the reward not of the Old, but of the New Testament, just as the same prophets indeed foretold that Christ himself would come, in whose blood the New Testament was consecrated. Of this testament the apostles became the ministers, as the most blessed Paul testi-

---

47. Gal 4.21–22, 24–26; some variations from Vg.
48. Gen 21.10.
49. Jer 38.31–32 (LXX). This, with some variations, is Jer 31.31–32 in Vg.
50. Dan 7.18.

fies, "Who also has made us fit ministers of the new testament, not in the letter, but in the spirit. For the letter kills, but the spirit gives life."[51] But in that testament which is properly called the Old, and was given on Mount Sinai, we do not find that anything but an earthly happiness is explicitly promised. Whence, that land, into which the people were led after having been led through the desert, is called the promised land, a land in which there were peace and a kingdom, the spoils of victories over their enemies, an abundance of children and of the fruits of the earth, and other benefits of this sort—these are the promises of the Old Testament. And even if by these are prefigured the spiritual goods which belong to the New Testament, nevertheless, whoever embraces God's law because of these earthly goods, he is the heir of the Old Testament. For those things are promised and given according to the Old Testament which are desired according to the old man; those things pertaining to the New Testament which are set forth figuratively in the Old require new men. The great Apostle knew well what he was saying when he declared that the two testaments were differentiated in the allegorical distinction of the bondswoman and the free woman,[52] attributing to the Old Testament the children of the flesh and to the New Testament the children of the promise. "Not they that are the children of the flesh," he says, "are the children of God, but they that are the children of the promise, are accounted for the seed."[53] Thus, the children of the flesh belong to the earthly Jerusalem, which is in bondage with her children, but the children of the promise [67] belong to the Jerusalem which is on high, our free and eternal mother in heaven.[54] From this it is evident who belongs to the earthly kingdom and who belongs to the heavenly kingdom. Even those in that distant age who through the grace of God perceived this distinction became the children of the promise, and they were designated heirs of the New Testament according to God's secret design, even though they appropriately observed the Old Law given by God, in his disposition of the times, to the people of old.

51. 2 Cor 3.6.   52. Cf Gal 4.23.
53. Rom 9.8.   54. Cf. Gal 4.26.

(15) How then would the children of promise, the children of the free and eternal Jerusalem in heaven, not with good reason be disturbed when this apostolic and catholic distinction appears to be abolished by the words of Pelagius, and Hagar is believed to be in some way the equal of Sarah? Therefore, with heretical impiety, he does no less harm to the Scripture of the Old Testament than[55] does someone who with an impious and sacrilegious effrontery denies that it is from the good, supreme, and true God, as do Marcion, Mani, and other scourges who think this. In order, then, I may express as briefly as I can my own views on this matter: just as harm is done to the Old Testament if it is denied to be from the good and supreme God, so also is harm done to the New Testament, if it is placed on a par with the Old. Hence, when Pelagius in his reply explained his reason for declaring that even in the Old Testament the kingdom of heaven is promised, citing the testimony of the prophet Daniel, who clearly prophesied that the saints would receive the kingdom of the most high, it was rightly judged that this statement of Pelagius was not contrary to the Catholic faith—not in accordance with that distinction by which the earthly things promised at Mount Sinai [68] are shown properly to pertain to the Old Testament, but appropriately according to the custom of speaking, by which all the canonical Scriptures delivered prior to the incarnation of the Lord were included under the name, "Old Testament." For the "kingdom of the most high" is not other than the kingdom of God. Or does anyone dare to contend that the kingdom of God is one thing and the kingdom of heaven another?

Sixth Objection: Possibility of Life without Sin?

6.(16) After this, the objection was raised that Pelagius said in the same book of his, *A man can, if he wishes, be without sin,* and also that, writing to a widow,[56] he said in flattery, *May piety find*

55. Reading, with BA: *scripturae veteris testamenti non minorem facit iniuriam quam qui eam;* PL, CSEL: *scripturae veteris testamenti facit iniuriam qui eam.*
56. This letter is cited by Jerome, *Dial. c. Pel.* 3.14–16. Marius Mercator quotes a letter in a similar vein to a widow named Livania (*Commonitorium super*

in you a place, such as she finds nowhere else; may justice, though every-where a stranger, find a home in you; may truth, although no longer known by anyone, become a member of your household and your friend; and may the law of God, which is despised by nearly everyone, be honored only by you.[57] He also writes to her, *How happy and blessed are you, if justice, which we must believe flourishes only in heaven, is found on earth in you alone.* And in another work addressed to her, after a prayer to our Lord and savior, in order to show how saints pray, he declares, *He worthily raises his hand to God and with a good conscience pours forth his prayer who can say, "You know, O Lord, how holy and innocent, how pure from all malice and iniquity and theft are the hands I stretch forth to you, how just and pure and free from all deceit are the lips by which I offer to you my prayer that you will have mercy on me."*[58] But to this Pelagius replied, "We stated that a man can be without sin and [69] keep the commandments of God, if he wishes,[59] for God has given him this possibility. On the other hand, we did not say that anyone could be found, who from infancy to old age had never sinned, but that whoever has turned away from sin, could by his own labor and the grace of God be without sin, yet nevertheless would not thereby be incapable of regression afterwards. But as for the other statements which they have brought forward against us,

---

nomine Caelestii 4.3; PL 48. 102), but Evans ("Pelagius, Fastidius," 93) challenges the identification of that letter with the one quoted here. The passages cited are of a sort customary in letters of the time; de Plinval refers to them by the name of *verba beatificantia* (BA 21. 631). The attribution to Pelagius is disputed.

57. This entire passage is in the subjunctive mood.

58. This passage is from *De vita christiana* 11 (PL 40. 1042), which Robert F. Evans argues is by Pelagius (see "Pelagius, Fastidius," and *Four Letters of Pelagius*). De Plinval suggests that, in denying that he said this and the preceding two passages quoted or that they are in his books, Pelagius may be engaging in a subtle mental reservation, taking a personal letter, such as the works cited, not to be a "book," and in anathematizing as "fools" those who hold the sentiments expressed may be labeling the interpretation of his opponents "foolish" (BA 21. 632). On this subject see Evans, "Pelagius' Veracity at the Synod of Diospolis."

59. In 30.54 below, Augustine refers to a letter in which Pelagius claims that this statement was approved by the bishops, but in quoting himself, adds the word "easily" (*facile*): "A man can be without sin and easily keep the commandments of God, if he wishes." This is apparently the form in which the statement appears in the *Liber capitulorum*, since both Jerome (*Dial. c. Pel.* 1.32) and Orosius (*Apol.* 11) quote it this way.

they are not in our books, and we have never said such things."
Upon hearing this, the synod declared, "Since you deny having
written such opinions, do you anathematize those who hold
them?" Pelagius replied, "I anathematize them as fools, not as
heretics, considering that there is no dogma involved." The
bishops then pronounced their judgment, saying, "Now, since
Pelagius has by his own words anathematized as foolishness the
statements introduced, and correctly responds that with the assistance and grace of God a man can be without sin, let him now
reply to the other charges."[60]

(17) Could, or should, the judges here condemn these un-
identified and vague statements, when no one was present
from the opposition to show that Pelagius had written these
blameworthy statements which were alleged to have been addressed to the widow? Certainly in this case it could not be sufficient to bring forward a manuscript and read these things as
his writings, unless there were also witnesses present, in case,
even when the words were read, he denied that they were his
writings. Still, in regard to these, the judges did what they could
do, when they asked Pelagius if he would anathematize those
who professed such sentiments, such as he denied having written or said. And when he did respond by anathematizing them
as fools, what right had the judges to press the inquiry further
on this point, in the absence of his opponents?

(18) Perhaps it is necessary to consider further whether it
was rightly said that those who hold these opinions should be
anathematized as fools, not as heretics, considering that there
is no dogma involved. But [70] under these circumstances the
judges had good reason to abstain from deciding at what point
someone is to be described as a heretic, a question that is not
easy. For example, if anyone were to say that young eagles,
when carried in the talons of the father bird and exposed to the
light of the sun, if they blink their eyes, are dropped to the
earth as unfit (as though the light were in some way a test of
their true nature), he ought not to be judged a heretic, if the

60. See *De pecc. orig.* 11.12, where Augustine reproduces the *acta* of the
synod from this point through the statement of Pelagius contained here at the
beginning of 11.24.

story happens to be false.[61] But since this story is found in the writings of learned men and it is commonly accepted in popular opinion, it should not be considered foolish to repeat it, even if it is not true, nor does it either hurt or help that faith, on account of which we are called "faithful." But if anyone, holding this opinion, went further and contended that birds possessed rational souls, because at times human souls were reincarnated into them, then it would certainly be necessary to banish from our ears and soul such a heretical idea, as if it were a plague. And, even if the stories about eagles were true (just as it is true that there are many marvelous things about bees which our eyes behold), it would be necessary for us to demonstrate that nevertheless far different from the powers of sense, however marvelous, of irrational animals of this sort, is reason, which is common, not to men and beasts, but to men and angels. For certainly many foolish things are said by ignorant and empty-headed persons, who are nonetheless not heretics—for example, the words of those who make rash judgments in unfamiliar disciplines, which they have not studied, or who with immoderate and blind fervor either praise those they love or attack those they hate, and whatever else in the ordinary practice of human discourse is not solidly grounded but here and there, as it may occur at the moment, is with foolish [71] levity either put forward in speech, or written down, or even put into books. Many people, once admonished even a little about these matters, have quickly regretted that they have said such things. They did not retain these things as if they were fixed in some act of belief, but rather they had poured them out as if they had taken them at random and not given them any consideration. It is scarcely possible, however, to be free of such faults, and who has not made a slip of the tongue and offended with words?[62] But it makes a difference to what extent and from what motive one has erred, and finally, whether one, once warned of his error, corrects, or by stubbornly defending it, makes a dogma out of that which he had declared,

61. Cf. Pliny, *Hist. Nat.* 10.3.3, and Lucan, *Pharsalia* 9.902.
62. Cf. Sir 19.16 and Jas 3.2.

not dogmatically, but in levity. Since, therefore, every heretic is consequently also a fool, but not every fool is right away to be labeled a heretic, the judges were quite right in saying that Pelagius had in his own voice anathematized the foolish discourse under consideration, because even if it was not a heresy,[63] undoubtedly it was foolish discourse. Therefore, whichever it was, they called it by a name indicating general blameworthiness. Whether these words were spoken from some dogmatic position, or not in fact from a fixed and established opinion, but in a loose and easily correctible way of speaking, it was not considered necessary at that time to settle, since the man who was on trial denied that they were his words, no matter in what sense they had been used.

(19) While we were reading this defense of Pelagius in the brief paper which we had received earlier, some of our holy brothers were present, who declared that they possessed some hortatory or consolatory letters which Pelagius had sent to a widow, whose name was not given, and suggested that we examine whether the words which he had refused to admit as his own might perhaps be written there, since they said that they themselves did not know this. And in fact when [72] these books were read through from the beginning, the words in question were sought and found. Moreover, those who had brought forward the copy declared that they had acquired the books almost four years previously as books of Pelagius, and that they had never heard any doubt expressed by anyone as to whether they were his. Therefore, considering that these servants of God, whose honesty is well-known to us, could not have lied concerning this matter, the alternative seems to remain that we should rather believe that Pelagius had lied at his trial before the bishops, unless perhaps we might think that something has been circulated under his name, even for so many years, which was not actually written by him. For these brothers did not say that they had received these books from Pelagius himself, nor that they had ever heard him say that they were his. For in my own case also, certain brothers of ours have informed me that

63. Reading, with BA, *etsi haeresis non esset;* CSEL, PL: *si haeresis esset.*

various writings have appeared in Spain under my name, which would not be recognized as mine by those who have read my other writings, but might nevertheless be believed by others to be mine.

(20) For that matter, even what Pelagius admits is his own is still obscure, but I think that what will follow in later parts of these proceedings will make it clearer. Thus, Pelagius declares, "We stated that a man can be without sin and keep the commandments of God, if he wishes, for God has given him this possibility. On the other hand, we did not say that anyone could be found, who from infancy to old age had never sinned, but that whoever has turned away from sin, by his own labor and the grace of God could be without sin, yet nevertheless would not thereby be incapable of regression afterwards." It is quite difficult to see in these words what he means by the grace of God; and indeed the catholic judges could not have understood grace as anything other than that which the doctrine of the Apostle so strongly recommends to us: this is that grace, by which [73] we hope we can be delivered "from the body of this death, by Jesus Christ our Lord."[64]

7. And it is to obtain this grace that we pray that we may not enter into temptation.[65] This grace is not nature, but that which supports a weak and corrupted nature. This grace is not knowledge of the law, but it is that of which the Apostle says, "I cast not away the grace of God, for if justice be by the law, then Christ died in vain."[66] Therefore this grace is not the letter which kills but the spirit which gives life.[67] For the knowledge of the law, without the grace of the Spirit, produces all concupiscence in man. As the Apostle says, "I do not know sin but by the law, for I had not known concupiscence, if the law did not say, 'Thou shalt not covet.' But sin, taking occasion by the commandment, wrought in me all manner of concupiscence."[68] Yet in saying this he does not blame the law; rather, indeed, he praises it, when he says, "The law indeed is holy, and the commandment holy, and just, and good. Was that then which is

64. Rom 7.24–25.   65. Cf. Matt 6.13.
66. Gal 2.21.   67. Cf. 2 Cor 3.6.
68. Rom 7.7–8.

good," he asks, "made death unto me? God forbid. But sin, that it may appear sin by that which is good, wrought death in me."[69] And again he praises the law in saying, "For we know that the law is spiritual; but I am carnal, sold under sin. For that which I do, I understand not. For I do not that which I will; but the evil which I hate, that I do. If then I do that which I will not, I consent to the law that it is good."[70] Behold, he knows the law, praises it and consents to it; that is, he acknowledges that the law is good, because what it commands, this he also desires, and what it forbids and condemns, this he also hates; yet nevertheless, what he hates, he does. [74] Therefore, he has in him a knowledge of the holy, but still his evil concupiscence is not healed; he has in him a good will, but evil action prevails. Thus it happens that in the struggle of the two laws within him, when the law in his members wars against the law of his mind and makes him captive to the law of sin, confessing this he exclaims and says, "Unhappy man that I am, who shall deliver me from the body of this death? The grace of God, by Jesus Christ our Lord."[71]

8.(21) Therefore, it is not nature (which, sold under sin and wounded by corruption, desires a savior and redeemer), nor is it knowledge of the law (through which comes the recognition, rather than the expulsion, of concupiscence) which delivers us "from the body of this death," but "the grace of God, by Jesus Christ our Lord."[72]

9. This grace is not the nature which dies, nor the letter which kills, but the life-giving spirit. For the Apostle already possessed nature with freedom of the will, since he said, "For to will is present with me;"[73] but he did not possess this nature in a sound state without corruption, for he said, "I know that there dwells not in me, that is to say, in my flesh, that which is good."[74] He already possessed a knowledge of the holy law, for he said, "I do not know sin, but by the law;"[75] but he did not possess the strength to practice and to accomplish justice, for he said, "I do

69. Rom 7.12–13.   70. Rom 7.14–16.
71. Rom 7.24–25.   72. Rom 7.24–25.
73. Rom 7.18.   74. Rom 7.18.
75. Rom 7.7.

not that which I will, but the evil which I hate, I do,"[76] and, "To accomplish that which is good, I do not find."[77] So it is not the choice of the will nor the precepts of the law whereby he is delivered from "the body of this death," because he already possessed both of these, the one by nature, the other through learning, but what he entreated was the help of "the grace of God, by Jesus Christ our Lord."[78]

10.(22) [75] The bishops believed that Pelagius confessed this grace, which they knew was commonly accepted in the catholic Church, when they heard him say, "A man who has turned away from his sins, by his own labor and the grace of God can be without sin." I personally, however, was uneasy, because of that book which had been given to me, in order that I might refute it, by some servants of God who had been followers of Pelagius,[79] and who, although they had a great affection for Pelagius himself, admitted that the words were his, where, when the question was put before him, because he had already offended many people by [seeming to] speak against the grace of God, he very explicitly admitted that he *understood by the "grace of God" that, when our nature was created, it received the possibility of not sinning, because it was created with a free will.* So I, because of this book, but also many of the brothers, because of his discussions, which they say are well known to them, are equally disturbed by the ambiguity of his words, lest there be a hidden meaning, and he might later tell his followers that he had spoken without prejudicing his own doctrine, explaining thus, "Without a doubt I asserted that a man is able by his own effort and the grace of God to be without sin, but you know quite well what I mean by 'grace,' and you may recall by reading, that grace is that in which we were created with a free will by God." And thus while the bishops understood him to mean by "grace," not that by which we humans were created, but that by which we have been made new creatures by adoption (since it is this latter grace which divine Scripture very

76. Rom 7.15.   77. Rom 7.18.
78. Rom 7.25.
79. Augustine is referring to *De natura*, given to him by Timasius and James, for whom he wrote *De natura et gratia*.

clearly commends), they, not realizing he was a heretic, acquitted him as a catholic. Also, it made me suspicious that, while, in the work which I answered, he very definitely stated that *The just Abel never sinned at all,*[80] he now states, "On the other hand, we did not say that anyone could be found who [76] from infancy to old age has never sinned, but that whoever has turned away from sin, by his own labor and the grace of God could be without sin." He did not say that Abel was just, because after having turned from his sins he became sinless for the rest of his life, but *because he never committed any sin.* Hence, if that book is his, then certainly it must be corrected on the basis of his present response. I do not wish to say that he was dissembling just now, for he might say that he had forgotten what he had said in that book. Accordingly, let us consider what remains. For statements followed in the ecclesiastical proceedings, from which, with the help of God, we can show that, even if Pelagius, as some think, was cleared in this examination and was certainly absolved by the judges, who were after all only human, his heresy, which is such that we wish it neither to be extended further nor to become yet worse, undoubtedly was condemned.

Seventh Objection: Propositions Associated with Caelestius

11.(23) For there follow certain objections made to Pelagius,[81] which are said to have been found in the doctrine of his disciple Caelestius: "That Adam was created mortal, and, whether he had sinned or not, he would have been going to die. That the sin of Adam injured only himself and not the human race. That the law leads to the kingdom just as does the gospel. That before the coming of Christ there were men without sin. That newborn infants are in the same condition in which Adam was before his transgression. That the race of man as a whole does not die through the death or transgression of

---

80. Cf. *De natura et gratia* 37.44.
81. In *De pecc. or.* 11.12, Augustine quotes the *acta* of the synod for this exchange, through the response of Pelagius, given here in 11.24.

Adam, nor does the race of man as a whole rise again through the resurrection of Christ." These statements were raised in objection, just as also [77] they are said to have been heard and condemned at Carthage by your holiness[82] and other bishops with you. As you will recall, I was not present there myself, but later, on my arrival in Carthage, I examined the acts of the synod, some of which I remember. But I do not know whether all the statements mentioned are contained in them. But does it really matter if some of them perhaps were not mentioned and thus not included in the synod's condemnation, when it is quite clear that they deserve condemnation? Next other charges were brought up against him, introduced with the mention of my name. These had been sent to me from Sicily, when some of our catholic brothers there were troubled by problems of this kind, to which I gave a reply that to me seemed sufficient, in a book which I addressed to Hilary,[83] who, in consulting with me, sent them to me in a letter. Here are the charges: "That a man can, if he wishes, be without sin. That infants, even if they are unbaptized, have eternal life. That rich people, even if they are baptized, unless they renounce all they have, should not be credited with whatever good they may seem to have done, nor can they possess the kingdom of God."

(24) To these charges that were brought up against him, as the proceedings testify, Pelagius responded as follows: "That a man can be without sin has already been explained," he said, "but, regarding the point that there were men without sin before the coming of the Lord, we also declare that before the coming of Christ, some people lived holy and just lives, according to the teaching of the sacred Scriptures. But the remaining things, even according to the testimony of my accusers, were not said by me, and I have no responsibility to answer for them. Nevertheless, to satisfy the holy synod, I anathematize those who hold, or have ever held, these opinions." [78] After this reply of Pelagius, the synod declared, "To the above-

82. Bishop Aurelius. For an account of the condemnation of Caelestius at Carthage in 411, see Introduction to *De nat. et gr.*, above.
83. *Ep.* 157. These propositions were probably put forward by radical followers of Caelestius in Sicily.

mentioned charges, Pelagius, here present, has given sufficient
and legitimate satisfaction in anathematizing those opinions
which were not his." Consequently, we see and maintain that
the most pernicious evils of this kind of heresy have been condemned not only by Pelagius but also by the holy bishops who
presided at this inquiry. [These evils are:] That "Adam was created mortal," to which, in order to demonstrate more fully the
meaning of this statement, it was added, "and, whether he had
sinned or not, he would have been going to die; that the sin of
Adam injured only himself and not the human race; that the
law leads to the kingdom just as does the gospel; that newborn
infants are in the same condition in which Adam was before
his transgression; that the race of man as a whole does not die
through the death or transgression of Adam, nor does the race
of man as a whole rise again through the resurrection of Christ;
that infants, even if they are unbaptized, have eternal life; that
rich people, even if they are baptized, unless they renounce all
they have, should not be credited with whatever good they may
seem to have done, nor can they possess the kingdom of God."
It is evident that all these propositions have been condemned
in the ecclesiastical tribunal, by the anathema of Pelagius and
by the interlocutory decree of the bishops.

(25) Many of our weak brothers were disturbed by these
questions and by the contentious assertion of these opinions,
which are still causing heated debate everywhere. For this reason, we were compelled, by the anxiety of that love which it is
proper for us to have toward the church of Christ through the
grace of Christ, to write also to Marcellinus of blessed memory,
who every day suffered from these most troublesome disputers
and who had consulted with me by letters, on some of these
questions, especially on the baptism of infants.[84] [79] Again, on
this subject, at your request, I endeavored to the best of my
ability, with the help of your prayers, in the Basilica Maiorum,
holding also in my hand a letter of the most glorious martyr

---

84. *De peccatorum meritis et remissione et de baptismo parvulorum*, written in 412.
Marcellinus was a Christian and the imperial official appointed by the Emperor
Honorius to preside over the Conference of 411 between the Catholics and
Donatists at Carthage.

Cyprian, reading and commenting on his words on this subject,[85] so that this dangerous error might be removed from the hearts of some people, who had been persuaded by these opinions, which, as we see, are condemned in these proceedings. These opinions are those of which certain persons, who agree with them, have tried to persuade some of the brothers, threatening them in the name of the Eastern churches, that unless they accepted these opinions they could be condemned by those churches. Now note that fourteen presiding bishops of the Eastern church in that land where the Lord manifested the presence of his incarnation would not have absolved Pelagius, unless he condemned these opinions as opposed to the catholic faith. Consequently, if he was absolved because he anathematized such opinions, undoubtedly these opinions were condemned. This will become more abundantly clear in what follows.

(26) So let us now look at those two points that Pelagius was unwilling to anathematize, because he acknowledged that they were his own, and how he explained the way that he understood them, in order to remove that in them which gave offense. "That a man can be without sin," he declares, "has already been asserted." It was indeed asserted, and we remember it, but in a mitigated way and with the approval of the judges, because Pelagius added to it the grace of God, of which nothing was said in those chapters under investigation. But it is necessary to examine more closely how he responded to the second charge, "Regarding the point that there were men without sin before the coming of the Lord, we also declare that before the coming of Christ some people lived [80] holy and just lives, according to the teaching of the sacred Scriptures." He did not dare to say, "We also declare that before the coming of Christ there were men without sin," although this objection had been raised to him from the statements of Caelestius—for he realized that this would be dangerous and a source of trouble—but he said, "We also declare that before the coming of Christ some

85. Sermon 294, preached at Carthage on June 27, 413. In it, Augustine quoted from Cyprian, *Ep.* 64.

people lived holy and just lives." Who would deny this? To say this is one thing, but to say they were without sin is another, for they lived holy and just lives, who nevertheless truly said, "If we say that we have no sin, we deceive ourselves, and the truth is not in us."[86] Today too there are many who live just and holy lives, and yet they do not lie in their prayers when they say, "Forgive us our debts, as we forgive our debtors."[87] In the sense in which Pelagius himself asserted he had said it, the statement under discussion was acceptable to the judges, but not in the sense in which it was charged that Caelestius had said it. Now we must examine the remaining topics to the best of our ability.

Eighth Objection: The Church "Without Spot or Wrinkle"

12.(27) It was raised as an objection to Pelagius that he said, *The Church here is without spot or wrinkle.*[88] It was on this very point that the Donatists were in constant conflict with us in our conference,[89] but we stressed in rebuttal against them the mixture of bad men with good, like that of the chaff with the wheat, relying on the parable of the threshing floor.[90] With this same parable we can reply also to our present opponents, unless they would have "the Church" be understood to mean only good people, whom they say have no sin at all, so that the Church here could be without spot or wrinkle. If this is their meaning,

86. 1 John 1.8.   87. Matt 6.12.
88. Cf. Eph 5.27. This is one of the points which Hilary brings to Augustine's attention in *Ep.* 156 as being taught by certain Christians in Sicily. Pelagius makes this point in passing in his commentaries on Paul (Souter 2, 128, 484, 515). It is raised here in an effort to connect Pelagius with Donatism, and in fact Pelagianism did share with the Donatists a perfectionistic concept of the Church and the use of this text to support it. However, for the Donatists, the purity of the Church was understood more in a ritual sense, while for the Pelagians it was understood in a moral sense. See Collinge, "Christian Community and Christian Understanding," 27–31. Bonner, noting that "the ecclesiology of Donatism and Pelagianism had remarkable affinities," suggests that the Pelagian movement may have found support among former Donatists in North Africa ("Rufinus the Syrian," 34–5, *Augustine and Pelagianism*, 36).
89. The conference at Carthage with the Donatists in 411. See Augustine, *Breviculus collationis cum Donatistis* (PL 43).
90. Cf. Matt 13.24–30.

then I repeat the same words which I have just quoted, for how can they be members of the Church, of whom [81] their truthful humility exclaims, "If we say that we have no sin, we deceive ourselves, and the truth is not in us"?[91] Or how will the Church pray that which the Lord taught it, "Forgive us our debts,"[92] if in this world it is without spot or wrinkle? Finally, they should ask themselves whether or not they admit that they themselves have any sins. If they deny that they have any, it should be said to them that they are deceiving themselves and the truth is not in them. If, however, they will admit that they have sins, then what is this but a confession of their own wrinkle or spot? Hence, they are not members of the Church, for the Church is without spot and wrinkle, while they have spot and wrinkle.

(28) To this objection, Pelagius replied with a prudent reserve which the catholic judges approved without hesitation. "That was said by me," he declared, "but in the sense that through baptism the Church is purified from every spot and wrinkle, as the Lord wishes her to remain." To which the synod said, "Of this we also approve." For who among us denies that the sins of all men have been remitted through baptism and that all the faithful arise without spot and wrinkle from the bath of regeneration? Or what catholic Christian is not pleased by that which pleases the Lord, and which will be, that the Church should remain without spot or wrinkle, since it is now being brought about by God's mercy and truth that the holy Church is being led to that perfect state in which it is to remain for eternity without spot and wrinkle? But between the baptismal waters, through which all past spots and wrinkles are removed, and the kingdom in which the Church will remain forever without spot or wrinkle, there is this intermediate time of prayer, when it is necessary to say, "Forgive us our debts."[93] On account of this, it is raised as an objection against them that they say, [82] "Here the Church is without spot and wrinkle," if by this opinion they dare to prohibit the prayer by which the Church, already baptized, pleads for itself day and night for

91. 1 John 1.8.   92. Matt 6.12.
93. Matt 6.12.

the forgiveness of sins. Regarding the intermediate time between the remission of sins that takes place in baptism and the
abiding state of sinlessness that will exist in the kingdom, nothing was discussed with Pelagius, and no decision was taken by
the bishops—except only this, that he thought he should briefly
indicate that he had not spoken in a sense which seemed objectionable. For when he said this, "That was said by me, but in
this sense," what else did he wish to be understood than that
he had not spoken in the same sense as he was believed by his
accusers to have spoken? However, that which led the judges
to declare that they were satisfied with his answer was baptism,
by which the holy Church is washed from its sins, and the kingdom, in which the Church, which is now being cleansed, will
remain without sin—this, so far as I can tell, is sufficiently clear.

Ninth Objection: We Do More than Is Commanded

13.(29) Next some objections were taken from a book of
Caelestius,[94] based on the contents of each chapter, but more
in accordance with the general sense than with the words.
Caelestius indeed developed ideas at greater length, but those
who brought the indictment against Pelagius said they were not
able at that time to supply all [of what Caelestius said]. So they
reported that the following statement was written in the first
chapter of Caelestius' book: "That we do more than is commanded in the law and the gospel." To which Pelagius responded, "This is what they have set forth, as if it were our
statement. But what we said was in accordance with the statement of the Apostle on virginity, of which Paul says, 'I have no
commandment of the Lord.' "[95] The synod said, "This also the
Church accepts." As for myself, I have read the interpretation
that Caelestius gives to this in his book, [83] at least if he does
not deny that the book is his. For it is clear that he says this to
persuade us that through the nature of our free will we have
so great an ability not to sin that we are able to do more even
than we are commanded to do, since perpetual virginity, which

94. This work is otherwise unknown.   95. 1 Cor 7.25.

is not commanded, is maintained by a great many persons, whereas in order not to sin it is sufficient to fulfill the commandments. But what Pelagius answered, in order that the judges might approve it, the latter did not understand as meaning that those persons observe all the commandments of the law and the gospel and, in addition, maintain virginity, which is not commanded. Rather, they understood it to mean only that the virginity which is not commanded is superior to the conjugal chastity which is commanded, and that to observe the former is indeed greater than to observe the latter, although neither of them can be maintained without the grace of God, for the Apostle in speaking of this says, "For I would that all men were even as myself, but every one has his proper gift from God, one after this manner, and another after that."[96] Furthermore, as the disciples said to the Lord himself, "If the case of a man with his wife be so, it is not expedient to marry,"[97] or, as it is better said in Latin, "It is not expedient to take a wife,"[98] and he said, "All men take not this word, but they to whom it is given."[99] The bishops therefore declared that the Church accepted this position, that the state of continual virginity, which is not commanded, is greater than the chastity of married life, which is commanded. But in what sense Pelagius or Caelestius said this, the judges were not aware.

Tenth Objection: Caelestius' Teaching on Grace

14.(30) After this, other teachings of Caelestius, [84] capital charges and without question worthy of condemnation, were brought against Pelagius, and if he had not anathematized them, Pelagius certainly would have been condemned along with them. In his third chapter Caelestius had written, "The grace and assistance of God is not given for individual acts, but consists in the freedom of the will, or in the law and doctrine," and also, "The grace of God is given according to our merits,

96. 1 Cor 7.7.   97. Matt 19.10.
98. *Non expedit ducere* [sc. *uxorem*]. Augustine regards *ducere* as a better rendition than *nubere* for the active infinitive γαμῆσαι.
99. Matt 19.11.

for if God were to give it to sinners, he would seem to be unjust." And he drew his conclusion in these words: "And grace itself has been placed in my will, in accordance with whether I have been worthy or unworthy. For if we do all things through grace, then when we are overcome by sin, it is not we who are overcome, but God's grace, which wanted to help us in every way but could not." And again, he states, "If, when we conquer sins, it is by the grace of God, then it is God who is at fault when we are conquered by sin, for either he was unable or unwilling to protect us altogether from sin." Pelagius responded to these charges, "Whether these are propositions of Caelestius, let them verify who say they are his. For my part, I have never held such views; rather, I anathematize anyone who holds them." The synod declared, "The holy synod approves you in thus condemning these words, worthy of censure." On all these points certainly the response of Pelagius anathematizing them, and the most unconditional judgment of the bishops in condemning them, are fully evident. Whether Pelagius or Caelestius, or both or neither of them, or others either together with them or in their name, have ever held or still hold these opinions may be doubtful or unclear; nevertheless, it is sufficiently manifest that by this judgment they have been condemned, and that Pelagius would have been condemned along with them, had he not himself also condemned them. Now, after this judgment, it is certain that, whenever we argue against opinions of this sort, it is against a condemned heresy that we are arguing.

(31) [85] I want to discuss one point at greater length. Above, I expressed apprehension that, when Pelagius declared, "With the help of the grace of God, a man can be without sin," he perhaps meant that this grace is a potentiality of our nature created by God with a free will, as it says in that book, which I received as his and to which I replied,[100] and in this way he was deceiving the judges, who were unaware of the book. But now, when he anathematized those who declare that the grace and assistance of God are not given for individual acts, but consist

100. The *De natura* of Pelagius. See above, 10.22.

in free will, or in the law and doctrine, it appears clearly enough that he is speaking of that grace which is preached in the church of Christ and is conferred through the support of the Holy Spirit,[101] so that we may be assisted in each of our actions. This is why we always pray for that favorable help, so that we may not be brought into temptation.[102] I no longer have that apprehension, that perhaps when he said, *No one can be without sin except one who has acquired a knowledge of the law,* and explained it thus, that there is help toward not sinning in the knowledge of the law,[103] he wished this knowledge of the law to be understood as the grace of God. Observe that he anathematizes those who hold this opinion, and also how he does not wish the nature of free will, or the law and doctrine, to be understood as that grace by which we are helped throughout our individual actions. What therefore remains for him but to understand grace as that which the Apostle tells us is given by the support of the Holy Spirit?[104] Concerning this the Lord said, "Take no thought how or what to speak, for it shall be given to you in that hour what to speak. For it is not you that speak, but the Spirit of your Father that speaks in you."[105] Again, there is no need for me to be apprehensive that perhaps, when he said, *All* [86] *are ruled by their own will,* and then explained that he had said this "because of free will, which God assists when it chooses the good,"[106] he here also was saying that God was helping through the nature of free will and the teaching of the law. For since he rightly anathematized those who say that God's grace and assistance is not given for individual acts but consists in free will or in the law and doctrine, it follows that the grace or help of God is given for individual acts (leaving out of account free will or the law and doctrine), and in this way we are ruled by God throughout our individual acts, when we act rightly. Nor is our prayer in vain, when we say, "Direct my ways according to your word, and let not iniquity have dominion over me."[107]

101. Phil 1.19.
102. Cf. Matt 6.13.
103. See above, 1.2.
104. Phil 1.19.
105. Matt 10.19–20.
106. See above, 3.5.
107. Ps 118.133.

Eleventh Objection: The Diversity of Graces

(32) But that which follows these things makes me uneasy once more. For when an objection from the fifth chapter of Caelestius' book was brought up against him, that "they say that each person can possess all virtues and graces, and they eliminate the diversity of graces, which the Apostle teaches," Pelagius replied, "This was said by us, but our opponents have criticized us with malice and ignorance. For we do not eliminate the diversity of graces, but we say that God gives all graces to him who has been worthy to receive them, just as he gave them to the Apostle Paul." At this the synod declared, "Therefore you also believe in accordance with what the Church believes about the gift of the graces, as they are contained in the holy Apostle." Here someone may ask, "What then disturbs you? Or do you deny that all the virtues and graces were in the Apostle?" For my part, in truth, if there are meant all those gifts which the Apostle himself mentions in one particular passage, which gifts I believe are what the bishops had in mind when they approved the answer of Pelagius and declared it to be spoken according to the belief of the Church, then I do not doubt that the Apostle possessed them all. For he says, "And indeed God has [87] set some in the Church: first the apostles, secondly prophets, thirdly teachers, after that miracles, then the graces of healings, helps, governments, kinds of tongues."[108] What then? Shall we say that the Apostle Paul did not possess all these gifts? Who would dare say this? For by the very fact that he was an apostle, he certainly possessed apostleship. But he also possessed prophecy. Or was this not a prophecy of his, "Now the Spirit manifestly says, that in the last times some shall depart from the faith, giving heed to the spirit of error, and the doctrines of devils"?[109] Furthermore, he was "a teacher of the gentiles in faith and truth."[110] Also, he performed miracles and healings, for he shook off from his unharmed hand a biting viper,[111] and, at a word from him, a paralytic stood upright, his

---

108. 1 Cor 12.28.   109. 1 Tim 4.1.
110. 1 Tim 2.7.   111. Acts 28.3.

health restored.[112] The gift of "helps," of which he speaks, is obscure, for it is a term of wide application. But who would say that he was lacking even in this grace, he through whose efforts assistance was so manifestly given toward the salvation of men? What is more outstanding than his "government," when the Lord not only in his time governed so many churches through him but even now governs them through his epistles? Further, what "kinds of tongues" could he have lacked, when he says of himself, "I thank God I speak with all your tongues"?[113] Hence, it is necessary to believe that the Apostle Paul lacked none of these gifts, and therefore the judges approved of that answer of Pelagius, when he said that all the graces were given to him. But there are other graces which were not mentioned here. For, although the Apostle Paul was a very eminent member of the body of Christ, he did not receive more and greater [88] graces than[114] the very head itself of the entire body, whether in his flesh or in his soul as a man, a created nature that the Word of God assumed as his own in the unity of his person, so that he might be our head and we might be his body. Indeed, if all the gifts could be in each member, the likeness which Paul offered in this connection, that of the members of our body, would seem useless. For there are some things which are common to all the members, such as health and life, but there are still others belonging to the individual members, so that the ear does not perceive colors, nor the eye sounds. Because of this it is written, "If the whole body were the eye, where would be the hearing? If the whole were hearing, where would be the smelling?"[115] This indeed is not said as if it were impossible for God to give to the ears the sense of seeing, and to the eyes that of hearing. But it is clear what God does in the body of Christ, which is the Church, and what diversity of churches, comparable to the various members of which there are gifts proper to each, the Apostle signified. Wherefore, it is by now clear both for what reason those who raised this objection did not want to eliminate the diversity of graces and for what reason the bish-

---

112. Acts 14.10 (Vg.: 14.9).   113. 1 Cor 14.18.
114. Reading, with BA, *accepit quam ipsum;* CSEL, PL: *accepit ipsum.*
115. 1 Cor 12.17.

ops, on account of the Apostle Paul, in whom we acknowledge all the gifts which he mentions in one passage, could approve what Pelagius said in his response.

(33) What is it therefore which caused me to say earlier that I was made uneasy by this chapter? Clearly, it is this statement of Pelagius, "God gives all graces to him who has been worthy to receive them, just as he gave them to the Apostle Paul." I would not have been made uneasy by this answer of Pelagius, were it not related to the issue about which we must take the greatest care, lest the grace of God undergo attack, while we remain silent and do not take seriously so great an evil. Therefore, since Pelagius does not say that God gives to whom he will, but that "God gives all graces to him who has been worthy to receive them," I could not, when I read this, [89] fail to be suspicious. For the very name of grace and the meaning of its name are taken away if it is not given gratuitously but is received by him who is worthy of it. Or will someone perhaps say that I insult the Apostle because I do not agree that he was worthy of grace? On the contrary, I then bring insult upon him and a punishment upon myself, if I do not believe what he himself says. For has he not defined grace in such a way as to show that it is called grace because it is given gratuitously? Did he not[116] himself say, "And if by grace, it is not now by works; otherwise grace is no longer grace."[117] This is why he also says, "Now to him that works, the reward is not reckoned according to grace, but according to debt."[118] Therefore, whoever is worthy of something, that thing is owed to him. However, if it is owed to him, it is not grace, for grace is *given*, but what is owed is *paid*. Hence, grace is given to those who are unworthy, in order that they will be paid what is their due when they are worthy. But it is God himself who arranges that they shall have whatever is due them when they become worthy, who gives them what they did not have when unworthy.

(34) Perhaps Pelagius will respond to this, "I have said that the Apostle was worthy of such great graces as were given him,

---

116. Reading *nempe* with CSEL; BA: *nemque*.
117. Rom 11.6.　　　　　　　　　118. Rom 4.6.

not because of his works, but because of his faith. It was not his works, which previously were not good, but rather his faith that merited this." What then? Are we to suppose that faith does not do work? Certainly faith truly works, which "works by charity."[119] However much the works of the unfaithful are extolled, we know that the statement of that same Apostle is true and irrefutable: "For all that is not of faith is sin."[120] And for this very reason he frequently says that justice is attributed to us, not because of our works, but rather because of our faith, even though faith "works by charity," lest anyone [90] think that he attains faith itself through the merit of his works, when faith itself is the beginning from which all good works proceed, since, as it is written, "All that is not of faith is sin." Hence, it is also said to the Church in the Song of Songs, "You will come and pass by from the beginning of faith."[121] Therefore, although faith obtains for us the grace to do good works, yet certainly we do not merit by any faith that we should have faith itself; rather, in giving faith to us, in which we follow the Lord, his mercy has gone before us.[122] Or was it we who gave it to ourselves, and we who made ourselves faithful? Here I must say very emphatically, "he made us and not we ourselves."[123] Unless perhaps the teaching of the Apostle commends something else to us when he says, "For I say, by the grace that is given to me, to all that are among you, not to be more wise than it is proper to be wise, but to be wise unto sobriety and according as God has divided to everyone the measure of faith."[124] Whence indeed also is the saying, "What do you have that you have not received?"[125] since we have received even that from which proceeds whatever good we have in our actions.

(35) What is the meaning, then, of that which the same Apostle writes, "I have fought a good fight, I have finished my course, I have kept the faith. As to the rest, there is laid up for me a crown of justice, which the Lord, the just judge, will ren-

119. Gal 5.6.
121. Cant 4.8 (LXX).
123. Ps 99.3.
125. 1 Cor 4.7.

120. Rom 14.23.
122. Cf. Ps 58.11.
124. Rom 12.3.

der to me in that day,"[126] if these things are not paid as rewards to the worthy, but bestowed as gifts on the unworthy? He who raises this question attends too little to the fact that the crown could not have been given to one who was worthy of it, unless grace had been given to him when still unworthy. For the Apostle says, "I have fought a good fight," but the same Apostle also says, "But thanks be to God who has given us the victory through [91] our Lord Jesus Christ."[127] He says, "I have finished my course," but the same Apostle also says, "It is not of him that wills, nor of him that runs, but of God that shows mercy."[128] He says, "I have kept the faith," but the same Apostle also says, "For I know whom I have believed, and I am certain that he is able to keep that which I have deposited with him, against that day"[129] (that is, what I have commended to him, for some copies do not have the word *depositum* but *commendatum*, which is clearer[130]). Now what do we commend to God's keeping save those things which we pray he will preserve? Is not our very faith among these? For what else did the Lord commend for the Apostle Peter, by his prayer for him, whence he said to him, "I have prayed for you, Peter, that your faith shall not fail,"[131] save that God would preserve his faith, and that it should not fail by giving way to temptation? For this reason, O blessed Paul, great preacher of grace, I will say without fear— for who will be less angry with me for saying these things than you who have said that these things are to be said and have taught that they are to be taught?—I will say without fear, I was starting to say, that the crown is indeed rewarded to you for your merits, but your merits are gifts of God.

(36) Therefore, due reward is given to the Apostle, who is worthy of it, but grace gave him the apostleship itself, which was not due him and of which he was not worthy. Or should I

<hr>

126. 2 Tim 4.7–8. 127. 1 Cor 15.57.
128. Rom 9.16. 129. 2 Tim 1.12.
130. Vg reads *depositum*. We have altered the translation in the Douai version, in order to bring out the contrast between *depositum* and *commendatum*. It is also possible to read the Greek, τὴν παραθήκην μου, as referring to what God has entrusted to Paul, as does NAB: "I am confident that he is able to guard what has been entrusted to me until that day."
131. Luke 22.32.

regret having said that? Not at all, for by his own testimony I shall be protected against this reproach, and no one will consider me audacious except him who would be bold enough to call the Apostle himself a liar. He himself exclaims, he himself testifies, he himself, who, in order to commend the gifts of God within himself, and to glory not in himself but in the Lord,[132] not only says that he had no [92] good merits, so that he might become an Apostle, but even declares his evil deserts, in order to make manifest and to proclaim the grace of God. "I am not fit," he says, "to be called an apostle."[133] What else can this mean but, "I am not worthy"? For this is how most Latin manuscripts put it.[134] This is exactly what we seek, for it is undoubtedly in the gift of apostleship that all those graces mentioned are contained. Indeed it was neither fitting nor proper that an apostle should not possess prophecy, or not be a teacher, or not be famed for miracles and the power of healing, or not furnish help, or not govern churches, or not excel in the varieties of languages.[135] The one name of apostleship embraces all of these. Let us, then, consult the man himself, let us rather listen to him. Let us say to him, "Holy Apostle Paul, Pelagius the monk declares that you were worthy to receive all the graces of your apostleship; what do you say?" He answers, "I am not worthy to be called an apostle." So, in order to give honor to Paul, shall I dare to believe Pelagius rather than Paul on the subject of Paul? I will not do so, for if I did this, I would be more onerous to myself than honoring to him.[136] Let us hear again why he says he is not worthy to be called an apostle: "because," he says, "I persecuted the Church of God."[137] Now if we would follow the normal sequence of ideas, who would not judge that he deserves to be condemned, rather than called, by Christ? Who would so love the preacher as not to detest the persecutor?

132. Cf. 1 Cor 1.31.   133. 1 Cor 15.9.
134. Augustine's text reads, *non sum idoneus*, to which he prefers, *non sum dignus*, which is the rendition of Vg.
135. Cf. 1 Cor 12.28 and the discussion above, 14.32.
136. We here borrow from the translation by Peter Holmes in NPNF. Holmes observes, "This is a poor imitation of Augustin's playful words: 'Me potius onerabo quam illum honorabo' " (NPNF 5. 200).
137. 1 Cor 15.9.

Therefore he says most rightly and truly, "I am not worthy to
be called an apostle, because I persecuted the Church of God."
Doing then so much evil, how could you have merited so much
good? [93] Let all people hear his reply, "But by the grace of
God, I am what I am."[138] For why else is it ascribed to grace,
except because it was given to someone unworthy? "And his
grace in me," he adds, "has not been in vain."[139] He enjoins this
upon others to show them the free choice of the will, when he
declares, "And we, enjoining,[140] beseech you, that you receive
not the grace of God in vain."[141] But how does he establish that
the grace of God in him was not in vain, except from that which
follows: "But I have labored more abundantly than all they"?[142]
Thus, he did not labor in order to receive grace, but he received
grace so that he might labor. And thus, though unworthy, he
received gratuitously the grace by which he might become worthy to receive his due reward. Nor did he even venture to claim
his labor for himself. For when he had said, "I have labored
more abundantly than all they," he at once added, "Yet not I,
but the grace of God with me."[143] O great teacher, confessor,
and preacher of grace! What does this mean, "I labored more,
but not I"? When the will exalted itself even a little, piety kept
watch and humility trembled, because weakness acknowledged
itself.

(37) John, the holy bishop of Jerusalem, as the proceedings
show, with good reason also used this testimony of the Apostle,
just as he himself recounted, when questioned by our brother
bishops, who were presiding with him in that trial, as to what
had taken place in his presence prior to the trial.[144] For at that
time, when some were murmuring and saying that Pelagius
said, "Without the grace of God, this could be accomplished,"
that is, as he had said earlier, *that man was able to be without sin,*
[94] he said that "censuring this statement, I also brought for-

138. 1 Cor 15.10.   139. 1 Cor 15.10.
140. Augustine's text here reads *praecipientes;* Vg, following Gk, *adiuvantes,*
'helping.'
141. 2 Cor 6.1.   142. 1 Cor 15.10.
143. 1 Cor 15.10.
144. In the meeting at Jerusalem on July 20, 415. This is reported in Orosius, *Apol.,* 3.6–4.1. See the Introduction.

ward on this question the fact that even the Apostle Paul, who labored so much, not by his own power but by the grace of God, said, 'I have labored more abundantly than all they. Yet not I, but the grace of God with me.'[145] And he also said, 'So then it is not of him that wills, nor of him that runs, but of God that shows mercy.'[146] And there is also this passage, 'Unless the Lord build the house, they labor in vain that build it.'[147] We also quoted many similar passages from the holy Scriptures. But to those who did not accept what we said from the holy Scriptures but continued to murmur, Pelagius said, 'This I also believe. Let him be anathema who believes that without the grace of God, man can advance to the achievement of all the virtues.' "

15.(38) Bishop John narrated all this within the hearing of Pelagius, who certainly might have politely responded, "Your holiness is mistaken, you are not remembering well. It was not in reference to the passages of Scripture which you have quoted that I said, 'This I believe,' since I do not understand them to mean that the grace of God works together with man, so that if he does not sin, this is the doing 'not of him that wills, nor of him that runs, but of God that shows mercy.' "[148]

16.(39) There are certain commentaries on the Epistle of Paul to the Romans, which are said to be the work of Pelagius himself, in which he asserts that the passage, "*not of him that wills, nor of him that runs, but of God that shows mercy,*"[149] *was not spoken by Paul in his own person, but rather he made use of the voice of someone questioning and countering him, when he said this, as if such a statement ought not in fact to be made.*[150] But when Bishop John clearly acknowledged that the passage in question was the opinion of the Apostle and cited it, so that Pelagius [95] would not think that anyone avoids sin without the grace of God, and said that Pelagius responded, "This also I believe," and when

145. 1 Cor 15.10. 146. Rom 9.16.
147. Ps 126.1. 148. Rom 9.16.
149. Rom 9.16.
150. See Souter 2. 76. According to de Plinval (BA 21. 635) this interpretation appeared in the earlier versions of Pelagius' commentaries, but in the latest version (contained in manuscript A of Reichenau), Pelagius revised his comment as follows: "Thus it is not only of him that wills or of him that runs, but also of God who helps."

Pelagius heard this reported in his presence [at the synod], he did not answer, "I do not believe this." He should either deny that that perverse interpretation, according to which he would have us understand that the Apostle did not hold this opinion but rather was attacking it, is his, or else he should not hesitate to correct and revise it. For whatever Bishop John said of our absent brothers, whether our brother bishops Heros and Lazarus, or the priest Orosius, or of still others whose names are not mentioned in the proceedings,[151] I believe that Pelagius understands that it would not be prejudicial to them. For if they had been present, perhaps they would have, I dare not say convicted him of lying, but maybe reminded him of something that he might have forgotten, or in which the Latin translator might have misled him, even though not out of a desire to deceive, but because of the difficulty of a foreign language imperfectly understood, especially since the question was not considered in the proceedings, which were drawn up to be useful in preventing evil men from deceiving, and good men from forgetting something. However, if someone brings an inquiry on this subject to bear upon our above-mentioned brothers, and summons them to appear before an episcopal tribunal, they will come to him, to the extent that they can. Therefore, what need do we have to pursue the point, when not even the judges themselves, after the testimony of our brother bishop, wished to pronounce a judgment on that basis?

17.(40) Since Pelagius, who was present for the reading of these testimonies of Scripture, acknowledged by his silence that he had said that he thus believed,[152] how then could it happen that, after considering that testimony of the Apostle a few words earlier and finding that he had said, "I am not worthy to be called an apostle, because I persecuted the Church of God, but by the grace [96] of God I am what I am,"[153] did he not see

151. Orosius mentions the priests Passerio and Avitus and also Domnus (*Apol.* 6.1).
152. That is, he believed in accordance with the statement attributed to him by John in 15.38.
153. 1 Cor 15.9–10. This passage comes a few words prior to the words from 1 Cor 15.10 which John had quoted.

that he ought not to have said, when he discussed the abundance of graces which the same Apostle received, that he was worthy to receive them, when the Apostle himself not only admitted, but demonstrated, supplying still another reason, that he was unworthy of them, and by that very fact commended grace as genuinely *grace*? But if perhaps Pelagius could not reflect upon or recall the testimony of Bishop John some time previous, then let him look back at his own very recent response and let him attend to that which he anathematized a little earlier from the opinions of Caelestius which had been cited against him. For among these are to be found the objection that Caelestius had said, "The grace of God is given according to our merits."[154] Now if Pelagius sincerely anathematized this statement, what does he mean by saying that all the graces were given to the Apostle because he deserved them? Is there a difference between being worthy to receive them and receiving them according to merit? And can it be shown by some subtlety of dialectic that someone is worthy, but does not merit? But Caelestius, or whoever else was the author of all the opinions which Pelagius previously anathematized, does not permit him to envelop this expression in a fog and hide himself therein. For he insists and declares, "And grace itself has been placed in my will, in accordance with whether I have been worthy or unworthy." Therefore, if Pelagius had rightly and sincerely condemned this statement, when it is said, "The grace of God is given according to merits and to those who are worthy," how could he think in his heart or utter with his mouth the words, "We say that God gives all graces to him who has been worthy to receive them"?[155] Who, if he paid careful attention to these things, would not feel some anxiety about Pelagius' answer or defense?

(41) Why, then, someone might ask, did the judges approve this? I confess that I am still uncertain about this myself. But it is not to be wondered at if some brief phrase too easily eluded the hearing and attention of the judges, or if, [97] thinking it could somehow be interpreted in a correct sense, since it was

154. See above, 14.30.   155. See above, 14.32.

spoken by one from whom they seemed to have clear affirmations of truth in this matter, they decided that no controversy
should be provoked with him over little more than a word. And
if we had sat with them at the trial, a similar sentiment might
also have occurred to us. For if, instead of the term "worthy,"
the term "predestined" or some other word of this sort had
been used, no misgiving would have touched, and touched
off,[156] our mind. But if it were asserted that he who is justified
by the election of grace, without any previous merits, but by a
[divine] determination, is called "worthy," just as he is called
"elect," it is difficult to judge whether this could be said rightly
or with only minimal offense to the intelligence. As far as I am
concerned, I might easily move on from a discussion of this
word, had not that book,[157] which I refuted, in which he says
that the grace of God is nothing at all except our own nature
with free will—the "grace" of created nature—made me uneasy concerning the meaning of the thought of Pelagius himself, whether he had perhaps inserted this word into the argument, not through negligence in use of language, but rather
with a certain doctrinal intention. Finally, the last remaining
statements had such an effect on the judges that, without waiting for Pelagius' answer, they judged them worthy of condemnation.

Twelfth Objection: Further Statements of Caelestius

18.(42) For it is objected that in the sixth chapter of the work
of Caelestius it is said, "No one can be called the children of
God except those who will in every way have been made free
from sin." Therefore, according to this statement, not even the
Apostle Paul is a child of God, since he said, "Not as though I
had already attained, or were already perfect."[158] In the seventh chapter it is written, "Forgetfulness and ignorance are not
counted as sin, for they do not occur through the will, but
through necessity," although David says, "The sins of my youth

156. *Tangeret atque angeret.*   157. The *De natura.*
158. Phil 3.12.

[98] and my ignorances do not remember,"[159] and in the law sacrifices are offered for ignorance as if for sin.[160] In chapter ten we read, "The will is not free if it needs the aid of God, since everyone possesses in his own will the power either to do something or not to do it." In chapter twelve we find, "Our victory comes, not from the help of God, but from free will," an inference which he was said to have drawn in these words, "The victory is ours, since it was with our own will that we took up arms, just as, on the contrary, it is ours if we are defeated, since it was of our own will that we neglected to arm ourselves." And he cited this testimony from the Apostle Peter, "We are partakers of the divine nature,"[161] and is said to have drawn out this syllogism: that "if the soul cannot be without sin, then God is also subject to sin, since a part of him, that is, the soul, is vulnerable to sin." In the thirteenth chapter he says, "That pardon is given to those who repent, not according to the grace and mercy of God, but according to their own merit and effort, who through repentance will have been worthy of mercy."

19.(43) After these statements were read, the synod said, "What does the monk Pelagius say to these statements which have been read in his presence? For the holy synod, and the holy catholic Church of God, rejects them." Pelagius replied, "Again I say that these statements, even according to the testimony of my accusers, are not mine. As I have said, I have no responsibility to answer for them. I have confessed the opinions which are genuinely my own, and I affirm them to have been said correctly, but those which I have said are not my own, I reject in accordance with the judgment of the holy Church, and I pronounce anathema on everyone who opposes and contradicts the doctrines of the holy catholic Church. [99] For I believe in the Trinity of one substance and all things in conformity with the teaching of the holy catholic Church; and if indeed anyone supposes opinions contrary to this, let him be anathema."

159. Ps 24.7.
160. Cf. Lev 4.2–3,13–14,22–23,27–28.
161. 2 Pet 1.4.

The Verdict of the Synod

20.(44) The synod declared: "Now that we have received satisfactory reply to the charges brought against Pelagius the monk, here present, and since he concurs with the holy doctrines, and rejects and anathematizes those things which are contrary to the faith of the Church, we recognize him to belong to the communion of the catholic Church."

21.(45) If these are the proceedings which led the friends of Pelagius to rejoice that he was acquitted, we, for our part—since he has taken considerable pains to establish the friendship we have for him, to the point of bringing forward and reading our personal letters, which were included in the proceedings—desire and wish beyond all doubt for his salvation in Christ. But, with respect to his acquittal, which is believed more than clearly demonstrated, we should not be too quick to rejoice. In saying this, I do not accuse the judges either of negligence or of connivance, nor—which would most certainly be very foreign to their minds—of the acceptance of impious doctrines. But, although their judgment is approved and praised on its own merits, it still does not seem to me that Pelagius is acquitted among those to whom he is more fully and certainly known. For the bishops tried him as one concerning whom they knew nothing, especially because of the absence of those who had prepared the indictment against him, and were unable to examine him with sufficient diligence, but even so they have completely destroyed the heresy itself, if those who were striving to defend this perversity would follow the bishops' judgment. However, those who know well what [100] Pelagius had been in the habit of teaching, either those who have contended against his arguments, or those who rejoice because they have been set free from this error, how can they help but suspect him, particularly when they read, not a simple confession of his, condemning past errors, but a defense claiming that he had never held any other opinions than what was approved by this tribunal in his response?

Augustine's Own Involvement with Pelagius

22.(46) For, to refer especially to my own case, I first became acquainted with Pelagius' name and the great reputation he had, when he was away and established at Rome. Later, reports began to reach us, that he was arguing against the grace of God. Although I deplored this and believed those by whom it was told to me, I still desired to observe something of this sort from him directly, or in one of his books, so that, if I began to refute it, he could not disavow it. But afterwards, when he arrived in Africa during my absence, he was received on our coast, that is, that of Hippo, where, as I learned from our friends, nothing of this nature was heard from him, for he left from there more quickly than was expected. Subsequently, as I remember, I saw his face once or twice at Carthage, when I was preoccupied with preparations for the conference which we were about to have with the heretical Donatists,[162] but he had hastened away from there across the sea. Meanwhile, these doctrines were seething, spread by the mouths of those who were regarded as his disciples, to the point where Caelestius appeared before an ecclesiastical tribunal and incurred a verdict worthy of his perverse opinions.[163] At any rate, we thought it a more helpful way of proceeding against them if, without mentioning the names of any individuals, we were to challenge and refute the errors themselves. Thus the individuals might be brought to their senses by a fear of ecclesiastical judgment, rather than punished by a judgment itself. [101] Hence we did not cease to argue against these evil doctrines either through books or by instructions to the people.

23.(47) But then, when that book was given to me by Timasius and James, good and honorable servants of God, in which Pelagius very openly put to himself as an objection, in his own words, but as if raised by an enemy, the question, which had already caused him to work under great opposition, of God's grace, and when he seemed to resolve it not otherwise than by

---

162. The Conference of 411. See note to 12.27 above and Introduction to *De nat. et gr.*
163. See above, 11.23 and note.

declaring that the grace of God is our nature created with a free will—adding at times, in an offhanded and unclear way, either the help of the law or the forgiveness of sins[164]—then without any doubt it was clear to me how much the poison of this perversity was inimical to salvation by Christ. However, I still did not include the name of Pelagius in the work in which I refuted his book, for I thought that I would succeed better if I continued to maintain a friendly relation with him and to spare him any personal offense, although I thought I ought no longer to spare his writings. This is why I now feel some annoyance with what he said at one point in his trial: "I anathematize those who hold or have ever held these opinions."[165] It would have been enough to say, "those who hold these opinions," in order that we might believe he was correcting himself; but when he added, "or have ever held them"—first, is it not quite unjust to dare to condemn those undeserving persons, who were free from that error,[166] which they had learned either from others, or from himself as teacher? Second, who among those who knew that Pelagius himself had not only formerly held but also taught these opinions, would not reasonably suspect that he had dissembled in anathematizing those who presently hold these opinions, since he did not hesitate to condemn in the same manner those who had previously held these opinions, among [102] whom they will remember that he himself was the teacher? Consider Timasius and James, not to mention others—how can he lay eyes on them, how can he face them, his admirers and onetime disciples, to whom I wrote the book in which I responded to his book? I thought I ought not to pass over in silence and to neglect the way they wrote to me in response, and so I have attached below a copy of their letter.

24.(48) Greetings in the Lord from Timasius and James to the truly blessed lord and deservedly venerable father, Bishop Augustine. The grace of God administered to us by your word has restored and re-

164. See *De nat. et gr.*, especially 44.52, 51.59, and 26.29.
165. See above, 11.24.
166. Here we follow CSEL and PL (and the French translation in BA) in reading *errore caruerunt*. BA emends: *errore non caruerunt*, which could be translated, 'who did not avoid this error.'

freshed us so much that we can say with complete sincerity, "He sent his word and healed them,"[167] most blessed lord and deservedly venerable father. Indeed, we have found that your sanctity has sifted the text of the little book of Pelagius with such diligence that we are stunned by the answers you made to even the slightest of his points, whether in matters which every Christian ought to challenge, detest, and shun, or in those in which he has not been found with sufficient certainty to have erred, although even in these cases, with some deviousness, he believed that the grace of God should be left unmentioned. Nevertheless, there is one thing which concerns us with respect to such a great benefit, and that is that this so outstanding gift of the grace of God has shone forth so late, for it happens that some are absent, whose blindness has had need of this illumination of such clear truth. But we do not doubt that this same grace will later find its way even to them through the favor of God, "Who will have all men to be saved and to come to the knowledge of the truth."[168] As for us, although long since, taught by the spirit of charity which is in you, we have thrown off our subjection to this error, we now offer our gratitude for the fact that what we have already believed, we have now [103] learned to make clear to others, for the very fruitful words of your holiness have opened the way which makes it easy.

And, in another hand: "May the mercy of God in all eternity glorify your blessedness in safety and keep you mindful of us."[169]

25.(49) Now if Pelagius also were to confess that at one time he had been caught up in this error as if it had taken possession of him, but that now he anathematized those who held such opinions, whoever would not congratulate him for now following the way of truth would himself lose all sentiment of charity. Now, however, it is bad enough that he has refused to affirm that he has been delivered from this plague, but in addition he has anathematized those who have been delivered, who love him so much that they wish for him also to be delivered. Among the latter are those persons who expressed their good will toward him in their letter which was sent to me. For they were thinking especially of him, when they declared that they were concerned that I might have written that work too late. "For it

---

167. Ps 106.20.   168. 1 Tim 2.4.
169. This is found among the letters of Augustine as *Ep.* 168.

happens," they wrote, "that some are absent, whose blindness has had need of this illumination of such clear truth. But we do not doubt," they add, "that this same grace will later find its way to them through the favor of God." But they too still thought it best to leave the name or names unmentioned, that, friendship surviving, the error of friends might more readily perish.

(50) But if Pelagius now thinks of God, if he is not ungrateful for his mercy, which brought him before the episcopal tribunal so that he would not dare later to defend these anathematized opinions, and so that he would now acknowledge them as deserving abhorrence and rejection, then he will more gratefully receive our [present] book, in which, by mentioning his name, we open the wound in order to cure it, [104] than that earlier one, where, since we feared to cause him pain, we caused the inflammation to increase, which we regret. However, should he have become angry with us, let him consider how unfairly he is angry, and, that he might conquer his anger, let him then, at last, ask for that grace of God, which he confessed during his trial to be necessary for each of our actions, so that with the help of God he may attain a true victory. For of what use to him are all those great praises in the letters of the bishops, which he considered it necessary to mention and even to read and to adduce as evidence in his favor—as if all who heard his vehement and, in some ways, passionate exhortations to a good life could easily have known that he held these perverse opinions?

26.(51) For my part, in my letter which he has brought forward, not only did I refrain from all praise of him, but I exhorted him as much as I could, without provoking any dispute over the grace of God, to think rightly. To be sure, I addressed him as "Lord," a term which in our epistolary style we are accustomed to write even to some persons who are not Christians, nor have I used it deceitfully, for we owe to everyone, in order to attain salvation, which is in Christ, a sort of free servitude. I said "most beloved" to him, which I even now say, and, even if he should become angry, I will still say it, for if I did not continue to maintain an affection for him on becoming angry, I would hurt myself more than him. I addressed him as "most

PROCEEDINGS OF PELAGIUS   161

longed-for," because I greatly desired to have a face-to-face conversation with him, for I had already heard that he was trying in public disputation to oppose that grace by which we are justified, whenever any reference was made to it. Finally, the brief [105] text of my letter indicated all this, for, after I had thanked him that he had cheered me by his letter, assuring me of his own well-being and that of his friends—for although we wish their thoughts to be made sound, we ought also to wish for their soundness in physical health—I expressed at once the wish that the Lord reward him with good things, not those pertaining to physical health, but rather those blessings which he thought, and perhaps still thinks, are situated in the choice of our will alone and in our own power, and at the same time, and on this account, I wished him "eternal life." And then, because in his letter, to which I was replying, he gave much kind praise to some good qualities of this sort in me, I also asked him to pray for me, that I might rather be made by the Lord such a man as he already believed me to be, in order that I might admonish him, against the view that he was maintaining, that the very justice he considered worthy to be praised in me, was "not of him that wills, nor of him that runs, but of God that shows mercy."[170] This is all that that brief letter of mine contains, and this was the intention with which it was dictated, for it reads as follows:

27.(52) "Augustine, to his most beloved lord and most longed-for brother Pelagius, greetings in the Lord."

28.[171] "I am very grateful that you have seen fit to cheer me with your letter and to have assured me of your well-being. May the Lord reward you with good things, and through them may you always be good, and live for all eternity with the eternal God, most beloved lord and most longed-for brother. As for me, although I do not recognize in myself the object of your high praises of me, which are contained in the letter of your

170. Rom 9.16.
171. Most manuscripts relied on in the CSEL text place the chapter number, "28," here. CSEL, following the 1614 printed edition of Franciscus Suarez, puts the number in the margin at this line.

Kindness,[172] still I cannot be ungrateful for the benevolent feelings you have expressed for my meager worth. At the same time I admonish you that you pray for me that the Lord would indeed make me such a man as you already account me to be." [106] And in another hand: "Be mindful of us, may you be safe and find favor with the Lord, most beloved lord and most longed-for brother."[173]

29.(53) Also, in what I included as a postscript, that he might find favor with the Lord, I meant that this would depend more upon the grace of God than only upon man's will, for I did not exhort, nor enjoin, nor instruct this, but merely expressed a wish for it. Just as, if I had exhorted, enjoined, or instructed him to show that all this pertains to the free will, I would nonetheless not be detracting from the grace of God, so, in expressing this as a wish, I indeed emphasized the grace of God, but did not snuff out the freedom of the will. Why, then, during the course of the proceedings, did he bring forward this letter, in accordance with which if from the beginning he had guided his thoughts, he would perhaps never have been called before this tribunal of bishops by our brothers, who, though men of good will, were nonetheless offended with the perversity of his arguments? Moreover, just as I have given an account of my letter, so if it were necessary would they whose letters he adduced explain what they thought, or what they were not aware of, or with what purpose they wrote. Therefore, whatever holy people of whose friendship he may boast, whatever letters in praise of him he may read, whatever proceedings declaring his exoneration he may bring forward—unless by his confession he has anathematized those things which he has been demonstrated by the testimony of reliable witnesses to have set forth in his books against the grace of God, by which we are called and justified, and unless he then has written and argued against these same things, Pelagius will not seem, in the eyes of those to whom he is best known, to have been corrected at all.

---

172. *Tuae benignitatis epistola.* Holmes notes that this phrase "is more than 'your kind letter.' 'Benignitas' is a complimentary abstract title addressed to the correspondent" (NPNF 5. 205).

173. This is Augustine's *Ep.* 146. It was written in 413.

The Aftermath of the Trial

30.(54) I will not remain silent about what occurred after the trial, and which greatly increased my suspicions. There came [107] into my hands a certain letter, coming, it was said, from Pelagius himself, writing to a friend of his, a priest, who, in a letter (according to what is contained in this letter) had kindly admonished him not to be for anyone an occasion to separate himself from the body of the Church. In this letter, among other things, which would be too long, and also unnecessary, to include here, Pelagius says, *The statement in which I maintained that 'a man can be without sin and easily keep the commandments of God, if he wishes,' has been approved by the verdict of fourteen bishops. This verdict,* he says, *has spread confusion over the faces of my opponents and has separated from one another the entire group that was conspiring together for evil.* Whether, therefore, Pelagius actually wrote this letter, or whether it was forged by someone else in his name, who could avoid seeing how this error glories, as if in a victory, even in this trial, wherein it was refuted and condemned? For he has taken the words we have just quoted in the terms in which they are stated in his book called *Testimonies*,[174] but not as read in the objections brought against him at his trial, or as repeated by him in his response. In fact, even his accusers, through some sort of oversight, omitted a word, about which there is no small controversy. For they declared that he had said that "a man can, if he wishes, be without sin, and keep the commandments of God, if he wishes."[175] Nothing is said here of this being done *easily.* Later, in his reply, he said, "We said that a man can be without sin and keep the commandments of God, if he wishes." He did not say "easily keep," but only, "keep." Again, in another place, among the statements about which Hilary consulted me and to which I replied,[176] an objection was raised that it was said, *A man can be without sin, if he wishes.* To this Pelagius himself responded thus: [108] "That a man can be without sin has already been explained." Here then we do not find that the word, "easily," is added, either by those

174. See note to 1.2 above.   175. See above, 6.16 and note.
176. See above, 11.23.

who raised the objection or by Pelagius himself in replying. Previously, in the narrative of Bishop John, this statement is cited as follows: "When his opponents were pressing him and saying that he is a heretic, because he says that 'a man can, if he has wished, be without sin,' and when we questioned him on this point, he declared, 'I did not say that man's nature has received the quality of being incapable of sinning; rather, I said that, whoever is willing, for his own salvation, to labor and struggle to abstain from sinning and to walk in the ways of the commandments of God, has the ability to do so from God.' At that time, when some were murmuring and saying that Pelagius said that, 'Without the grace of God, this could be accomplished,' censuring this statement, I also brought forward on this question the fact that even the Apostle Paul, who labored so much, not by his own power but by the grace of God, said, 'I have labored more abundantly than all they. Yet not I, but the grace of God with me,' "[177] and so on, as I have already quoted.[178]

(55) What is the significance, then, that in this letter they dared to glorify themselves, boasting that they have convinced the fourteen bishops who presided at the trial not only that we have the "possibility of not sinning," but that this can be done *easily*, as it is asserted in the *Book of Testimonies* of the same Pelagius, although this sentence, so many times brought up and repeated in the proceedings, is never found to contain that word? Besides, how can this word not be contrary to the defense and response itself that Pelagius gave, [109] since both Bishop John asserted that Pelagius had responded in his presence that "he wished it to be understood that a person could be without sin, who was willing to labor and struggle for his salvation," and Pelagius himself, in the course of the Acts of the synod, defending himself had said that "by his own labor and the grace of God a man can be without sin"?[179] But how could it be done *easily*, if it requires *labor* to be done? For I am sure that all human sentiment agrees with us that wherever there is

177. 1 Cor 15.10.   178. See above, 14.37.
179. See above, 6.16.

labor there is no ease. Nevertheless, a sleazy, windy, and pomp-
ous letter takes to the air and, arranged to exceed in speed the
slow circulation of the proceedings, lands in men's hands to say
that fourteen bishops in the East have agreed, not only that a
man can be without sin and keep the commandments of God,
but that he can keep them "easily," without mentioning, "with
the assistance of God," but only, "if he (the individual) wishes."
Thus, the divine grace, for which we were struggling so
strongly, is left unmentioned, so that the only thing that is read
in this letter is human pride, unhappy and self-deceiving, for it
represents itself as victorious. All this as though Bishop John
had not stated that he had censured this statement and had not,
with three texts of divine Scripture, like bolts of lightning, de-
molished the gigantic mountains piled up against the supereminence
of celestial grace.[180] Or as if the other bishops who were
with him could have been able to bear Pelagius either in their
minds or even with their ears when he said, "We stated that a
man can be without sin and keep the commandments of God, if
he wishes," if he had not gone on at once to say, "For God has
given him this possibility" (but they did not know that he was
speaking of nature, and not of that grace which they had
learned from the preaching of the Apostle), and then [110]
added, "On the other hand, we did not say that anyone could
be found, who from infancy to old age had never sinned, but
that whoever has turned away from sin, by his own labor and
the grace of God could be without sin." Considering that in their
verdict they used these words, "He has answered correctly,
'with the assistance and grace of God, a man can be without
sin,' " what else did they fear except that, by denying this, they
would seem to be doing wrong, not to human ability, but to
God's grace itself? Nonetheless, it has not been defined when a
man may become without sin, although it has been judged that
this can happen through the helping grace of God. It has not
been defined, I say, whether, in this flesh, which lusts against
the spirit,[181] there has ever been, now is, or will be anyone who,
making use of reason and the free choice of the will—whether

180. Cf. Eph 3.19.   181. Cf. Gal 5.17.

in the bustle of society or in the solitude of monks—has no need to offer up the prayer, not for others, but also for himself, "Forgive us our debts,"[182] or whether in fact this favor is obtained when "We shall be like to him," when "we shall see him as he is"[183]—when it will be not said by those that are fighting, "I see another law in my members, fighting against the law of my mind,"[184] but by those in triumph, "O death, where is your victory? O death, where is your sting?"[185] But this is not a question that ought to be discussed between catholics and heretics, but rather, perhaps, peacefully among catholics themselves.

31.(56) Assuming that this letter is in fact his, how can it be believed that Pelagius has both sincerely confessed the grace of God, which is not our nature with its free will, nor the knowledge of the law, nor simply the remission of sins, but that which is necessary for each of our actions, and sincerely [111] anathematized everyone who held the contrary opinion—considering that in his letter he affirmed an "easiness" in the avoidance of sin, regarding which no question had arisen during the investigation, as if even this word was agreeable to the judges, and he did not affirm the grace of God, by the confession and addition of which he escaped ecclesiastical condemnation?

32.(57) There is another matter which I ought not to pass over in silence. In a brief paper containing his defense, which he sent to me through a certain friend of ours, Charus, a citizen of Hippo, but a deacon in the eastern Church, Pelagius has given an account which is different from that which is contained in the proceedings of the bishops. The contents of the proceedings are far better, and stronger, and in all respects more thorough in the defense of the catholic truth in opposition to the plague of this heresy. For when I read his paper, before the proceedings reached me, I was not aware that he had not[186] used the exact words, which he had employed when speaking on his own behalf before the tribunal, for there are

182. Matt 6.12. 183. 1 John 3.2.
184. Rom 7.23. 185. 1 Cor 15.55.
186. We follow the emendation in BA: *nesciebam eum non ea ipsa verba posuisse;* CSEL: *nesciebam eum ea ipsa verba posuisse;* PL, codd.: *nesciebam ea ipsa verba posuisse.*

few and only slight differences, about which I do not feel much anxiety.

33. However, I was annoyed that he may seem to have reserved for himself the option of defending certain opinions of Caelestius, which, it is clear from the proceedings, he had anathematized. Some of these statements he denied were his, merely saying that he had no responsibility to answer for them, but he was unwilling to anathematize them in the same paper. The following are the statements: "That Adam was created mortal, and, whether he had sinned or not, he would have been going to die. That the sin of Adam injured only himself and not the human race. That the law leads to the kingdom of heaven just as also does the gospel. That newborn infants are in the same condition in which Adam was [112] before his transgression. That the race of man as a whole does not die through the death or transgression of Adam, nor does the race of man as a whole rise again through the resurrection of Christ. That infants, even if they are unbaptized, have eternal life. That rich people, even if they are baptized, unless they have renounced all they have, should not be credited with whatever good they seem to have done, and will not possess the kingdom of heaven."[187] Now to all this he replies thus in his paper: "All these statements, according to the testimony of my accusers themselves, were not made by me, and I have no responsibility to answer for them." But in the proceedings he responds to the same propositions as follows: "According to the testimony of my accusers themselves, these things were not said by me, and I have no responsibility to answer for them. Nevertheless, to satisfy the holy synod, I anathematize those who hold, or have ever held, these opinions."[188] Why then is it not written thus in his paper? It would not, I think, have cost much ink, or writing, or time, or taken up much space in the paper itself, if it had been done thus. But who can help believing that it had been arranged that this paper would circulate everywhere as if it were an abridgement of the proceedings? Consequently, it

187. See above, 11.23, where the wording is slightly different.
188. See above, 11.24.

might be thought that the right to defend any of these opinions had not been taken away, on the grounds that they had only been raised as objections and were not demonstrated to be his, but were not anathematized and condemned.

(58) Later in this same paper, he gathered together many of the points from the book of Caelestius which had been raised against him as objections, nor has he inserted his two responses, by which he anathematized these propositions, separated by the intervals which the proceedings indicate, but has substituted one reply for them, once and for all. I might think that this had been done out of a desire for brevity, if I had not perceived that this has great relevance to the issue which concerns us. For he concludes, "Again I say [113] that these statements, even according to the testimony of my accusers, are not mine. As I have said, I have no responsibility to answer for them. I have confessed the opinions which are my own, and I affirm that I spoke them correctly, but those which I have said are not my own, I reject in accordance with the judgment of the holy Church, and I pronounce anathema on everyone who opposes the doctrines of the holy and catholic Church,[189] and also on those who by inventing untrue opinions have brought false accusations upon us." The proceedings do not contain this last clause; however, it has no bearing on the matter about which we ought to be anxious. So indeed may they be anathema who by inventing untrue opinions have brought false accusations upon them. But when I first read, "But those which I have said are not my own, I reject in accordance with the judgment of the holy Church," I was unaware that that judgment had already been made by the Church, since he is silent about it and I had not yet read the proceedings. I thought he meant nothing else than that he promised to accept the same views about these points as the Church, which had not yet passed judgment, but whenever it might pass judgment, and that he would reject the opinions, which it had not yet rejected but might one day reject, and also that this was the bearing of, "I pronounce anathema on everyone who opposes or contradicts the doctrines of the holy and catholic Church." But in fact, as the proceedings

189. See above, 19.43.

witness, a judgment of the Church had already been declared by the fourteen bishops on these opinions, a judgment in accordance with which he said he rejected all these assertions and anathematized all those persons who, professing such opinions, went counter to the judgment, which, the proceedings show, had already been rendered. For the judges had already said, "What does the monk Pelagius say to these statements, which have been read in his presence? For the holy synod, and the holy catholic Church of God, rejects them." But those who are unaware of this verdict, and who read this paper, will think that some of these assertions can be legitimately [114] defended, as if they had not been judged contrary to catholic doctrine, and as if Pelagius had declared himself ready to adopt the same judgment concerning them, which the Church had not yet determined but would determine. Therefore, Pelagius has not written in this paper, with which we are now concerned, in such a way that a reader can recognize that to which the proceedings bear witness—namely, that all these doctrines by means of which this heresy has been creeping along and has grown in strength and contentious audacity, have been condemned by fourteen bishops presiding in an ecclesiastical synod! Now if he was afraid to reveal this matter as it is, then let him correct himself rather than be angry at our admittedly late vigilance, such as it is. However, if it is false that he was afraid of this, and if we are being overly suspicious, as people are inclined to be, let him forgive us, but let him from now on oppose the opinions which are anathematized and rejected in the proceedings of the trial, when he was given a hearing. For in sparing them, he would appear not only to have believed them before, but still to believe them.

Concluding Review of the Affair of Pelagius

34.(59) That is why I wished to dedicate this book, lengthy, but perhaps not unreasonably so, on such a serious and important matter, to your reverence,[190] in order that, if it does not

190. Bishop Aurelius.

offend your sentiments, it may become known, under the recommendation of your authority, which is far superior, rather than by the labor of our humble estate, to such persons as you think necessary. It may in this way help to suppress the vain and contentious ideas of those who suppose that, since Pelagius was acquitted, those eastern bishops who pronounced the judgment approved of those teachings which are springing up in a most pernicious way against the Christian faith and the grace of God, by which we are called and justified. Christian truth always condemns these teachings, and it has condemned them again by the authority of these fourteen bishops, who on that occasion would have condemned Pelagius together with them, if they had not been anathematized by him. Now, bearing in mind that we have already extended to this man the concern of brotherly charity and have expressed in good faith our anxiety concerning him, and on his behalf, [115] let us observe briefly how it can be shown that, even though, as is clear, he has been acquitted in the eyes of men, nevertheless the heresy itself has always been considered worthy of condemnation by divine judgment, and has also been condemned by the judgment of these fourteen bishops of the eastern Church.

35.(60) This is the final verdict of that trial. The synod declared, "Now that we have received satisfactory reply to the charges brought against Pelagius the monk, here present, and since he is also in agreement with the holy doctrines and rejects and anathematizes those things which are contrary to the faith of the Church, we recognize him to belong to the communion of the catholic Church."[191] The holy bishops who gave this judgment have brought together in the brevity of their judgment two points, both adequately clear, concerning the monk Pelagius: on the one hand, that "he is in agreement with the holy doctrines," and, on the other hand, that "he rejects and anathematizes those things which are contrary to the faith of the Church." Because of these two points, Pelagius was declared to belong to "the communion of the catholic Church." Therefore, let us see, by briefly reviewing everything, in what

191. See above, 20.44.

words he at that time clarified both points, as far as men were able to judge on that occasion, on the basis of what was clearly evident. For among those things which were raised as objections against him, the ones which he said were not his, he was said to reject and anathematize as "contrary." Briefly, therefore, let us summarize this whole case, if we can, as follows.

(61) Since it was necessary that what the Apostle Paul predicted should be fulfilled: "For there must also be heresies, that they also who are approved may be made manifest among you."[192] After the old heresies, [116] a heresy has also recently been invented,[193] not by bishops or priests, or any clergy, but by a certain sort of monk, which, under the guise of defending free will, has disputed against that "grace of God," which we have "through Jesus Christ our Lord"[194] and endeavored to overthrow the basis of the Christian faith, of which it is written, "For by one man came death, and by one man the resurrection of the dead. And as in Adam all die, so also in Christ all shall be made alive."[195] And he has denied God's help in our actions, saying that, in order to avoid sin and to attain complete justice, human nature, which has been created with a free will, can be sufficient, and that God's grace consists in our having been created so that we can do this by the will, and also in that God gave us the assistance of the law and his commandments, and that he forgives of their past sins those who turn to him. In these things alone God's grace should be regarded as consisting, not in help given for our individual actions, for a man can be without sin and easily keep God's commandments, if he wishes.

(62) After this heresy had deceived many persons and disturbed our brothers, although it did not deceive them, a certain Caelestius, who held such opinions, was brought to trial before the Church of Carthage and condemned by a verdict of the bishops. Then, some years later, when charges of this heresy were raised against Pelagius, who was considered to be the teacher of Caelestius, he himself was also brought before an

192. 1 Cor 11.19.
193. Following the emendation in BA: *inventa est etiam modo haeresis;* CSEL: *inlata est etiam modo haeresis,* PL: *invecta etiam modo haeresis.*
194. Rom 7.25.   195. 1 Cor 15.21.

episcopal tribunal. When all the charges which the Gallic bishops, Heros and Lazarus, had set forth in their brief against him
had been read (they themselves were absent, excusing themselves owing to the illness of one of them), and when Pelagius
had responded to all of them, the fourteen bishops of the province of Palestine, [117] judging on the basis of his responses,
declared him free from the perversity of this heresy, while condemning without hesitation the heresy itself. For they gave
their approval to him in accordance with what he replied to the
objection: "Through knowledge of the law, a man is assisted in
not sinning, as it is written, 'He gave them his law for help.' "[196]
However, they did not on this basis judge that this knowledge
of the law is that grace of God, of which Scripture says, "Who
shall deliver me from the body of this death? The grace of God
by Jesus Christ our Lord."[197] Nor did they judge that Pelagius
said, *All are ruled by their own will,* as if God did not rule them,
for he answered that he had said this "because of free will,
which God assists when it chooses the good; but man when he
sins is himself at fault, since his will is free."[198] Moreover, they
approved his statement, *On the day of judgment no mercy will be
shown to the wicked and the sinners, but they will be punished in the
eternal fires,*[199] for he declared that he had said this in accordance with the gospel, where it is written, "And these shall go
into everlasting punishment, but the just, into life everlasting."[200] But he did not say that *all* sinners are destined for eternal punishment, so that he would provide no cause to seem to
have spoken counter to the statement of the Apostle, who said
that some "will be saved, yet so as by fire."[201] They also approved his statement, *The kingdom of heaven was promised even in
the Old Testament,*[202] for he brought forward the testimony of
the prophet Daniel, where it is said, "And the saints shall receive the kingdom of the most high."[203] They understood "Old
Testament," as used here by Pelagius, not merely as the testa-

196. See above, 1.2. Scripture quotation is Isa 8.20 (LXX).
197. Rom 7.24–25.   198. See above, 3.5.
199. See above, 3.9.   200. Matt 25.46.
201. 1 Cor 3.15.   202. See above, 5.13.
203. Dan 7.18.

ment that was established on Mount Sinai, but as all the canonical Scriptures that were delivered prior to the coming of the Lord. But the statement, *A man can be without sin*, [118] *if he wishes*, was not approved by the bishops in the sense in which Pelagius apparently meant it in his book, that is, as if this was in the power of man alone, through free will, for this is what he was accused of having thought, when he said, *if he wishes*. Rather, it was approved in the sense in which he now responded, or better yet, in the sense in which the episcopal judges very concisely and clearly restated it, "That, with the assistance and grace of God, a man can be without sin."[204] Nevertheless, it was not determined when the saints might attain this state of perfection, whether in "the body of this death,"[205] or when death shall be swallowed up in victory.[206]

(63) From the statements Caelestius had spoken or written and which were raised as objections against Pelagius inasmuch as they were teachings of his disciple, Pelagius acknowledged that some of them were his own, but he answered that he held them in a different sense from that which was alleged in the indictment. Among these statements was the following, "Before the coming of Christ, some people lived holy and just lives."[207] Caelestius, however, was held to have declared that "they were without sin."[208] Likewise, it was objected that Caelestius had declared, "The Church is without spot or wrinkle."[209] But Pelagius said that he himself had indeed said this, "but in the sense that through baptism the Church is purified from every spot and wrinkle, as the Lord wishes her to remain."[210] Likewise, Caelestius' statement, "That we do more than is commanded in the law and the gospel,"[211] [was presented as an objection], but Pelagius replied that he had said this concerning virginity, "of which Paul says, 'I have no commandment of the Lord.' "[212] It was also objected that Caelestius had maintained, "Each person can possess all virtues and graces," thus eliminat-

204. See above, 6.16.
206. Cf. 1 Cor 15.54.
208. See above, 11.23.
210. See above, 12.28.
212. 1 Cor 7.25.

205. Rom 7.24.
207. See above, 11.24.
209. See above, 12.27.
211. See above, 13.29.

ing the diversity of graces which the Apostle teaches. Pelagius, however, replied that he did "not eliminate the diversity of graces, but" said [119] "that God gives all graces to him who has been worthy to receive them, just as he gave them to the Apostle Paul."[213]

(64) These four propositions, presented under the name of Caelestius, were not approved by the episcopal judges in the sense in which Caelestius was said to have held them, but in that which Pelagius gave them in his reply. For they saw that it is one thing to be without sin, and another to live a holy and just life, as Scripture testifies that some people lived even before the coming of Christ. And they saw that, although the Church here is not without spot or wrinkle, yet she is cleansed from every spot and wrinkle by the bath of regeneration, and the Lord wishes her to remain in this state—for so she will remain, since she will indeed reign without spot and wrinkle in eternal felicity. And they saw that perpetual virginity, which is not commanded, is undoubtedly greater than marital chastity, which is commanded—although virginity is maintained by many people, who nevertheless are not without sin. Finally, they recognized that the Apostle Paul possessed all those graces which he enumerates in one particular passage. Still, either they understood the claim that he was worthy to receive them in some sense to mean that he was worthy, not according to his merits, but rather according to predestination—for he himself says, "I am not worthy" or "I am not fit to be called an apostle"[214]—or the word escaped their attention, and Pelagius himself will have to see to the sense in which he meant it. These are the points on which the bishops declared that Pelagius was in agreement with the holy doctrines.

(65) Now, recapitulating in a similar way, let us look a little more intently at the points which they said he rejected and anathematized as contrary to the faith. It is in these, especially, that the entire heresy consists. Leaving aside, therefore, those things he is reported to have said in his books in flattery of a certain widow—since he responded that they are not in his

213. See above, 14.32.   214. 1 Cor 15.9.

books and that he [120] had never said such things, and he anathematized those who held such opinions, not as heretics but as fools[215]—these are the main points, it grieves me to say, by which the brambles of this heresy are spreading every day to the point where they are now becoming a real thicket:

That Adam was created mortal, and, whether he had sinned or not, he would have been going to die; that the sin of Adam injured only himself, and not the human race; that the law leads to the kingdom, just as does the gospel; that newborn infants are in the same condition in which Adam was before his transgression; that the race of man as a whole does not die through the death or transgression of Adam, nor does the race of man as a whole rise again through the resurrection of Christ; that infants, even if [at death] they are unbaptized, have eternal life; that rich people, even if they are baptized, unless they renounce all they have, should not be credited with whatever good they may seem to have done, nor can they possess the kingdom of God;[216] that the grace and assistance of God is not given for individual acts, but consists in the freedom of the will, and in the law and doctrine; that the grace of God is given according to our merits, so that this grace has been placed in the will of a man, in accordance with whether he has been worthy or unworthy;[217] that no one can be called a child of God except he who will have been made absolutely free from sin; that forgetfulness and ignorance are not counted as sin, for they do not occur through the will, but through necessity; that the will is not free, if it needs the aid of God, since everyone possesses in his own will the power either to do something or not to do it; that our victory comes, not from the help of God, but from free will; that from what Peter says, "We are partakers of the divine nature,"[218] it follows that the soul can be without sin, in the same way as God is.[219]

I myself have read this in the eleventh chapter of the book, which does not carry the name of its author but is generally held to be the work of Caelestius, in these words: "How can anyone," he says, "become a partaker of that thing, from the condition and quality of which he is defined as alien?" For this reason, the brothers who raised these objections understood

215. See above, 6.16.   216. See above, 11.23–24.
217. See above, 14.30.   218. 2 Pet 1.4.
219. See above, 18.42.

him in this sense: as if he had said that the soul and God are of the same nature, and that the soul is part of God, for they took this statement to mean that he thought the soul is of the same "condition and quality" as God. Finally, in the last of these objections it was set forth "That pardon is given to those who repent, not according to the grace and mercy of God, but according to their own merit and effort, who through repentance will have been worthy of mercy."[220] The judges expressed their approval of Pelagius in denying these to be his own and in anathematizing all these propositions and the arguments introduced in support of them, and therefore declared that, in rejecting and anathematizing them, he had condemned them as contrary to the faith of the Church. And therefore, in whatever way Caelestius may or may not have set them forth, or Pelagius may or may not have believed them, let us rejoice that these great errors of this heresy, so new on the scene, have been condemned by a judgment of the Church, and let us give thanks and proclaim our praises to God.

Postscript: The Raid on Jerome's Monastery

(66) After this judgment, certain crimes are said to have been committed with incredible audacity by some band of rabble, who were held to have strongly supported Pelagius in his perversity. It is said that the servants and handmaidens of God, residing under the direction of the holy priest Jerome, were set upon in a most wicked onslaught, that a deacon was killed, that the buildings of the monastery were burned, and that only [122] a well-fortified tower managed to protect Jerome himself, by the mercy of God, from the attack and assault of these impious people. About these matters, I see that it becomes us to be silent, but rather to wait and see what our brothers the bishops there think should be done about such evils,[221] for who

220. See above, 18.42.
221. This raid occurred late in 416 in Bethlehem at the monastery where not only Jerome but also the virgin Eustochium, daughter of Paula, lived. There is no evidence to connect Pelagius with this attack, but the report of it contributed to the discrediting of Pelagius in the West. Pope Innocent, who on doctrinal grounds had on January 27, 417, pronounced Pelagius and Caelestius excom-

would think they could ignore them? For the impious teachings of such persons ought to be refuted by all catholics, even those who live far away from these lands, so that they cannot do damage anywhere where they have been able to spread. But impious actions, whose suppression belongs to episcopal discipline in the place where they are committed, should ordinarily be punished there, with pastoral diligence and pious severity, by those in authority in that place or nearby.[222] Therefore, we, who live so far away, can only hope that such an end be put to these matters that there be no necessity for further adjudication about it anywhere, but rather an end which it is fitting for us to proclaim, so that the souls of all who have been seriously wounded by the report, winging about everywhere, of those crimes, may be healed by the mercy of God, following afterward. And so let this be the conclusion of this book, which if, as I hope, it has merited the favor of your approval, will with the help of the Lord be of service to its readers, commended to them more by your name than by mine, and, through your diligence, better known to a wider audience.

---

municated until they could give satisfaction, shortly afterward wrote two strongly worded letters, one of reproof to John of Jerusalem and one to Jerome, assuring him of future protection (Innocent, *Epp.* 42 and 43, included among the letters of Jerome as *Epp.* 136 and 137; CSEL 56. 263–65).

222. Cf. the letter of Innocent to five bishops, included among the letters of Augustine as *Ep.* 183.

ON THE PREDESTINATION
OF THE SAINTS
and
ON THE GIFT OF
PERSEVERANCE

INTRODUCTION

The last two works—really two parts of one work—contained in this volume represent one of the final phases of the Pelagian controversy during Augustine's lifetime. The scene of the conflict has shifted to Gaul, although North Africa is directly involved and the East indirectly, through the person of John Cassian. Augustine's opponents now are not Pelagians, as Augustine himself acknowledges, but they take exception to the more extreme positions to which Augustine has been led in the course of the Pelagian controversy. Since the seventeenth century they have commonly been known as "Semi-Pelagians," but, as will be discussed below, this term is something of a misnomer.

Background: The Controversy at Hadrumetum

(2) In 426 or 427, Florus, a monk of Hadrumetum (modern Sousse in Tunisia), was visiting his native city of Uzalis. There, in the library of Bishop Evodius,[1] he came upon a copy of Augustine's *Letter* 194, written in 418 to the Roman presbyter Sixtus, later to become Pope Sixtus III (432-440). Florus had the work copied and sent the copy back to his monastery as a gift, by way of his companion Felix, while he himself went on to Carthage. Felix, upon his return, circulated the work among the monks, unknown to the Abbot Valentinus, and sharp controversy broke out.[2]

(3) What was it about *Ep.* 194 that was so provocative? The

1. Evodius, who came from Augustine's native town of Thagaste, was a companion of Augustine in his early years as a Christian and later resided in Augustine's monastic communities at Thagaste and Hippo. He is Augustine's dialogue partner in *De libero arbitrio*.
2. Valentinus to Augustine, *Ep.* 216.2.

letter had been written at the height of the Pelagian controversy, as part of Augustine's campaign to convince the Italian Church of the dangers of Pelagianism. Its recipient, Sixtus, had earlier been regarded as sympathetic to the Pelagian party, but had more recently joined in its condemnation.[3] In this letter, Augustine presents his theory of grace and predestination in uncompromising terms. Why, from among the human *massa damnationis*,[4] does God call and justify some people and not others? Certainly not because of their merits; "what else but his gifts does God crown when he crowns our merits?"[5] Even faith, the foundation of all good works, is not to be attributed to the human free will nor seen as a reward for prior merits.[6] Augustine returns to his theology of election, worked out in his replies to Simplicianus in 397, which had not up to this point played much role in the Pelagian controversy. He uses the case of infants—why is one baptized and saved, while another perishes unbaptized?—as a paradigm to show that election is gratuitous, and, for the first time since *Ad Simplicianum,* he gives extensive treatment of the case of Esau and Jacob, born at the same time of the same parents, the one called at the moment of birth, before there could be any question of merit, the other left behind.[7]

(4) In one important respect, as J. P. Burns has argued, *Ep.* 194 represents a development in Augustine's theology of election, in the direction of exclusion of human autonomy.[8] *Ad Simplicianum* had put forward the theory of the "congruous call," which held that what distinguished the elect is that God issued a call and manipulated external circumstances in a way that was so adapted to their prior dispositions that they would respond to their call by their own free will.[9] Now, however, he sees conversion, the beginning of faith, as the result of the Holy Spirit working upon the human will from within.[10] "The grace of con-

3. Augustine, *Ep.* 191.1, 194.1.
4. *Ep.* 194.4. See note to *De nat. et gr.* 5.5 above.
5. *Ep.* 194.19.   6. *Ep.* 194.9.
7. *Ep.* 194.34-41.   8. Burns, *Development,* 141-58.
9. See above, Introduction to *De nat. et gr.,* and below, note to *De dono pers.* 14.35.
10. *Ep.* 194.15.

version is operative: it produces human willing and consent."[11]

(5) In the aftermath of the reading of *Ep.* 194 at Hadrumetum, some monks maintained a doctrine of grace so strong that they "deny man's free will, and, what is more serious, they say that on the Day of Judgment God will not render to every man according to his works," while others "confess that our free will is aided by the grace of God to know and do what is right."[12] Abbot Valentinus only learned of the controversy from Florus, upon the latter's return. He first wrote to Evodius, then later to the priest Sabinus for advice, but their responses did not satisfy the dissident monks.[13] So two monks, Cresconius and Felix (not the Felix who first brought *Ep.* 194 to Hadrumetum), were dispatched to Hippo. Later they were joined by the other Felix, and the three returned to Hadrumetum, bearing *Epp.* 214 and 215 to Valentinus, as well as the treatise, *De gratia et libero arbitrio.*[14] *Epp.* 214 and 215 request that Florus be sent to Hippo, and *Ep.* 216A indicates that this was done.[15]

(6) In *De gratia et libero arbitrio* (*On Grace and Free Will*), Augustine defends both grace and free will, continuing his insistence on God's interior working on the human will: "The will is not destroyed by grace, but is changed from a bad will to a good will, and is aided by grace once it becomes good."[16] "God works in men's hearts to incline their wills to whatsoever way he wills: either to good in accordance with his mercy, or to evil in accordance with their evil merits, and this, indeed, by his own judgments, sometimes manifest, sometimes hidden, but always just."[17] Augustine concludes by again citing the case of

---

11. Burns, *Development*, 158.	12. Augustine, *Ep.* 214.1.

13. *Ep.* 216.3. The replies of Evodius and of another priest, Januarianus, were published by Morin, *Revue Bénédictine* 18 (1901) 241-56, and reprinted, PLS 2. 332-34. Evodius' letter is published, with a facing French translation, in BA 24 46-53; the letter of Januarianus is published, with French translation, in the same volume, 228-45.

14. Translation by Robert P. Russell, O.S.A., *On Grace and Free Will*, FOTC 59 (1968) 250-308. For more information, see the translator's introduction to that work, pp. 245-48.

15. This account is based on *Epp.* 214.1, 215.1, 216.3, and 216A (FOTC 32. 74). On Augustine's invitation to Florus, see *Epp.* 214.6 and 215.9.

16. *De grat. et lib. arb.* 20.41.

17. *De grat. et lib. arb.* 21.43.

infants and appealing, as often, to the inscrutability of God's judgments and the unsearchability of God's ways.

(7) Augustine's reply was not enough. Florus came bearing a letter from Valentinus relating that some at Hadrumetum had drawn the conclusion that "no one should be admonished for not observing the commandments of God, but that prayer alone should be offered for him so that he would observe them."[18]

(8) Augustine responded with the treatise *De correptione et gratia*. His judgment with regard to rebuke or admonishment is that it is fully appropriate. If the person rebuked is among the elect, its effect may be salutary—the rebuke itself is part of the economy of grace.[19] If, on the other hand, the person rebuked does not belong to the number of the predestined, the rebuke is for him a penal infliction.[20] It is in this work that Augustine begins to give sustained attention to the grace of perseverance.[21] Augustine's treatment of this subject (further elaborated in *De dono perseverantiae*) represents, according to Burns, the final stage of the development of his theology of operative grace. On the model of the operative grace of conversion, worked out in *Ep.* 194, Augustine identified a distinct operative grace of perseverance. Previously, he had understood the grace of perseverance as a strengthening of charity, given in response to the believer's striving and prayer, for the willing and performance of good works. Now, however, he identifies a distinct grace, whereby believers are preserved from the sin which would separate them from eternal life. This grace produces the willing and performance of good actions. Without it, one will inevitably fall into sin and lose eternal life.[22] "Finally, he asserted that this grace of perseverance is given without regard for the prior merits of good willing and performance based on charity. Thereby he defined a fully gratuitous predestination, distinct and separable from the prior gifts of faith and charity."[23] In connection with the grace of perseverance, Au-

---

18. *Retr.* 2.93.1. On Valentinus' letter, see *De corr. et gr.* 1.1.
19. *De corr. et gr.* 9.25.   20. *De corr. et gr.* 14.43.
21. *De corr. et gr.* 6.10-8.17.   22. Burns, *Development*, 172-73.
23. Burns, *Development*, 176. See *De corr. et gr.* 8.17.

gustine develops at length a distinction between the grace given to Adam and that given to those saved in Christ. Adam was given the *posse non peccare*, the possibility of not sinning, grace providing his free will with the *adiutorium sine quo non*, the assistance whereby he was able to avoid sin and to choose and perform the good. "But now to the saints predestinated to the kingdom of God by God's grace, the aid of perseverance that is given is not such as the former, but such that to them perseverance itself is bestowed; not only so that without that gift they cannot persevere, but, moreover, so that by means of this gift they do, in fact, persevere."[24]

The Conflict in Provence

(9) It was in Gaul that an articulate opposition arose to Augustine's ideas on predestination and grace; there the controversy continued off and on for over a hundred years.

(10) We first learn of the conflict in Gaul from the writings of Prosper of Aquitaine, the leading defender of the Augustinian position during the controversy's first phases. Prosper, born in Aquitaine toward the end of the fourth century, was living at Marseille at this time. He was a layman, associated with the monastery of St. Victor in Marseille. Around 440 he moved to Rome, where he died some time after 455. He wrote a number of treatises defending the Augustinian theory of grace, most notably the *Contra collatorem* (433), a rebuttal of Cassian's Thirteenth Conference, as well as a *Chronicon* of world history.[25] His earliest extant writing is a letter to a certain Rufinus, who is otherwise unknown. The letter, which is known to predate his letter to Augustine from the fact that it does not mention *De corr. et gr.*, can be dated to around 427. It reports the opinion of some that Augustine "completely sets aside free will and under cover of grace upholds fatalism" and "wants us to believe," as

24. *De corr. et gr.* 12.34 (NPNF translation altered).
25. The writings of Prosper may be found in PL 51. For English translations of Prosper's theological writings, see the two volumes edited by P. de Letter, S.J., *The Call of All Nations*, ACW 14 (1952), and *Defense of Saint Augustine*, ACW 32 (1963).

did the Manichaeans, "that there are in the human race two different substances and natures."[26] Later, after the arrival of a copy of *De corr. et gr.* has provoked still more opposition, he wrote to Augustine for help, and at the same time a layman, otherwise unknown, named Hilary, wrote a similar letter. These are letters 225 and 226 among the letters of Augustine, and they are reprinted in translation below. From them, we know that other letters from Prosper and Hilary have been lost.[27] It was in reply to these letters, both *Epp.* 225 and 226 and the lost letters, that Augustine wrote *De praedestinatione sanctorum* and *De dono perseverantiae.* Before considering Augustine's response, we must attend more closely to the letters of Prosper and Hilary and ask, When were they written? Who were those whom Prosper and Hilary opposed? What were the ideas which Prosper and Hilary opposed?

(11) The dating of these letters, and consequently of *De praed. sanct.* and *De dono pers.*, is a subject of some difficulty. Clearly *De praed. sanct.* and *De dono pers.*, since they quote the *Retractationes,* are later in date than that work, usually assigned to 427. Traditionally, a date of 429 has been given, based on the following passage in Prosper's letter: "Your beatitude must know that one of them [those he opposes], a man of eminent authority and ability in spiritual studies, the saintly Hilary, Bishop of Arles, is an admirer and follower of your teaching in all other matters, and that he has long been anxious to consult your Holiness on his attitude to this question, which has brought him into the controversy."[28] Since Hilary is thought to have become bishop in 429, the letters cannot be dated before this, and in light of Augustine's own death in 430, 429 itself has seemed the most probable date. In 1945, however, Owen Chadwick, in the course of attempting to resolve a problem with the chronology of John Cassian's works which it occasioned, challenged this dating. He noted that all manuscripts of *Ep.* 225 read *Hilarium* in the passage quoted above (the reading accepted in the CSEL text and followed in the English transla-

---

26. *Ep. ad Rufinum* 3 (translation by de Letter).
27. See *Epp.* 225.1 and 226.9.   28. *Ep.* 225.9.

tion reproduced here), except one (Parisinus nov. acq. 1449) which reads *elladium*. This manuscript, although not the oldest, represents a different textual tradition than do the four older manuscripts. Moreover, the earliest list of the bishops of Arles, dating from the ninth century, lists a "Euladius" between Patroclus and Honoratus, that is, in 426-27. The principle of the *lectio difficilior*, together with the more plausible chronology which results, persuaded Chadwick to adopt the reading *elladium*, and several commentators writing in English have followed him.[29] Elie Griffe supposes that this Elladius or Euladius may be the Helladius to whom Cassian dedicates his *Conferences* 1-10, who is mentioned as a bishop in the preface to *Conferences* 11-17.[30] I follow Chadwick's conjecture here (but follow Griffe in adopting the spelling, "Helladius"[31]), and thus propose for *Epp.* 225 and 226 a date of late 427, and for Augustine's reply a date of 428. This allows more time for these works in Augustine's last years, a time when he was also engaged in writing *De haer.* and *C. Iul. op. impf.*, and more particularly, more time before the arrival of the Vandals in Africa cut off communications with Gaul.

(12) Prosper writes to Augustine of the opposition to the latter's theories of grace and predestination which has arisen among "the servants of Christ who live in the city of Marseille,"[32] while Hilary adds that it has spread to other areas of Gaul.[33] Prosper's reference is to the monastery of Saint Victor, whose founder (in 415 or 416) and abbot was John Cassian. The "other areas of Gaul" mentioned include Arles and, especially, the monastery of Lérins, situated on an island in the Mediterranean near Cannes. The only individual mentioned

---

29. Chadwick, "Euladius of Arles." See also Chadwick, *John Cassian*, 128, where the spelling, "Helladius," is preferred; Bonner, *St Augustine*, 350; Rees, *Pelagius*, 104, who says, "It seems to be generally accepted now that Euladius was the bishop in question." Chéné, after reporting the evidence in favor of Chadwick's hypothesis, concludes noncommittally, "Nous n'avons pas à nous prononcer sur cette conjecture: nous la signalons seulement au lecteur" (BA 24. 808).

30. Griffe, *La Gaule chrétienne*, 2. 241.

31. According to Griffe, "Euladius est une forme aberrante ou plutôt fautive" (241).

32. *Ep.* 225.2.   33. *Ep.* 226.2.

by name by Prosper and Hilary as opposing Augustine's theory of predestination is Helladius, but it is clear that the central figure in this opposition is Cassian. Also among this party were St. Vincent of Lérins and, at a later date, Faustus, abbot of Lérins and later bishop of Riez (c.408-c.490). Aside from these figures, it is difficult to identify Augustine's opponents by name, but "they were not a little clique. The party contained not only Cassian and St. Vincent of Lérins, but the leading bishops, priests and monks of Provence."[34]

(13) The ecclesiastical context of this opposition was the monastic movement, which had become prominent in southern Gaul.[35] The theological context was the same as that of the original Pelagian controversy (and indeed, that of the later revival of this controversy at the time of the Reformation): a perception of the incompatibility between the Augustinian theology of grace and the practice of Christian asceticism. The monastic practice of Gaul was shaped less by Augustinian theology than by the theology of the East, where, as seen earlier, Pelagius received a much more friendly reception than in North Africa.

(14) Nevertheless, Augustine's opponents in Gaul were not Pelagians. Prosper notes that they hold that "All men have sinned in the sin of Adam and no one can be saved by regeneration through his own efforts, but through the grace of God."[36] As we have seen, Helladius is said to have agreed with Augustine in all matters other than predestination. Since the early seventeenth century, this group has been commonly labeled "Semi-Pelagians,"[37] but, as Chadwick points out, "The name is wrong. The leaders of the school were not half-way to being disciples of Pelagius"—they were in fact far nearer to Au-

---

34. Chadwick, *John Cassian*, 127.   35. Brown, *Augustine of Hippo*, 401.
36. *Ep.* 225.3.
37. According to Lesousky, who bases her statements on M. Jacquin, "A quelle date apparaît le terme 'Semipélagien'?" *Revue des sciences philosophiques et théologiques* 1 (1907) 506-08, "Semipelagian" was first used during the late sixteenth-century controversy *de auxiliis*, on grace and freedom, which arose over the teachings of the Jesuit Luis de Molina and the Dominican Domingo Bañez. The term appeared in the meetings of the "Congregatio de Auxiliis," appointed by Pope Clement VIII in 1597, and gained currency through its use by the theologian Diego Alvarez early in the following century (see Lesousky, *The* De dono perseverantiae, 37).

gustine.[38] The earlier name, "Massilians" (people from Marseille), is preferable.[39]

(15) The leading figure in this party, John Cassian (c.360-435), is described by Gennadius as a native of Scythia. At an early age, around A.D. 380, he travelled to Palestine and settled at a monastery in Bethlehem. Two years later, he travelled to Egypt and for the better part of seventeen years lived there, chiefly among the monks of the Scete. Around 399, he went to Constantinople, where John Chrysostom ordained him a deacon. When Chrysostom was exiled, Cassian came to Rome, and by around 415, he was at Marseille, where he founded monasteries for men and women.[40]

(16) Had Augustine never written on grace, it is likely, Chadwick says, that Cassian's doctrine of grace would have remained unsystematic, as generally was that of the eastern monastic writers. These writers, and Cassian with them, tended to hold that "God's grace was offered freely to everyone who wanted it. But it could hardly enter the human soul because of the barricade of passions and vices, such a clutter within the soul as to make a man almost incapable of wanting God's help. Therefore cut away the passions, then grace will be enabled to flow."[41] The cutting away of the passions was the human work of ascesis, but counteracting this emphasis on the human will was the monks' strong condemnation of human pride. "Whenever they wrote about pride, the monks wrote eloquently about the soul's absolute dependence upon the grace of God."[42] This as-

---

38. Chadwick, *John Cassian*, 127.

39. The Massilian, or Semi-Pelagian, controversy continued in Gaul up to the Council of Orange in 529. For an account of its course after Augustine's death, see Lesousky, *The* De dono perseverantiae, 70-81, or, in more detail, Amann, "Semi-Pélagiens," 1817-49.

40. Information on Cassian's life is from Quasten, *Patrology* 4, 512-13. An irony is that Lazarus, one of the accusers of Pelagius, spent the end of his life at Saint Victor with Cassian, the leader of the "Semi-Pelagians" (Griffe, *La Gaule chrétienne*, 2. 255, basing the statement on a funerary inscription). Griffe's conjecture, "Il est vraisemblable que Cassien soit venu d'Orient, en 416, en compagnie de l'ancien évêque d'Aix," (256) is falsified by Augustine's Letter 19*, which has Lazarus travelling to Hippo at that time. No visit of Cassian to Hippo is recorded.

41. Chadwick, *John Cassian*, 110.   42. Chadwick, *John Cassian*, 111.

sertion of dependency was strengthened by the monks' emphasis on the need to pray in order to be transformed. All of this is taken over into Cassian's earlier writings to form a theology of grace which, at some cost to consistency, combines an assertion of the absolute dependence of human conversion and progress on grace with an assertion that grace follows upon the human effort of "asking, seeking, and knocking."[43]

(17) Perceiving in Augustine's teaching, perhaps especially that of *De correptione et gratia*, a threat to human free will, Cassian set out, in an irenic spirit, to rebut it in *Conference* 13, presented as a discourse by the Abbot Chaeremon. Here Cassian states clearly that "Men always have need of God's help, and . . . human weakness cannot accomplish anything that has to do with salvation by itself alone."[44] In some cases, as in Augustine's paradigm case of Paul, the grace of conversion simply overturns a will that was contrary to God. But Cassian's paradigm case is the Good Thief, who is saved after asking for mercy. Thus, "When he sees in us some beginnings of a good will, he at once enlightens it and strengthens it and urges it on towards salvation, increasing that which he himself has implanted or which he sees to have arisen from our own efforts."[45] Cassian thinks it blasphemy to think that God wills to save not *all* but only *some* human beings.[46] Nor has the Fall destroyed all human capacity to know and choose the good.[47] We always retain some freedom to "neglect or delight in the grace of God."[48] Grace, then, is not irresistible; those who are lost are lost because they refuse grace, not because God did not predestine them to be among the elect and thus did not offer it to them.

(18) Prosper and Hilary probably had not yet seen *Conference* 13 when they wrote their letters to Augustine. There are relatively few direct verbal echoes of the Conference in the letters. Still, Prosper at least would have had much opportunity to be-

43. For Cassian's theology of grace prior to *Conference* 13, see Chadwick, *John Cassian*, 112-17.
44. *Coll.* 13.6, translated by Edgar C. S. Gibson, NPNF, Second Series, vol. 11.
45. *Coll.* 13.8.   46. *Coll.* 13.7.
47. *Coll.* 13.12.   48. *Coll.* 13.12.

come acquainted with Cassian's teaching, and he responds to Cassian's central themes in his letter. However, as Prosper notes, the Massilians did not all speak in unison,[49] and some of the ideas which Prosper and also Hilary report, notably the whole question of God's basing his election on his foreknowledge of human merits, and particularly the hypothetical merits of infants, are not found in *Conference* 13.[50] It is also very probable that Prosper and Hilary may report the ideas they oppose in a form less nuanced than that in which they were put forward by their proponents.

(19) Following are the theses of the Massilians, as presented by Prosper and Hilary, more or less in the order in which they appear in *Epp.* 225 and 226:

(a) All have sinned in Adam, and none are reborn except through God's grace (225.3, 226.2). This agrees with Augustine.

(b) Reconciliation in Christ is offered to all without exception, so that all who are willing to come to faith and be baptized can be saved (225.3, 226.7). God determined to admit to his kingdom none except the baptized, yet all "are called to this gift of salvation either by natural law or by written law or by the preaching of the gospel" (225.4). God's universal salvific will is thus affirmed with Cassian over against Augustine.

(c) God predestined to his kingdom those whom he foresaw would be worthy of election and would depart from this life by a good death (225.3). More particularly, predestination is equated with God's foreknowledge of a person's faith, as Augustine himself said in his early *Expositio quarundam propositionum ex epistola ad Romanos* (226.3).

(d) A theory of predestination whereby God either from the beginning of the world or from the foundation of the human race distinguished the elect from the reprobate, the vessels of honor from the vessels of dishonor, deprives unbelievers and sinners of a motive for conversion and gives good Christians an excuse for lukewarmness. In general, this preaching under-

49. *Ep.* 225.4.
50. Chadwick, *John Cassian*, 129. For a detailed comparison of Cassian's *Coll.* 13 with the letters of Prosper and Hilary, see Amann, "Semi-Pélagiens," 1811.

mines Christian moral striving (225.3,6, 226.5). The theory of predestination, even if true, should not be preached, because of its spiritual danger to those who hear it (225.3).

(e) Augustine's theory of predestination leads to a fatalism or dualism, as if the human race were divided into two different kinds of nature, and no one can change the condition as elect or reprobate in which he was created (225.3)

(f) Romans 9.14-21, which Augustine quotes in support of the thesis that the grace of God precedes the merits of the elect, has not previously been understood by ecclesiastical writers in that sense (225.3).

(g) Some, Prosper says, hold that the initial grace of conversion comes as a consequence of the good use of the "grace" of created nature, the natural ability to "ask, seek, and knock" (225.4,6). Hilary develops this position in a more nuanced manner: the one thing still possible for human nature, injured by sin, is to have faith in God and ask for healing. Thus, "he who has begun to will is helped" by God toward an increase in faith and full restoration, and it is not the case that "grace is given to make him will, while others equally guilty are excluded from this gift, who could likewise be saved if the will to believe were imparted to them" (226.2,4).

(h) Children who die before they can gain merits of their own are brought to baptism and saved, or left unbaptized and lost, in accordance with God's foreknowledge of the merits they would have had if they had lived longer (225.5). Alternatively, the question of the fate of infants should be left open, as Augustine had done in his early work, *De libero arbitrio* (226.8).

(i) Likewise, Christ is preached, or not preached, to the nations, in accordance with God's foreknowledge of whether they would or would not believe (a suggestion which Augustine himself made in his *Ep.* 102) (225.5, 226.3).

(j) The idea of a "fixed number of elect and reprobate" (226.7) is opposed (225.6, 226.7).

(k) The grace of perseverance does not prevent all sinning, but is something from which one can fall away through one's own will. It should not be preached in any sense which implies "that it cannot be won by prayer or lost by obstinacy" (226.4).

(l) Augustine's theóry, put forward in *De corr. et gr.*, that Adam was given a gift of perseverance that was necessary but not sufficient, while the saints now are given a grace that is both necessary and sufficient for perseverance, is opposed (226.6).

De praedestinatione sanctorum *and* De dono perseverantiae

(20) *De praed. sanct.* and *De dono pers.* are Augustine's answer to *Epp.* 225 and 226, as well, in some measure, to the lost letters from Prosper and Hilary. Above, a date of 428 was proposed for them. Augustine's repeated references in *De dono pers.* to *De praed. sanct.* as "the former book" (or some other equivalent term) (see, e.g., 1.1) make clear that he sees the two books as one work. Prosper, in the introduction to his *Pro Augustino responsiones ad excerpta Genuensium*, refers to them as "the books of Bishop Augustine of saintly memory entitled *On the Predestination of the Saints*".[51] The sixth-century writer Eugippius gives *De dono perseverantiae* as a title for the second book of the work, and from the ninth century on, the two books are treated as separate works, with *De bono perseverantiae* (*The Good of Perseverance*) rather than *De dono perseverantiae* the more common title for the latter.[52]

Synopsis of On the Predestination of the Saints

(21) In 1.1–2.3 Augustine acknowledges his opponents in Gaul as "brothers," fellow catholic Christians, who agree with him in much that is essential. He undertakes to show against them that the faith by which one becomes a Christian is itself a free gift of God.

(22) In 2.4–6 he cites scriptural texts, chiefly by or about Paul, on the absolute gratuity of all gifts of God and on faith as a gift of God. He argues that we do not bring before our own minds the thoughts which must precede the will to believe; that is God's doing (2.5).

51. PL 51. 187, English translation by P. de Letter, ACW 32. 49.
52. Lesousky, *The* De dono perseverantiae, 95-96; BA 24. 437.

(23) In 3.7–8, quoting from his *Retractationes,* Augustine notes the change in his own position between the *Expositio quarundam propositionum ex epistola ad Romanos* (around 394) and the *Ad Simplicianum de diversis quaestionibus* (397). Writing the latter book, he became persuaded by the Epistle to the Romans, especially chapter 9, together with 1 Cor 4.7 ("What do you have that you have not received?") that even the beginning of faith is a gratuitous gift of God.

(24) In 5.9–7.12 he gives further textual argument that Paul meant for faith to be included in the reference of 1 Cor 4.7.

(25) In 8.13–16 Augustine argues on the basis of John 6 that no one comes to Jesus in faith "unless the Father draw him" by grace, given through the Spirit. That the turning of unbelievers and even persecutors to faith is a gift of God is shown by the fact that the Church prays to God to bring it about. Those who are not given this gift are condemned justly.

(26) In 9.17–11.22 Augustine addresses the objection that in *Ep.* 102 (A.D. 405) he had suggested that Christ was preached or not preached to nations in accordance with God's foreknowledge of whether or not they would believe. This answer, he says, was an *ad hoc* proposal for the sake of argument. When in the same letter he said that Christian salvation "was never lacking to him who was worthy of it," this worthiness was that of grace or predestination. Predestination is simply God's foreknowledge of what he himself was going to do. To say that God would offer the grace of good works if the human person first had faith is to make God's ability to carry out his intentions depend on human works.

(27) In 12.23–14.29 Augustine says that the case of infants provides an outstanding example of God's predestination. He rebuts the argument that they are baptized and saved, or left unbaptized and lost, on the basis of the merits they would have gained had they lived longer. First, why could God not forgive those hypothetical sins, as he forgives genuine ones (12.24)? Second, this argument leaves no role for original sin, if infants are saved or damned on the basis of foreseen actual sins, and thus is tantamount to the Pelagian denial of original sin (13.25). Third, analogously to this argument, we could reason that a

timely death would not—contrary to what is upheld by Cyprian and by Wisdom 4.11—be spiritually beneficial to a person, for one would be judged on the basis of what one would have done if one had lived longer.

(28) In 15.30–31 Augustine argues that another outstanding example of predestination is the human Jesus of Nazareth, who did not merit the grace of the incarnation by means of prior works or faith. "Just as that one man was predestined to be our head, so we, being many, are predestined to be his members" (15.31).

(29) In 16.32–33 Augustine notes that God calls people in two different ways. Some, such as the guests in the parable who refused to come to the wedding, are called although God foreknows they will reject the call. The predestined, however, are called by a call which makes them into believers (16.32).

(30) In 17.34–18.37 the point is made that the elect are not chosen because they have believed but in order that they might believe. Relying on Ephesians 1.4-11, Augustine argues that God chose them by that predestination by which he foreknew their future faith, not as if it originated from them, but as his own future action.

(31) In 19.38–20.42 Augustine turns to his opponents' position that God chose people on the basis of his foreknowledge, not of any of their good works, but only of their initial act of faith. He reiterates his earlier argument based on Eph 1.4-11 and adds to it arguments based on Pauline texts to the effect that we thank God for faith and we pray for faith in those who lack it, both implying that faith is God's gift. He cites numerous texts to establish that God works in human hearts to cause them to will the good.

(32) In 21.43 he concludes this book, emphasizing that he has shown that not only the increase but even the beginning of faith is a gift of God.

Synopsis of On the Gift of Perseverance

(33) De dono perseverantiae divides into two major sections, one on the gift of perseverance (2.2–13.33) and one on the

preaching of predestination (14.34–23.65), between an introduction and a general conclusion to both books.

(34) In 1.1 Augustine establishes his topic: final perseverance, the perseverance to the end, not a "perseverance" that is
temporary and eventually fails.

(35) In 2.2–13.33 Augustine argues that final perseverance
is a gift of God. He begins with Paul's statement that to suffer
for Christ is a gift (Phil 1.29), applying this to martyrdom. If
the martyr's perseverance is a gift, so also is that of others
(2.2). Moreover, we pray for perseverance, which shows that
we regard it as a gift of God (2.3). The Lord's Prayer, as the
commentary of Cyprian shows, is an extended prayer for
perseverance (2.4–6.12), especially the petition, "Bring us not
into temptation."[53] Just as God brings it about that we approach him, so he brings it about that we not depart from him
(7.14).

(36) Augustine returns to Eph 1.4-11 (7.15) to argue that
perseverance is a gratuitous gift, without regard to merit.
Those who are not given this gift are condemned justly. The
case of infants, even twins, shows the utter gratuity of the gift
of salvation (8.17). As to why one is saved and one lost, or why
one is given perseverance and another not, God's judgments
are inscrutable, but we know they are just (8.18, 9.21, 11.25).
The division of the human race into the elect and non-elect
does not reintroduce a dualism of two human natures, contrary
to what Augustine's opponents argue. Indeed, if there were
such a dualism, there would be no grace; those saved would be
saved because of the goodness of their nature (8.19). As our
thoughts are not in our power, so also our faith and perseverance (8.20).

(37) Augustine again raises the issue of those rescued
by God through death, preventing them from undergoing
a temptation whereby they would fall away, and he again
attacks the theory that people would be judged for sins
they did not commit but would have committed if they had
lived longer. He cites the example of the condemnation of

53. On this wording, see note to *De nat. et gr.* 53.62, above.

Tyre and Sidon, even though those people would have repented if the gospel had been preached there[54] (9.22–10.24).

(38) He next considers his opponents' claim that the case of infants should not be used as a model for adults and their use of a passage from *De libero arbitrio* against Augustine's later theory (11.26–27). In the earlier work, Augustine says, he had confined himself to what was necessary to refute the Manichaeans, but the fact that there is original sin shows that the cases of infants and adults are similar, that the grace of salvation is equally gratuitous in either case (12.30–31). What applies to the grace of baptism applies equally well to that of perseverance: they are not given on the basis of any merits, actual or hypothetical, but according to the secret, yet just, predestination of God.

(39) In 14.34–23.65 Augustine turns to his opponents' claim that the doctrine of predestination is harmful or dangerous to Christian preaching. He begins with the case of Paul, whose teaching of predestination hardly undermined his zeal for preaching (14.34). Jesus himself both said that it is God who draws people to him and exhorted people to believe in him (14.35). The preaching of predestination is salutary for the curbing of human pride (14.36). The same objections which are raised against the preaching of predestination could equally well be raised against the proclamation of God's foreknowledge, which no one denies (15.38). God has so arranged things that only the one who prays for perseverance will be granted it (16.39). Our silence on this and related subjects could be more harmful than our preaching openly (16.40). The only alternative to a gratuitous predestination is to hold that the grace of God is given according to our merits, which was condemned at Diospolis (16.41). Augustine's opponents themselves admit that they consider to be gifts of God some other things to which at the same time they exhort their audience: such things as chastity, charity, and piety. Why not then also perseverance (17.42–45)?

54. Matt 11.21-22.

(40) Augustine now addresses his opponents' contention that predestination is a dangerous innovation, by arguing that it has always been taught in the Church, although not necessarily by name. When Paul speaks of "foreknowledge" in Rom 11.2, for instance, it is clear that he is speaking of predestination, God's foreknowledge of what he was going to do (18.47). When Cyprian proclaimed that nothing is our own, and Ambrose said that our hearts and thoughts are not within our power, they were preaching the gratuity of grace and thus implicitly they were preaching predestination. Clearly, in their cases the doctrine of predestination did not hamper their commitment to exhortation (19.48). Augustine cites further texts to show that Cyprian and Ambrose taught a gratuitous grace of faith and perseverance and adds a misquoted passage from Gregory of Nazianzus, which he understands to the same effect (19.49–50). As repeatedly in the treatises contained in this volume, Augustine responds sharply to his opponents' use of his own earlier writings, in this case to the claim that he defended the faith quite well in them without the doctrine of predestination.[55] He cites his teaching on the gratuity of grace from *Ad Simplicianum* on, especially in the *Confessiones,* and the doctrine of predestination there implicit (20.52–53). The teaching of *De correptione et gratia,* that perseverance to the end is a distinct gift of God, is set out more clearly than before, but is nothing new. It follows from Augustine's earlier teaching, as well as that of Cyprian (21.55).

(41) Predestination should be preached carefully, and not so as to give unnecessary offense, certainly not in such a way as to state that some of one's hearers are inevitably going to be damned (22.57–61). One's audience should always be exhorted to trust God and to pray for perseverance (22.62). The Church has always prayed that unbelievers come to faith and believers persevere in it, evidence of the belief that these things are in God's hands (23.63). This prayer itself is given to us by God in his Spirit (23.64).[56]

---

55. Hilary, *Ep.* 226.8.
56. Burns observes, "The preaching [Augustine] advised, however, was not in full accord with the theology he had developed: trust in God's love and

(42) In 24.66–68 Augustine prays that his opponents will be given a greater understanding of the gratuity of grace (24.66). He recurs to the example of the predestination of the human Jesus (24.67), and concludes by commending his work to the judgment of the "teachers of the Church" (24.68).

Texts and Translations

(43) The text of Letters 225 and 226 was edited by A. Goldbacher in CSEL 57 (1911) 454-81, reprinted with French translation in BA 24 (Paris: Désclee de Brouwer, 1962) 392-435. The Benedictine text is reprinted in PL 33. 1002-12. We here reproduce the translation, made from the Goldbacher text, of Sister Wilfrid Parsons, S.N.D., FOTC 32 (1956) 119-39, but we have introduced many significant alterations. In rendering quotations from *Epp.* 225-226 within the text of *De praed. sanct.* and *De dono pers.*, we have provided a fresh translation. Another translation of *Ep.* 225, the letter of Prosper, appears in Prosper of Aquitaine, *Defense of St. Augustine*, translated and annotated by P. de Letter, S.J., ACW 32 (1963) 38-48.

(44) There is no modern critical edition of *De praedestinatione sanctorum* and *De dono perseverantiae*. This translation has been made from the Benedictine text, which is found, for *De praed. sanct.*, in PL 44. 959-992, and, for *De dono pers.*, in PL 45. 993-1034, as reprinted with French translation by M. J. Chéné in BA 24, 464-597 (*De praed. sanct.*) and 600-765 (*De dono pers.*). Except as noted (and some silent corrections of obvious typographical errors), we have followed the BA text in this translation. In preparing this translation, we have consulted the French translations in BA 24, the earlier English translation of both works by Rev. Robert Ernest Wallis, NPNF 5 (1887) 497-519 and 526-52, and the translation of *De dono perseverantiae*, with introduction, notes, and facing text, by Sister Mary Alphonsine Lesousky, *The* De dono perseverantiae *of Saint Au-*

---

prayer for assistance, for example, are explained as the work of the Holy Spirit in the Christian, which neither earn nor dispose for the distinct grace and operation of perseverance" ("Confessing the Glory of God," 139).

gustine (Washington, D.C.: The Catholic University of America Press, 1956).

(45) There is a German translation by Adolar Zumkeller, with text, in Augustinus, *Schriften gegen die Semi-pelagianer* (Würzburg: Augustinus-Verlag, 1955) 241-327 (*Die Vorherbestimmung der Heiligen*) and 329-439 (*Die Gabe der Beharrlichkeit*). A Spanish translation, with text, of *De praed. sanct.* (*De la predestinacion de los Santos*), by P. Emiliano Lopez, can be found in BAC 50 (Madrid, 1956) 479-567, and a translation, with text, of *De dono pers.* (*Del don de la Perseverancia*), by P. Toribio de Castro, in the same volume, 573-671.

APPENDIX: LETTERS 225 (Prosper) and 226 (Hilary)

225. Prosper to Augustine, his saintly lord, indescribably wonderful and incomparably honorable prelate and illustrious patron

(1) Although I am not personally acquainted with you, I am known to you to some extent, if you remember, in mind and speech, for I have sent and received letters through my holy brother, the deacon Leontius. Now, however, I take the liberty of writing to your Blessedness, not only for the pleasure of greeting you as I did then, but because of my zeal for the faith by which the Church lives. Knowing that your watchful care is ever on guard to protect all the members of the body of Christ against the snares of heretical doctrines, and ever ready to fight in the strength of truth, I think I need not fear being burdensome to you or importunate in a matter which touches the salvation of many and therefore is of concern to your Piety. In fact, I believe I should incur guilt if I failed to bring such an extremely dangerous situation to the attention of the outstanding defender of the faith.

(2) Many of the servants of Christ who live in the city of Marseille, having read the writings which your Holiness published against the Pelagian heretics, think that your argument on the calling of the elect according to the design of God is contrary to the opinion of the Fathers and the tradition of the Church.

And while they have chosen for some time past to blame their own slowness of comprehension rather than criticize what they do not understand, and some of them wanted to request of your Blessedness a plainer and clearer explanation of this matter, it happened, by the disposition of God's mercy, that you published a book, full of divine authority, on *Amendment and Grace*,[1] at a time when similar doubts assailed certain monks in Africa. When this work had been brought to our knowledge by an unhoped-for chance, I thought that all the complaints of our opponents would be quieted, because your answer in that work was as complete and as final, on all points on which your Holiness had been consulted, as if you had in mind the special aim of allaying the disturbance that had arisen among us. But after they had studied this book of your Blessedness, those who had formerly followed the holy and apostolic authority of your teaching became more enlightened and much better instructed, while those who were held back by the darkness of their own prejudice went away more opposed than they had previously been. We have to fear this headlong separation of theirs, first for their own sake, lest the spirit of Pelagian impiety make sport of men so clear-minded and so exemplary in the pursuit of all virtues; and second, for the more ordinary souls, who hold the former in high esteem because they see their uprightness, lest they think that the safest opinion they can hold is the one they hear asserted by the others whose authority they follow without reflection.

(3) This is a summary of what they profess: All men have sinned in the sin of Adam and no one can be saved by regeneration through his own efforts, but through the grace of God. Moreover, the propitiation which is found in the mystery of the blood of Christ was offered for all men without exception; hence, all who are willing to approach to faith and baptism can be saved. God foresaw before the foundation of the world[2] those who would believe or who would stand firm in the faith, which thereafter would be seconded by grace; and he predestined to his kingdom those whom he called freely, of whom he

1. *De correptione et gratia.*   2. Eph 1.4; Matt 25.34.

foresaw that they would be worthy of election and would depart from this life by a good death. Therefore, every man is warned by divine enactments to believe and to perform good works, so that none need despair of laying hold on eternal life, since a reward is prepared for voluntary consecration. But they claim that this calling by God according to his design by which a distinction between the elect and the reprobate is said to have been made—either before the beginning of the world or in the act of creating the human race, so that, according to the pleasure of the creator, some are created vessels of honor, others vessels of dishonor[3]—deprives the lapsed of a motive for rising from their sins, and affords good Christians an excuse for lukewarmness, if the reprobate cannot enter heaven by any effort of his own, or the elect be cast out for any negligence. However they act, the outcome for them cannot be other than what God has determined, and in this uncertainty of hope there can be no constant course of action, because the effort of man's striving is useless if the choice of God's predestination rules otherwise. This has the effect of undermining effort and doing away with the virtues, if the purpose of God is antecedent to the human will, and thus under the name of predestination a certain inevitably of fate is introduced; or else the Lord is described as the Creator of different natures, if no one can become different from what he was made. To sum up briefly and completely what these men think: whatever your Holiness has set down in this book from the thought of your opponents as something to refute, and whatever you have quoted in the books against Julian of his own words on this question, as something to be most powerfully attacked, all of this these holy men most vehemently proclaim. And when to refute them we offer writings of your Blessedness, furnished with the most cogent and innumerable proofs from the divine Scriptures, and when we imitate the form of your reasoning by building up an argument strong enough to hem them in, they defend their obstinacy by an appeal to antiquity. Quoting what is brought forward from the Epistle of the Apostle Paul, writing to the Romans,[4] as proof

3. Rom 9.21.   4. Rom 9.14–21.

of divine grace antecedent to the merits of the elect, they declare that these words have never been understood by any ecclesiastical writer as they are now understood. When we ask them to explain this passage as it is understood by those to whom they refer, they say they have not found the statement they want, and they enforce silence about those whose lofty heights no one can scale. They have reached such a pitch of stubbornness that they define our faith in a way to disedify their hearers, saying things which, even if true, ought not to be said aloud; they make dangerous statements which are not to be accepted, and without any risk they pass over in silence what is unintelligible.

(4) Some of them, indeed, are so far from forsaking Pelagian paths that when they are forced to admit that the grace of God forestalls all human merits—because if it is given as a reward of merit it is wrongly called grace—they hold that it comes to each single man in this way. Before man exists, and therefore before he is capable of merit, the grace of the creator makes him a rational being endowed with free will; then, through his ability to discern good from evil,[5] he can direct his will to the knowledge of God and the observance of his commandments; by asking, seeking, and knocking,[6] through the use of that natural faculty, he attains to that grace by which we are reborn in Christ, and he receives, he finds, and he enters in because he makes a good use of a good gift of nature; thus, with the help of the initial grace he merits to attain to the grace of salvation. The proposition of the grace of election they define entirely in this way: that God has determined to admit none to his kingdom without the sacrament of regeneration, but that all men without exception are called to this gift of salvation either by natural law or by written law or by the preaching of the gospel; that all who will may become sons of God, and that there is no excuse for those who refuse to be of the number of his faithful; that the justice of God consists in this, that those who do not believe in him are doomed, but his goodness is shown by the fact that he excludes no one from life, but 'will have all men'

5. Heb 5.14.　　　　6. Matt 7.7,8; Luke 11.9–10.

without distinction 'to be saved and to come to the knowledge of the truth.'[7] At this point they offer evidence according to which the admonition of the divine Scripture rouses the wills of men who, of their free choice, either do what they are commanded or fail to do it. They think it follows that, as the sinner's disobedience is attributed to his lack of will, so there is no doubt that the faithful man has been obedient because he willed it; that each one has as much potentiality for evil as for good, and that the mind moves with equal inclination to vice and to virtue; that, finally, the grace of God supports the soul when it seeks what is good, but a just condemnation overtakes the one who pursues evil.

(5) When we offer as an objection to these arguments the unnumbered throng of little children who are cut off by a decree of God, who, except for the taint of original sin under which all men are equally born to share in the condemnation of the first man, have as yet no will, no actions of their own, who are to be carried off before any experience of this life gives them a discernment of good and evil, of whom some are enrolled among the heirs of the heavenly kingdom because of their regeneration, while others, without baptism, pass over as debtors to eternal death, they say that such children are lost or saved according to what the divine knowledge foresees they would have been in their adult years if they had been preserved to an active life. They do not observe that they are thereby debasing the grace of God which they represent as a companion, not a forerunner, of human merits, making it subject to those wills which they admit are forestalled by it according to their own fanciful idea. But in making the free choice of God subject to certain imaginary merits they invent a future which is not going to exist, as the past also does not exist, and by a new kind of absurdity God foresees what is not going to happen and what is foreseen does not happen. Certainly, they imagine they are affirming this foreknowledge of God in human merits, according to which his grace of election operates, when they come to consider those nations of past ages which were given

7. 1 Tim 2.4.

up and allowed to enter upon their own ways, or which are even now going to destruction in the impiety of an ancient ignorance, without any enlightenment of law or gospel to shine upon them. But when and inasmuch as the gate is opened and a way made for preachers [of truth], when the people of the gentiles who sat in darkness and in the shadow of death have seen a great light,[8] and those who were not his people are now the people of God, while those on whom he had no mercy, on them he now has mercy,[9] these objectors say that the Lord foresaw that they would believe and that he dispensed to each nation the times and services of teachers so that the faith of their collective good will should come into being. Nor, they say, does this undermine the principle that God will have all men to be saved and to come to the knowledge of the truth; for there is no excuse for those who are indeed able to be instructed by their natural intelligence in the worship of the one true God, but who do not hear the gospel because they would not accept it if they heard it.

(6) Our Lord Jesus Christ, they say, died for the whole human race, and thenceforth no one is excluded from the redemption wrought by his blood, not even a man who should spend his whole life in a state of hostility to him, because the mystery of divine mercy includes all men. The reason why many do not receive a new life is because God foresees that they have not the will to receive it. Therefore, as far as God is concerned, eternal life is prepared for all; but as far as the freedom of the will is concerned, eternal life is won by those who believe in God by their own choice and who receive the help of grace as a reward of their belief. Those whose contradictions displease us turned eagerly to that manner of preaching grace, although they previously had held a better opinion about it, because, if they were to admit that grace was antecedent to all those good merits and that these are made possible and conferred by it, they would necessarily have to concede that God acts according to his plan and the determination of

8. Isa 9.2; Matt 4.16.
9. Hos 2.24; Rom 9.25; 1 Peter 2.10.

his will by a hidden purpose and a manifest act 'to make one vessel unto honor, another unto dishonor,'[10] because none is justified except by grace and none is born except in sin. But they shrink from admitting this and they have a dread of designating the merits of the saints as the work of God; they do not agree that the predestined number of the elect can be neither increased nor diminished, because in that case they would have no ground among unbelieving and careless souls for the incentives of their preaching; the injunction to effort and industry would be fruitless in the case of those whose zeal would be brought to nought if they are not among the elect. For they assert that anyone can be roused to conversion or to spiritual progress only if he knows that he can be good by his own effort, and that therefore his liberty will be assisted by the help of God if he chooses what God commands. Thus, as in those who have reached the age of free choice there are two causes which bring about human salvation, namely, the grace of God and the obedience of man, they insist that obedience comes before grace. In this case we should have to believe that salvation is initiated by the one who is saved, not by the one who saves, and that the will of man procures for itself the help of divine grace, not that grace subordinates the human will itself.

(7) As we have learned by the enlightening mercy of God and the instruction of your Blessedness that this is a most evil belief, we can indeed be firm in refusing to accept it, but we are no match for the authority of those who hold such theories, because they far surpass us in the merits of their lives, and some of them outrank us by having recently been raised to the honor of the episcopate, nor does anyone except a few fearless lovers of perfect grace readily dare to refute the arguments of men so far above us. As a consequence, there is increasing danger not only for those who listen to them, but even for themselves, because of their rank, since respect for them holds many in an unprofitable silence or carries them along in an uncritical assent, so that statements which are not challenged by any refutation seem to them perfectly safe. Since, then, there is no small

10. Rom. 9.21.

trace of poison in these survivals of Pelagian error, if the beginning of salvation is wrongly ascribed to man; if the human will is impiously set above the divine will so as to claim that man is helped because he has willed it, not that he wills because he is helped; and if it is wrongly believed that man, sinful in his origin, receives the first beginnings of good, not from the Supreme Good but from himself; if it is true that man can please God only through the bounty of God, grant us your help in this cause, most holy prelate and excellent father; let your piety put forth its utmost effort with the Lord's help, and be so good as to expound to us with your clearest explanations all that is obscure in these questions and too hard to understand.

(8) In the first place, as there are many who think that the Christian faith is not harmed by this difference of opinion, I should like you to make clear the danger in this point of view; next, explain how the freedom of our will is not hindered by this forestalling and co-operating grace; next, whether the foreknowledge of God remains constant according to his purpose, so that those same things which are determined by him are to be accepted as foreknown, or whether they undergo change through different kinds of causes and varieties of persons, so that, because there are different ways of election, in those who are saved without any future activity on their part, the purpose of God would seem to stand alone, whereas in those who are destined to perform good works the purpose could depend on the foreknowledge; or, on the other hand, whether these two forces act in one and the same manner, and although the foreknowledge cannot be separated from the purpose by a distinction of time, yet the foreknowledge in point of order depends on the purpose; and, as there is no form of activity which the divine foreknowledge has not foreseen, so there is nothing good in which we take part which is not originated by God. Finally, if those who are preordained to eternal life become believers through this preaching of the purpose of God, how is it that none of those who are to be exhorted are hindered or have any opportunity of being negligent if they despair of being predestined? We ask you, then, to bear with our foolishness and show us how that argument can be demol-

ished, because, after reviewing the opinions of our predecessors on this matter, we find that almost all of them are reducible to one and the same statement in which they set forth the purpose and predestination of God according to his foreknowledge, in the sense that he made some to be vessels of honor and others vessels of dishonor because he foresaw the end of each one and knew beforehand what each would be like in will and action under the help of his grace.

(9) After you have disentangled all these knotty points and discussed many others over and above which, with your deeper insight, you see have a bearing on this case, we believe and hope that not only will our insufficiency be strengthened by the strong protection of your arguments, but also that those men, distinguished by merits and honors, whom the fog of this opinion wraps in darkness, may receive the most pure light of grace. Your Beatitude must know that one of them, a man of eminent authority and ability in spiritual studies, the saintly Hilary,[11] Bishop of Arles, is an admirer and follower of your teaching in all other matters, and that he has long been anxious to consult your Holiness on his attitude to this question, which has brought him into the controversy. But as it is not certain whether he will do this, or for what purpose he will do it, and as the weariness of all of us is refreshed by the vigor of your charity and your knowledge, under the provident grace of God in the present age, lend your learning to the humble, give your rebuke to the proud. It is necessary and even useful to write what has been written, lest we esteem too lightly what is infrequently debated. People think that absence of pain betokens health and they do not feel a wound covered over with skin, but let them understand that the body which has a swelling tumor will have to be cut. May the grace of God and the peace of our Lord Jesus Christ crown you for all time and glorify you forever as you progress from virtue to virtue, my lord and most blessed prelate, my indescribably wonderful and incomparably honorable, most illustrious patron.

11. Or Helladius (Euladius). See the introduction to *De praed. sanct.* and *De dono pers.*, (11).

226. Hilary to his father, Augustine, his most holy lord, longed for with all affection and greatly cherished in Christ

(1) If, in the absence of objections posed by opponents, the inquiries of those desirous to learn are generally pleasing to you, even when they desire to learn things of which they could without peril remain ignorant, I think the care we have devoted to our report will be still more acceptable. For this report, while it points out things mentioned by certain men which are contrary to the truth, busies itself in making provision, not so much for its own sake as for the sake of those who are both the disturbers and the disturbed, by recourse to the advice of your Holiness, most saintly lord, worthy of all our affection, and our greatly cherished father.

(2) These, then, are some of the views that are being aired at Marseille or even in some other places in Gaul: that it is a new theory and one useless for preaching which says that some are to be of the elect according to the purpose [of God], but that they are able neither to grasp nor to hold this salvation except through the will to believe which has been given to them. They think that all the force goes out of preaching if it is said that there is nothing left in man which can be aroused by it. They agree that all men died in Adam and that no one can be saved from that death by his own will, but they assert that it is consistent with truth, or at least consonant with preaching, to say that when the opportunity of gaining salvation is made known to human nature, laid low and never likely to rise by its own strength, it can be cured of its weakness through the merit by which it wills and believes, and that an increase of faith and a complete restoration follow as an effect. But they admit that no one can be fully capable of beginning any other good work, much less of carrying it through to completion. The fact that everyone who is sick wills, with a frightened and suppliant will, to be cured, should not, they think, be regarded as part of the work of curing. Taking the words, 'Believe and you shall be saved,'[1] they assert that one of these represents something demanded as payment, the other something offered; with the re-

---

1. Rom 10.9.

sult that if there is payment of what is demanded, then what is offered is attributed to it. They think it follows that faith is to be manifested by man, since this concession has been made to his nature by the will of the creator, and that this nature is not so debased or destroyed that it ought not or cannot will to be healed. Therefore, man is either cured of his illness or, if he does not will it, he is punished by being left with it. They say it is not denying grace to predicate such an act of will as its precursor, a will which only seeks its physician but is not able to do anything for itself. Referring to passages such as: 'According as God hath divided to every one the measure of faith,'[2] and the like, they try to make them mean that he who has begun to will is helped, not that the grace is given to make him will, while others equally guilty are excluded from this gift, who could likewise be saved if the will to believe were imparted to them as it is imparted to others equally unworthy. According to them, if such a will exists in all men so that each one is able to reject or to obey it, they think that the final casting up of accounts of the elect and the reprobate depends on the use that each one makes of the merit of free will which is given to him.

(3) When they are asked why the faith is preached or not preached to some or in some places, or why it is now preached, although in the past nearly all peoples were left without preaching, as some are today, they say it is a consequence of the divine foreknowledge and that truth was or is made known at that time and place and to those people when and where God foresaw that it would be believed. They claim to prove this not only from the testimony of other Catholics, but even by an earlier argument of your Holiness in which with no less transparency of truth you expounded this same grace, as, for instance, in that passage where your Holiness refuted Porphyry on the question of the temporal beginning of the Christian religion and said that 'Christ willed to appear among men and to preach his doctrine to them at the time when and the place where he knew there would be souls to believe in him.'[3] In that other passage from your book on the Epistle to the Romans at this

2. Rom 12.3.   3. Cf. Letter 102.

place: 'Thou wilt say therefore to me: Why doth he then find fault? for who resisteth his will?'[4] you say: 'He answers this query so as to make us understand that the first merits of faith and impiety are clear to spiritual men, and even to men who do not live like carnal men, and he shows God in his foreknowledge chooses those who will believe and condemns unbelievers, yet does not choose the former according to their works, nor condemn the latter according to their works, but makes it possible for the faith of the former to do good works and hardens the impiety of the latter by abandoning them to their evil works.'[5] Again in the same book you say in an earlier passage:[6] 'All are equal prior to the existence of merit, and among things that are equal it is utterly impossible to speak of choice. But since the Holy Spirit is given only to believers, God does not indeed choose the works which he himself makes it possible for us to do when he gives the Holy Spirit that we may do good works through love; nevertheless he does choose the faith of the recipient, because unless a man believes and is steadfast in his will to receive he does not receive the gift of God, that is, the Holy Spirit, through whose infused love he is able to do good works. Therefore, by his foreknowledge he does not choose anyone for the works which are to be his own gift, but he chooses according to his foreknowledge of a man's faith, and he chooses the one whose faith he foreknows in order to give him the Holy Spirit, that by performing good works he may attain eternal life. For the Apostle says: "It is the same God who worketh all in all."[7] But nowhere does he say: "God believes all in all, for what we believe is our own doing but what we do is his." ' There are other passages in the same work which they say they accept and approve as being in accord with the truth of the gospel.

(4) For the rest, they assert that foreknowledge and predestination or purpose amount to this, that God foreknows or predestines or proposes to choose those who will believe. Of this belief it is not possible to say, 'What hast thou that thou hast not

4. Rom 9.19.
5. *Expositio quarundam propositionum ex epistula ad Romanos* 62 (PL 35.2080).
6. Ibid. 60 (PL 35.2078).   7. 1 Cor 12.6.

received?'[8] since it remains in the same nature which was whole and perfect when it was given but is now vitiated. When your Holiness says that no one perseveres unless he receives the strength to persevere, they accept it in a limited sense as meaning that when this grace is given even to a sluggish soul it is to be attributed to a prior will of man's own, which they say is free only to this extent that it can will or not will to admit its physician. They profess to abominate and condemn those who think that any strength remains in anyone by which he can return to health. But they do not want this perseverance preached in the sense that it cannot be won by prayer or lost by obstinacy. They are unwilling to yield themselves to the unknown purpose of God's will when it is evident to them, as they think, that they have some beginning of will, whatever it may be, by which they may obtain or receive [grace]. That other quotation you gave as proof: 'He was taken away lest wickedness should alter his understanding,'[9] they dispose of as being uncanonical and therefore to be disregarded. Thus, the foreknowledge which they accept is to be understood as a foreknowledge of a future faith, and they claim that the perseverance which is granted to anyone is not a grace to keep him from sinning, but a grace from which man of his own will can fall away and thus become weakened.

(5) They assert that the custom of exhorting anyone is useless if it is said that nothing was left in man which could be aroused by correction. They admit an innate residue left in nature[10] in virtue of which, when truth is preached to the ignorant, this is credited as the benefit of a grace already present. For, they say, if men are so predestined to either side that no one can go from one to the other, what is the use of that external pressure of correction unless by it is roused in a man, even if not perfect faith, at least sorrow and compunction for his weakness, or he is frightened by the demonstrated danger of death? If a man cannot fear where there is cause for fear, except by that will which is received, no blame is to be attached to him because of

8. 1 Cor 4.7.   9. Wisd 4.11.
10. That is, after original sin.

his present unwillingness, but there is blame in and with the one who at one time was unwilling, so that he deserves this punishment for himself and his posterity of never willing to seek what is upright but always what is depraved. But if there is some kind of sorrow which is aroused by the exhortation of the preacher who rebukes, they say this is the very reason why one man is rejected and one is saved, and thus there is no need of setting up two classes of men to or from which it is impossible either to add or to subtract.

(6) In the next place they are displeased because a distinction is made between the grace given in the beginning to the first man and that which is now given to all, and that Adam received perseverance 'not as something to make him such that he would persevere, but as something without which he could not persevere of his own free will, whereas now the perseverance given to the saints predestined by grace for the kingdom [of heaven] is not that kind of help, but the perseverance given to them is not only such that they could not persevere without that gift, but it is even such that they would in fact persevere through that gift.'[11] They are so disturbed by these words of your Holiness that they say a kind of despair is thereby set before men. For, they say, if Adam was helped so that he could remain steadfast in justice or fall away from justice, and if now the saints are helped so that they cannot fall away if once they have received that perseverance of will which prevents them from doing anything else, or if some are left unhelped so that they either do not approach [to the faith], or if they have approached they also fall back, they say that the usefulness of preaching or of threatening appeals to that will which maintains the free power of persevering or of giving up, but not to the will which is constrained by the inevitable necessity of refusing justice, except for those who were created, along with those condemned as part of the universal clay, with the provision that they would be saved through the grace of redemption. Hence, they are willing to make this single distinction between the first man and the rest of human nature that this grace, with-

---

11. Augustine, *De correptione et gratia* 12.34 (PL 44.937).

out which he could not persevere, aided in him a will acting with unimpaired vigor; but for the rest of mankind with lost and ruined strength it not only raises up believers when they are prostrate, but also supports them as they walk. Outside this, they contend that whatever help is given to the predestined can be lost or retained by the force of their own will. This conclusion would be false if they thought it true that certain souls received such a grace of perseverance as made it impossible for them not to persevere.

(7) That is why they do not accept that view which admits a fixed number of elect and reprobate,[12] and that they do not support the explanation of that opinion which you set forth. Their view holds that God wills that all be saved, not merely those who will belong to the number of the saints, but absolutely all, making no exception of any. And in this there is no danger of anyone saying that some are lost against God's will; but, they say, in the same way that he does not will sin to be committed or goodness forsaken, yet it is constantly forsaken and sin is committed contrary to his will, so he wills to save all men, yet all men are not saved. The proofs from Scripture which you adduced concerning Saul or David[13] have nothing to do with this question which concerns preaching, they say, but they offer others which, according to their interpretation, favor grace in this sense that each one is helped after his will has acted, even to that election which is offered to the unworthy. They profess to prove this by passages both from your works and from those of others, which it would take too long to enumerate.

(8) They do not admit that the case of children can be used as an example for adults. They say that your Holiness carried the argument to the point of wishing it to be undecided and preferring to leave the question of their penalty in doubt. You remember that in Book III of your treatise *Free Will* you left it so phrased that it could give them this ground.[14] They do this also with the works of others whose authority is recognized by

---

12. Ibid. 13.39; 14.44.   13. Ibid. 14.45.
14. *De libero arbitrio* 3.23,66–68.

the Church, and, as your Holiness observes, this can be no slight help to the other side unless we produce greater, or at least equal authorities. Your most prudent Piety is not unaware how many there are in the Church who hold their opinions or change them according to the weight of names. Finally, now that all of us are weary of it, their discussion or, rather, their complaint comes to this, that they say—and those who do not venture to disapprove of this definition of doctrine agree with them—what need was there to disturb the hearts of the less intelligent by an unresolved argument like this? They also say that the Catholic faith was no less usefully defended without this definition for so many years, by so many writers of treatises, in so many previous books both yours and others', against other heretics and especially against the Pelagians.

(9) These are some of the things they say, my father, and there is an endless list of others which, to avow my inmost wish, I should have preferred to have you receive through me, or, since I have not deserved this honor, at least to have more ample time in which to collect and send you all the arguments by which they are influenced, so that I might hear what rebuttal is made on these matters, how far they can be refuted, or, if that is not possible, how much of it is allowable. But, since neither of these plans has worked out according to my wish, I have decided to do the best I could and send you this summary rather than remain entirely silent about this great opposition on the part of several. Some of them are persons of such importance that laymen are required by Church custom to show them the greatest respect. With God's help, we have tried to observe this without, at the same time, passing over in silence the points which our limited ability has been gathering together in order to give you a general idea of this question. So now, by way of reminder, I have sketched out these points in a summary fashion, as far as the haste of the bearer has allowed. It will be for your holy Prudence to discover what has to be done if the charge of these men, of such character and influence, is to be overcome or modified. I think it will be of little use for you to plead your case unless some authority is adduced which their tireless passion for argument cannot withstand. Certainly I

ought not to refrain from telling you that they profess to admire your Holiness in all your deeds and words with this exception. You will have to decide how this opposition of theirs is to be met. Do not be surprised that I have added something of a different tenor in this letter which, as far as I can recall, I did not include in my last one. This is the nature of their present pronouncement, except for what I have perhaps omitted through haste or forgetfulness.

(10) I ask that as soon as they are published we may deserve to have the books in which you are revising all your writings;[15] their authority will be of the greatest use to us, and in our anxiety to safeguard the honor of your name we shall no longer have to suppress anything that may not have been satisfactory to you. We have no copy of your *Grace and Free Will;* it remains for us to deserve to receive it, because we trust it will be of use in this controversy. However, I should not like your Holiness to think that I am writing this as if I were doubtful of the works which you have just published. Let it be penalty enough for me, exiled as I am from the sweetness of your presence which I used to drink in as life-giving nourishment, to be tormented by my separation from you as well as by the inflexibility of certain men who not only reject what is evident but even criticize what they do not understand. But I free myself from this suspicion so far as to reflect that my own weakness is so excessive that it makes me bear such men with too little patience. However, as I said, I leave it to your wisdom to decide what kind of measures to take. On my side, I have felt that as a return for that charity which I owe to Christ and to you I should not fail to speak of these matters which are in controversy. We shall gratefully welcome as an expression of that grace which all of us, both little and great,[16] admire in you, whatever decision you wish or are able to make, and it shall have for us a most beloved and revered authority. Because of the urgency of the bearer I greatly fear that I have not been able to cover everything, or that I have not done justice to what I have said, for I am aware of my own limited ability; consequently, I have arranged with a man[17] re-

15. The *Retractationes.*   16. Ps 103.25.
17. Prosper, writer of Letter 225.

nowned for character and fluency of style and learning to include all the details he could collect in his letter. I have taken steps to despatch his letter with mine. He is a man whom your Holiness might well judge worthy of your acquaintance, even aside from this emergency. The holy deacon Leontius, an admirer of yours, joins with my parents in sending you cordial greetings. May your Paternity be mindful of me and may our Lord Christ deign to give you to his Church for many years, my lord and father.

(11) I should like your Holiness to know that my brother and his wife, for whose sake we are leaving here, have vowed perfect chastity to God by mutual consent, and we ask your Holiness kindly to pray that the Lord may deign to strengthen and preserve them in this holy purpose.[18]

18. Indicated by editors as a postscript.

ON THE PREDESTINATION OF THE SAINTS

TO PROSPER AND HILARY

Introduction: The Opinions of Those in Provence

E KNOW that the Apostle has said in the Epistle to the Philippians, "To write the same things to you, to me indeed is not wearisome, but to you is necessary."[1] But the same Apostle, writing to the Galatians, when he saw that he had done enough among them by the ministry of his word to accomplish what he saw as necessary, said, "For the rest, let no one cause me difficulty," [PL 44.960] or, as it reads in most manuscripts, "Let no one be troublesome to me."[2] Now I confess that it troubles me that the divine words in which the grace of God (which is in no way grace if it is given in accordance with our merits) is preached, words which are so many and so manifest, are not yielded to. Still, I love the zeal and fraternal affection, my most beloved sons Prosper and Hilary, [961] which makes you wish such persons not to be in error, so that after so many books and letters of mine on this subject, you would have me write on it again—I love it more than I can say, and yet I dare not say I love it as much as I ought. This is why I write again to you,[3] and although I am now not with you, yet through you I continue to do what I believed I had already done sufficiently.

(2) After having closely read your letters, I seem to see these brothers, on whose behalf you show such pious solicitude that they not adhere to the thought of the poet, "Each man has hope in himself,"[4] and thus incur that which is declared not poeti-

---

1. Phil 3.1.
2. Gal 6.17. Vg agrees with "most manuscripts": *nemo mihi molestus sit.*
3. *Rescribo vobis:* apparently a reference to a lost letter.
4. Vergil, *Aeneid* 11.309.

cally but prophetically, "Cursed be the man who places his hope in man,"[5] should be treated as the Apostle treats those to whom he said, "And if in anything you be otherwise minded, this also God will reveal to you."[6] Certainly they still remain in the dark concerning the question of the predestination of the saints, but they have the source from which, if "in anything" in this matter they are "otherwise minded," God may reveal this also to them, if they walk in that to which they have come. Because of this, when the Apostle said, "If in anything you be otherwise minded, this also God will reveal to you," he added, "Nevertheless whereunto we have come, let us walk therein."[7] Now those brothers of ours on whose behalf your devout charity is disturbed, "have come" to believe with the Church of Christ, that all humankind are liable to punishment for the sin of the first man, and that no one is delivered from this evil save through the justice of the second man.[8] They also "have come" to confess that men's wills are anticipated by the grace of God[9] and to agree that each person can be sufficient to himself neither to begin nor to complete any good work.[10] Therefore, these truths, to which they "have come" and which they hold fast, separate them considerably from the error of the Pelagians. And further, if they "walk in" them and if they pray to him who gives understanding, and if "in anything" about predestination they "are otherwise minded," this also he "will reveal to" them. But let us also expend upon them the affection of our love and the ministry of our word, according as he gives, to whom we have prayed, that we might say in these letters those things which are suitable and useful to them. For whence do we know whether perhaps our God wishes to accomplish this purpose through our service, in which we become their servant in the free love of Christ?

2.(3) Therefore we ought first to show that the faith by which we are Christians is a gift of God, if indeed we can do this any more painstakingly than we have already done in so many large volumes. But now I see that I must reply to those who contend

5. Jer 17.5.   6. Phil 3.15.
7. Phil 3.16.   8. Prosper, *Ep.* 225.3.
9. Prosper, *Ep.* 225. 5.   10. Hilary, *Ep.* 226.2.

that the divine testimonies which we have cited regarding this
matter mean this: that we may know that we have faith itself
from ourselves, but its increase is from God, as if faith were not
given to us by him but was only increased in us by him, in virtue
of the merit by which it began from us.[11] Now this does not
depart from that opinion which Pelagius himself, before the
tribunal of the bishops of Palestine, as its own Proceedings testify, [962] was obliged to condemn, "That the grace of God is
given according to our merits,"[12] if it does not belong to the
grace of God that we begin to believe, but rather, because of
this beginning, an addition is made to us so that we may believe
more fully and perfectly, and thus we first give the beginning
of our faith to God, in order that we may receive in return from
him a greater completion of faith and any other goods that we
may ask for in faith.

Refutation from Scriptural Texts

(4) But against this error, why do we not instead listen to
these words: "Who has first given to him, and what recompense
shall be made to him? For of him, and by him, and in him are
all things."[13] And therefore, that very beginning of our faith—
from whom is it, if not from him? For it is not the case that, with
this excepted, all other things are from him, but "of him, and
by him, and in him are all things." But who would say that he
who has already begun to believe does not merit anything from
him in whom he has believed? From which it results that other
divine gifts are said to be added in recompense to him who
already has merit, and hence that God's grace is given according to our merits—a statement which Pelagius, when it was
raised in objection to him, himself condemned, so that he
might not be condemned. Therefore, whoever wishes in every
way to avoid this condemnable opinion, let him understand
that the Apostle spoke truly when he said, "Unto you it is given
for Christ not only to believe in him but also to suffer for

11. Prosper, *Ep.* 225.4, 6. Hilary, *Ep.* 226.4.
12. *De gest. Pel.* 14.30.   13. Rom 11.35-36.

him."[14] Both of these he shows to be the gifts of God, because both he says are given. He does not say, "to believe in him more fully and perfectly," but "to believe in him." Nor does he say that he himself had obtained mercy in order to be more faithful, but to be faithful,[15] because he knew that he had not first given the beginning of his faith to God, and had its increase returned to him by God, but had been made faithful by God, by whom he was also made an apostle. For the beginning of his faith is recorded in Scripture,[16] and the account is very well known, for it is read in our churches on a solemn occasion.[17] Thus, he felt an aversion to the faith to which he was laying waste and, being vehemently adverse toward it, he was suddenly converted to it by a more powerful grace, converted by him to whom, as the one who would do it, the prophet said, "You will turn and bring us to life."[18] Thus, not only from one who refused to believe did he become a willing believer, but even from a persecutor he came to suffer persecution in defense of that faith which he had persecuted. For it was given him by Christ, not only to believe in him, but also to suffer for him.

(5) And therefore commending this grace, which is not given according to any merits, but causes all good merits, he says, "Not that we are sufficient to think anything as from ourselves, but our sufficiency is from God."[19] Let them consider this well and weigh these words, who believe that the beginning of faith is of our doing and that only the supplementing of faith is from God. For who would not see that thinking comes before believing? For no one believes anything, unless he has first thought that it is to be believed. [963] However hastily, however speedily, some of our thoughts fly before the will to believe, and even if this will follows them in such a manner that it appears to accompany them, as though they were inseparable, still it is

14. Phil 1.29.
15. Cf. 1 Cor 7.25. *Fidelis* ('faithful') is always used here in the usual Christian sense, 'having faith.'
16. Acts 9.1-9.
17. Acts was read on Easter Sunday and immediately afterward. See Augustine, *Sermo* 315.1.
18. Ps 84.7.   19. 2 Cor 3.5.

222 PREDESTINATION OF THE SAINTS

necessary that all things which are believed, are believed after thought has preceded. Yet even to believe is in fact nothing other than to think with assent. For not everyone who thinks, believes, for many think in order that they may not believe, but everyone who believes, thinks, and in believing thinks, and in thinking believes. So in that which concerns religion and piety (of which the Apostle was speaking), if we are not "sufficient to think anything as from ourselves, but our sufficiency is from God," it follows that we are not capable of believing anything, as from ourselves, for we cannot believe anything without thought, but "our sufficiency" by which we begin to believe "is from God." Therefore, just as no one is sufficient unto himself for the beginning or the completion of any good work (which these brothers, as your letters indicate, already believe is true), so that in the beginning as well as in the perfecting of every good work, our sufficiency is from God, so no one is sufficient to himself either to begin or to perfect faith, but "our sufficiency is from God." For faith, if it is not thought, is nothing, and we are not "sufficient to think anything as from ourselves, but our sufficiency is from God."[20]

(6) Take care, brothers beloved of God, that a man does not raise himself up in opposition to God, when he says that he himself does what God has promised. Was not the faith of the nations promised to Abraham, and he, giving glory to God, believed most fully that that which God has promised, "He is able also to perform."[21] He therefore brings about the faith of the nations, who is able to perform what he has promised. Further, if it is God who produces our faith, acting in a wondrous manner in our hearts so that we believe, surely we should not

20. The idea here seems to be that we cannot control what thoughts come before our minds, and yet we cannot believe without some thought coming before our minds, so in that sense the act of belief cannot be up to us. This echoes Augustine's analysis of the act of faith in *Ad Simpl.* 1.2.21-22 (A.D. 396): "Who can welcome in his mind something which does not give him delight? But who has it in his power to ensure that something that will delight him will turn up, or that he will take delight in what turns up? If those things delight us which serve our advancement toward God, that is due not to our own whim or industry or meritorious works, but to the inspiration of God and to the grace which he bestows." See TeSelle, *Augustine the Theologian*, 179.

21. Rom 4.20-21.

fear that he cannot do the entire work, and because of this does man claim for himself the first part of this work in order to merit receiving the last from God? See if this leads anywhere else than to the contention that the grace of God is given wholly according to our merits, and thus that grace ceases to be grace. For in this way it is paid as something owed, not given gratuitously, for to the person who believes, it is owed that that same faith of his be increased by the Lord, and faith increased be the reward of faith begun, and it is overlooked, when this is said, that this reward is credited to believers not as grace but as something owed. And I fail altogether to see why in this case we do not attribute everything to man, so that he who could initiate for himself what he did not have could himself also increase what he had initiated—were it not for the fact that it is impossible to go against the most manifest divine testimonies, by which faith also, in which piety has its beginning, is shown to be the gift of God. Among such texts are the statement, "God has divided to everyone the measure of faith,"[22] and this, "Peace be to the brothers and charity with faith, from God the Father and the Lord Jesus Christ,"[23] and other similar statements. Not wishing therefore to contradict such clear testimonies, and yet desiring it to be his own [964] doing that he believes, man forms a sort of composite with God, so that he claims a portion of faith for himself and leaves a part for God. And, what is more arrogant, he takes the first part and gives the following to God, and in that which he says belongs to both, he puts himself first, God second.

Changes in Augustine's Own Position

3.(7) Such was not the sentiment of that pious and humble doctor, I am speaking of the most blessed Cyprian, who said, "We must take glory in nothing, since nothing is our own."[24] And in order to show this, he cited the Apostle, who said, "Or what do you have that you have not received? And if you have

22. Rom 12.3.   23. Eph 6.23.
24. Cyprian, *Ad Quirinum*, 3.4 (the title of that chapter). This work, written before A.D. 249, was a compendium of Scripture passages on various topics.

received, why do you glory, as if you had not received it?"[25] It was principally this testimony that also convinced me, when I was involved in a similar error, thinking that the faith by which we believe in God is not the gift of God, but that it is in us from ourselves, and through it we obtain the gifts of God by which we "may live temperately, and justly, and piously in this world."[26] For I did not think that faith was preceded by the grace of God, so that through it, it might be given to us that we might ask usefully. Except for the fact that we could not believe unless the proclamation of the truth had preceded, I thought that once the gospel was preached to us our assent was our own doing, and came to us from ourselves. This error of mine is sufficiently evident in some small works of mine written before my episcopate. Among these is that which you mentioned in your letters,[27] that is, my *Exposition of Certain Propositions from the Epistle to the Romans*. Eventually, when I was reconsidering all of my works and when I was putting that reconsideration into writing—a project of which I had already completed two books before I received your lengthy letters—and when in the first volume I had arrived at the reconsideration of this book, I spoke as follows:

Likewise, when I was discussing what God chose in a man not yet born, whom he said his elder brother would serve, and what he rejected in this elder brother, likewise not yet born—in relation to whom, on that account, I called to mind the testimony of the prophet, although it was uttered a long time afterwards: "Jacob I have loved, but Esau I have hated"[28]—I continued my explanation to the point where I said, "God, then, in his foreknowledge, has not chosen the works of any man, which he himself would give, but in his foreknowledge, he has chosen faith, so that he chose him whom he foreknew would believe in him, to give him the Holy Spirit, so that, by performing good works, he would obtain eternal life."[29] I had not yet sought diligently enough or discovered up to this time what is the nature of "the election of grace," concerning which the same Apostle says, "There is a remnant saved according to the election of grace."[30] This certainly is not grace if any

25. 1 Cor 4.7.
26. Titus 2.12.
27. Hilary, *Ep.* 226.3.
28. Rom 9.13; Mal 1.2-3.
29. *Propp. ex Ep. ad Rom.* 60.
30. Rom 11.5.

merits precede it; indeed then, what is given not according to grace but according to debt is recompense for merits rather than gift. Hence, I would not have written what I said immediately afterwards: "In fact, the same Apostle says, 'The same God who works all things in all';[31] but it has not been said anywhere: 'God believes all things in all';" and what I added: "What we believe, therefore, is ours; but what good we do is his who gives the Holy Spirit to those who believe,"[32] [965] if, at the time I knew that this faith also is found among the gifts of God which are given "in the same Spirit."[33] Both are ours, then, because of free choice of will, and both, moreover, have been given because of a "spirit of faith"[34] and charity. And it is not charity alone, but as is written, "love with faith from God the Father and our Lord Jesus Christ."[35]

And what I said shortly afterwards, "For it is ours to believe and will, but his to give to those who believe and will, the power of doing good 'through the Holy Spirit' through whom 'charity is poured forth in our hearts,' "[36] is indeed true, but true according to the same rule—both are his, because he himself "prepares the will,"[37] and ours also, because they are not done unless we are willing. For this reason too, what I also said later is certainly very true: "We cannot will if we are not called, and when, after the call, we have willed, our will and our course do not suffice if God does not give strength to the runners and lead whither he calls," and what then I added is absolutely true: "It is clear, therefore, that it is 'not of him who wills nor of him who runs, but of God showing mercy'[38] that we do good."[39] But I said little about the call itself, which is given according to the purpose of God,[40] for this is not true of all who are called, but only of the elect. And so what I said a little later, I said most truly: "For just as in those 'whom God has chosen,'[41] not works initiate merit but faith, so that they do good through the gift of God, so in those whom he condemns, infidelity and impiety initiate the penalty of chastisement, so that they also do evil because of the very penalty."[42] But that the merit of faith is also a gift of God, I did not think should be inquired into, nor did I say it.

And in another place, I said, "For him on whom he has mercy he causes to do good and him 'whom he hardens'[43] he abandons to do

31. 1 Cor 12.6.   32. *Propp. ex Ep. ad Rom.* 60.
33. 1 Cor 12.9.   34. 2 Cor 4.13.
35. Eph 6.23.
36. *Propp. ex Ep. ad Rom.* 61, citing Rom 5.5.
37. Prov 8.35 (LXX).   38. Rom 9.16.
39. *Propp. ex Ep. ad Rom.* 62.   40. Cf. Rom 9.11.
41. Cf. Mark 13.20, Acts 1.2.   42. *Propp. ex Ep. ad Rom.* 62.
43. Rom 9.18.

evil. But indeed this mercy is given to the preceding merit of faith and this hardness to the preceding impiety."[44] This is certainly true, but it was still necessary to inquire whether the merit of faith, too, comes from the mercy of God, that is, whether this mercy, then, is shown only to a man because he is faithful, or whether, in truth, it has been shown so that he has become faithful. For we read what the Apostle says, "I have obtained mercy to be faithful;"[45] he does not say, "because I was faithful." It is therefore in truth given to a faithful man—but that he has become faithful, has also been given. Very correctly, then, I have said in another place in the same book, "Since if, in truth, it is not according to our works, but by the mercy of God that we are called to believe, and that it is granted to those who believe to do good, we should not envy the gentiles this mercy."[46] However, there I did not discuss with sufficient care that call which is given according to the purpose of God.[47]

4.(8) You see clearly what my thoughts then were concerning faith and works, although I was struggling to commend the grace of God. I see that those brothers of ours are now of that opinion, because they did not take the same care, with which they read my books, also to join me in my progress in them. [966] For if they had taken such care, they would have discovered that this question is resolved in accordance with the truth of the divine Scriptures in the first of the two books which I addressed at the very beginning of my episcopate to Simplicianus of blessed memory, bishop of the Church of Milan and successor to blessed Ambrose. Unless perhaps they did not know of this work—in this case, see to it that they do know it. Thus, of the first of these two books I spoke at the beginning of the second book of the *Retractationes,* and what I said is as follows:

The first two books which I wrote as a bishop are addressed to Simplicianus, bishop of the Church of Milan who succeeded the most blessed Ambrose. They deal with various questions. I put into the first book two of these on the Epistle of Paul the Apostle to the Romans. The

44. *Propp. ex Ep. ad Rom.* 62.   45. 1 Cor 7.25.
46. *Propp. ex Ep. ad Rom.* 64.
47. *Retr.* 1.22.2-4. Here and in the following chapter, we quote, with considerable revisions, the translation of Sister Mary Inez Bogan, FOTC 60. 98-103.

first question is on the passage, "What shall we say, then? Is the law sin? By no means!"[48] up to the place where he says, "Who will deliver me from the body of this death? The grace of God through Jesus Christ our Lord."[49] In this question,[50] the words of the Apostle, "The law is spiritual, but I am carnal,"[51] and other words where he shows that the flesh wars against the spirit, I have explained as though he were describing a man still "under the law" and not yet living "under grace."[52] Long afterwards, I thought—and this is more probable—that these words could also refer to the spiritual man. The second question in this book deals with the passage where the Apostle says, "Not she only, but Rebecca also who conceived in one act of intercourse [two sons] of Isaac our father,"[53] up to where he says, "Unless the Lord of Hosts had left us a posterity, we should have become as Sodom, and should have been like Gomorrah."[54] In the solution of this question, I indeed labored in defense of the free choice of the human will, but the grace of God conquered, and only thus was I able to arrive at the point where I understood that the Apostle spoke with the clearest truth, "For who singles you out? Or what do you have that you have not received? And if you have received it, why do you glory as if you had not received it?"[55] Cyprian the martyr too, wishing to show this, embraced all this under the heading: "We must take glory in nothing, since nothing is our own."[56]

That is why I said above that it was especially this testimony of the Apostle by which I myself was convinced, when I thought otherwise about this matter; God revealed this to me, as I have said, when I was writing to Bishop Simplicianus, trying to resolve this question. Therefore, this testimony of the Apostle, when, in order to suppress man's conceit, he said, "What do you have that you have not received?"[57] does not permit any believer to say, "I have faith which I did not receive." These words of the Apostle completely suppress all the pride of such a reply. Nor can even this be said: "Although I have not a perfected faith, yet I have its beginning, by which I first believed in Christ." For here also the reply is "But what do you have that

---

48. Rom 7.7.
50. *Ad Simpl.* 1.1.7-9.
52. Rom 6.14.
54. Rom 9.29.
56. Cyprian, *Ad Quirinum*, 3.4; *Retr.* 2.27.1.
57. 1 Cor 4.7.

49. Rom 7.25.
51. Rom 7.14.
53. Rom 9.10.
55. 1 Cor 4.7.

you have not received? And if you have received, why do you glory, as if you had not received it?"

"*What Do You Have That You Have Not Received?*"

5.(9) [967] Regarding that opinion which they hold, that "of this faith it cannot be thus said, 'What do you have that you have not received?' for it has remained in the same nature, although corrupted, which when originally given was healthy and perfect,"[58] if it is considered why the Apostle said this, then one can see that it has no force for the purpose they desire. For he was concerned that no one should take glory in man, because dissensions had arisen among the Christians of Corinth, to the point where people were saying, "I indeed am of Paul; and another: I am of Apollos; and another: I am of Cephas;"[59] and from this he went on to say, "But the foolish things of the world God has chosen, that he may confound the wise; and the weak things of the world God has chosen, that he may confound the strong. And the base things of the world, and the things that are contemptible, God has chosen, and things that are not, as if they were, that he might bring to naught things that are, that no flesh should glory in God's sight."[60] Here the Apostle's intention is perfectly clear: to attack the pride of man, so that no one should take glory in man, and therefore no one should take glory in himself. Then after he had said, "that no flesh should glory in God's sight," he promptly added, in order to show in whom man ought to take glory, "But of him are you in Christ Jesus, who of God is made unto us wisdom, and justice, and sanctification, and redemption, that, as it is written, 'He that glories, let him glory in the Lord.' "[61] Now his intention has arrived at a point from which he goes on to say, rebuking them, "For you are yet carnal. For whereas there is among you envy and contention, are you not carnal, and do you not walk according to man? For while one says, 'I indeed am of Paul,' and

---

58. Hilary, *Ep.* 226.4. Hilary's opponents' point here is that our power to believe belongs to our nature and is a grace only in the sense that our nature is a grace or gift from God.   59. 1 Cor 1.12.
60. 1 Cor 1.27-29.   61. 1 Cor 1.30-31, citing Jer 9.23-24.

another, 'I am of Apollos,' are you not men? What then is Apollos, and what is Paul? Ministers through whom you have believed; and to everyone as the Lord has given. I have planted, Apollos watered, but God gave the increase. Therefore, neither he who plants is anything, nor he who waters, but God who gives the increase."[62] Is it not evident that the Apostle has no other concern than that man be humbled, so that God alone may be exalted? For in all those things which are planted and watered, he declares that the planter and the waterer themselves are nothing, but only the one who gives the increase, God—and even the fact that that person plants and this one waters, the Apostle attributes not to themselves but to God, saying, "to everyone as the Lord has given, I have planted, Apollos watered."[63] Thence, continuing with the same intention, the Apostle arrives at the point where he says this: "Let no man therefore glory in man."[64] For he had already said, "He that glories, let him glory in the Lord."[65] After these words and some other points that are connected with them, this same intention of his brings him to this conclusion: "But these things, brethren, I have in a figure transferred to myself, and to Apollos, for your sakes; that in us you may learn, that one be not puffed up against the other for another, above that which is written. For who distinguishes you? Or what do you have that you have not received? And if you have received, why do you glory, as if you had not received it?"[66]

(10) In this most evident intention of the Apostle, whereby he speaks against man's pride, so that man should not take glory in man but in God, it is, in my view, completely absurd to suppose that the Apostle has in mind the natural gifts of God, whether of our whole and perfect nature, such as was given to us in our original state, [968] or its vestiges, whatever they may be, in our fallen nature. For how can it be by gifts such as these, which are common to all men, that men are distinguished from one another? Thus the Apostle first said, "For who distinguishes you?" and then he added, "Or what do you have that

62. 1 Cor 3.2-7.   63. 1 Cor 3.5-6.
64. 1 Cor 3.21.   65. 1 Cor 1.31.
66. 1 Cor 4.6-7.

you have not received?" For a man swollen with pride in comparison to another might say, "My faith distinguishes me," or "my justice," or whatever else. It is to forestall such ideas that the good teacher asks, "But what do you have that you have not received?" And from whom if not from him who distinguishes you from another, to whom he did not give what he gave to you? "But if you have received, why do you glory as if you had not received it?" Now I ask, is the Apostle concerned here with anything else than that "He who glories should glory in the Lord"? But nothing is so contrary to this sentiment than for anyone to glory in his own merits as if he and not the grace of God were responsible for them—but a grace that distinguishes the good from the wicked, not one which is common to the good and the wicked. Therefore, let the grace by which we are living and rational creatures and distinguished from beasts be ascribed to nature. Let also be ascribed to nature that grace by which among men themselves the beautiful are distinguished from the ugly, or the intelligent from the stupid, and anything else of that kind. But that person whose pride the Apostle was trying to restrain was not puffing himself up in comparison to the beasts, nor in comparison to another man because of any gift of nature that might exist even in the worst of men. Rather, he was puffed up because he attributed some good thing which pertained to the morally good life to himself and not to God, when he merited to hear the rebuke, "For who distinguishes you? Or what do you have that you have not received?" For though the ability to possess faith belongs to our nature, is that also true of the actual possession of faith? "For not all men have faith,"[67] although all men have the possibility of having faith. But the Apostle does not say, "What can you have, the possibility of having which, you did not receive?" But he says, "What do you have that you have not received?" Accordingly, the possibility of having faith, like the possibility of having charity, belongs to the nature of man, but actually to have faith, as actually to have charity, belongs to the grace of the faithful. Hence that nature which is given to us and by which we have the possibility

67. 1 Thess 3.2.

of having faith does not distinguish one man from another; rather, faith itself distinguishes the believer from the unbeliever. Hence, when it is said, "For who distinguishes you? Or what do you have that you have not received?" whoever has the audacity to reply, "I have faith from myself, hence I did not receive it," straightway contradicts this very evident truth—not because it is not in the free choice of the human will either to believe or not to believe, but because in the elect the will is prepared by God.[68] Hence, also to that very faith, which is in the will, the passage applies, "Who distinguishes you? Or what do you have that you have not received?"

6.(11) "Many hear the word of truth, but some believe and others speak against it. Therefore the former will to believe, but the latter do not will." Who would not know this? Who would deny it? But since in some persons the will is prepared by God and in others it is not, we must indeed distinguish [969] what comes from his mercy and what comes from his judgment. "That which Israel sought," says the Apostle, "he has not obtained, but the election has obtained it, and the rest have been blinded. As it is written, 'God has given them the spirit of insensibility: eyes that they should not see, and ears that they should not hear, until this present day.' And David says, 'Let their table be made a snare, and a recompense, and a stumbling block unto them. Let their eyes be darkened, that they may not see; and bow down their back always.' "[69] Behold mercy and judgment: mercy upon the elect, who have obtained the justice of God, but judgment upon the others who have been blinded. And yet the former have believed, because they have willed, while the latter have not believed, because they have not willed. Hence, mercy and judgment were brought about in their own wills. Clearly, this election is through grace, not at all through merits. As the Apostle had earlier said, "Even so then at this present time also, there is a remnant saved according to the election of grace. And if by grace, it is not now by works; otherwise grace is no more grace."[70] Therefore, it is by grace that the

68. Prov 8.35 (LXX).
69. Rom 11.7-10, citing Isa 6.9-10 and Ps 68.23.
70. Rom 11.5-6.

elect have obtained what they have obtained; there preceded nothing which they might first give so that it might be given to them in recompense. God saved them for nothing. As to those others who were blinded, as it is clearly stated here, it was done in retribution. "All the ways of the Lord are mercy and truth."[71] But "his ways" are "unsearchable."[72] Hence, the mercy by which he freely liberates and the truth by which he justly judges are both unsearchable.

7.(12) But perhaps our opponents may say, "The Apostle distinguishes faith from works; indeed, he says that grace is not given because of works. However, he does not say that it might not be given because of faith." Indeed this is so, but Jesus says that faith itself is also the work of God, and he commands us to do this work. For the Jews said to him, " 'What shall we do, that we may work the work of God?' Jesus answered and said to them, 'This is the work of God, that you believe in him whom he has sent.' "[73] The Apostle thus distinguishes faith from works, in the way in which, in the two kingdoms of the Hebrews, Judah is distinguished from Israel, though Judah itself is [part of] Israel. But he says that man is justified "by faith . . . not by works,"[74] in this sense, that faith is first given, and from it the other things may be obtained, which are properly called "works", by which one lives justly. For he himself also says, "For by grace you are saved through faith, and that not of yourselves, for it is the gift of God,"[75] that is to say, "And when I said 'through faith,' even that faith is not from you but is God's gift." "Not of works," he says, "that no man may glory."[76] It is often said, "He deserved to believe, because even before he believed he was a good man." This may be said of [970] Cornelius, whose alms were accepted and whose prayers were heard before he had faith in Christ.[77] Yet he neither gave alms nor prayed without faith of some kind. For how did he call on him, in whom he had not believed?[78] For if he could have been saved without faith in Christ, the Apostle Peter would not have been sent like

71. Ps 24.10.
73. Jn 6.28-29.
75. Eph 2.8.
77. Cf. Acts 10.4.

72. Rom 11.33.
74. Gal 2.16.
76. Eph 2.9.
78. Cf. Rom 10.14.

an architect to build him up, although "Unless the Lord build the house, they labor in vain that build it."[79] And it is said to us, "Faith is from us, the other things pertaining to the works of justice are from the Lord," as if faith did not pertain to the building of which I speak, as if the foundation of a building did not belong to that building! But if this belongs to it first and foremost, then he labors in vain who seeks to build up faith by preaching, unless the Lord build it up from within by having mercy. Hence, whatever good works Cornelius performed, whether before he believed in Christ or when he believed or after he had believed, should all be attributed to God, lest perchance anyone exalt himself.

The Words of Jesus in John 6

8.(13) This is why our only teacher and Lord, after he said that which I quoted above, "This is the work of God, that you believe in him whom he has sent,"[80] adds a little later in the same discourse, "But I said unto you, that you also have seen me, and you believe not. All that the Father gives to me shall come to me."[81] What does "shall come to me" mean, but "shall believe in me"? But that this may happen is the gift of the Father. A little further on he says, "Murmur not among yourselves. No man can come to me except the Father, who has sent me, draw him; and I will raise him up on the last day. It is written in the prophets, 'And they shall all be taught by God.' Everyone that has heard from the Father, and has learned, comes to me."[82] What does "Everyone that has heard from the Father, and has learned, comes to me," mean except that there is no one who hears from the Father, and learns, and does not come to me? For if everyone who has heard from the Father and has learned comes, it follows that everyone who does not come has not heard from the Father and learned, for if he had heard and learned he would have come. Thus no one has heard and learned and yet does not come, but, as the Truth says, "Every-

---

79. Ps 126.1.   80. John 6.29.
81. John 6.36-37.   82. John 6.43-45, citing Isa 54.13.

one who has heard from the Father, and has learned, comes."
Far removed from the senses of the flesh is this school, in which
the Father is heard and teaches, that we may come to the Son.
The Son himself is also there, because he is the Word of the
Father, through which he teaches thus, and he does not do this
through the ear of the flesh but that of the heart. The Spirit of
the Father and the Son is also present there at the same time,
for it is not the case that he does not teach, or that he teaches
separately, for we have learned that the works of the Trinity
are inseparable. And he is indeed the Holy Spirit, of whom the
Apostle says, "But having the same Spirit of faith."[83] But this
teaching is attributed especially to the Father because from him
is begotten the only-begotten, and from him proceeds the Holy
Spirit. But it would take too long to treat of this subject in
greater depth. Also, I think that my work, in fifteen books, *On
the Trinity*, which God is, has already reached you.[84] Far removed, I say, from the senses of the flesh is this school, in which
God is heard and teaches. We see many come to the Son, because we see many believe in Christ, but we do not see when
and how they have heard this from the Father [971] and
learned. This grace is a very great secret—but who can doubt
that it is grace? Therefore, this grace, which out of the divine
generosity is bestowed secretly in human hearts, is rejected by
no one, no matter how hard-hearted he may be. For it is given
so that hardness of the heart may first be taken away. Therefore, when the Father is heard within and teaches, so that one
may come to the Son, he takes away the heart of stone and bestows a heart of flesh, as he promised by the word of the
prophet.[85] For it is thus that he makes them children of the
promise and vessels of mercy which he has prepared for
glory.[86]

(14) Why, then, does not the Father teach all people, in order
that they might come to Christ, unless it is that all those whom

83. 2 Cor 4.13.
84. The question of how certain actions can be ascribed particularly to one
person of the Trinity, although the Trinity always acts as one, is dealt with
especially in Book 1 and Book 2 of *De Trin.*
85. Cf. Ezek 11.19.   86. Cf. Rom 9.23.

he teaches, he teaches because of mercy, but those whom he does not teach, because of judgment he does not teach? "Therefore he has mercy on whom he will, and whom he will he hardens."[87] But when he has mercy, he endows with good things; when he hardens, he repays what is deserved. Or if, as some would prefer to distinguish them, these words are those of him to whom the Apostle says, "You say therefore to me," so that he may be regarded as having said, "Therefore he has mercy on whom he will, and whom he will he hardens," as well as the words which follow, namely, "Why does he then find fault? For who resists his will?"[88] it does not matter, for does the Apostle reply, "O man, what you have said is false"? No— rather he replies, "O man, who are you that you reply against God? Shall the thing formed say to him that formed it, 'Why have you made me thus?' Or has not the potter power over the clay, of the same lump"[89] and what follows, which you know well. Nevertheless in a certain sense the Father does teach all to come to his Son. For not in vain is it written in the prophets: "And they shall all be taught by God."[90] Jesus cited this testimony, then added, "Everyone who has heard from the Father and has learned comes to me."[91] Just as, therefore, we speak correctly when we say of a teacher of literature who is the only one in a city, "This man teaches literature here to everyone," not because all learn, but because no one, among those who learn literature there, learns from anyone other than him, so we rightly say, "God teaches all to come to Christ," not because all come, but because no one comes in any other way. But why he does not teach all, the Apostle revealed, insofar as he judged it was to be revealed, as follows: "[God], willing to show his wrath, and to make his power known, endured with much patience, vessels of wrath, fitted for destruction, that he might show the riches of his glory on the vessels of mercy, which he has prepared unto glory."[92] Hence it is that "The word of the

87. Rom 9.18.   88. Rom 9.19.
89. Rom 9.20.
90. Isa 54.13, cited according to John 6.45.
91. John 6.45.
92. Rom 9.22-23. Augustine omits the first words of vs. 22, *Quod si Deus* ('What if God'), thus changing the passage from a question into a statement.

cross, to them indeed that perish is foolishness, but to them that are saved, it is the power of God."[93] God teaches all these to come to Christ, for "He wills all" these "to be saved, and to come to the knowledge of the truth."[94] For if God had willed to teach even those to whom the word of the cross is foolishness, so that they would come to Christ, undoubtedly they too would have come. For when he says, "Everyone who has heard from the Father, and has learned, comes to me,"[95] he neither deceives nor is deceived. Perish the thought, then, that anyone does not come who has heard from the Father and has learned.

(15) "Why," they say, "does he not teach everyone?" If we reply that those whom he does not teach are not willing to learn, we shall be given this answer: And what happens to that which is said to him, "You will turn, O God, and bring us to life"?[96] Or if [972] God does not make men willing who are not willing, why does the Church, in accordance with the Lord's commandment, pray for her persecutors?[97] For in this sense also the blessed Cyprian[98] wanted it to be understood when we say, "Thy will be done on earth as it is in heaven,"[99] that is, just as for those who have already believed and are in a sense "heaven," so too for those who do not believe and for this reason are still "earth." What then do we pray for those who do not will to believe, except that God shall work in them that they will?[100] Certainly, the Apostle spoke of the Jews when he said, "Brethren, the good will of my heart indeed, and my prayer to God, is for them unto salvation."[101] What does he pray for those who

93. 1 Cor 1.18.
94. 1 Tim 2.4. This verse, in Augustine's text, reads, *Omnes vult salvos fieri, et in agnitionem veritatis venire.* Augustine precedes these words with *Hos enim,* thus reducing "all" (*omnes*) to "all these" (*hos omnes*). Vg accurately renders the Greek πάντας ἀνθρώπους, *omnes homines* ('all men'). For other attempts on Augustine's part to weaken the sense of 1 Tim 2.4, see *De corr. et gr.* 14.44 and 15.47. Augustine's opponents in Provence took this text literally; see Prosper, *Ep.* 225.5-6, and Hilary, Ep. 226.7.
95. John 6.45.   96. Ps 84.7.
97. Cf. Matt 5.44.
98. Cyprian, *De dominica oratione* 18 (written A.D. 251-2). See *De dono pers.* 2.4 and note.
99. Matt 6.10.   100. Cf. Phil 2.13.
101. Rom 10.1.

do not believe, except that they may believe? For in no other way do they obtain salvation. Therefore if the faith of those who pray precedes the grace of God, then does the faith of those for whom we pray that they might believe precede the grace of God? Not at all, since this is the very thing that is sought for them, that to those who do not believe, that is, those who do not have faith, faith itself be given. Therefore, when the gospel is preached, some believe and some do not, but those who believe, when they hear the voice of the preacher from without, hear from the Father and learn within, while those who do not believe hear the external word, but inwardly do not hear nor learn. That is to say, to the former it is given to believe, to the latter it is not given. For "No one can come to me, except the Father, who has sent me, draw him."[102] This is stated more clearly later. For after a little while, when he was speaking of eating his flesh and drinking his blood, even some of his disciples said, " 'This saying is hard, and who can hear it?' But Jesus, knowing in himself that his disciples murmured at this, said to them, 'Does this scandalize you?' "[103] And a little later he said, "The words I have spoken to you are spirit and life. But there are some of you who believe not." And the Evangelist adds, "For Jesus knew from the beginning who they were who would be believers,[104] and who he was that would betray him. And he said, 'Therefore did I say unto you that no one can come to me, unless it be given him by my Father.' "[105] Hence, to be drawn toward Christ by the Father, and to hear and learn from the Father that one might come to Christ, is nothing other than to receive from the Father the gift by which one believes in Christ. For it was not to distinguish those who hear the gospel from those who do not hear, but those who believe from those who do not believe, that Christ said, "No one can come to me, unless it be given to him by my Father."[106]

(16) Faith, then, both in its beginning and in its completion, is a gift of God, and let it not be doubted by anyone who does

102. John 6.44.   103. John 6.61-62.
104. Augustine's text here reads, *qui essent credentes* ('who would be believers'). In Gk and Vg, this phrase is negative, 'who would not be believers.'
105. John 6.64-66.   106. John 6.66.

not wish to contradict the most evident sacred writings that this gift is given to some, but to others it is not given. Why this gift is not given to all should not disturb the believer, who believes that from one man, all have gone into condemnation, a condemnation undoubtedly most just, so much so that even if no one were freed therefrom, there would be no just complaint against God. It is evident from this that it is a great grace that many are delivered and recognize, in those who are not delivered, that which they themselves deserved, so that "he who glories may glory" not in his own merits, which he observes as equalled in those who are condemned, but "in the Lord."[107] As to why God delivers this person rather than that one, [973] "How incomprehensible are his judgments, and how unsearchable his ways."[108] For it is better for us here to listen or to say, "O man, who are you that replies against God?"[109] than to dare to explain, as if we knew, what God has chosen to keep a secret—God who in any event could not will anything unjust.

Augustine's Response to Porphyry

9.(17) But that which you note[110] that I said in my small work against Porphyry,[111] titled *On the Time of the Christian Religion,* I wrote in order to bypass the present more painstaking and toilsome argument concerning grace, although its meaning, which could be developed elsewhere or by others, was not entirely omitted, even though in that treatise I had not wished to explain it. For among other matters, I spoke there in answer to the question proposed, "Why did Christ appear after so long a time?":

Hence, since they do not raise this objection against Christ, that not all follow his teaching (for they themselves are aware that this objection

107. 1 Cor 1.31.   108. Rom 11.33.
109. Rom 9.20.   110. Hilary, *Ep.* 226.3.
111. This is Porphyry the Neoplatonic philosopher (c. 232-c. 303), disciple and biographer of Plotinus and editor of his *Enneads.* In *Retr.* 2.57.1, Augustine expresses doubts that this question actually is the work of the famous philosopher Porphyry; however, modern scholars agree that it is from the latter's work, *Against the Christians* (Κατὰ Χριστιανῶν), which survives only in fragments. See the article, "Porphyre," DTC 12. 2561-74.

could truly, but vainly, be raised against the wisdom of their philoso-
phers or the divinity of their gods), what will they reply, if for the sake
of brevity in discussing this question—leaving aside any consideration
of the depth of the wisdom and the knowledge of God, where perhaps
some other divine plan is hidden in even deeper secrecy, and without
prejudice to other possible causes that the wise can search out—we say
only this, that Christ wished to appear to men and wanted his doctrine
to be preached among them at a time when and a place where he knew
that there would be some who would believe in him? Christ foreknew
that in those times and places in which his gospel was not preached,
all would respond to the preaching of the gospel as, not indeed all,
but nevertheless many people responded in his bodily presence, who
would not believe in him even after he had raised the dead. Even now,
when the declarations of the prophets about him are so evidently fulfilled, we see many such who are still unwilling to believe and who
would rather resist by human cleverness than to yield to divine authority, so clear and evident, so sublime and sublimely proclaimed far and
wide, so long as the human mind is small and weak in approaching
divine truth. Is it any wonder, then, if Christ knew that in earlier ages
the world would be so full of unbelievers, that he would with good
reason not wish to appear or to be preached to those whom he foreknew would believe neither his words nor his miracles? Nor is it incredible that at that time all were such as we have seen with astonish-
ment that so many, from his coming on up to the present time, have
been and continue to be. And yet from the beginning of the human
race, sometimes more obscurely, sometimes more openly, according
as it seemed to the divine judgment was more fitting to the times, he
did not cease to be prophesied, nor were there lacking those who believed in him, both from Adam to Moses, [974] and in the people of
Israel itself, which by some special mystery was a prophetic nation,
and in other nations before he came in the flesh. For considering that
the sacred books of the Hebrews mention some, as early as the time of
Abraham, who were neither of the offspring of his flesh, nor of the
people of Israel, nor of those who happened to be associated with the
people of Israel, yet who shared in this mystery [sacramentum], why
may we not believe that there were others elsewhere among other peoples here and there, although we do not find any mention of them in
the same authorities? Thus the salvation offered by this religion, the
only true religion, through which true salvation is truly promised, was
never lacking to him who was worthy of it, and whoever lacked it was
unworthy of it. And from the beginning of the human race even to

the end, salvation is preached, to some for reward, to some for judgment. And for this reason those to whom it was not announced at all were foreknown not to be going to believe; and those to whom it was announced nonetheless, although they would not believe, are given as an example of [what would have happened had it been preached to] the former; while those to whom it is announced and who will believe, these are being prepared for the kingdom of heaven and the company of the holy angels.[112]

(18) Do you see that, without prejudging the hidden design of God or other explanations, I wished to say as much concerning Christ's foreknowledge as might seem sufficient to refute the unbelief of the pagans who had put forward this question? For what is more true than that Christ foreknew who would believe in him, and when and in what places they would believe? But whether, when Christ was preached to them, they would have faith from themselves or they would receive it as a gift from God, that is, whether God only foreknew them or also predestined them, I did not consider it necessary to inquire or discuss at that time. Hence, that which I said, "that Christ wished to appear to men and wanted his doctrine to be preached among them at a time when and a place where he knew there would be some who would believe in him," can also be stated this way, "that Christ wished to appear to men and wanted his doctrine to be preached among them at a time when and a place where he knew there would be some who had been elected in him before the foundation of the world."[113] But since, if it had been expressed this way, it would have turned the attention of the reader to those problems, which only now, in order to correct the Pelagian heresy, we have been obliged to submit to a more lengthy and laborious discussion, it seemed best to me to say briefly what was sufficient for the question at hand—setting aside, as I said, the depth of the wisdom and the knowledge of God, and without prejudice to other explanations, which I thought should be discussed not then but at some other, more appropriate time.

112. *Ep.* 102.2.14-15 (written c. 409). In preparing this translation, we have made some use of the translation by Sister Wilfrid Parsons, FOTC 18, 157-59.
113. Cf. Eph 1.4.

10.(19) Similarly, when I said, "The salvation offered by this religion was never lacking to him who was worthy of it, and whoever lacked it was unworthy of it," if it is discussed and is asked how anyone can be worthy, there is no lack of those who will say, by the human will. But we say, by grace or divine predestination.[114] And between grace and predestination the only difference is this, that predestination is the preparation for grace, while grace is the gift itself. Thus, when the Apostle says, "Not of works, that no man may glory. For we are his [975] workmanship, created in Christ Jesus in good works," he speaks of grace, but when he says what follows, "which God has prepared that we should walk in them," [115] he speaks of predestination. This cannot exist without foreknowledge, though there can be foreknowledge without predestination. By predestination God indeed foreknew that which he himself was going to do, whence it was said, "He has made that which shall be."[116] Furthermore, he can foreknow even those things which he himself does not do, such as whatever sins there may be.[117] For, even though there are certain things that are sins and at the same time punishment for sins, so that it is written, "God delivered them up to a reprobate mind, to do those things which are not fitting,"[118] this is not the sin of God, but the judgment of God. Wherefore, the predestination of God, which has the good for its object, is, as I have said, the preparation of grace, and grace in turn is the effect of that predestination. Hence, when God promised Abraham that the faith of nations was in his seed, saying, "I have established you as a father of many nations,"[119] on which basis the Apostle says, "Therefore is it of faith that according to grace the promise might be firm to all the seed,"[120] such a promise was based, not upon the power of our will, but upon his predestination. For he promised what he himself would do, not what men would do. For

114. Augustine gives a similar explanation of this passage in *Retr.* 2.57.2.
115. Eph 2.9-10.   116. Isa 45.11 (LXX).
117. On Augustine's treatment of divine foreknowledge, see Kondoleon, as well as the literature cited in that article.
118. Rom 1.28.   119. Gen 17.5.
120. Rom 4.16.

even though men do good works which pertain to the honoring of God, it is he who brings it about that they do what he has ordered; it is not they who bring it about that he does what he has promised. Otherwise, the accomplishment of God's promises would not be in the power of God, but in that of men, and what was promised by the Lord, would be rendered to Abraham by men themselves. This was not what Abraham believed, but rather "He believed, giving glory to God, that whatsoever he has promised, he is able also to perform."[121] He does not say, "to foretell;" he does not say, "to foreknow;" because God can foretell and foreknow also what others do, but he says, "He is able also to perform." And thus the deeds are not those of another, but his own.

(20) Or perhaps God promised to Abraham the good works of the nations in his seed, so that he promised that which he himself would do, yet did not promise the faith of the nations, which men accomplish for themselves, but rather foreknew that men would accomplish it, so that he could promise what he himself does?[122] The Apostle certainly does not speak in this way, for what he very clearly says is that God promised to Abraham children who would follow in the footsteps of his faith. [123] But if God promised the works, and not the faith, of the nations, still, since works are not good unless they are from faith (for "The just shall live by faith"[124] and "All that is not of faith is sin"[125] and "Without faith it is impossible to please"[126]), we must nonetheless conclude that the fulfillment of what God has promised is in the power of men. For [in this case] unless man did that which without the gift of God belongs to man, God will not bring about that which he gives; that is, unless man first possesses faith from himself, God does not fulfill what he has promised, that works of justice are given by God. And this would mean that God's ability to fulfill his promises is not in

121. Rom 4.20-21.
122. See especially Hilary, *Ep.* 226.2, for the idea that the human will has the power to turn to God in faith but must rely on God's grace to do any good works.
123. Rom 4.12.   124. Hab 2.4.
125. Rom 14.23.   126. Heb 11.6.

God's power, [976] but in man's. But if truth and piety prevent
us from believing this, let us believe with Abraham that what
God has promised he is also able to perform. But he promised
children to Abraham, which people cannot be if they do not
have faith; therefore, he himself gives faith also.

11.(21) Truly, when the Apostle says, "Therefore is it of faith
that according to grace the promise might be firm to all the
seed,"[127] I am amazed that men would rather trust in their own
weakness than in the strength of God's promise. "But I am uncertain," someone might say, "of God's will toward me." What
then? Are you certain of your own will toward yourself, and do
you not fear, "Wherefore, he that thinks himself to stand, let
him take heed lest he fall"?[128] Therefore, since both wills are
uncertain, why does not man commit his faith, hope, and love
to the stronger rather than to the weaker?

(22) "But," they say, "when it is said, 'If you believe, you will
be saved,'[129] one of these is required and the other is offered.
What is required is in the power of man; what is offered is in
the power of God."[130] Why are not both in God's power, that
which he commands and that which he offers? For we pray that
he give what he commands. Those who believe ask that their
faith be increased, and for those who do not believe they ask
that faith be given to them. Thus faith is a gift of God, both in
its increase and in its beginnings. So, "If you believe, you will
be saved," is said, rather, in the same sense as it is said, "If by
the Spirit you mortify the deeds of the flesh, you shall live."[131]
For here also, of these two things, one is required and the other
is offered. "If by the Spirit," the Apostle says, "you mortify the
deeds of the flesh, you shall live"—thus, that by the Spirit we
mortify the deeds of the flesh is required, but that we may live
is offered. Shall we therefore agree to say that the mortification
of the flesh is not a gift of God, and not to confess it to be a gift
of God, since we hear that it is required of us, with life offered
as a reward to us if we have done it? May this be far from agreeable to the partakers and defenders of grace! For this is the

127. Rom 4.16.
129. Rom 10.9.
131. Rom 8.13.

128. 1 Cor 10.12.
130. Cf. Hilary, *Ep.* 226.2.

condemnable error of the Pelagians, whose mouths the Apostle right away shuts by adding, "For whosoever are led by the Spirit of God, they are the sons of God,"[132] so that we would not believe that we mortify the deeds of the flesh by our own spirit, rather than by God's. Furthermore, it was this Spirit of God of whom he was speaking, where he says, "But all these things, one and the same Spirit works, dividing to everyone according as he will."[133] And, as you know, among all these things, he also named faith. Therefore, just as the mortification of the deeds of the flesh, even though it is a gift of God, is nonetheless required of us, with life offered as a reward, so also faith is a gift of God, although when it is said, "If you believe, you will be saved," it also is required of us, with salvation offered as a reward. For these things are both commanded of us and shown to be gifts of God, so that we may understand not only that we do them, but that God brings it about that we do them, as he says very clearly through the prophet Ezekiel. For what could be clearer than when he says, "I will cause you to do"?[134] Read with care this passage from Scripture, [977] and you will see that God promises that he will cause them to do those things which he commands to be done. Nor indeed does he here overlook the merits, but rather the evil deeds, of those to whom he shows that he will return good things for evil, by the very fact that he causes them to have good works from that point on, when he causes them to carry out the divine commands.

The Predestination of Infants

12.(23) But this entire argument, by which we have defended "the grace of God by Jesus Christ our Lord"[135] as being truly grace, that is, have contended that it is not given according to our merits, although it is most evidently asserted in the testimony of the divine Scriptures, still creates some difficulty among those who believe that they are completely restrained from all zeal for piety, unless they can attribute something to

132. Rom 8.14.
134. Ezek 36.27.
133. 1 Cor 12.11.
135. Rom 7.25.

themselves, which they first give so that they may in turn be compensated. This difficulty has some relevance to the case of adults, who already exercise the choice of the will. But when we come to the case of little children, and to that of the very mediator between God and Man, the man Christ Jesus,[136] it is impossible to assert the existence of human merits that precede the grace of God. For surely it is not in virtue of any prior merits that some children are distinguished from the rest, so that they belong to the liberator of men, nor was Christ, being himself also a man, made the liberator of men by virtue of any preceding human merits.

(24) For who can understand what they say, that children leave this life still in infancy but baptized, by reason of their future merits, while others are said to die in the same stage of life unbaptized, because their future deserts are foreknown, but as evil, so that God rewards or condemns, not their good or evil life, but no life at all?[137] The Apostle indeed set a limit, which, to put it mildly, man's rash suspicions should not transgress. For he says, "We will all stand before the judgment seat of Christ, that everyone may receive according to what he has done through the body, whether it be good or evil."[138] "Has done," he said, and he did not add, "or would have done." But how it ever occurred to such men to think that the future merits of infants, which are not really future, should be punished or honored, I do not know. But why is it said that man is to be judged according to his bodily activities, when many things are done by the soul alone, not through the body, nor through any member of the body? Frequently these are so serious that such thoughts deserve the most just punishment, such as, to say nothing of other instances, when "The fool has said in his heart, There is no God."[139] Hence, what does it mean to say, "That everyone may receive, according to what he has done through

---

136. Cf. 1 Tim 2.5.   137. Prosper, *Ep.* 225.5.
138. 2 Cor 5.10. Augustine's text here differs significantly from Vg, which reads, "For we must all be manifested before the judgment seat of Christ, that every one may receive the proper things of the body, according as he has done, whether it be good or evil."
139. Ps 13.1.

the body," if not, "according to what he has done in that time while in the body," so that we may understand "through the body" as "throughout the time of the body"? For after the body no one will be in the body, except at the final resurrection, and then not to obtain any merits, but to receive a reward for good merits, or to suffer punishment for evil deserts. But in the intermediate time between the [978] laying down and the taking up again of the body, souls, according to what they have done throughout the time of the body, live either in torment or in rest. To this time of the body belongs also that which the Pelagians deny, but which the Church of Christ confesses, namely, original sin. Whether this sin is absolved by the grace of God, or by his judgment not absolved, then, when infants die, they either pass by the merit of regeneration from evil things to good, or by the merit of their origin from evil things to evil. This the Catholic faith knows, and on this point even some heretics agree, without any objection. And, though I marvel and wonder, I cannot understand how men, whose intelligence your letters indicate is by no means contemptible, could think that anyone might be judged not according to the merits which he had during the time when he was in the body, but rather according to the merits which he would have had if he had lived longer in the body; and I would not dare to believe that there were such men, if I could dare not to believe you. Nevertheless, I hope that God will help them, so that when they are admonished, they will immediately perceive that if those sins which they say would have occurred can, in those who have not been baptized, rightly be punished by God's judgment, they can also, in those who have been baptized, be remitted by God's grace. For anyone who says that future sins can only be punished by the judgment of God but cannot be forgiven by the mercy of God should consider how great a wrong he is doing to God and his grace—as if a future sin could be foreknown, but could not be forgiven. And if this is absurd, it is all the more reason to believe that, by means of the waters which wash away sins, God would help, when they die early in life, those who would have been sinners if they had lived a longer time.

13.(25) Perhaps our brothers will say that sins are remitted to those who repent, and therefore if those who die in their infancy are not baptized, it is because it has been foreknown that, if they lived, they would not do penance, while God foreknows that those who are baptized and depart from the body while still little ones would have done penance had they lived. Let our brothers note that, if this is so, it is no longer original sin that God punishes in the infants who die without baptism, but rather the sins which each one would have committed had he lived. Similarly for the baptized infants, it is not original sin that is washed away, but the sins which they would have committed had they lived. For they could not have sinned except at a more mature age, but God foreknew that some would do penance, and others would not do penance; therefore, some left this life baptized, and others without baptism. If the Pelagians dared to maintain this, they would no longer have to exert themselves to seek, in view of their denial of original sin, on behalf of unbaptized infants some place outside the kingdom of God where they enjoy I know not what kind of happiness of their own—especially when they are convinced that infants cannot possess eternal life, because they have not eaten of the flesh nor drunk of the blood of Christ,[140] and because for those who have not sinned at all, baptism, which is given for the remission of sins, would be a contradiction.[141] For then they could say straightforwardly that there is no original sin, but that it is in virtue of their future merits, had they lived, that those who

140. Cf. John 6.54.
141. On the opinion that unbaptized infants go to some place which is neither damnation nor the Kingdom of God, see *C. duas epp. Pel.* 1.22.40. Julian of Eclanum asserts this position explicitly (*C. Iul. op. impf.* 1.50). Pelagius himself was more cautious: "As for infants who die unbaptized, I know indeed whither they do not go [sc., the kingdom of heaven], yet whither they go, I know not" (*De pecc. or.* 21.23, translation NPNF 5. 244). The opinion that unbaptized infants go to some "middle" place of beatitude within the kingdom of heaven was condemned at the Council of Carthage in 418 (CCSL 149.70), but something not far from it or from Julian's position became standard in Medieval Latin theology as the doctrine of limbo (see, for instance, Thomas Aquinas, ST [Suppl.] 3.69.4-6). The opinion attributed to Caelestius, that infants who die unbaptized have eternal life, was condemned by Pelagius at the Synod of Diospolis (*De gest. Pel.* 11.23-24). Pope Innocent quotes John 6.54 in support of the condemnation of this proposition, in his reply to the Synod of Milevis of 416 (among the letters of Augustine, *Ep.* 182.5).

are separated from the body as infants either are or are not baptized, and that it is in virtue of their future merits [979] that they either receive or do not receive the body and blood of Christ, without which they could in no way possess life. And thus they are baptized for a true remission of sins, although they derived no sin from Adam, since the sins are forgiven them for which God foreknew that they would do penance. Thus with the greatest of ease the Pelagians could plead and win their case, in which they deny that there is original sin, and contend that the grace of God is given only according to our merits. But because the future merits of men, which are not really future, are unquestionably not merits at all, and this is very easy to see, not even the Pelagians were able to say this, and so all the more ought these people not to say it. For it cannot be said how upset it makes me that what the Pelagians have seen to be most false and absurd, these people, who with us, on the basis of Catholic authority, condemn the error of these heretics, have not seen.

14.(26) Cyprian wrote a book, *On Mortality*,[142] known and esteemed by many if not all of those who love the literature of the Church. In this book he teaches that death is not only not to the disadvantage of believers, but is even found to be to their advantage, for it removes a man from the risk of sinning and establishes him in the security of sinning no more. But what advantage is it if even future sins, which have not been committed, are punished? But Cyprian argues at great length and with great cogency that the risks of sinning are not lacking in this life and that they do not continue after it. And there he also cites this testimony from the Book of Wisdom: "He was taken away, lest wickedness should alter his understanding."[143] I also have cited this passage,[144] but you said that these brothers of ours had rejected it because it had not been brought forward

142. *De mortalitate*, written after a plague at Carthage, A.D. 252, which followed shortly upon the Decian persecution.

143. Wis 4.11.

144. Among the places where Augustine cites this passage in his anti-Pelagian writings are *Ep.* 217.15 (to Vitalis), *De grat. et lib. arb.* 23.45, and *De corr. et gr.* 8.19.

from a canonical book,[145] as if, even apart from the question of the attestation of this book, the truth itself which I maintained was taught from it were not clear. For what Christian would dare to deny that a just man, taken prematurely by death, shall find rest?[146] Whoever may have said this, what man of sound faith will think it should be resisted? Furthermore, if he should say that the just man who has deviated from the just life in which he has long lived, and has died in impiety, in which he has lived, I do not say for a year but only for a day, will suffer the punishment owed to the wicked, and that his past justice will avail him nothing,[147] who among the faithful will contradict this evident truth? Further, if we are asked whether, if he died at that time when he was just, he would have found punishment or repose, shall we hesitate to reply that he will find repose? Undoubtedly this is the complete reason why it was declared, no matter who may have said it, "He was taken away, lest wickedness should alter his understanding." This was said in view of the perils of this life, and not in view of the foreknowledge of God, who foreknew what would be, not what would not be—foreknew, that is, that he would bestow on him an untimely death, so that he might be withdrawn from the uncertainty of temptations, not that he would sin, for he was not going to remain in temptation. For concerning this life we read in the Book of Job, "Is not the life of man upon earth a temptation?"[148] Now why it should be given to some to be taken away

145. Hilary, *Ep.* 226.4. The canonicity of Wisdom, as that of other works not included in the Palestinian Hebrew canon (fully determined in the late first or early second centuries A.D.) but included in the LXX, was debated among the Fathers (NJBC, 1037-1043). Clement of Rome, Irenaeus, and Tertullian cite or allude to it, Clement of Alexandria refers to it as Scripture, Origen normally quotes it as Scripture while noting that the book "is not held by all to have authority" (*De princ.* 4.4.6), but Jerome excludes it from the canon (see David Winston, *The Wisdom of Solomon*, vol. 43 of *The Anchor Bible* [Garden City: Doubleday, 1979] 66-70). It was accepted as canonical by councils at Hippo in 393 and Carthage in 397 (CCSL 149. 43) and Carthage in 419 (CCSL 149. 108) (see Albert C. Sundberg, Jr., "The 'Old Testament': A Christian Canon," *Catholic Biblical Quarterly* 30 [1968] 143-55). An oddity of the history of the canon is that the Muratorian Fragment (from Rome, late second century) lists Wisdom among the canonical books of the *New* Testament.
146. Cf. Wis 4.7.   147. Cf. Ezek 18.24.
148. Job 7.1.

from the perils of this life while they are just, [980] while other just people are kept in the same perils for a more extended life, until they fall from justice—"Who has known the mind of the Lord?"[149] And yet from this it can be understood that even the just who maintain pious and virtuous ways of life up to the maturity of old age and the last day of this life should glory not in their merits but in the Lord.[150] For he who took the just man away through brevity of life, "lest wickedness should alter his understanding," is he who protects the just man, no matter how long his life may be, so that wickedness may not alter his understanding. But why God should have kept the just man here to fall, when he might have taken him before his fall—his judgments are perfectly just, but inscrutable.

(27) Since these things are so, one should not repudiate the statement of the Book of Wisdom, a book which has merited to be read over a long period of time from the platform of the lectors[151] of the Church of Christ, and to be heard by all Christians, from the bishops down to the lowliest faithful laity, penitents, and catechumens, with the respect that is owed to the divine authority. For certainly if I were to appeal to the commentators on the divine Scriptures who came before us to establish a defense of this judgment, which we are now compelled more fully and assiduously than previously to defend against the new error of the Pelagians—the judgment, that is, that the grace of God is not given according to our merits but rather is given freely to whom it is given (for it does not depend upon him who wills, nor upon him who runs, but upon God who shows mercy[152]), but by his just judgment it is not given to those to whom it is not given (for there is no injustice with God[153])—

---

149. Rom 11.34.   150. Cf. 1 Cor 1.31.
151. "The African (or Roman) plan uses the arrangement of the civil basilica without adapting it. In the African plan the presiding platform is divided into a place for presiding ministers and a place for the proclamation of the word. The presider and his assistants take seats in the apse which had been designated for the civil magistrate. The two legal stands on either side of the apse where the lawyers presented their cases became the lectern as well as the place for the music schola. The altar (often portable as Augustine indicates) was located in the center of the nave" (James Notebaart, "Lectern," NDT).
152. Rom 9.16.   153. Rom 9.14.

if I were to put forward a defense of this judgment from the words of the Catholic commentators on the holy Scriptures who came before us, the brothers for whom I write this work would certainly acquiesce, for you have indicated this in your letters.[154] But what need is there for us to scrutinize the writings of these authors, who, since the Pelagian heresy had not yet arisen, had no need to become involved with this question, which is so difficult to resolve? Doubtless they would have treated it had they been compelled to respond to such people. Thus it happened that briefly and in passing in some places in their writings they touch on what they thought of God's grace, but they dwell at length on those topics about which they were disputing against the enemies of the Church and on exhortations to those virtues by which we serve the living and true God in order to attain eternal life and true happiness. But what the grace of God meant to them is clearly and simply revealed in the frequency of their prayers, for they would not have prayed to God that the things he commands be done, unless it were given by him that they be done.

(28) But those who wish to be instructed by the opinions of commentators should prefer this Book of Wisdom, where we read, "He was taken away, lest wickedness should alter his understanding,"[155] over all commentators. For even those eminent commentators who lived near the time of the apostles, if they cited it, preferred it to themselves, because they believed that they were making use of nothing else than divine testimony. In any case, it is clear that the most blessed Cyprian, in order to show the value of an earlier death, declared that those who come to the end of this life, in which sin is possible, are removed from the dangers of sin. In the same treatise he declares among other things, [981] "Why, when you are about to be with Christ and assured of the promise of the Lord, not embrace the fact that you are called to Christ and rejoice that you are escaping the devil?"[156] Elsewhere he says, "Children escape the danger of their unsteady youth."[157] And in another

---

154. Hilary, *Ep.* 226.9.
156. Cyprian, *De mortalitate* 3.

155. Wis 4.11.
157. *De mortalitate* 15.

place he says, "Why do we not hasten and run, that we may
see our fatherland, that we may greet our ancestors? A great
number of those who are dear to us await us there, parents,
brothers, sons; a dense and vast crowd yearns for us; already
secure in their own safety, they are still much concerned about
our salvation."[158] By these and similar statements, that teacher
witnesses quite openly, in the clearest light of the Catholic faith,
that up to the laying down of this body the risks of sin and temptations are to be feared, but afterwards no one will suffer any
such things. And even if he had not so testified, when would
any Christian have had any doubt about this? How then would
it not have been to the advantage of a man who, fallen, ends
this life wretchedly in his fall from grace, and then passes into
the punishments owed to such persons, how, I ask, would it
not have been to his highest and greatest advantage if he were
snatched away by death from this place of temptation, before
he fell?

(29) And therefore, if we want to avoid reckless contention,
this whole question concerning the man who "was taken away,
lest wickedness should alter his understanding"[159] is closed.
And therefore the Book of Wisdom, which has deserved to be
read in the Church of Christ for so many years, and in which
this text is also read, ought to suffer no abuse because it resists
those who go astray on behalf of men's merits and thus oppose
the most evident grace of God. This divine grace appears above
all in the case of infants, in whom, since some of them reach the
end of this life baptized and others unbaptized, the mercy and
the judgment of God are sufficiently revealed to us—a mercy
that is wholly gratuitous, a judgment that is due. For if men
were judged according to the merits of the life which they did
not have, because they were prevented by death, but would
have had if they had lived, there would be no advantage for
him who "was taken away, lest wickedness should alter his understanding," and there would have been no advantage to
those who died after falling from grace, if instead they had died
before their fall—things which no Christian will dare to say.

158. *De mortalitate* 26.   159. Wis 4.11.

Hence, our brothers who, with us, on behalf of the Catholic faith, attack the pernicious error of the Pelagians, should not agree with this opinion of the Pelagians, that the grace of God is given according to our merits, to the point of seeking to invalidate—something which the Pelagians themselves could not dare to do—a proposition which is clearly true and Christian from antiquity, "He was taken away, lest wickedness should alter his understanding," and to set up instead something which we ought to think no one would, I do not say believe, but even dream of, that anyone among the dead is to be judged according to those things which he would have done had he lived for a longer time. Hence, let what we say, that the grace of God is not given according to our merits, be clearly seen to be irrefutable, from the fact that talented men who contradict this truth are led into saying these things, which must be banished from the ears and thoughts of everyone.

The Predestination of the Man Jesus

15.(30) There is another most illuminating example of predestination and grace, and that is the savior himself, "the mediator of God and men, the man Christ Jesus."[160] By what prior merits of his, whether of works or of faith, did the human nature which is in him attain this status? Let there be an answer to my question: Whence has this man [982] merited to be the only-begotten Son of God, assumed by the Word co-eternal with the Father into the unity of one person?[161] What good of his, of any kind whatever, preceded this union? What did he do beforehand, what did he believe, what did he ask, in order to arrive at this ineffable excellence? Was it not by the action of the Word assuming him that this man himself, from the time when he began to be, began to be the only Son of God? Did not that woman, full of grace, conceive the only Son of God? Was not the only Son of God born of the Holy Spirit and the Virgin Mary, not by the concupiscence of the flesh but by a unique gift

160. 1 Tim 2.5.
161. *Ille homo, ut a Verbo Patri coaeterno in unitatem personae assumptus, Filius Dei unigenitus esset, unde hoc meruit?*

of God? And was it to be feared that this man as he grew older might sin through free will? Or for that reason was his will not free, instead of being so much the more free, as he was the more unable to be a slave to sin? Certainly, all these uniquely admirable gifts, and whatever other gifts may most truly be said to be proper to him, human nature—that is, our nature—received uniquely in him, without any prior merits of its own. Suppose a man, if he dares, challenges God at this point and asks, "Why not I also?" And if he has heard in answer, "O man, who are you that you reply against God?"[162] suppose he does not restrain himself, but becomes more impudent, and says, "What is the meaning of what I hear, 'Who are you, O man?' Since I am that which I hear you to say, that is, a man, and he of whom I speak is also a man, why should not I also be what he is? But it is by grace that he is such and so great: why this diversity of grace, when the nature is common? Surely, 'There is no respect of persons with God.' "[163] Would anyone, I do not just say any Christian, but any madman, say these things?

(31) Therefore, in him who is our head, let there appear for us the very fountain of grace, whence he pours himself out through all his members according to the measure of each one. For the grace that makes any man a Christian from the time he begins to believe is the same grace by which one man from his beginning became Christ. That Spirit by which the Christian is reborn is the same Spirit by which Christ is born. It is the same Spirit that brings about in us the remission of sins as brought about in Christ that he had no sin.[164] These things God beyond all doubt foreknew that he would accomplish. This then is that predestination of the saints, which appeared most clearly in the saint of saints. Who can deny this predestination, who rightly understands the words of the truth? For we learn that the very Lord of glory was predestined, inasmuch as he was a man who was made the Son of God. This is what the teacher of the gentiles proclaims in the beginning of his Epistles: "Paul, a servant

162. Rom 9.20.   163. Col 3.25.
164. Augustine returns to this point below, at *De dono pers.* 24.67. See also *Enchiridion* 11.36 and *C. Iul. op. impf.* 1.138.

of Jesus Christ, called to be an apostle, separated unto the gospel of God, which he had promised before, by his prophets, in the holy Scriptures, concerning his Son, who was made to him of the seed of David, according to the flesh, who was predestined the Son of God in power, according to the Spirit of sanctification, by the resurrection from the dead."[165] Therefore, Jesus was predestined, so that he who was to be the Son of David according to the flesh should nonetheless be in power the Son of God, according to the Spirit of sanctification, for he was born of the Holy Spirit and the Virgin Mary. This is that unique act, performed in an ineffable manner, the assumption of a man by the Word of God, so that he might be truly and properly be called at once the Son of God and the Son of Man—the Son of Man because of the man who was assumed, the Son of God [983] because of the only-begotten God who assumed him— lest not a Trinity but a Quaternity be believed in. Such an uplifting of human nature was predestined, an elevation so great, so lofty, and so sublime that our nature could not be raised higher, just as for us the divinity could not humble itself more profoundly than by taking on a man's nature with the infirmity of the flesh, even to death on a cross.[166] Therefore, just as that one man was predestined to be our head, so we, being many, are predestined to be his members. Here let human merits, which have perished through Adam, be silent, and let reign that grace of God which reigns through Jesus Christ our Lord, the only Son of God, and the one Lord! Anyone who can discover in our head the merits which have preceded his unique generation, let him seek in us his members those merits which preceded our multiple regeneration. For that generation was not given to Christ as a recompense, but rather given, so that he should be born of the Spirit and the Virgin, apart from all the bonds of sin. And likewise our being born again by water and the Spirit is not a recompense for any merit but is freely given. And if faith has led us to the bath of regeneration, we ought not for that reason to think that we have first given something, so that our saving regeneration might be given us in return. For he has

165. Rom 1.1-4.   166. Cf. Phil 2.8.

made us believe in Christ who made for us the Christ in whom we believe. He made in men the beginning and the completion of their faith in Jesus, who made the man Jesus "the author and finisher of faith,"[167] for this is what he is called, as you know, in the Epistle to the Hebrews.

The Twofold Call

16.(32) For God calls his many predestined children to make them members of his predestined only Son, and not with that call by which those who did not wish to come to the wedding were called,[168] for with that call the Jews also were called, to whom Christ crucified is a scandal, and the gentiles were called, for whom Christ crucified is foolishness.[169] Rather, he calls the predestined by that call which the Apostle distinguished when he declared that he preached Christ, the Wisdom and the Power of God, to those who were called, Jews as well as Greeks. For he speaks thus: "But unto those who are called,"[170] to show that those others were not called, for he knows that there is a special and certain call reserved for those who are called according to God's purpose, "whom he foreknew and predestined to be conformable to the image of his Son."[171] This is the calling which he means when he says, "Not of works, but of him who calls, was it said to her, 'The elder shall serve the younger.' "[172] Did the Apostle say, "Not of works but of him who believes"? No, for he took this entirely away from man, so that he might give it all to God. Hence he said, "But of him who calls," not by any kind of call but by that call whereby one becomes a believer.

(33) This is also what the Apostle had in mind when he said, "For the gifts and the calling of God are without repentance."[173] Consider briefly also what subject he is treating here. For when he had said, "For I would not have you ignorant,

---

167. Heb 12.2.
169. 1 Cor 1.23.
171. Rom 8.28-29.
172. Rom 9.12, citing Gen 25.23 (spoken by God to Rebecca).
173. Rom 11.29.

168. Cf. Luke 14.16-20.
170. 1 Cor 1.24.

brothers, of this mystery (lest you should be wise in your own conceits), that blindness in part has happened in Israel, [984] until the fullness of the gentiles should come in. And so all Israel should be saved, as it is written, 'There shall come out of Sion he that shall deliver, and turn away ungodliness from Jacob. And this is to them my covenant,' when I shall take away their sins,"[174] he immediately added something that must be carefully understood: "As concerning the gospel, indeed, they are enemies for your sake: but as touching the election, they are beloved for the sake of the fathers."[175] What is meant by, "As concerning the gospel, indeed, they are enemies for your sake," except that their enmity, which led them to put Christ to death, has, as we see, indubitably served the purpose of the gospel? And the Apostle shows that this came about by God's design, who knows how to use even evil things for good; not that the vessels of wrath might be of benefit to him, but rather that by his own good use of them they might be of benefit to the vessels of mercy. For what could be said more clearly than these words: "As concerning the gospel, indeed, they are enemies for your sake"? Hence, it is in the power of the wicked to sin; but that, by sinning, they accomplish this or that in their malice is not in their power, but in the power of God, who divides the darkness [from the light][176] and orders it. Hence, even what men do that is contrary to the will of God, is not accomplished unless it be God's will. We read in the Acts of the Apostles that when the Apostles had been sent away by the Jews and had come to their own people and made known to them all that the priests and the elders had related to them, they all raised their voices in unison to the Lord and said, "Lord, you are he who made heaven and earth, the sea, and all things that are in them. Who, by the mouth of our father David, your holy servant, has said, 'Why did the gentiles rage, and the people meditate vain things? The kings of the earth stood up, and the princes assembled together against the Lord and against his Christ.' For in truth there assembled together in this city

174. Rom 11.25-27, citing Isa 59.20-21.
175. Rom 11.28.   176. Cf. Gen 1.4.

against your holy servant Jesus whom you anointed, Herod and Pilate and the people of Israel, to do what your hand and your counsel predestined to be done."[177] Behold what is said: "As concerning the gospel, indeed, they are enemies for your sake." For the hand and counsel of God predestined that such things be done by the enemy Jews as were necessary for the gospel for our sake. But what is the meaning of what follows: "As touching the election, they are beloved for the sake of the fathers"? Are those enemies who died in their enmity, and those from among the Jews who still die as adversaries of Christ, are they elected and beloved? Not at all, and what person, however stupid, would say this? But both of these terms, though contrary to one another, that is, "enemies" and "beloved", apply, not indeed to the same individuals, but nonetheless to the same Jewish people and to the same posterity of Israel according to the flesh, insofar as some of them belong to the laming and others to the blessing of Israel itself.[178] The Apostle explained this point more clearly earlier, when he said, "That which Israel sought, he has not obtained, but the election has obtained it, and the rest have been blinded."[179] Yet in both instances it was the same Israel. Hence, when we hear, "Israel has not obtained" or "the rest have been blinded," we should understand these words to mean the "enemies for our sake," but when we hear, "but the election has obtained it," we should understand this to mean those who "are beloved for the sake of the fathers," to which fathers these things indeed were [985] promised. "To Abraham were the promises made and to his seed."[180] Thus it is onto this olive tree that the wild olive tree of the gentiles is grafted.[181] Now, moreover, regarding the election of which the Apostle speaks, we should recall that it is according to grace and not according to debt, for "there is a remnant saved according to the election of grace."[182] The election

177. Acts 4.24-28, citing Ps 2.1-2. There are significant differences between Augustine's text and the Vulgate.
178. Augustine here alludes to Gen 32.25-33, in which Jacob wrestles with God, is lamed and then blessed, and given the name Israel.
179. Rom 11.7.   180. Gal 3.16.
181. Rom 11.17.   182. Rom 11.5.

obtained what they sought, while the others were blinded. According to this election the Israelites were "beloved for the sake of the fathers." For they were called, not by that calling of which it is said, "Many are called,"[183] but by that by which the elect are called. And thus after he had said, "As touching the election, they are beloved for the sake of the fathers," he immediately added the words from which this discussion arose: "For the gifts and the calling of God are without repentance," that is, they are irrevocably fixed and not subject to change. Those who belong to this calling are all "teachable by God"[184] and none of them can say, "I believed in order that I might be thus called." For the mercy of God preceded him, because he was thus called in order that he might believe. For all who are "teachable by God" come to the Son, for they have heard and learned from the Father through the Son, who states very clearly, "Everyone who has heard from the Father and has learned comes to me."[185] And of these none shall perish, because of all that the Father has given him, he will lose nothing.[186] Therefore, whoever is of their number does not perish at all, nor was anyone who perished one of their number. Because of this it is said, "They went out from us, but they were not of us. For if they had been of us, they would no doubt have remained with us."[187]

The Call of the Elect

17.(34) Therefore, let us understand the nature of this calling, by which they become elect—they are chosen not because they have believed, but they are chosen so that they may believe. For this calling the Lord himself sets forth clearly enough, when he says, "You have not chosen me, but I have chosen you."[188] For if the apostles had been elected because they had believed, certainly they themselves would have previously chosen him by believing in him, so that they would have merited to be elected. But the Lord removes altogether this

183. Matt 20.16.
185. John 6.45.
187. 1 John 2.19.

184. John 6.45.
186. John 6.39.
188. John 15.16.

possibility, when he says, "You have not chosen me, but I have chosen you." And yet they themselves undoubtedly chose him when they believed in him. Whence, for no other reason does he say, "You have not chosen me, but I have chosen you," than because they did not choose him so that he could choose them, but he chose them in order that they might choose him, for his mercy preceded them[189] according to grace, not according to debt. Hence, he chose them out of the world, when he lived here in the flesh, but they were already chosen in him before the foundation of the world. This is the unchangeable truth of predestination and grace. For what does the Apostle say? "As he chose us in him before the foundation of the world."[190] But if this is said because God foreknew that they would believe, not because he himself was going to make them believers, then the Son is speaking against this foreknowledge when he says, "You have not chosen me, but I have chosen you," [986] when in fact God foreknew this: that the apostles themselves would choose Christ, so that they might deserve to be chosen by him. Therefore, they were chosen before the foundation of the world by that predestination by which God foreknew his future actions, but they were chosen out of the world by that calling, by which God fulfilled that which he predestined. "For those he predestined, he also called," that is, with that calling which is according to his purpose. Therefore, not others, but "those whom he predestined, he also called"; not others, but "those whom he" thus "called, he also justified"; not others, but "those whom he" predestined, called, and "justified, he also glorified,"[191] to that end indeed which has no end. So God elected the faithful, but in order that they might be faithful, not because they already were faithful. The Apostle James says, "Has not God chosen the poor in this world, rich in faith, and heirs of the kingdom which God has promised to them who love him?"[192] It is by choosing them, therefore, that he makes them rich in faith, just as he makes them heirs of the kingdom. It is indeed rightly said that he chose this faith in them, since it was

189. Cf. Ps 58.11.   190. Eph 1.4.
191. Rom 8.30.   192. Jas 2.5.

in order to bring it about that he chose them. I ask, who could hear the Lord saying, "You have not chosen me, but I have chosen you," and dare to say that men believe in order to be elected, when rather they are elected in order to believe, lest, contrary to the statement of the truth, they be found to have first chosen Christ, to whom Christ says, "You have not chosen me, but I have chosen you."

18.(35) Listen to these words of the Apostle: "Blessed be the God and Father of our Lord Jesus Christ, who has blessed us with spiritual blessings in heavenly places, in Christ, as he chose us in him before the foundation of the world, that we should be holy and unspotted in his sight in charity, predestining us unto the adoption of children through Jesus Christ unto himself, according to the pleasure of his will, in which[193] he has graced us in his beloved Son. In whom we have redemption through his blood, the remission of sins, according to the riches of his grace, which has abounded in us in all wisdom and prudence, that he might show to us the mystery of his will, according to his good will, which he has set forth in him, in the dispensation of the fullness of times, to reestablish all things in Christ, that are in heaven and on earth, in him. In whom we also have obtained our lot, being predestined according to the purpose of him who works all things according to the counsel of his will, that we may be unto the praise of his glory."[194] Is there anyone who can listen carefully and intelligently to these words and then dare to have any doubt concerning that truth, so clear, which we are defending? God chose in Christ, before the foundation of the world, those who were to be his members, and how would he choose those who did not yet exist, unless by predestining them? Therefore he chose us by predestining us. And would he choose the impious and the impure? If the question is proposed, whether God would choose such people, [987]

193. Augustine omits the words preceding this relative pronoun, *in laudem gloriae gratiae suae*, thus changing its antecedent from 'his grace' to 'his will.' However, his discussion of this verse in section 36, below, seems to presuppose at least some of the missing words, and in 19.38, below, as well as in *De dono pers.* 7.15, he quotes, *gratiae suae, qua gratificavit nos in dilecto Filio suo*.
194. Eph 1.3-12.

or would not rather choose the holy and the spotless, who would hesitate which of them to answer, and not at once to render judgment in favor of the holy and the spotless?

(36) "Therefore God has foreknown," says the Pelagian, "who would be holy and spotless through the choice of their free will, and on that account chose them before the foundation of the world in his foreknowledge, by which he knew that they would be such. Therefore," he continues, "God elected them before they existed, predestining them to be children whom he foreknew would be holy and spotless, but he certainly did not make them such, nor did he foresee that he would make them such, but rather that they would be such." Let us consider, then, the words of the Apostle, and let us see whether God chose us before the foundation of the world because we were going to be holy and spotless, or that we might be so. "Blessed," he says, "be the God and Father of our Lord Jesus Christ, who has blessed us with spiritual blessings in heavenly places, in Christ, as he chose us in him before the foundation of the world, that we should be holy and unspotted."[195] He therefore does not say, "because we were going to be" so, but "that we should be" so. It is evidently certain, it is evidently manifest. Clearly, we were going to be holy and spotless, because God chose us, predestining us that we might be such through his grace. Thus, God "has blessed us with spiritual blessings in heavenly places, in Christ Jesus, as he chose us in him before the foundation of the world, that we should be holy and un-spotted in his sight in charity, predestining us unto the adoption of children through Jesus Christ unto himself." Consider what the Apostle next adds: "According to the pleasure," he says, "of his will," lest in such a benefit of grace, we take glory in the pleasure of our own will. "In which he has graced us," he says, "in his beloved Son," for certainly it is by his own will that he has graced us. Thus it is said that he has graced us by grace, just as it is said, he has justified us by justice. "In whom we have redemption through his blood, the remission of sins, according to the riches of his grace, which has abounded in us all wisdom

195. Eph 1.3-4.

and prudence, that he might show to us the mystery of his will, according to his good will." In this mystery of his will, he placed the riches of his grace, according to his good will, not according to ours, which could not be good, unless God himself, in accordance with his own good will, should assist it, that it become so. Then, after having said, "According to his good will," he added, "which he has set forth in him," that is, in his beloved Son, "in the dispensation of the fullness of times, to reestablish all things in Christ, that are in heaven and on earth, in him, in whom we also have obtained our lot, being predestined according to the purpose of him who works all things according to the counsel of his will, that we may be unto the praise of his glory."

(37) It would take too long to argue these points one by one. But certainly you must see with what evidence of apostolic testimony this grace is defended, against which human merits are exalted, as if a man should first give something to God in order to be compensated for it. Therefore, God "chose us in" him "before the foundation of the world, predestining us unto the adoption of children," not because we were going to be holy and [988] spotless through ourselves, but he chose and predestined us that we might become so. This he has done "according to the pleasure of his will," so that no one might take glory in his own will, but because of the will of God toward him. He did this "according to the richness of his grace," "according to his good will, which he has set forth" in his beloved Son, "in whom we have obtained our lot, being predestined according to his purpose," not ours, "who works all things" to the point that he works in us to will also.[196] Furthermore, he works "according to the counsel of his will, that we may be unto the praise of his glory." This is why we cry out, "Let no man glory in man,"[197] and accordingly not in himself, but "He that glories, let him glory in the Lord,"[198] in order that we may "be unto the praise of his glory." Indeed, God works according his purpose, "that we may be unto the praise of his glory," by being indeed holy

196. Cf. Phil 2.13.   197. 1 Cor 3.21.
198. 1 Cor 1.31.

and spotless, for which reason he called us, predestining us before the foundation of the world. From this decree of his proceeds that call which belongs to the elect, for whom "he works all things together unto good,"[199] because "they are called according to his purpose,"[200] and "the gifts and the calling of God are without repentance."[201]

The Question of the Beginning of Faith

19.(38) But these brothers of ours, concerning whom and on whose behalf we are now writing, will perhaps say that the Pelagians are refuted by this apostolic testimony, namely, that we are chosen in Christ and predestined before the foundation of the world, in order that we might become holy and spotless in his sight in love. For the Pelagians think, "We can, through our own power, once we have received God's commandments, become, by the choice of our free will, holy and spotless in his sight in love. And," they say, "since God foreknew that this would be the case, he chose and predestined us in Christ before the foundation of the world." Yet the Apostle says that God did not elect us because he foreknew that we would be such, but in order that we might be such through that very election of "his grace, in which he has graced us in his beloved Son."[202] Therefore, when he predestined us, he foreknew his own work, by which he makes us holy and spotless. And so the Pelagian error is duly refuted by this testimony: "But we say," they say, "that God has foreknown nothing of ours but our faith, that faith by which we begin to believe, and that he chose and predestined us before the foundation of the world, so that we might be holy and spotless through his grace and his work." But let our brothers also hear that passage in this testimony, where the Apostle says, "In whom we also have obtained our lot, being predes-

---

199. Rom 8.28. Here and elsewhere, Augustine reads the verb in this text in the singular, *cooperatur*, making its subject be "God." The Vulgate, followed by Douai, reads, "All things work together [*cooperantur*] unto good." In the Gk, the verb is singular, because the subject, πάντα ["all things"], is neuter plural.

200. Rom 8.28.   201. Rom 11.29.

202. Eph 1.6, including the words, *gratiae suae*, omitted from the quotation of this passage in 18.35 above.

tined according to the purpose of him who works all things."[203]
He, therefore, "who works all things" brings it about that we
begin to believe. Clearly, this faith does not precede that calling, of which it is said, "For the gifts and the calling of God are
without repentance,"[204] and of which it is said, "Not of works,
but of him who calls"[205] (although the Apostle could [if he had
wished] have said, "of him who believes"), and the election
which the Lord meant when he said, "You have not chosen me,
but I have chosen you."[206] For he chose us, not because we have
believed, but that we might believe; otherwise, we would be said
to have chosen him first, and it would be false (and who could
admit this?) that, "You have not chosen me, but I have chosen
you." Nor are we called because we have believed, but that we
might believe, and by that calling, which is without repentance,
it is brought about and accomplished that we believe. Nor must
these many things we have said about this be repeated.

(39) [989] Finally, following this testimony, the Apostle gives
thanks to God for those who have believed, thanking him not
indeed because the gospel has been proclaimed to them, but
because they have believed. For he says, "In whom you also,
hearing the word of truth, the gospel of your salvation, in
whom believing, you were signed with the Holy Spirit of promise, who is the pledge of our inheritance, unto the redemption
of acquisition, unto the praise of his glory. Wherefore, I also,
having heard of your faith in Christ Jesus, [and of your love][207]
towards all the saints, cease not to give thanks for you."[208] Their
faith was new and recent, after the gospel was preached to
them, and the Apostle, on hearing of their faith, gives thanks
to God on their account. If one were to give thanks to a man
for that which one either thought or knew he had not given,
this would be called flattery or mockery rather than gratitude.
"Be not deceived: God is not mocked,"[209] for even the begin-

---

203. Eph 1.11.   204. Rom 11.29.
205. Rom 9.12.   206. John 15.16.
207. "And of your love" (*dilectione*) is omitted in Augustine's citation of Paul's
text, but is here supplied as being necessary to the sense. It is present in Augustine's citation of this text at *Ep.* 217.28.
208. Eph 1.13-16.   209. Gal 6.7.

ning of faith is the gift of God, unless the Apostle's thanksgiving be rightly judged to be either erroneous or dishonest. And what about this next passage? Is it not apparently the beginning of the faith of the Thessalonians for which this same Apostle nevertheless gives thanks to God, when he says, "Therefore, we also give thanks to God without ceasing, because when you had received of the word of the hearing of God, you received it not as the word of men, but (as it truly is) the word of God, which works in you, in which you have believed"?[210] Why does he give thanks here to God? Certainly, it would be vain and meaningless if the person to whom he gives thanks for something is not the person who did it. But since this is not vain and meaningless, then certainly God, to whom he gives thanks for this work, is the one who brought it about that the Thessalonians, when they had received from the Apostle the word of the hearing of God, received it not as the word of men, but, as it truly is, the word of God. Therefore, God works in the hearts of men, by that calling which is according to his purpose and of which we have said much, so that they would not hear the gospel in vain, but, having heard it, they would be converted and believe, receiving it not as the word of men, but, as it truly is, the word of God.

20.(40) The Apostle also informs us that that beginning of men's faith is the gift of God, indicating it in his Epistle to the Colossians, when he declares, "Persevere in prayer, watching in it with thanksgiving, praying besides for us also, that God may open to us the door of his word to speak the mystery of Christ (for which also I am bound), that I may make it manifest as I ought to speak."[211] In what way is the door of the word opened, except when the understanding of the listener is opened so that he may believe, and once the beginning of faith is made, may accept those things which are preached and taught to build up in him the doctrine of salvation, so that, with a heart closed through unbelief, he does not reject and spurn those things which have been spoken? For this reason, the Apostle also says to the Corinthians, "But I will tarry at Ephesus

210. 1 Thess 2.13.   211. Col 4.2-4.

until Pentecost. For a great and evident door is opened to me, and many adversaries."[212] Can this be understood in any other way than that, when the gospel had been first preached there by him, many had believed, and many adversaries of the same faith [990] had arisen, according to the saying of the Lord, "No one can come to me, unless it be given him by my Father,"[213] and, "To you it is given to know the mystery of the kingdom of heaven, but to them it is not given"?[214] Therefore, the door is open in those to whom it is given, but there are many adversaries among those to whom it is not given.

(41) And again, in his second letter to the Corinthians, the same Apostle says, "When I had come to Troas for the gospel of Christ, and a door was opened unto me in the Lord, I had no rest in my spirit, because I found not Titus my brother, but bidding them farewell, I went into Macedonia."[215] To whom did he declare farewell except to those who had believed, that is to say, to those in whose hearts a door was opened for him to preach the gospel? But note well what he adds: "Now thanks be to God, who always makes us triumph in Christ, and manifests the odor of his knowledge by us in every place. For we are the good odor of Christ unto God, in those who are saved and in those who perish; to some indeed the odor of death unto death, but to others the odor of life unto life."[216] Behold why this most intrepid soldier, this most invincible defender of grace, gives thanks. Behold why he gives thanks—that the apostles are the good odor of Christ unto God, both in those who are saved by his grace and in those who perish in virtue of his judgment. But to lessen the irritation of those who have difficulty understanding these things, he adds this admonition: "And for these things who is sufficient?"[217] But let us return to that "opening of the door," by which the Apostle signifies the beginning of faith in his hearers. For what is the point of "Praying besides for us also, that God may open to us the door of his word,"[218] except to reveal to us most clearly that the very

212. 1 Cor 16.8-9.
214. Matt 13.11.
216. 2 Cor 2.14-16.
218. Col 4.3.

213. John 6.66.
215. 2 Cor 2.12-13.
217. 2 Cor 2.16.

beginning of faith is a gift of God? For we would not ask God for something in prayer, unless we believed that it was given by him. This gift of heavenly grace descended upon that seller of purple, of whom Scripture says, in the Acts of the Apostles, "God opened her heart, and she attended to those things which were said by Paul."[219] For she was called in such a way that she would believe. For God does what he wishes in the hearts of men, either through his help or his judgment, so that even through their own means there may be accomplished that which his hand and his counsel have predestined to be done.[220]

(42) In vain also do they object that what we have established from Scripture in the books of Kings and Chronicles—that when God wills the accomplishment of something which ought not to be done except by men who will it, their hearts will be inclined to will this, with God producing this inclination, who in a marvellous and ineffable way works also in us that we will— is not pertinent to the subject with which we are dealing.[221] What else is this but to contradict without saying anything? Unless perhaps they gave you some explanation of why it seems this way to them, but you have chosen not to mention it in your letters. But what that explanation could be, I do not know. Do our brothers perhaps think that, because we have shown that God so acted in the hearts of men and led the wills of those whom it pleased him to lead, that Saul or David was established as king, these examples are not pertinent to the subject, since it is one thing to reign temporally in this world and another to reign eternally [991] with God? Do they suppose, accordingly, that God moves the wills of those whom he has wished to the creation of earthly kingdoms, but that he does not move them to the attainment of a heavenly kingdom? But I think that it was in reference to the kingdom of heaven, rather than to an earthly kingdom, that it was said, "Incline my heart into your testimonies,"[222] or, "By the Lord shall the steps of a man be

219. Acts 16.14.   220. Cf. Acts 4.28.
221. Hilary, *Ep.* 226.7. Hilary refers to *De corr. et gr.* 14.45, where Augustine cites 1 Sam (Vg: 1 Kgs) 10.25-27 and 1 Chr 12.18, in reference to the establishment of Saul and David as kings.
222. Ps 118.36.

directed, and he shall like well his way,"[223] or, "The will is prepared by the Lord,"[224] or, "The Lord our God be with us, as he
was with our fathers, and not leave us, nor turn us from himself, but may he incline our hearts to himself, that we may go
in all his ways,"[225] or, "I will give them a heart to understand
me and ears which hear,"[226] or, "I will give them another heart
and a new spirit."[227] Let them also hear this: "I will put my spirit
in the midst of you, and I will cause you to walk in my just ways,
and to keep my judgments, and to do them."[228] Let them hear,
"The steps of a man are guided by the Lord, but how does a
mortal understand his own ways?"[229] Let them hear, "Every
man seems just to himself, but the Lord directs the hearts."[230]
Let them hear, "As many as were ordained to life everlasting,
believed."[231] Let them hear these words, and whatever others I
have not quoted, by which it is shown that God prepares and
converts men's wills also for the kingdom of heaven and for
eternal life. And think how strange it would be for us to believe
that God moves men's wills for the establishment of earthly
kingdoms, but that for the attainment of the kingdom of
heaven men move their own wills.

Conclusion

21.(43) We have said a great deal, and perhaps we could long
ago have persuaded you of what we wished, and yet we continue speaking to such intelligent minds as if they were obtuse
ones, to whom even that which is too much is not enough. But
let them forgive us, for a new question has compelled us to do
this. For, although in our earlier treatises we had sufficiently
established, with suitable [992] testimonies from Scripture,
that faith is a gift of God, a ground for objection was found,
namely that those testimonies were sufficient to show that the
increase of faith was a gift of God, but that the beginning of

223. Ps 36.23.   224. Prov 8.35 (LXX).
225. 1 Sam (1 Kgs) 8.57-58.   226. Bar 2.31.
227. Ezek 11.19.   228. Ezek 36.27.
229. Prov 20.24.   230. Prov 21.2 (LXX).
231. Acts 13.48.

faith, by which one first believes in Christ, is from the man himself, and is not a gift of God. But, the objection continues, God requires this beginning, so that after it has appeared, other things may follow, based, as it were, on its merit, and these are the gifts of God—but none of them is given gratuitously, even though in them God's grace is proclaimed, which is not grace unless it is gratuitous. You see how absurd this is. Therefore, we undertook, as far as we could, to show that even this very beginning of faith is a gift of God. And if we have done this at greater length than might have been desired by those for whom it was written, we are ready to be reproached by them for it, provided that they nevertheless will admit that, even if at much greater length than they would like, even at the cost of boredom and weariness on the part of those who understand, we have accomplished what we set out to do: that is, have shown that even the beginning of faith, like continence, patience, justice, piety, and other things of which there is no dispute with our brothers, is a gift of God. Therefore, let us conclude this volume, that too great a length of one book may not be displeasing to the reader.

ON THE GIFT OF PERSEVERANCE

TO PROSPER AND HILARY

Introduction

HE SUBJECT of perseverance is now to be considered more carefully (in the former book we have already said something about it when dealing with the beginning of faith[1]). What we maintain, then, is that the perseverance by which we persevere in Christ to the end is a gift of God. And by "the end" I mean the time at which this life is finished, during which alone there is the peril of falling. Thus, it is uncertain whether anyone has received this gift so long as he is still living. [PL 45.994] For if he falls before his death, he is said, and quite rightly said, not to have persevered. How, therefore, could he who has not persevered be said to have received or possessed perseverance? Now if a man were to have continence, and later fall away and become incontinent, or likewise were to have justice, or patience, or faith itself, and fall away, he would rightly be said to have had it but not to have it now. For he was continent, or just, or patient, or faithful, [995] for a time. But when he has ceased to be so, he no longer is what he was. But he who has not persevered, how could he have been "persevering," when it is only by persevering that a person can show that he is persevering, and he has not done this? Now someone might resist this argument by saying, "Suppose that after a person became a believer, he lived, let us say, ten years, and that halfway through that period he fell away from his faith—did he not persevere for five years?" I will not argue about words, if someone thinks that this should also be called perseverance, for however long it lasted. But certainly a person

1. See, for instance, *De praed. sanct.* 8.16 and 14.26–29.

271

who did not persevere to the end can in no way be said to have
had that perseverance of which we are now speaking, by which
one perseveres in Christ to the end. Someone who was a believer for only a year, or as much shorter a time as one may
think, if he lived faithfully until death, possessed this perseverance, rather than one who believed for many years, but then a
short time before death fell away from steadfastness of faith.

The Grace of Final Perseverance

2.(2) This being established, let us consider whether this perseverance, of which it is said, "He that shall persevere unto the
end, shall be saved,"[2] is a gift of God. For if it is not, how is that
statement of the Apostle true, "Unto you it is given for Christ,
not only to believe in him, but also to suffer for him"?[3] Now of
these things, the one relates to the beginning and the other to
the end. Nevertheless, both are said to be gifts of God, for both
are said to be given, as we have already said above.[4] For what is
more truly the beginning for a Christian than to believe in
Christ? What better end than to suffer for Christ? Nevertheless, in that which concerns faith in Christ, whatever sort of
objection has been raised, that not the beginning but the increase of faith should be called the gift of God—to this opinion,
with the help of God, I have responded sufficiently above.[5] But
what argument could be made that perseverance to the end is
not given in Christ to the one to whom it is given to suffer for
Christ, or, to put it more precisely, to whom it is given to die
for Christ? For the Apostle Peter also shows us that this is the
gift of God when he says, "It is better doing good (if such be the
will of God) to suffer, than doing evil."[6] When he says, "If such
be the will of God," he shows that it is a divine gift, but not one
given to all the saints, to suffer for the sake of Christ. Nor do
those whom the will of God does not wish to arrive at the experience and glory of suffering fail to attain the kingdom of God,
if they have persevered in Christ to the end. But who would say

2. Matt 10.22.   3. Phil 1.29.
4. De praed. sanct. 2.4.   5. De praed. sanct., passim.
6. 1 Pet 3.17.

that this perseverance is not given to those who die in Christ from bodily sickness or some accident, although a far more difficult perseverance is given to those who suffer even death itself for the sake of Christ? [I say "more difficult"] for it is much more difficult to persevere when a persecutor is endeavoring that one not persevere, and on this account one is sustained in perseverance unto death. The latter perseverance is more difficult to have, the former easier, but for him to whom nothing is difficult, it is easy to give either one. For God has promised this in saying, [996] "I will give my fear in their heart, that they may not revolt from me."[7] And what else do these words mean but, such and so great shall be my fear, which I will give into their heart, that they will adhere with perseverance to me?

(3) Moreover, why is this perseverance asked for from God, if it is not given by God? Is not this petition a mockery, when that is asked of him which it is known he does not himself give, but which is in the power of a man without his gift? Just as it is also a mockery to give thanks, if one gives thanks to God for that which he did not give or do. But what I have said of the latter case,[8] I say also here of the former: "Be not deceived," says the Apostle, "God is not mocked."[9] O man, God is a witness not only of your words, but also of your thoughts; if you ask sincerely and faithfully anything of one who is so rich, believe that you will receive that which you ask from him from whom you ask it. Do not honor him with your lips, and in your heart extol yourself over him, by believing that you already possess from yourself what you are pretending to ask from him. Or do we perhaps not ask for this perseverance from him? Anyone who says this is not to be refuted by my arguments, but rather must be overwhelmed by the prayers of the saints. But is there really anyone among them who does not ask of God that he persevere in him, considering that in that very prayer which is called the Lord's Prayer, because the Lord taught it, when it is prayed by the saints, almost nothing else is understood to be prayed for but perseverance?

7. Jer 32.40.
9. Gal 6.7.

8. *De praed. sanct.* 19.39.

(4) Read a little more attentively the commentary on this prayer in the book on this subject, titled, *On the Lord's Prayer*,[10] by the blessed martyr Cyprian, and see what an antidote he had prepared, and how many years ahead of time, against the future poisons of the Pelagians. As you know, there are three points which the catholic Church especially defends against them. The first of these is that the grace of God is not given according to our merits, for even all the merits of the just are gifts of God and conferred by his grace. The second is that no one, no matter how just he may be, lives in this corruptible body without some kind of sin. The third is that a man is born answerable for the sin of the first man and held by the bond of condemnation, unless the guilt contracted through generation is absolved through regeneration. Of these three, the one of which I have spoken last is the only one which is not discussed in the above-mentioned work of that glorious martyr, but the other two are developed with such penetrating clarity there that the heretics of whom I have spoken, the new enemies of the grace of Christ, are found to have been convicted long before they were born. Thus, among the merits of the saints, which are nothing if not gifts of God, he asserts that perseverance also is a gift of God, declaring, "We say, 'Hallowed be thy name,'[11] not because we wish, for God, that he be hallowed by our prayers, but rather because we ask of him that his name be hallowed in us. Besides, by whom is God sanctified, he who himself sanctifies? But because he himself said, 'Be you holy because I am holy,'[12] we ask and beg [997] that we who were sanctified in baptism may persevere in that which we have begun to be."[13] A little later, still discussing the same subject and teaching that we should ask for perseverance from the Lord,[14]

10. Cyprian, *De dominica oratione*. When controversy broke out at Hadrumetum (see Introduction to this and the preceding work), Augustine read through this work of Cyprian with three of the monks, who had come to him (*Ep.* 215.2). He also commends it to Valentinus, the abbot of Hadrumetum, as showing how Cyprian appeals to the free will of his readers to show "that they are to ask in prayer for help to fulfill all that the law commands" (*De grat. et lib. arb.* 13.26, translation by Robert P. Russell, O.S.A., FOTC 59.280).
11. For the text of the Lord's Prayer, see Matt 6.9–13.
12. Lev 19.2. 13. Cyprian, *De dom. or.* 12.
14. Correcting BA: *Domini* to *Domino*.

which he could in no way rightly and truly do, unless this was also God's gift, he says, "We pray that this sanctification may remain in us, and because our Lord and judge admonishes the man who was healed and revived by him not to sin, lest something worse happen to him,[15] we make this entreaty with continual prayers, day and night we ask, that the sanctification and vivification which is received through the grace of God may be preserved in us by his protection."[16] Thus it is perseverance in sanctification, that is, that we should persevere in sanctification, that this teacher understands us to be asking from God when we who are sanctified declare, "Hallowed be thy name." For what does it mean to ask for that which we have already received, unless to ask that it be secured for us not to cease to possess it? Hence, just as the saint, when he prays to God that he may be holy, is certainly asking that he may continue to be holy, so also the chaste person, when he asks that he may be chaste, the continent, that he may be continent, the just, that he may be just, the pious, that he may be pious, and so on for the other things, which we maintain against the Pelagians are gifts of God—undoubtedly these persons are asking that they may persevere in those good things which they acknowledge that they have received. And if they receive this, surely they also receive perseverance itself, the great gift of God by which his other gifts are preserved.

(5) What do we understand by these words, "Thy kingdom come"? Do we not ask that that come also to us which we do not doubt will come to all the saints? Here too, then, what do they who are already holy pray for except that they may persevere in that holiness which has been granted to them? For only in this way will the kingdom of God come to them, which certainly will come, not to others, but to those who persevere to the end.

3.(6) The third petition is, "Thy will be done in heaven and on earth," or, as it is read in most manuscripts and more often used by those praying, "on earth as it is in heaven," which most interpret to mean, "May we also like the holy angels do your will." But our teacher and martyr wishes it understood that

15. Cf. John 5.14.
16. Cyprian, *De dom. or.* 12.

"heaven and earth" refers to the spirit and the flesh, and that we are praying that we do the will of God with both of them in harmony.[17] He also notes in these words another meaning in conformity with the soundest faith, of which we have already spoken above,[18] namely, that believers, who, being clothed with the heavenly man, are not without justice designated by the name of "heaven," are understood to be praying for unbelievers, who are still "earth," carrying only the earthly man from their first birth. Here he clearly shows that even the beginning of faith is a gift of God, since the holy Church prays not only for believers, that faith may be increased or persevere in them, but also for unbelievers, that they may begin to have that which they did not possess in any way, and against which, moreover, they were venting their hostility. But now I am not arguing about the beginning of faith, with which I have already dealt at some length in the first book, but rather about that perseverance which must be had unto the end. [998] For this indeed the saints, who do the will of God, also pray, saying in the Prayer, "Thy will be done." Since it has already been accomplished in them, why do they still ask that it be done, unless that they may persevere in that which they have begun to be? Nevertheless it may here be said that the saints do not ask that the will of God be done in heaven, but that it be done on earth as in heaven, in other words, that earth may imitate heaven, that is, that a man may imitate an angel, or an unbeliever a believer, and thus that the saints pray that that may be, which is not yet, not that that which is may persevere. So no matter how much men may excel in sanctity, they are still not equal to the angels of God, and thus the will of God is not yet accomplished in them as it is in heaven. If we grant this, then in that part where we ask that men may from unbelievers become believers, we seem to be desiring not perseverance but rather the beginning [of faith]. But in that part where we ask that men may be made equal to the angels of God in doing the will of God, when the saints pray for this, they are shown to be praying for perseverance, for no one arrives at that supreme beatitude, which is in the kingdom, unless

17. Cyprian, *De dom. or.* 16.   18. *De praed. sanct.* 8.15.

he persevere to the end in that sanctity which he has received on earth.

4.(7) The fourth petition is, "Give us this day our daily bread." Here too the blessed Cyprian shows how perseverance is understood to be asked for. Among other things he says the following: "But we request that this bread be given to us every day, so that we who are in Christ and every day receive the eucharist as the food of salvation, may not, through the occurrence of some rather grave sin, be separated from the body of Christ by being excluded from communion and prevented from partaking in the heavenly bread."[19] These words of the holy man of God make it perfectly clear that the saints implore God for perseverance, when they say, "Give us this day our daily bread," with this intention, that they not be separated from the body of Christ, but may continue in the sanctity by which they admit no offense whereby they would deserve to be separated from it.

5.(8) In the fifth petition we say, "Forgive us our debts as we also forgive our debtors." This is the only petition in which perseverance is not found to be requested. For the sins for which we ask forgiveness belong to the past, while perseverance, which saves us for eternity, is indeed indispensable for the period of this life, not for that time which is past, but rather for that which remains, even to the end. Nevertheless, it is worth the effort to consider briefly how even in this petition the heretics who were to appear much later were even then transfixed by the tongue of Cyprian as by the most invincible lance of truth. For the Pelagians are bold enough to say that the just man is entirely without sin in this life and that in the person of such just men there is already present among us the Church which has no spot or wrinkle or anything similar[20] and is the one and only spouse of Christ, as if the Church which repeats throughout all the earth these words learned from him, "Forgive us our debts," were not really his spouse. But consider how the most glorious Cyprian demolishes these heretics. Commenting on this passage of the Lord's Prayer, he says

19. Cyprian, *De dom. or.* 18.   20. Eph 5.27. See *De gest. Pel.* 12.27.

among other things: "But how necessary, provident, and salutary it is that we are [999] admonished that we are sinners, who are compelled to ask forgiveness for our sins, so that while indulgence is asked of God, the soul is recalled to awareness of itself. In order that no one be pleased with himself as if he were innocent, and perish all the more by exalting himself, he is instructed and taught that he sins every day, when he is told every day to ask forgiveness for his sins. Furthermore, John, writing in his epistle, spoke thus: 'If we say that we have no sin, we deceive ourselves, and the truth is not in us.' "[21] And [Cyprian goes on to say] more, which would be too long to include here.[22]

(9) Now indeed when the saints say, "Bring us not into temptation, but deliver us from evil,"[23] what do they pray for except that they may persevere in sanctity? And certainly once that gift of God is granted to them (and that it is God's gift is sufficiently clearly shown by the fact that it is asked of him)—I say, once that gift of God is granted to them, that they may not be brought into temptation, then not one of the saints fails to hold on to perseverance in sanctity even to the end. For no one ceases to persevere in Christian commitment unless he is first brought into temptation. Hence, if that which he prays for, that he not be brought into temptation, is granted to him, then certainly, in sanctification, which by the gift of God he has obtained, by the gift of God he also persists.

6.(10) "But," you write, "these brothers do not want this perseverance to be preached as if it can neither be merited by prayers nor lost through obstinacy."[24] Here they give inadequate attention to what they say. For we speak of that perseverance by which one perseveres to the end; and if it has been given, one has persevered to the end, but if one has not persevered to the end, then it has not been given—a point which I have already discussed sufficiently above.[25] Consequently, people should not say that perseverance is given to anyone to the end,

21. 1 John 1.8.   22. Cyprian, *De dom. or.* 22.
23. On Augustine's preference for the wording, *Ne nos inferas in tentationem* for Matt 6.13a, over the more common, *Ne nos inducas in tentationem*, as in Vg, see note to *De nat. et gr.* 53.62.
24. Hilary, *Ep.* 226.4.   25. See above, 1.1.

save when the end itself has come, and the person to whom it has been given has been found to have persevered to the end. Certainly, we call someone chaste whom we know to be chaste, whether or not he will remain in that same chastity, and if he should possess any other divine gift which may be kept or lost, we say that he has it for as long as he has it, and if he has lost it, we say he *had* it. But perseverance to the end, because no one has it except a person who perseveres to the end, many can have, but no one can lose. For it is not to be feared that if a man has persevered to the end, some evil will may arise in him, so that he does not persevere to the end. Therefore, this gift of God may be merited through prayer but, once it has been given, it cannot be lost through obstinacy. For when anyone has persevered to the end, this gift cannot be lost, nor can others which might have been lost before the end. Therefore, how can that be lost, through which it comes about that even that which could be lost is not lost?

(11) Perhaps this may be said: Undoubtedly final perseverance cannot be lost once it has been given, that is to say, when a person has persevered to the end, but in a certain sense it can be lost, when a person, through some [1000] obstinacy, makes it impossible to attain it, just as we say that someone who has not persevered to the end has lost eternal life, or the kingdom of God, not because he had already received or possessed it, but because he would have received or possessed it had he persevered. Let us put aside controversies of words, and declare that some things which are not even possessed, but are hoped to be possessed, can be lost. But if anyone dares, let him tell me whether God cannot give that which he has ordered to be asked of him. Surely, anyone who thinks this, is, I do not say foolish, but mad. But God commanded that his saints say to him in prayer, "Bring us not into temptation." Therefore, whoever asks this and is favorably heard, is not brought into the temptation of obstinacy, by which he becomes capable or deserving of the loss of his perseverance in sanctity.

(12) But [the objector might continue], "It is by his own will that each person abandons God, and is deservedly abandoned by God." Who would ever deny this? And the reason why we

ask not to be brought into temptation is that this may not happen. And if we are heard, then this indeed does not happen, because God does not allow it to happen. For nothing happens except what God either does himself or permits to occur. Therefore, he has the power both to turn wills from evil to good and to turn them back when they are inclined toward a fall, as well as to direct their steps in ways which are pleasing to him. It is not in vain that we say to him, "You will turn us, O God, and bring us to life."[26] It is not said in vain, "Do not suffer my feet to be moved."[27] It is not said in vain, "Give me not up, O Lord, from my desire, to the wicked."[28] Finally, not to increase the number of citations, since more may well occur to you, it is not said in vain, "Bring us not into temptation." For whoever is not brought into temptation is evidently not brought into the temptation of his own evil will, and he who is not brought into the temptation of his own evil will is certainly not brought into any temptation at all. For, as it is written, "Every man is tempted by his own concupiscence, being drawn away and allured," but "God tempts no one,"[29] that is, by a harmful temptation. For there is also the useful temptation, by which we are not deceived or overcome but put to the proof, according to that which is said, "Prove me, O Lord, and tempt me."[30] Hence, with that harmful temptation, of which the Apostle speaks when he says, "Lest perhaps he that tempts should have tempted you, and our labor should be made vain,"[31] God, I repeat, tempts no one, that is, brings or leads no one into temptation. For to be tempted and not to be brought into temptation is not evil, indeed it is even good, for this is to be put to the proof. Therefore, when we say to God, "Bring us not into temptation," what else do we say but, "Permit us not to be brought into temptation"? For this reason, some do pray in these terms, and this is the reading in many manuscripts, and it is thus that the most blessed Cyprian has put it, "Suffer us not to be led into temptation." Nevertheless, in the gospel in Greek I have never found

26. Ps 84.7.
28. Ps 139.9.
30. Ps 25.2.

27. Ps 65.9.
29. Jas 1.14, 13.
31. 1 Thess 3.5.

it other than, "Bring us not into temptation."³² Therefore we
live more securely if we give up everything to God and do not
rather entrust ourselves partly to him and partly to ourselves,
as this venerable martyr saw. For in commenting on that passage of the prayer, he says, after other things the following:
"When we request that we not come into temptation, we are
reminded of our own infirmity and weakness, while we [1001]
ask thus, lest anyone exalt himself insolently, lest anyone with
pride and arrogance assume anything to himself, lest anyone
take the glory either of confession or of suffering as his own.
For the Lord himself in teaching humility said, 'Watch and
pray that you enter not into temptation. The spirit indeed is
willing, but the flesh is weak.'³³ So after we have confessed with
humility and submission and given all to God, everything that
we ask and implore with fear of God we shall obtain from his
loving kindness."³⁴

7.(13) Therefore, if there were no other proofs, this Lord's
Prayer would alone be sufficient for us in behalf of that grace
which I am now defending, for it leaves us nothing in which we
may glory as if it were our own, since it shows that even our not
departing from God is given only by God, when it shows that it
is to be asked for from God. For he who is not brought into
temptation does not depart from God. This is not at all in the
powers of our free will, such as they now are; it was in the power
of man before he fell. How much power the freedom of our
will had in the excellence of our original state was manifested
in the angels who, when the devil and his angels fell, remained
firm in the truth, and thus merited the attainment of that perpetual security of not falling, a state in which we are most certain that they are now. But, after the fall of man, God willed
that it belonged only to his grace that a man approach him, and
it belonged only to his grace that a man not depart from him.³⁵

(14) This grace he has placed in him "in whom we have obtained our lot, being predestined according to the purpose of

32. See note to *De nat. et gr.* 53.62, above.
33. Matt 26.41.   34. Cyprian, *De dom. or.* 26.
35. On the themes of the latter part of this paragraph, see the more extensive
discussion in *De corr. et gr.* 10.26–12.38.

him who works all things."[36] And accordingly, just as he likewise brings it about that we should approach him, he brings it
about that we not depart from him. For this reason it was said
to him by the prophet, "Let your hand be upon the man of
your right hand, and upon the son of man whom you have
confirmed for yourself, and we depart not from you."[37] This
man is certainly not the first Adam, in whom we departed from
God, but the second Adam, upon whom is placed the hand of
God, that we not depart from him. For Christ is complete, with
all his members, because of the Church, which is his body and
his fullness.[38] So when the hand of God is upon him, that we
not depart from God, then the work of God (for this is what is
meant by his hand) reaches indeed to us. For in Christ "we have
obtained our lot, being predestined according to the purpose
of him who works all things." Therefore it is by God's hand,
not our own, that we depart not from God. This is his hand, I
say, who declared, "I will give my fear into their heart, that they
may not revolt from me."[39]

(15) This is also why God willed that he should be asked that
we may not be brought into temptation, because if we are not
so brought, [1002] it is impossible that we should depart from
him. This perseverance could have been given to us even if we
did not pray for it, but he willed that we, by our prayer, be
reminded of him from whom we might receive these benefits.
For from whom do we receive them, save from him whom we
have been commanded to ask? The Church has indeed no need
here to look for laborious arguments—let it simply consider its
own daily prayers. It prays that those who do not believe may
believe; hence, it is God who converts people to faith. It prays
that those who believe may persevere; hence, it is God who
gives perseverance to the end. This God foreknew that he
would do; this is the predestination of the saints, whom "God
chose in Christ before the foundation of the world, that they
should be holy and unspotted in his sight in charity, predestining them unto the adoption of children through Jesus Christ

36. Eph 1.11.   37. Ps 79.18–19.
38. Cf. Eph 1.23.   39. Jer 32.40.

unto himself, according to the pleasure of his will, unto the praise of the glory of his grace,[40] in which he has graced them in his beloved son. In whom they have redemption through his blood, the remission of sins, according to the riches of his grace, which has abounded in them in all wisdom and prudence, that he might show to them the mystery of his will, according to his good will, which he has set forth in him, in the dispensation of the fullness of times, to reestablish all things in Christ, that are in heaven and on earth, in him. In whom we also have obtained our lot, being predestined according to the purpose of him who works all things."[41] Against such a clear trumpet of truth what man of sober and vigilant faith would admit any human arguments?

8.(16) "But why," it may be asked, "is not the grace of God given according to men's merits?" I reply, "Because God is merciful." "Then why," it is asked, "is it not given to all?" And here I reply, "Because God is a judge." Thus, on the one hand, grace is given freely by God, and, on the other, by his just judgment in the case of others it is revealed what benefit grace confers on those to whom it is given. Therefore, let us not be ungrateful that "according to the pleasure of his will, unto the praise of the glory of his grace" the merciful God delivers so many from a perdition so well deserved that, even if he delivered no one therefrom, he would not be unjust. Indeed, through one man, all have been sentenced to go into a condemnation that is not unjust, but just. So let him who is delivered love his grace, and him who is not delivered acknowledge his desert. If there is understood to be goodness in remitting a debt, and justice in requiring its payment, then never is injustice found to be with God.

(17) "But why," it is asked, "not only in one and the same case of infants but even twin children[42] is the judgment so differ-

40. Here Augustine includes the words, *in laudem gloriae gratiae suae*, omitted in his citation of the same passage in *De praed. sanct.* 18.35.
41. Eph 1.4–11. Augustine changes the grammatical person from first to third plural, except in the last verse.
42. Augustine's earliest sustained treatment of the question of predestination, in *Ad Simpl.* 1.2 (A.D. 397), endeavors to explain Rom 9.10–29 (which is cited in the present paragraph), on the different treatment by God of the twins

ent?" Is it not a similar question, why the judgment is the same
when the case is different? Let us recall here those workers in
the vineyard who worked all day, and those who worked for an
hour—surely, the situation is different as regards labor ex-
pended, and yet the judgment is the same in the payment of
wages. In this case, did those who protested hear anything else
from the head of [1003] the household except, "This is my
will"? Thus he indeed showed generosity to some without
showing any injustice toward the others. Indeed, both of these
groups are among the good, but with respect to justice and
grace it can be rightly said to the guilty person who is condemned, of the guilty person who is delivered, " 'Take what is
yours and go your way,' but I wish also to give to this one what
he is not owed. 'Or is it not lawful for me to do what I will? Is
your eye evil because I am good?' "[43] And if the condemned
should ask, "Why not me also?" he will deservedly hear, " 'O
man, who are you that reply against God?[44] Although clearly
in the case of the one of you, you behold a most generous bene-
factor, and in your own case a most just exactor, in neither case
do you behold an unjust God." For, since he would be just even
if he were to punish both, the one who is delivered has reason
to give thanks, while the one who is condemned has no ground
for complaint.

(18) "But if," it is said, "it was necessary that God, in not condemning all, should show what all merited, and thus commend
more freely the grace he has given to the vessel of mercy, why
in the same situation will he punish me rather than another or
deliver him rather than me?" I cannot answer, if you ask me
why, because I confess that I do not find anything to say. And
if you ask why I do not, it is that in this matter, even as his anger
is just and his mercy is great, so his judgments are inscrutable.

(19) But suppose someone goes on and asks, "Why is it that
to some who worshipped him in good faith, he did not give
perseverance to the end?" Well, why, except because he does

Esau and Jacob. Concerning this text, see *Retr.* 2.27.1, which Augustine quotes
above, *De praed. sanct.* 4.8. Augustine returned to the question of Esau and
Jacob in *Ep.* 194.34–41.

43. Matt 20.14,15.   44. Rom 9.20.

not lie who says, "They went out from us, but they were not of us. For if they had been of us, they would no doubt have remained with us."[45] Are there then two natures of men?[46] Not at all. If there were two natures, there would be no grace, for gratuitous deliverance would be given to no one, if it were paid as a debt to nature. But it seems to men that all who appear to be good and faithful ought to receive the gift of final perseverance. God, however, has judged it better to mingle some who will not persevere with the certain number of his saints, so that those for whom security in the temptations of this life is not helpful cannot be secure. For these words of the Apostle restrain many from pernicious pride: "Wherefore he who thinks himself to stand, let him take heed lest he fall."[47] But he who falls, falls by his own will, and he who stands, stands by God's will. "For God is able to make him stand"[48]—not, therefore, he himself, but God. And yet it is good not to think lofty thoughts, but to fear. It is always through his own thought that each person falls or stands. But, according to the words of the Apostle, which I have quoted in the preceding book,[49] "We are not sufficient to think anything as of ourselves, but our sufficiency is from God."[50] And the blessed Ambrose, following the Apostle, ventures also to say, "For our heart is not within our own power, nor our thoughts."[51] And everyone who is humbly and truly pious feels this to be most true.

(20) When Ambrose said this he was speaking in his book, [1004] *On Flight from the World*, teaching that this world must be fled not in the body but in the heart, and he argued that this could not be done without God's help. For he says the following:

Often we hear talk about fleeing from this world, and I wish that the mind were as careful and circumspect as talk is easy! But, what is worse, the allurement of earthly lusts frequently creeps in, and an influx of vanities takes over the mind, so that what you endeavor to avoid, you think about and turn over in your mind. It is difficult for a

45. 1 John 2.19.   46. Cf. Prosper, *Ep.* 225.3.
47. 1 Cor 10.12.   48. Rom 14.4.
49. *De praed. sanct.* 2.5.   50. 2 Cor 3.5.
51. See long quotation in next paragraph.

man to guard against this, but impossible for him to get rid of it. Indeed, in this matter the wish exceeds the accomplishment, as is attested in these words of the prophet: "Incline my heart unto your testimonies and not to covetousness."[52] For our heart is not within our own power, nor our thoughts, which, poured out unexpectedly, swamp the mind and soul, and draw you in a different direction from that which you have proposed. They recall us to temporal things, they introduce worldly concerns, they suggest pleasures, they weave enticements, and in the very time when we are preparing to elevate our minds, we are usually enveloped with vain thoughts and cast down to earthly things.[53]

Therefore it rests not in the power of men, but of God, that men have the "power to be made the sons of God."[54] They receive it from him who inspires in the human heart devout thoughts,[55] through which it possesses "faith which works through love."[56] For acquiring and retaining this good, and for progressing perseveringly in it to the end, "We are not sufficient to think anything as of ourselves, but our sufficiency is from God,"[57] in whose power are our heart and our thoughts.

9.(21) Therefore, of two infants equally bound by original sin, why the one is taken and the other left behind, and of two adults living in impiety, why the one is called in such a way as to follow him who calls, while the other is not called at all, or not called in such a way—the judgments of God are inscrutable. And of two people of piety, why perseverance to the end should be given to the one and not given to the other, the judgments of God are even more inscrutable.[58] But this should be most certain to the believer: that the former belongs to the predestined and the latter does not. "For if they had been of us," says one of the predestined, who had drunk this secret from the breast of the Lord, "they would no doubt have remained with us."[59] What does this mean, I ask: "They were not of us, for if

52. Ps 118.36.
53. Ambrose, *De fuga saeculi* 1.1 (written between 387 and 394).
54. John 1.12.
55. Reading *cogitationes* in place of BA: *cogitationis*.
56. Gal 5.6.   57. 2 Cor 3.5.
58. Reading *inscrutabiliora* in place of BA: *inscrutabilior*.
59. 1 John 2.19.

they had been, they would no doubt have remained with us"? Had not both been created by God, born of Adam, and made from the earth, and had not both received from him who said, "All breath I have made,"[60] souls of one and the same nature? Finally, had not both been called and followed him who called? Had not both been made just from among the wicked and been renewed by the bath of regeneration? But if he were to hear this, who beyond any doubt knew what he was saying, he could say in reply, "These things are true. According to all of them, they *were* of us. But, with respect to another kind of distinction, they were not of us, for if they had been of us, they would certainly have remained with us." What, then, is this distinction? The Books of God lie open; let us not turn our sight from them. The divine Scripture calls out; [1005] let us turn our ear to it. They were not "of" them, because they had not been "called according to his purpose," they had not been elected "in Christ before the foundation of the world," they had not "obtained their lot" in him, they had not been "predestined according to the purpose of him who works all things."[61] For if they had been all this, they would have been "of" them, and they would no doubt have remained with them.

(22) Indeed, without trying to say how possible it may be for God to convert to his faith the wills of men that were turned away from or turned against him, and to act in their hearts so that they yield to no adversities and are not overcome by any temptation so as to depart from him (since he can also do what the Apostle says, not permit them to be tempted beyond their abilities[62])—without going into all this, one thing is certain: God, foreknowing that they would fall, was able to take them away from this life before that could happen. Or should we return to the point of continuing to argue[63] how absurd it is to say that dead people are judged even for the sins which God foreknew they would have committed if they had lived? This is so abhorrent to Christian or even to human sensibilities that

60. Isa 57.16. Augustine here agrees with the Hb in reading *feci* ('I have made'); Vg has *faciam* ('I will make').
61. Eph 1.4,11.   62. Cf. 1 Cor 10.13.
63. See *De praed. sanct.* 12.23–14.29.

one is ashamed even to refute it. For why not say that the Gospel itself has been preached, with so much labor and suffering on the part of the saints, in vain, or even that it is still preached in vain today, if men, even though they have not heard the Gospel, can be judged according to the obstinacy or docility which God foreknew they would have had if they had heard it? Tyre and Sidon would not have been condemned—not even condemned less severely than those cities in which miraculous signs were performed by Christ the Lord, without their believing—since if these signs had been accomplished in them they would have repented in ashes and sackcloth.[64] Thus the declarations of the truth express it, in which the Lord Jesus has shown to us in his own words the deeper mystery of predestination.

(23) For if we are asked why such great miracles were performed among those who would not believe when they saw them, and were not performed among those who would have believed if they had seen them, what shall we reply? Shall we say what I said in that book where I responded to some six questions of the pagans, but without wishing to preclude other explanations which the wise can discover? Indeed, as you know, when it was asked why Christ came after so long a time, I replied that, "Christ foreknew that in those times and places in which his Gospel was not preached, all would respond to the preaching of the Gospel, as many people responded in his bodily presence, who would not believe in him, even after he had raised the dead." A little further on in this same book, and on this same question, I said, "Is it any wonder, then, if Christ knew that in earlier ages the world would be so full of unbelievers, that he would with good reason not wish to be preached to those whom he foreknew would believe neither his words nor his miracles?"[65] Certainly we cannot say this of Tyre and Sidon, and in their case we recognize that the divine judgments pertain to those reasons for predestination, without prejudice to

64. Cf. Matt 11.21–22, quoted in the next paragraph.
65. *Ep.* 102.2.14. These two passages are included in the longer passage quoted above, *De praed. sanct.* 9.17, although Augustine makes some slight modifications here.

which hidden reasons I said I was then responding. It is quite
easy to accuse the Jews of infidelity; it arose from their own
free will, [1006] for they refused to believe when such great
wonders were done among them. The Lord himself, rebuking
them, declares this, when he says, "Woe to you, Corozain and
Bethsaida, for if in Tyre and Sidon had been worked the miracles that have been worked in you, they would long ago have
done penance in sackcloth and ashes."[66] But how could we say
that Tyre and Sidon would have refused to believe when such
great miracles had been worked among them, or would not
have believed if they were worked, when the Lord himself testifies of them that they would have repented with great humility
if those signs of divine power had been performed among
them? And yet they will be punished on the day of judgment,
although with less punishment than those cities which refused
to believe when miracles were done in their presence. For the
Lord goes on to say, "But I say to you, it shall be more tolerable
for Tyre and Sidon on the day of judgment than for you."[67]
The latter will be punished more severely, the former less severely, but still they will be punished. Now if the dead are
judged even for the deeds which they would have done if they
had lived, then since these people would have been believers if
the Gospel had been preached to them with such great miracles, they should certainly not be punished. But they will be
punished, and therefore it is false that the dead will be judged
even for those things which they would have done if the Gospel
had come to them while were living. And if this is false, then
there is no reason for saying of those infants who perish because they die without baptism that this has happened to them
because of this merit: that God foreknew that if they had lived
and the Gospel had been preached to them, they would have
heard it without faith. It remains, therefore, that they are held
in bondage by original sin alone, and because of this alone go
into damnation. And we see that in others in the same situation
this sin is not remitted save by regeneration through the gratuitous grace of God, and that by God's hidden yet just judgment,

66. Matt 11.21.   67. Matt 11.22.

for there is no injustice with God,[68] some even after baptism who are on the way to perishing for their most evil life are still kept in this life until they perish, although they would not have perished if the death of the body had come to their aid by preventing their fall into sin. For no dead person is judged by the good or evil things which he would have done had he not died. Otherwise, the inhabitants of Tyre and Sidon would not have suffered punishment for what they did, but rather, according to what they would have done if those miracles of the Gospel had been done among them, they would have obtained salvation through their great repentance and their faith in Christ.

10.(24) A certain Catholic commentator of some reputation[69] has interpreted this passage of the Gospel as follows: the Lord foreknew that the Tyrians and Sidonians, although they would have believed when miracles had been performed among them, would later have departed from faith, and so instead, out of mercy, he did not perform his miracles there, for they would have been subject to more severe punishment if they had given up the faith which they had embraced than if they had never held it. In this opinion of a man of learning and considerable insight, some questions might well still be open to investigation, but what point is there in my addressing them now, when this view as it stands supports me in the question which I am now considering? For if in his mercy the Lord did not perform miracles among them, through which they could have become [1007] believers, lest they be punished more severely when afterwards they became unbelievers, which he foreknew that they had been going to become, it is sufficiently and clearly shown, that no dead person is judged for those sins which God foreknew he would [otherwise] have committed, when in fact he is in some way helped not to commit them. In such a way, Christ, if that opinion is true, is said to have intervened in behalf of the Tyrians and Sidonians, whom he preferred should not come to faith, rather than depart from it in a much greater offense, as he foresaw they would have done

68. Cf. Rom 9.14.
69. The identity of this author is unknown.

if they had come to faith. However, if it is asked, "Why was it not arranged that they would believe, and have this help supplied to them, that before they abandoned the faith they would depart from this life?" I do not know what answer can be given. For anyone who says that to those who would abandon the faith, it were granted as a favor not to begin to have that which they would later in a more serious impiety abandon, adequately shows that a man is not judged by an evil which it is foreknown he was going to commit, when in fact he is helped by some favor so that he does not commit it. Thus, he likewise was helped, who "was taken away lest wickedness should alter his understanding."[70] But why the Tyrians and Sidonians were not helped in this way, so that they might believe and be taken away, so that wickedness should not alter their understanding, he might perhaps answer, who chose to resolve the question at hand in the way we have been discussing. But in that which concerns the subject I am now discussing, I find it is sufficient that, according to this opinion also, men are shown not to be judged with respect to those things which they have not done, even if they were foreseen to have been going to do them. However, as I have said, the opinion, according to which, in the dying or the dead, sins are punished, which they were foreknown to have been going to commit if they had lived, is one which I am ashamed even to refute, lest I seem also to have judged it to be of some importance, because I preferred to resist it by argument rather than to pass over it in silence.

11.(25) Hence, as the Apostle says, "It is not of him that wills, nor of him that runs, but of God who shows mercy."[71] God also comes to the aid of such infants as he wishes, even though they do not will or run, whom he chose in Christ before the foundation of the world,[72] to whom he intended to give his grace freely, that is, with no prior merits on their part, either of faith or of works. And those who are older, even those whom he foresaw would believe in his miracles if they were performed among them, whom he does not wish to help, he does not help,

70. Wis 4.11.   71. Rom 9.16.
72. Cf. Eph 1.4.

since in his predestination he has, secretly indeed, but justly, determined otherwise concerning them. For there is no injustice with God, but, "Incomprehensible are his judgments, and unsearchable his ways,"[73] and, "All the ways of the Lord are mercy and truth."[74] Thus his mercy is unsearchable, through which he has mercy on whom he will, independent of prior merits on that person's part, and his truth is unsearchable, by which he hardens whom he will,[75] whose deserts have indeed preceded, but deserts for the most part held in common with him on whom he has mercy. Thus, in the case of twins, of whom one is taken and the other left, their end is not equal, though their merits are common, yet in their case one is delivered by the great goodness of God, in such a way that the other is condemned without any injustice on God's part. For is there injustice with God? In no way—but his ways are unsearchable. Therefore, let us believe without hesitation in his mercy with respect to those who are delivered and [1008] in his truth with respect to those who are punished, and let us not try to comprehend the incomprehensible, nor to search out the unsearchable. For "out of the mouths of infants and sucklings" he has "perfected" his "praise,"[76] and what we see in the case of those infants whose deliverance no merits of their own have preceded, and in the case of those whose condemnation is preceded only by the original sin common to both groups, let us not hesitate at all to believe also occurs in adults. Let us not, that is, think either that grace is given to anyone according to his merits, or that anyone is punished except for what he deserved, whether those who are saved and those who are punished are equally deserving or whether they have unequal degrees of evil. So, "He who thinks himself to stand, let him take heed lest he fall,"[77] and, "He that glories, let him glory" not in himself, but "in the Lord."[78]

(26) But why, as you write, do these men "not allow the case of infants to be used as a model for adults,"[79] since they do not

73. Rom 11.33.   74. Ps 24.10.
75. Cf. Rom 9.18.   76. Ps 8.3.
77. 1 Cor 10.12.   78. 1 Cor 1.31.
79. Hilary, *Ep.* 226.8.

hesitate to declare against the Pelagians that there is original sin, which entered the world through one man, and that from this one man all have gone into condemnation?[80] The Manichaeans also do not accept this, for they not only do not hold the Old Testament[81] Scriptures to have any authority, but also accept those which belong to the New Testament in such a way that, by some privilege, or rather sacrilege, of their own, they take what they want and reject what they do not want. I opposed them in my books, *On Free Choice of the Will,* from which my present opponents consider they may have grounds for objection against me.[82] [In that work] I was not willing to deal precisely with the very laborious questions which arose, lest my work might become too long, especially since the authority of the divine Scriptures would not be available to me for use in argument against such perverse people. And yet I was able— as I in fact did, whatever may be true among those things which I did not definitely assert therein—to conclude by certain reasons that in all things God is to be praised, without any necessity to believe, as they insist, that there are two co-eternal substances mixed together, the one good and the other evil.

(27) Also, in the first book of the *Retractationes,* a work of mine

80. Cf. Rom 5.12–16.
81. Augustine actually speaks here of the *Vetus Instrumentum* or 'Old Document.' In *C. duas epp. Pel.* 3.4.12, he contends that *Vetus Instrumentum* is a more accurate name.
82. Hilary, *Ep.* 226.8, referring to *De lib. arb.* 3.23.66, which reads as follows: "An insidious objection is often levelled against this line of reasoning by ignorant men concerning the death of young children and the bodily sufferings with which we often see them afflicted. What need, they ask, was there for a child to be born when it departed this life before it could set out to merit in life? Or, what will be its destiny in the future judgment, seeing that it has no place either among the just, since it performed no good deeds, or among the wicked, since it did nothing sinful? Here is my answer to their objection. Viewing the universe as a whole and the perfect order prevailing throughout the entire creation spread over time and place, it is impossible that the creation of any man would be superfluous in a universe where not even the creation of a single leaf of a tree is superfluous. What is really superfluous is any inquiry about the merits of one who has acquired no merits. We need have no fear that there may be a life in between virtue and vice, or that the Judge may pass a sentence halfway between reward and punishment" (translation by Robert P. Russell, O.S.A., FOTC 59.225).

which you have not yet read, when I came to revising the same books, that is, *On Free Choice of the Will*, I said as follows:

So many subjects were discussed in these books that some incidental questions, which either I could not solve or which required lengthy discussion at the time, were postponed, but in such a way that from both sides or from all sides of those questions, where what was more in harmony with the truth was not clear, our reasoning, nevertheless, came to the conclusion that no matter what was true about them, it was believed, or even made clear, that God is to be praised. Now this discussion was undertaken because of those who deny that the source of evil lies in the free choice of the will and who contend that, if this is so, God, as the creator of all natures, is to be blamed. In this way, according to the error of their impiety (for they are the Manichaeans), they wish to introduce a kind of evil nature, unchangeable and co-eternal with God.[83]

Again, a little further on, I say this:

Then the question was taken up: [1009] from what misery most justly imposed on sinners is man freed by the grace of God, because man could fall of his own will, that is, by free choice, but could not also rise? The ignorance and difficulty which every man experiences from the beginning of his life belong to this misery of a just condemnation, and no one is freed from this evil except by the grace of God. The Pelagians, who deny original sin, refuse to believe that this misery comes from a just condemnation. However, even if ignorance and difficulty belonged to man's primordial state, God should not in that event be blamed but praised, as we argued in that same third book. This argument is to be considered as directed against the Manichaeans, who do not accept the holy Scriptures of the Old Testament, where an account of original sin is given, and who maintain, with detestable arrogance, that what is read about it in the apostolic letters was interpolated by corrupters of the Scriptures, as though it had not been said by the apostles themselves. Against the Pelagians, on the other hand, we must defend this doctrine, which both Testaments teach, for they profess to accept both.[84]

83. *Retr.* 1.8.2. Here as elsewhere in this volume we have based our translation on that by Sr. Mary Inez Bogan, but we have introduced many alterations. See FOTC 60.32, 39.
84. *Retr.* 1.8.6.

I said these things in the first book of my *Retractationes*, in reviewing my treatise, *On Free Choice of the Will*. These are by no means the only remarks I made there on this work; indeed, there were also many others, which I thought were too long to insert in this work for you, and also not necessary. I am sure that you will reach a similar judgment when you have read them all. Therefore, although in the third book of *On Free Choice of the Will* I spoke of little children in such a way that, even if what the Pelagians say were true, that ignorance and difficulty, without which no man is born, are conditions of our nature and not punishments, still the Manichaeans would be vanquished, who wish to maintain that there are two co-eternal natures, one of good and one of evil, is the faith on that account to be called into question or abandoned—that faith which the Church defends against these same Pelagians, which asserts that there is original sin, the guilt of which is contracted by generation and washed away by regeneration? And since our brothers also admit this truth with us, so that together on this issue we destroy the error of the Pelagians, why do they think it is to be doubted that God delivers from the power of darkness and transfers into the kingdom of his beloved Son[85] even infants, to whom he gives his grace through the sacrament of baptism? And therefore, in that he gives grace to some but not to others, why will they not sing mercy and judgment to the Lord?[86] But why it should be given to these rather than to those—"Who has known the mind of the Lord?"[87] Who can comprehend the incomprehensible? Who can search out the unsearchable?

12.(28) It is settled, then, that God's grace is not given according to the merits of those who would receive it, but according to the pleasure of his will, to the praise and glory of that same grace of his,[88] so that "He who glories" may by no means glory in himself but "in the Lord."[89] He gives his grace to those men to whom he wishes to give it, for he is merciful. And even if he does not give it, he is just. And he does not give

---

85. Cf. Col 1.13.
86. Cf. Ps 100.1.
87. Rom 11.34.
88. Cf. Eph 1.5.
89. 1 Cor 1.31.

it to to those to whom he does not wish to give it, "That he might show the riches of his glory on the vessels of mercy."[90] In giving to some what they did not deserve, clearly [1010] he willed that his grace be gratuitous and thus truly grace, and in not giving it to all, he showed what all deserved. He is good in the benefit given to certain people, and just in the punishment of the others, but good in all things, for it is good when that which is deserved is given, and just in all things, for it is just when that which is not merited is given without injury to anyone.

(29) Also, this unmerited grace of God, that is, true grace, can be defended even if, as the Pelagians believe, baptized infants are not delivered from the power of darkness (because, as the Pelagians think, they are not held responsible for any sin), but are only transferred into the kingdom of the Lord. For even so, without any good deserts the kingdom is given to those to whom it is given, and without any evil deserts it is not given to those to whom it is not given. We are accustomed to say this in opposition to the same Pelagians, when they object to us that we attribute God's grace to fate, when we say that it is not given in accordance with our merits.[91] For it is rather they who, in the case of infants, attribute God's grace to fate, when they say that where there is no merit, it is fate. And certainly, even according to the Pelagians themselves, no merits can be found in infants, such as would explain why some of them should be admitted into the kingdom but others should be excluded from it. But, just as now, in order to show that the grace of God is not given according to our merits, I believed it better to defend this truth in accordance with both points of view—our own, whereby we say that infants are bound by original sin, and that of the Pelagians, who deny that there is original sin—and yet I cannot for that reason doubt that infants have something which he pardons who saves his people from their sins,[92] so, in the third book of *On Free Choice of the Will*, I opposed the Manichaeans

90. Rom 9.23.
91. See Prosper, *Ep.* 225.3. There Prosper makes reference to Augustine's *C. Iul.*, dating from around 421, in which see especially 4.8.46. Augustine treats this topic at greater length in *C. duas epp. Pel.* 2.5.9–6.12 (circa A.D. 420).
92. Cf. Matt 1.21.

according to both opinions—whether the ignorance and difficulty without which no one is born are punishments or basic
elements of our nature—and yet I hold one of these (and this
also I expressed clearly enough in that book[93]): that these
things are not part of the nature of man as created, but his
punishment, as condemned.

(30) In vain, then, is objection raised against me from that
old book of mine, that I may not argue the case of infants as I
ought to argue it and to demonstrate by it with the light of clear
truth that the grace of God is not given according to men's merits. For if, when as a layman I began the books, *On Free Choice
of the Will,* and when as a priest I finished them, I still had
doubts about the condemnation of infants that are not born
again and the salvation of infants that are born again, no one,
I think, would be so unfair and hostile as to stay my progress
and to judge that I must remain in that uncertainty. But it could
be more accurately thought that I ought not to be believed to
have had doubts on this question, since it seemed to me that
those against whom my argument was directed were to be refuted in such a way that, whether there is punishment for original sin in infants (as is the truth), or there is not (as some erron-
eously think), in no way [1011] could it be believed that there
is a mixture of two natures, one good and one evil, such as the
Manichaean error introduces. Far be it from us therefore so to
forsake the cause of infants as to say that it is uncertain to us
whether those reborn in Christ pass into eternal salvation if
they die in infancy, but those not reborn pass into the second
death. For that which is written, "By one man sin entered into
the world, and by sin death, and so death passed upon all
men,"[94] cannot be correctly understood in any other sense.
And from this eternal death, a most just retribution for sin, no
one delivers any person, infant or adult, except him who died
for the remission of our sins, both original and personal, without any sin of his own, either original or personal. But why did
he deliver these rather than those? Again and again we say, and

93. See *De lib. arb.* 3.18.52, 3.20.55–58, 3.23.71.
94. Rom 5.12.

we are not ashamed to say, "O man, who are you who reply against God?"[95] "Incomprehensible are his judgments, and unsearchable his ways."[96] And let us add, "Seek not the things that are too high for you, and search not into things above your ability."[97]

(31) You see then, beloved, how absurd it is, how contrary to soundness of faith and purity of truth, for us to say that, when infants die, they are judged in accordance with those things which it is foreknown they would do if they were to live. Yet this opinion, which certainly all human sentiment, if it have any rational foundation, however small, and especially Christian sentiment, rejects with horror, they have been driven to hold, who wished to separate themselves from the error of the Pelagians in such a way that they nevertheless think that they must believe and also put forward in argument that "the grace of God, by Jesus Christ our Lord,"[98] by which alone, after the fall of the first man, in whom we all fell, we are helped, is given to us according to our merits. This opinion Pelagius himself condemned before the eastern bishops, in fear of his own condemnation.[99] But if we cannot say this, that is, that the dead are judged according to the works, good or evil, they would have done if they had lived, in other words, works which do not exist and, in God's foreknowledge itself, will not exist—if we cannot say this, which, as you see, would be a grievous error to say, then what will remain for us but to confess, with the darkness of disputation removed, that the grace of God is not given according to our merits, the position which the catholic Church defends against the Pelagian heretics, and to recognize this as all the more evidently true in the case of infants? For neither is God constrained by fate to come to the aid of these infants, but not of those, when the situation is the same for both, nor shall we think that human affairs, in the case of infants, are governed, not by divine providence but by chance, when these are rational souls which are to be saved or condemned, and yet not a sparrow falls to the ground without the will of our Father in

95. Rom 9.20. 96. Rom 11.33.
97. Sir 3.22.   98. Rom 7.25.
99. See *De gest. Pel.* 14.30.

heaven.[100] Neither is it to be attributed to parental negligence, when infants die without baptism, so that heavenly judgments are taken to have nothing to do with it, as though those who die badly in this way had of their own free will chosen those negligent parents, of whom they were born. And what shall I say about an infant [1012] who expires some time before he can be aided by the ministry of one who baptizes? For frequently the parents are eager and the ministers are ready that baptism be given to the infant; nonetheless, because God is unwilling, it is not given, for he has not kept the infant in this life for a short time so that it might be given. Again, why has it happened at times that the children of unbelievers could be given the aid of baptism so that they would not go into perdition, and yet the children of believers could not? Clearly this shows that there is no respect of persons with God;[101] otherwise, he would deliver the children of his worshippers rather than those of his enemies.

13.(32) And indeed, since we are treating here of the gift of perseverance, why is it that one unbaptized person about to die is given assistance, lest he die without baptism, while another person who is baptized and about to fall is not given assistance so that he might die before his fall? Or shall we perhaps listen again to that absurdity which declares that it is of no advantage for a person to die before his fall, since he will be judged according to those actions which God foreknew that he would have done had he lived? Who could have the patience to listen to an assertion so perverse, so violently contrary to the soundness of faith? Who could bear it? Yet this is what they are driven to say, who will not profess that the grace of God is not given according to our merits. But those who, perceiving the obvious falsity and absurdity of such a statement, refuse to say that anyone who has died is judged according to what God foreknew he would have done had he lived, have no further reason to say what the Church condemned in the Pelagians and caused to be condemned by Pelagius himself: that the grace of God is given according to our merits. For they see that some infants not re-

---

100. Cf. Matt 10.29.   101. Cf. Rom 2.11, Col 3.25.

born are taken from this life to eternal death, while others, reborn, are taken to eternal life; and of those who are reborn, that some leave this world after persevering to the end, while others are retained in this life until they fall, who certainly would not have fallen if they had been taken hence before their lapse; and again that some who fall do not depart from this life until they return [to grace], who, if they had died before their return, would certainly have perished.

(33) Thus, we have shown with sufficient clarity that the grace of God, both of the beginning [of faith] and of perseverance to the end, is not given according to our merits, but according to his most secret, and at the same time most just, wise, and benevolent will, for "those whom he predestined, he also called,"[102] by that calling of which it is said, "The gifts and the calling of God are without repentance."[103] And no one can be said with any degree of certainty by men to belong to this calling, until he has left this world, but in this "human life," which "is a temptation upon earth,"[104] "he who thinks to stand, let him take heed lest he fall."[105] For indeed (as I have already stated[106]), those who will not persevere are mingled, by the most provident will of God, with those who will persevere, so that we may learn to be "not minding high things but consenting to the humble,"[107] and that we may "with fear and trembling" work out our salvation; "For it is God who works" in us "both to will and to accomplish, according to his [1013] good will."[108] Therefore, we will, but God also works in us to will; we work, but God also works in us to work, according to his good will. This is useful to us both to believe and to affirm; this is pious and true, that our confession should be humble and submissive, and everything should be given to God. Thinking, we believe; thinking, we speak; thinking, we do whatever we do; but in that which concerns the way of piety and the true worship of God, "we are not sufficient to think anything as of

102. Rom 8.30.
103. Rom 11.29.
104. Job 7.1.
105. 1 Cor 10.12.
106. See above, 8.19.
107. Rom 12.16.
108. Phil 2.12–13.

ourselves, but our sufficiency is from God."[109] For "our heart is
not within our own power, nor our thoughts,"[110] whence Ambrose, who says this, also states, "Yet who is so blessed as always
to rise up in his heart? But how can this be done without divine
help? In absolutely no way. Finally," he says, "the same Scripture earlier[111] affirms, 'Blessed is the man whose help is from
you; he is ascended in his heart.' "[112] Certainly Ambrose said
this, not only because he read it in sacred Scripture, but also
because, as we should undoubtedly believe about the man, he
felt their truth in his own heart. Hence, that which we say in
the mysteries of the faithful, that we may have our hearts lifted
up to the Lord, is a gift of the Lord, and it is for this gift that
those who have said this are admonished by the priest after
these words to give thanks to the Lord our God, to which they
reply that it is fitting and just.[113] For, since our heart is not in
our power, but with the help of God is lifted up so that it arises
and tastes of "the things that are above, where Christ is sitting
at the right hand of God," not "the things that are upon the
earth,"[114] to whom should we give thanks for so a great a thing,
unless to the Lord our God who does this, who has chosen us

109. 2 Cor 3.5.   110. Ambrose, *De fuga saeculi* 1.1.
111. Ambrose has earlier cited Ps 118.36: "Incline my heart into your testimonies."
112. *De fuga saeculi* 1.2, quoting Ps 83.6.
113. Here Augustine is referring to the ancient dialogue (found in Hippoly-
tus [d. 235], but doubtless older) which precedes the Preface to the Eucharistic
Prayer in the eucharistic liturgy (see Jungmann, *Mass of the Roman Rite*, 2.110–
15, which contains several references to Augustine). This dialogue belongs to
that part of the liturgy which came to be called the "Mass of the Faithful" (Augustine's words are *sacramenta fidelium*), because catechumens were excluded
and only the baptized (the "faithful") were admitted. The dialogue proceeds:
Priest: The Lord be with you.
People: And with your spirit.
Priest: Lift up your heart.
People: We have, to the Lord.
Priest: Let us give thanks to the Lord, our God.
People: It is fitting and just.
Augustine always quotes 'Lift up your heart' (*Sursum cor*), rather than the more
familiar 'Lift up your hearts' (*Sursum corda*). See Van der Meer, *Augustine the
Bishop*, 639.
114. Col 3.1,2.

by delivering us from the depths of this world by such a gift, and has predestined us before the foundation of the world?[115]

The Preaching of Predestination

14.(34) But they say that this "doctrine of predestination is opposed to the usefulness of preaching."[116] As if indeed it had been an obstacle to the preaching of the Apostle! Did not that teacher of the Gentiles in faith and truth both frequently commend predestination and not cease to preach the word of God? For because he said, "It is God who works in you both to will and to accomplish, according to his good will,"[117] did he fail to exhort us both to will and to do what is pleasing to God? And because he said, "He who has begun a good work in you will perfect it unto the day of Christ Jesus,"[118] did he for this reason not persuade men to begin and to persevere to the end? Undoubtedly the Lord himself commanded men to believe, and said, "Believe in God, believe also in me,"[119] but his statement was not for that reason false nor his doctrine vain when he declares, "No one can come to me," that is to say, no one can believe in me, "unless it has been given him by my Father."[120] Nor, again, because the latter doctrine is true, is the former precept in vain. Why, then, do we think that the doctrine of predestination is disadvantageous for preaching, commandment, exhortation, rebuke—all of which are amply cited in Scripture—[1014] when it is a doctrine that the same divine Scripture commends?

(35) Would anyone dare to say that God did not foreknow those to whom he would give the gift of believing, or whom he would give to his Son so that he should lose none of them?[121] And indeed if he foreknew this, certainly he foreknew his own gifts, by which he would deign to deliver us. This and nothing else is the predestination of the saints, namely, the foreknowl-

115. Cf. Eph 1.4.
116. Hilary, *Ep.* 226.2; see also Prosper, *Ep.* 225.3,6.
117. Phil 2.13.   118. Phil 1.6.
119. John 14.1.   120. John 6.66.
121. Cf. John 18.9.

edge and the preparation of God's favors, by which those who are delivered are most certainly delivered. And where are the others, if not left by the just divine judgment[122] in the mass of perdition?[123] There the Tyrians and Sidonians were left, who could have believed, if they had seen the wonderful signs of Christ. But since it was not given them to believe, that through which they would have believed was also denied to them. From this it appears that some have naturally in the understanding itself a divine gift of intelligence which would move them to faith, if either they heard the words or perceived the signs fitted to their minds,[124] but nonetheless if, by the loftier judgment of God, they were not separated from the mass of perdition by the predestination of grace, then neither those divine words nor deeds reach them, through which they might believe, if only they heard or saw such things. Those Jews also were left in the same mass of perdition, who were unable to believe in such great and evident works that were performed in their sight. Nor has the gospel been silent concerning why they could not believe, for it says, "And whereas he had done so many miracles before them, they believed not in him, so that the saying of Isaiah the prophet might be fulfilled, which said, 'Lord, who has believed our hearing? And to whom has the arm of the Lord been revealed?' And therefore they could not believe, because Isaiah said again, 'He has blinded their eyes, and hardened their heart, that they should not see with their eyes, nor understand with their heart, and be converted, and I should

122. Restoring the word *iudicio*, omitted from BA.

123. See note to *De nat. et gr.* 5.5, above.

124. *Ex quo apparet habere quosdam in ipso ingenio divinum naturaliter munus intelligentiae, quo moveantur ad fidem, si congrua suis mentibus, vel audiant verba, vel signa conspiciant.* This is the theory of the "congruous call," first developed in *Ad Simpl.* 1.2.13. See Introduction to *De nat. et gr.* in this volume. However, here that which enables a response to the congruous call is not, as in *Ad Simpl.*, a natural desire for God present in all, but a special divine gift not given to all. Burns notes that this passage is a unique reference to the congruous call in Augustine's latest works, and that "in the single instance in which a congruous call might have worked, it was not given," whereas "those who did hear the preaching needed not a different set of miracles, but an interior grace which would soften their hardness and illuminate their blindness of heart" (Burns, *Development*, 166–67, compare 37–49).

heal them.' "[125] Hence the eyes of the Tyrians and Sidonians were not blinded, nor their hearts hardened in that way, because if they had seen such signs as the Jews saw, they would have believed. Yet the fact that they could have believed did not help them, for they were not predestined by him whose "judgments are incomprehensible and whose ways are unsearchable."[126] Nor would the fact that the Jews were unable to believe have been an obstacle to their faith if they had been predestined in such a way that God would enlighten them when they were blind and would wish to take away their heart of stone, when they had been hardened. Perhaps indeed what the Lord said of the Tyrians and Sidonians could be understood in a different sense,[127] but that no one comes to Christ, except one to whom it has been given, and that it is given to those who have been elected in him before the foundation of the world, he beyond any doubt confesses, the ears of whose heart are not deaf when he hears with the ears of the flesh. Yet this doctrine of predestination, which is clearly enough expressed in the words of the gospel itself, did not prevent the Lord from saying both regarding the beginning of faith, these words which I mentioned a little earlier, "Believe in God, believe also in me,"[128] and regarding perseverance, "We ought always to pray and not to faint."[129] For they hear these things and do them, to whom it is given; but they to whom it is not given do not do them, whether they hear them or not. "Because to you," he says, "it is given to know the mystery of the kingdom of heaven, but to them it is not given."[130] One of these refers to the [1015] mercy and the other to the judgment of him to whom our soul says, "Mercy and judgment I will sing to you, O Lord."[131]

(36) Thus, the preaching of predestination should not hinder the preaching of perseverance and progress in faith, in order that those to whom it has been given that they should obey, should hear that which they ought to hear. For, "how will they

---

125. John 12.37–40.   126. Rom 11.33.
127. See above, 10.24.   128. John 14.1.
129. Luke 18.1.   130. Matt 13.11.
131. Ps 100.1.

hear without a preacher?"[132] And, conversely, to preach of progress in faith and perseverance in it to the end should not hinder the preaching of predestination, in order that one who lives in faith and obedience should not be exalted because of that very obedience, as by a good which is one's own and not one which is received, but rather, "He who glories, let him glory in the Lord."[133] For "we must take glory in nothing, since nothing is our own."[134] This Cyprian saw most faithfully and explained most fearlessly, and thus he declared predestination to be most certainly true. For if "we must take glory in nothing, since nothing is our own," then we ought not to boast of the most persevering obedience, nor should we attribute it to ourselves, as if it were not given to us from above. Thus it is a gift of God, which, as all Christians profess, God foreknew that he would give to those who were called by that calling of which it is said, "The gifts and the calling of God are without repentance."[135] And this, therefore, is that predestination which we preach in faith and humility. And nevertheless that same teacher and worker, who believed in Christ and who lived in holy obedience with the utmost perseverance even to suffering death for Christ, did not cease to preach the gospel, to exhort to faith and to devout living and to that very perseverance to the end, in consequence of having said, "We must take glory in nothing, since nothing is our own." In these words Cyprian states without any ambiguity the true grace of God, that is, grace which is not given according to our merits. And since God foreknew that he would give this grace, beyond doubt predestination is proclaimed in these words of Cyprian. And if predestination did not prevent Cyprian from preaching obedience, it certainly ought not to prevent us.

(37) Therefore, although we say that obedience is a gift of God, still we exhort people to it. But to those who listen obediently to the exhortation of truth, this very gift of God is given, that is, to listen obediently, while to those who do not so listen, it is not given. For it was not just anyone, but Christ who said,

132. Rom 10.14.   133. 1 Cor 1.31.
134. Cyprian, *Ad Quirinum* 3.4, also quoted above, *De praed. sanct.* 3.7.
135. Rom 11.29.

"No one comes to me, unless it has been given him by my Father,"[136] and, "To you it is given to know the mystery of the kingdom of heaven, but to them it is not given."[137] And on the subject of continence, "Not all receive this word, but those to whom it is given."[138] And the Apostle, in exhorting married people to conjugal chastity, says, "I would that all men were even as myself, but everyone has his proper gift from God, one in this way, but another in that."[139] This suffices to show that not only continence is a gift from God, but also the chastity of those who are married. Although all this is true, [1016] nevertheless we exhort others to the practice of these virtues, to the extent that it is given to each of us to be able to exhort, for this also is a gift of him in whose "hand are both we and our words."[140] Therefore, the Apostle says, "According to the grace that is given to me, as a wise architect, I have laid the foundation."[141] And elsewhere, "To everyone as the Lord has given: I have planted, Apollos watered, but God gave the increase. Therefore, neither he who plants is anything, nor he who waters, but God who gives the increase."[142] And therefore, just as only he who has received this gift exhorts and rightly preaches, so certainly he who obediently hears him is he who has received this gift. This is why the Lord, when he was speaking to those whose bodily ears were open, nevertheless said, "He that has ears to hear, let him hear."[143] Undoubtedly, he knew that they did not all have "ears to hear." But the Lord himself shows by whom those who have them, have them, when he says, "I will give them a heart to understand me and ears which hear."[144] Ears to hear are the gift of obedience itself, whereby those who possess it come to him, to whom "no one comes unless it has been given to him by my Father." Hence, we exhort and preach, but only those who have ears to hear, hear us obediently, while to those who do not have them, it happens as it is written, "and hearing they hear not."[145] They hear, that is, with

136. John 6.66.
137. Matt 13.11.
138. Matt 19.11.
139. 1 Cor 7.7.
140. Wis 7.16.
141. 1 Cor 3.10.
142. 1 Cor 3.5–7.
143. Luke 8.8.
144. Bar 2.31. Augustine's text differs somewhat from Vg.
145. Matt 13.13.

the bodily sense, but not with the heart's assent. But as to why these have ears to hear and those do not, that is, why to these it has been given by the Father that they come to the Son, while to those it has not been given—"Who has known the mind of the Lord? Or who has been his counselor?"[146] Or, "O man, who are you who reply against God?"[147] Must that which is evident be denied, because that which is hidden cannot be understood? I ask, shall we say that what we see to be so, is not so, because we cannot discover why it is so?

15.(38) But they say, as you write,[148] "No one can be aroused by the stimuli of rebuke if in the assembly of the Church it is declared to numerous hearers: On predestination the set determination of the will of God is such that some of you, having received the will to obey, have passed from unbelief to faith, or, having received perseverance, remain in faith, but others of you, who remain in the delights of sin, have not yet arisen, because the assistance of pitying grace has not yet raised you. But if any of you have not yet been called, whom God by his grace has predestined to be elected, you will receive this grace, whereby you will wish to be and will be elected. And from any of you who obey, if you have been predestined to be rejected, the strength to obey will be withdrawn, so that you will cease to obey." When these things are said, they ought not to keep us from confessing the true grace of God, that is, grace which is not given according to our merits, and from confessing in accordance with it the predestination of the saints, even as we are not deterred from confessing God's foreknowledge, if someone should speak thus to the people concerning it: "Whether you do or do not live rightly now, you will later be such as God has foreknown that you will be, either good if he has foreknown you as good, or evil if he has foreknown you as evil." If upon hearing this, some should become torpid and sluggish, [1017] and falling away from their labor into a quest for pleasure, should pursue their lustful desires, ought we for that reason to

146. Rom 11.34.   147. Rom 9.20.
148. This passage does not appear in the letters of Prosper and Hilary which we possess, but a similar idea is found in Hilary, *Ep.* 226.5. The text quoted here is discussed in greater detail in 22.58–61 below.

think that what has been said about the foreknowledge of God
is false? Will they not be good if God has foreknown that they
will be good, no matter in what degree of evil they now live?
But if God has foreknown them to be evil, will they not be evil,
no matter in what degree of goodness they may now appear to
live? There was a brother in our monastery who, when he was
upbraided by the brothers and asked why he did some things
which should not have been done, and did not do things which
should have been done, replied, "Whatever I may now be, I
shall be such as God has foreknown that I shall be." Surely he
both spoke the truth and did not become any better by this
truth, but instead he progressed so far in evil that he deserted
the monastic community and became like a dog returned to his
vomit[149]—and yet, what he will later be remains uncertain. Are
the truths that are taught concerning God's foreknowledge to
be either denied or held back for the sake of such souls, at a
time when, if we do not speak them, people will pass over into
other errors?

16.(39) Furthermore, there are those who either do not pray,
or who pray without fervor, for they have learned from the
teaching of the Lord that God knows what our needs are before
we ask him.[150] Shall we suppose that on account of such people
the truth of this statement is to be abandoned or deleted from
the gospel? Not at all, since it is the case that God has prepared
some things to be given even to those who do not pray for them,
such as the beginning of faith, but other things to be given only
to those who pray for them, such as perseverance to the end;
clearly, he who thinks that he possesses this from himself does
not pray for it. So let us take care, lest, while we are afraid that
exhortation will grow cold, prayer should be extinguished and
arrogance inflamed.

(40) Therefore, let the truth be spoken, above all when some
question moves us to declare it. And let those who can, grasp
it, lest perhaps, while we are being silent on account of those
who cannot grasp it, they not only be deprived of truth but be
themselves grasped by error, who can grasp the truth by which

149. Cf. Prov 26.11.   150. Cf. Matt 6.8.

the error is guarded against. For it is easy, and indeed useful, to be silent about some truth for the sake of those who are incapable of comprehending it. For why else did the Lord say, "I have yet many things to say to you, but you cannot bear them now,"[151] and the Apostle say, "I could not speak to you as to spiritual, but as to carnal persons. As to little ones in Christ, I gave you milk to drink, not solid food, for you were not able as yet. But neither are you now able"?[152] However, in a certain manner of speaking, it can happen that what is said should be both milk for infants and solid food for adults, as for example, "In the beginning was the Word, and the Word was with God, and the Word was God."[153] What Christian can be silent about this? Who can grasp it? And what more sublime[154] truth can be discovered in sound doctrine? Nonetheless, it is not withheld from children nor from adults, nor is it hidden from children by adults. Yet the reason for withholding the truth is one thing, the necessity for speaking it another. It would be tedious to inquire into or to include all the reasons for withholding the truth, but one of them is this, that [if we spoke it] [1018] we might make worse those who do not understand it, while we wish to make those who understand it more learned, who indeed do not become more learned when we withhold such a thing, but also do not become worse. But when a truth is of such a quality that he who cannot grasp it is made worse by our speaking it, while he who can grasp it is made worse by our silence, what do we think should be done? Ought we not speak the truth, so that he who can grasp it may grasp it, rather than be silent, so that not only may neither grasp it, but also he who is more intelligent should himself be made worse? For if he should hear it and grasp it, more people would also learn it from him. For the more capable someone is of learning, the more suitable he is of teaching others. The enemy of grace presses upon us and in every way urges us to believe that grace

151. John 16.12.   152. 1 Cor 3.1–2.
153. John 1.1.
154. There is a play on words here, relying on two meanings of *grandis:* on the one hand, used of persons, 'adult' or 'grown up', on the other hand, used of words or ideas, 'sublime.'

is given according to our merits, and thus grace is no longer
grace, and are we unwilling to say what we can say, from the
testimony of Scripture? Are we afraid lest by speaking we offend him who cannot grasp the truth, and not also afraid lest
through our silence he who can grasp the truth be grasped by
falsehood?

(41) For either predestination must be preached in the way
in which holy Scripture clearly declares it, that in the predestined the gifts and calling of God shall be without repentance,[155] or it must be admitted that the grace of God is given
according to our merits, as the Pelagians hold, although this
opinion, as I have often said already, may be read in the proceedings of the eastern bishops to have been condemned even
by the mouth of Pelagius himself.[156] In any case, those on account of whom I am writing this work are removed from the
heretical perversity of the Pelagians to this extent, that, although they do not want to say that those who through the
grace of God become and remain obedient are predestined,
still they confess that this grace precedes the will of those to
whom it is given,[157] lest indeed this grace be thought to be given
not freely, as the truth declares, but rather in accordance with
the merits of a preceding will, as the Pelagian error maintains
in contradiction to the truth. Thus grace also precedes faith,
for if faith precedes grace, then undoubtedly the will also precedes it, for there cannot be faith without the will. But if grace
precedes faith, since it precedes the will, then clearly it precedes all obedience, and it also precedes love, by which alone
God is truly and agreeably obeyed, and grace works all these
things in him to whom it is given, all of whose own doing in
these things it precedes.

17. There remains among these benefits final perseverance,
which will be requested in vain every day from the Lord, unless
the Lord brings it about through his grace in him whose prayers he has heard. Now observe how far from the truth it is to
deny that perseverance to the end of this life is a gift of God,

155. Cf. Rom 11.29.   156. See *De gest. Pel.* 14.30.
157. See *De praed. sanct.* 1.2.

since it is he who brings this life to an end when he has so willed, and if he does so before someone's imminent fall, he causes that person to persevere to the end. But an even more wondrous and, to believers, remarkable act of the generosity of God's goodness is that this grace is given even to infants, who are not of such an age that obedience can be given. But to whomever God gives these gifts of his, undoubtedly he has foreknown that he will give them, and in his foreknowledge he has prepared them for them. "Those," therefore, "whom he predestined, [1019] he also called,"[158] with that call which I am not reluctant to mention often, and of which it is said, "The gifts and the calling of God are without repentance."[159] For to order his future works in his foreknowledge, which cannot be deceived or changed, is entirely, and nothing other than, to predestine. But just as he whom God has foreknown to be chaste, although this may be uncertain to him, acts in such a way as to be chaste, so he whom God has predestined to be chaste, although this may be uncertain to him, does not, simply because he hears that by God's gift he will be what he will be, fail to act so as to be chaste. Indeed, his charity is delighted, and he is not puffed up, as if he had not received it. Not only is he not hindered from the work of chastity by the preaching of predestination, but on the contrary he is helped in this task, so that when he glories, he may glory in the Lord.[160]

(42) But what I have said about chastity can also be said of faith, piety, love, and perseverance, and, without enumerating them individually, it can most truly be said of all the forms of obedience by which we obey God. However, those who place only the beginning of faith and perseverance to the end in our own power, in such a way that they do not consider that they are gifts of God, nor that God acts on our thoughts and wills in order that we may acquire and retain these gifts, do grant that he gives other things, since they are obtained from him by the faith of the believer. Why, then, are they not afraid that exhortation to these other things, and the preaching of them, will be

---

158. Rom 8.30.   159. Rom 11.29.
160. Cf. 1 Cor 1.31.

hindered by the doctrine of predestination? Will they perhaps say that these things are not predestined? But then they are not given by God, or else God did not know that he would give them. But if they are given, and if he foreknew that he would give them, then certainly he predestined them. Therefore, just as our brothers exhort others to chastity, charity, piety, and the other things which they confess to be gifts of God, and cannot deny that these things are foreknown by him, and therefore are predestined, and do not say that their exhortations are hindered by the preaching of the predestination of God, that is, by the preaching of God's foreknowledge concerning these future gifts of his—so let them see that their exhortations to faith and perseverance are not hindered if these things also are said to be, as truly they are, God's gifts and that they were foreknown, that is predestined, to be given. Let them see, rather, that what is hindered and overthrown by this preaching of predestination is that most pernicious error, whereby it is said that the grace of God is given according to our merits, so that he who glories may glory, not in the Lord, but in himself.

(43) Because I would like to develop this point more clearly for the benefit of those who are slow in apprehension, I ask that those who have been gifted with an intelligence that leaps ahead bear with me in my delay. The Apostle James says, "If any of you need wisdom, let him ask it of God, who gives to all abundantly and does not upbraid, and it shall be given to him."[161] It is also written in the Proverbs of Solomon, "Because the Lord gives wisdom."[162] And on the subject of continence, we read in the Book of Wisdom, whose authority has been invoked by great and learned men who long [1020] before us have commented on the divine Scriptures, thus: "And I knew that no one could be continent, except God gave it, and this also was a point of wisdom, to know whose gift it was."[163] Therefore, these are gifts of God, that is, wisdom and continence, not to mention others. And our brothers agree, for they are not Pelagians and would not oppose this obvious truth with obstinate

---

161. Jas 1.5.   162. Prov 2.6.

163. Wis 8.21; slightly different from Vg. On the authority of the Book of Wisdom, see note to *De praed. sanct.* 14.26, above.

and heretical perversity. "But," they say, "that these things are given to us by God is obtained by faith, which has its beginning from us." They contend that this faith, both insofar as we begin to have it and insofar as we remain to the end in it, depends upon us, as though we do not receive it from the Lord. Obviously this contradicts the Apostle when he says, "For what do you have that you have not received?"[164] It also contradicts the martyr Cyprian, who says, "We must take glory in nothing, since nothing is our own."[165] When we have said these things and many others, which it would be tedious to repeat, and have shown that both the beginning of faith and perseverance to the end are gifts of God, and that it is impossible that God should not foreknow any of his future gifts, both what things are to be given and to whom they are to be given, and therefore those whom he delivers and crowns have been predestined by him, they believe that they ought to reply, "The doctrine of predestination is opposed to the usefulness of preaching, for when it is heard, no one can be aroused by the stimuli of rebuke."[166] Those who say these things do not wish it to be taught to men that, when one comes to faith and remains in faith, these are gifts of God, lest more despair than encouragement should appear to be introduced, when those who hear this think it is uncertain, to human ignorance, on whom God bestows or does not bestow these gifts.[167] Why, then, do they preach, along with us, that wisdom and continence are gifts of God? For if, when these virtues are declared to be gifts of God, there is no impediment to the exhortation whereby we encourage people to be wise and continent, what reason is there for them to think that the exhortation whereby we encourage people to come to faith and to remain in it to the end will be impeded, if these also are said to be gifts of God, as they are proven to be by the witness of his Scriptures?

(44) Now—to put aside the topic of continence and speak

164. 1 Cor 4.7.
165. Cyprian, *Ad Quirinum* 3.4, cited above, 14.36.
166. See above, 14.34 and 15.38, and the references to the letter of Hilary found there.
167. Cf. Hilary, *Ep.* 226.6.

here only of wisdom—note what the Apostle James, already cited, says: "But the wisdom that is from above, first indeed is chaste, then peaceable, modest, easy to be persuaded, full of mercy and good fruits, without judging, without dissimulation."[168] Do you not see, I implore, that wisdom, abounding with so many great and good things, descends from the Father of lights? Indeed, as the same Apostle says, "Every best gift and every perfect gift is from above, coming down from the Father of lights."[169] To put aside the other qualities mentioned, why do we rebuke the unchaste and the contentious, to whom nevertheless we preach that chaste and peaceable wisdom is a gift of God? Nor do we fear that, motivated by uncertainty about the divine will, they may find in this preaching more despair than exhortation, or that they should be moved, [1021] by the stimuli of rebuke, against us rather than against themselves, since we reproach them for not possessing these things, which we ourselves say are not brought about by the human will, but rather given by the divine generosity. Finally, why did not the preaching of this grace deter the Apostle James himself from reproaching the troublesome by saying, "If you have bitter zeal, and there are contentions in your hearts, glory not and be not liars against the truth. For this is not wisdom descending from above, but earthly, sensual, devilish. For where there is envy and contention, there is inconstancy and every evil work"?[170] Hence, the troublesome are to be rebuked both by the testimony of the divine Scriptures and by those practices which these brothers have in common with us, and this rebuke is not hindered by the fact that we proclaim that the peaceable wisdom, by which the contentious are corrected and remedied, is a gift of God. In the same way, unbelievers or those who fail to remain in faith are to be rebuked, without any impediment to this rebuke from the preaching of God's grace, although that preaching commends that very faith and the continuation in it as gifts of God. For, although wisdom is obtained through faith—as the Apostle James himself has attested, when he said,

168. Jas 3.17.   169. Jas 1.17.
170. Jas 3.14–16.

"If any of you need wisdom, let him ask it of God, who gives to all abundantly and does not upbraid, and it shall be given to him,"[171] and added immediately, "But let him ask in faith, wavering in nothing"[172]—nevertheless, because faith may be given before it is requested by him to whom it is given, it does not follow that it is not a gift of God, but derives from us, simply because it is given to us without our asking for it. For the Apostle [Paul] says very clearly, "Peace be to the brothers and charity with faith from God the Father, and the Lord Jesus Christ."[173] Therefore, from him from whom peace and charity are given, faith is also given, and this is why we pray to him not only that faith may be increased in those who possess it, but also that it may be given to those who do not possess it.

(45) Nor do these brothers, on whose account I am saying these things, who complain that our doctrine of predestination and grace hinders exhortation, exhort only to those gifts which they hold are not given by God but come from us, such as the beginning of faith and perseverance to the end. This indeed is what they should do, that is, only exhort unbelievers to believe and believers to continue to believe. But as to those things which, along with us, they do not deny are gifts of God, so that together with us they work to destroy the error of the Pelagians, that is to say, concerning modesty, continence, patience, and the other virtues, by which we live rightly, and which are obtained from the Lord through faith, they ought simply to pray for them or to show that they should be prayed for, either for oneself or for others, but not to exhort anyone to acquire and retain them. When, nonetheless, they exhort others to these things, as far as they are able, and admit that people ought so to be exhorted, they show adequately enough that exhortations either to faith or to perseverance to the end are not hindered by that preaching, that is, by the fact that we teach that these things also are gifts of God and are bestowed on anyone, not by oneself, but by God.

(46) "But," it is said, "whoever abandons faith does so

171. Jas 1.5.   172. Jas 1.6.
173. Eph 6.23.

through his own fault, when he yields and consents to the temptation which causes him to abandon faith." Who denies this? But it cannot on this basis be said that perseverance in faith is not a gift of God. For this perseverance each person requests every day, who prays, [1022] "Bring us not into temptation,"[174] and if this is favorably heard, he receives it. And thus, in asking every day to persevere, clearly one is placing one's hope of perseverance not in oneself, but in God. However, I do not wish to belabor the point with my words; instead, I leave it to them to reflect upon, that they might realize the sort of opinion of which they have persuaded themselves, saying "that by the preaching of predestination more despair than exhortation is impressed upon those who hear." For this is equivalent to saying that a man despairs of his salvation when he has learned to place his hope not in himself but in God, although the prophet proclaims, "Cursed be the man who has his hope in man."[175]

(47) Therefore, these gifts of God which are given to the elect who are called according to his purpose, among which gifts are both to begin to believe and to persevere in faith to the end of this life (as I have shown, with so much evidence both of reason and authority)—these gifts, if there is no such predestination as I defend, are not foreknown by God. But they are foreknown. This, therefore, is the predestination which I defend.

18. Thus sometimes this same predestination is also designated by the name of foreknowledge, as when the Apostle says, "God has not cast away his people, whom he foreknew."[176] The words here, "he foreknew," can only be understood correctly as "he predestined," as the context of this passage shows. For the Apostle was speaking of the remnant of the Jews, who were saved, while the rest perished. For he had earlier cited these words of the prophet to Israel, "All the day long have I spread my hands out to a people that believes not and contradicts me,"[177] and, as if the reply were given, "What then has become of the promises made by God to Israel?" immediately went on,

174. Matt 6.13.   175. Jer 17.5.
176. Rom 11.2.   177. Rom 10.21, citing Isa 65.2.

"I say then, has God cast away his people? Far from it. For I also am an Israelite of the seed of Abraham, of the tribe of Benjamin," by which he meant, "For I also am from the same people." Next he added the words now under discussion: "God has not cast away his people, whom he foreknew." And to show that the remnant had been left by God's grace, not by the merits of their works, he went on to add, "Do you not know what the Scripture says of Elias, how he calls on God against Israel?" and so on.[178] "And what," he asks, "does the divine answer say to him? 'I have left me seven thousand men that have not bowed their knees to Baal.' "[179] God does not say, "There have been left for me," or "They have left themselves for me," but "I have left me" [*reliqui mihi*]. "Even so then," the Apostle continues, "at this present time also, there is a remnant made through[180] the election of grace. And if by grace, it is not now by works, otherwise grace is no longer grace." And bringing together those things which I have already quoted, he asks, "What then?" and in reply to this query says, "That which Israel sought, it has not obtained, but the election has obtained it, and the rest have been blinded."[181] Therefore, in speaking of this election and this remnant, which was made through the election of grace, the Apostle meant that people which God did not reject, because he foreknew them. This is that election by which those whom he willed, he chose in Christ [1023] "before the foundation of the world," that they "should be holy and unspotted in his sight in charity," predestining them "unto the adoption of children."[182] Thus, no one who understands these words can deny or doubt that, when the Apostle says, "God has not cast away his people, whom he foreknew," he intends to signify predestination. For God foreknew the remnant which he was going to make according to the election of grace. That is, there-

---

178. Rom 11.2.   179. Rom 11.4, citing 1 Kgs 19.18.
180. Augustine's text here reads, *reliquiae per electionem gratiae factae sunt.* Vg reads, *reliquiae secundum electionem gratiae salvae factae sunt,* translated in the Douai version as, 'There is a remnant saved according to the election of grace.' Augustine's reading is closer to the Gk than is the Vg.
181. Rom 11.5–7.   182. Eph 1.4.

fore, he predestined them, for undoubtedly he foreknew, if he predestined; but to have predestined is to have foreknown that which he was going to do.

19.(48) What, then, prevents us, when in certain commentators on the word of God we read of God's foreknowledge, in passages which are concerned with the calling of the elect, from understanding this same predestination to be meant? For perhaps they preferred to use this word ["foreknowledge"], which is both more easily understood and not inconsistent with but indeed in accordance with the truth which is declared concerning the predestination of grace. This I know, that no one has been able, without falling into error, to argue against this predestination, which we defend according to the holy Scriptures. But I think such holy men, renowned with praise everywhere for their faith and Christian learning, as Cyprian and Ambrose, whose clear testimonies I have set forth, should suffice for those who request the opinions of commentators on this subject.[183] And they should suffice for both doctrines, that is, [first], that they should in all circumstances believe and preach, as they ought to believe and preach, that the grace of God is gratuitous, and, [second], that they should not think this preaching is incompatible with the preaching by which we exhort the indolent or rebuke the evil. For these men, although they preached the grace of God in such a way that one of them said, "We must take glory in nothing, since nothing is our own,"[184] and the other said, "Our heart is not within our power, nor our thoughts,"[185] nevertheless did not cease to exhort and rebuke, so that the divine commandments might be obeyed. And they did not fear that it would be said to them, "Why do you exhort us? And why do you rebuke us, if nothing good that we have is from us, and if our heart is not in our power?" In no way could these saints fear that such things should be said to them, since they understood that it is given to very few to receive the teaching of salvation from God himself, or from the

183. Cf. Hilary, *Ep.* 226.8.
184. Cyprian, *Ad Quirinum* 3.4, first cited in this book at 14.36.
185. Ambrose, *De fuga saeculi* 1.1, first cited in this book at 8.19.

angels of heaven, without any human preaching to them, but that rather it is given to many to believe in God through [the ministry of] men. Yet in whatever way the word of God is addressed to a man, beyond doubt that he hears it in such a way as to obey it is a gift of God.

(49) Thus, the most eminent commentators on the divine Scriptures that I have just mentioned have both preached the true grace of God as it ought to be preached, that is, as a grace which no human merits precede, and urgently exhorted their audience to carry out the law of God, so that those who might have the gift of obedience should hear what commandments they ought to obey. For if any of our merits precede grace, then it is clearly the merit of some action, or word, or thought, in which is understood also the good will itself, but he [1024] very briefly encompassed every kind of merit, who said, "We must glory in nothing, since nothing is our own." And he who said, "Our heart is not within our power, nor our thoughts," did not indeed pass over our actions and words, for there is no human action or word which does not proceed from the heart and thought. What more could the most glorious martyr and brilliant teacher Cyprian do in this regard than when he admonished us that we must pray, in the Lord's Prayer, even for the enemies of the Christian faith? Then he showed what he thought about the beginning of faith, that even this is a gift of God. And as to perseverance to the end, he has shown us that the Church of Christ prays every day for it, because this also, no one grants but God, to those who have persevered. Likewise, the blessed Ambrose, commenting on the passage from Luke the evangelist, "It seemed good to me also,"[186] writes:

What he says seemed good to him cannot have seemed good to him alone. For it is not simply the human will to which it seemed good, but he likewise has found it good, "Christ, who speaks in me,"[187] who brings it about that that which is good can also seem good to us. For him upon whom he has mercy he also calls. Therefore, he who follows Christ can answer, when he is asked why he wished to be a Christian,

186. Luke 1.3.   187. 2 Cor 13.3.

"It seemed good to me also." When he says this, he does not deny that it seemed good to God, for "by God is prepared the will of man."[188] For it is by the grace of God that God is honored by a saint.[189]

Furthermore, in this same work, that is, in his Exposition of the same gospel, when he had come to that passage where the Samaritans refused to receive the Lord when he was going to Jerusalem, he declared the following:

Learn at the same time that he would not be received by people who were not converted in simplicity of heart. For if he had wished, he would have made them devout, who had not been devout. But the Evangelist himself noted why they would not receive him, saying, "because his face was of one going to Jerusalem."[190] Now the disciples earnestly desired to be received in Samaria. But God calls those whom he deems fit, and makes him whom he wishes religious.[191]

What teaching more evident and manifest do we seek in the commentators on God's word, if we are pleased to hear from them also what is clear in the Scriptures? But to these two writers, who ought to have been sufficient, let us add also a third, Saint Gregory, who testifies that both to believe in God and to confess what we believe are God's gift, saying, "Confess, I beg you, to the Trinity of one God, or, if you prefer to say it otherwise, say that it is of one nature, and God will be asked that a voice be given you by the Holy Spirit," that is, God will be asked to permit a voice to be given to you, [1025] by which you may confess what you believe. "For he will give it, I am sure; he who gave you what is first will also give you what is second. He who gave it to you to believe will also give it to you to confess your faith."[192]

188. Prov 8.35 (LXX).

189. Ambrose, *Exp. ev. sec. Luc.* 1.10. Augustine also quotes this passage at *De nat. et gr.* 63.75. There he omits "also" (*et*) from the Lucan passage under discussion.

190. Luke 9.53.

191. Ambrose, *Exp. ev. sec. Luc.* 7.27. Augustine also cites this passage at *De grat. Chr.* 46.51.

192. "Saint Gregory" here is Gregory of Nazianzus (329–389). The quotation is from a sermon delivered at Constantinople in 380 or 381 on the feast of Pentecost, *Oratio* 41 *in Pentecostem*. Augustine has cited the translation made by Rufinus around the year 400. There are significant differences between what

(50) When such great teachers as these say that there is nothing in which we may glory as if it were our own and God did
not give it to us, and that our own heart and our thoughts are
not within our power; when they credit all these things to God
and confess that we have received them from him, that we are
converted to him in such a way that we will remain faithful, that
that which is good also appears good to us and we desire it, that
we honor God and receive Christ, that from being people who
were not devout we are made devout and religious, that we
believe in the Trinity itself, and that we also confess with our
voice what we believe—all these things they ascribe to the grace
of God, they acknowledge as gifts of God, they testify are from
him to us, not from ourselves. Now will anyone venture to say
that they confessed the grace of God in such a way that they
dared to deny his foreknowledge, which not only the learned
but also the unlearned confess? Moreover, if they knew that
God gave all these things, and they knew it in such a fashion
that they did not overlook the fact that he foreknew that he
would give them and that he could not be unaware of who it
was to whom he would give them, beyond any doubt they knew

Gregory said and what Augustine took him to be saying. The Greek original
reads: Μιᾶς θεότητος, ὦ οὗτοι, τὴν Τριάδα ὁμολογήσατε, εἰ δὲ βούλεσθε, μιᾶς
φύσεως· καὶ τὴν θεὸς φωνὴν παρὰ τοῦ πνεύματος ὑμῖν αἰτήσομεν. Δώσει, γὰρ,
εὖ οἶδα, ὁ τὸ πρῶτον δούς, καὶ τὸ δεύτερον (PG 36.440): "Confess, I beg you,
the Trinity of one God, or if you prefer, of one nature, and we will ask for you
from the Holy Spirit the word, 'God.' For he who gave you the first gift, will, I
know well, give you also the second." This is directed against the "Pneumato-
machoi," who, while sharing the faith of the Church about the Father and the
Son, and that the Holy Spirit participates in the attributes of the Father and the
Son, refused to give the Holy Spirit the name, "God," because the Scriptures do
not do so. Rufinus' translation is more wordy, but captures the sense of the
Greek; he adds the gloss at the end, "He who gave it to you to believe will also
give it to you to confess your faith" (CSEL 46.150). Augustine, however, alters
Rufinus' *et Dei vocem dari vobis a sancto Spiritu deprecabimur*, "and we will pray
that the word, 'God', be given to you by the Holy Spirit," which conveys the
meaning of the Greek. What Augustine reads instead is, *et Deus vocem dari vobis
a sancto Spiritu deprecabitur*, "and God will be asked [a rare non-deponent use of
deprecor] that a voice be given you by the Holy Spirit." Augustine proceeds to
interpret the passage, which in Gregory asks that his opponents be given a
language, or the willingness to use a language, appropriate to what they believe
about the Holy Spirit, as if it instead were commending to believers that they
pray for the power to proclaim their faith. See the notes in Lesousky, *The De
dono perseverantiae*, 286–87, and by M.J. Chéné, BA 24, 831–35.

of predestination, which was preached by the apostles and which we defend so laboriously and carefully against the new heretics. Nevertheless, when they were preaching obedience and were fervently exhorting everyone to practice it to the best of their ability, it would not with any justification have been said to them, "If you do not wish that obedience, to which you enkindle us, to grow cold in our hearts, then do not preach to us that grace of God, by which you confess that God grants that which you are exhorting us to do."

20.(51) For this reason, if the Apostles and the teachers of the Church who succeeded them and followed their example have done both of these things, namely, have both truly preached the grace of God, which is not given according to our merits, and taught a pious obedience to the salutary precepts, how does it happen that these brothers of ours believe themselves rightly constrained by the invincible force of truth to say, "Even if what you say about the predestination of God's favors is true, it nevertheless must not be preached to the people"?[193] Indeed it must be preached, so that "he who has ears to hear may hear."[194] But who has them, if he has not received them from him who says, "I will give them a heart to understand me, and ears which hear"?[195] By all means let him who has not received them reject [the Word], while he who receives, let him take and drink, let him drink and live. For, just as piety must be preached, so that by him who has ears to hear, God may be rightly worshipped, and chastity must be preached, so that by him who has ears to hear, no illicit act may be committed with the sexual organs, and charity must be preached, so that by him who has ears to hear, God and neighbor may be loved, so also it is necessary to preach this predestination of God's favors, so that he who has ears to hear may glory, not in himself, but in the Lord.

(52) Our brothers say, "It was not necessary to trouble so many hearts of people of less intelligence with the obscurity of this kind of disputation, [1026] since the catholic faith has been

193. See Prosper, *Ep.* 225.3, and Hilary, *Ep.* 226.2.
194. Luke 8.8.   195. Bar 2.31.

defended to no less advantage for so many years without the benefit of this doctrine of predestination, at first against others, then especially against the Pelagians, in so many books by other catholic authors as well as your own earlier books."[196] I am quite astonished that they say this; that they give no attention (to pass over the works of others here) to the books that I wrote and published even before the Pelagians began to appear; and that they fail to see how in so many places in those treatises I was destroying the future Pelagian heresy, of which I was ignorant, by teaching of grace, whereby God sets us free from our evil errors and habits, without any preceding merit on our part, accomplishing this through his gratuitous mercy. I began to realize this truth more fully in that treatise which I wrote to Simplicianus of blessed memory, the bishop of the Church of Milan, at the beginning of my own episcopate, when I recognized and affirmed that even the beginning of faith is a gift of God.[197]

(53) And which of my works has been able to be more widely and agreeably known than the books of my *Confessions*? Although I also published this work before the Pelagian heresy arose, certainly I said in it to God, and said often, "Give what you command, and command what you will."[198] When these words of mine were quoted one day at Rome in Pelagius' presence by a fellow bishop and brother of mine, Pelagius was not able to bear them and, attacking them with considerable emotion, came close to fighting with him who had quoted them.[199] Yet what does God command first and foremost but that we believe in him? And this, therefore, he gives, if it is well said to him, "Give what you command." And also in this same work, when I recounted my conversion, how God converted me to that faith which I was laying waste with most miserable and raging loquacity, do you not remember how I told the story in such a way as to show that it was granted to the faithful and

196. Hilary, *Ep.* 226.8.   197. See *De praed. sanct.* 3.7–4.8.
198. *Conf.* 10.29.40, 10.31.45, 10.37.60. The *Confessions* date from 397–401.
199. On the identity of this bishop, see Introduction to *De nat. et gr.*, p. 12, note 51, above.

daily tears of my mother that I should not perish?[200] Certainly, I taught there that God, by his grace, converts men's wills, not only those turned away from right faith but also those turned against it, to that faith. And how I besought God for growth in perseverance, you know, and you can review when you wish.[201] But all the gifts of God which in that work I either requested or praised, who would dare, I do not say to deny, but even to doubt, that God foreknew that he would give them, and could never have failed to know to whom he would give them? This is the evident and certain predestination of the saints, which necessity later compelled me to defend more carefully and laboriously when I was already arguing against the Pelagians. For I have learned that each particular heresy raises in the Church its own peculiar challenges, against which the holy Scripture is to be defended more carefully than if no such necessity required. What compelled me to defend more fully and precisely by this labor of mine those passages of Scripture in which predestination is commended, if not the fact that the Pelagians say that God's grace is given according to our merits? And what else is this but a complete denial of grace?

21.(54) Therefore, in order to destroy this doctrine, which is displeasing to God and opposed to the gratuitous benefits of God by which we are [1027] delivered, I defend, in accordance with the Scriptures, from which I have already cited numerous texts, the position that both the beginning of faith and perseverance in it to the end are gifts of God. For if we say that the beginning of faith comes from us and that by it we merit to receive the other gifts of God, then, the Pelagians conclude, the grace of God is given according to our merits. And this view the Catholic faith so abhors, that Pelagius, fearing lest he be condemned, himself condemned it. And again, if we say that our perseverance is from ourselves, not from the Lord, they respond that we have the beginning of faith from ourselves, just as we have the end, arguing as follows: If we have the

200. See *Conf.* 3.11.20–12.21, 8.12.30.
201. The reference is probably to *Conf.* 10.28.39–43.70, where Augustine reviews his state of soul at the time of writing. This constitutes, in effect, an extended prayer for perseverance.

power, of ourselves, to continue to the end, all the more do we have from ourselves the beginning of faith, since it is a greater thing to complete a work than to begin it. And thus they repeatedly conclude that the grace of God is given according to our merits. But if both are gifts of God, and God has foreknown that he would give these gifts of his (and who can deny this?), it is necessary to preach predestination, so that the true grace of God, that is, grace which is not given according to our merits, may be defended by an insurmountable bulwark.

(55) And indeed, in the book titled, On Rebuke and Grace, which was not able to satisfy all my friends, I think that I set forth so clearly and evidently as (if my memory does not deceive me) I had never, or almost never, before written, that even perseverance to the end is a gift of God.[202] But it is not the case that no one before me has expressed this idea as I have in this present book. For the blessed Cyprian so explained our petitions in the Lord's Prayer, as I have already pointed out, as to affirm that in the very first petition we are asking for perseverance; he said this is what we pray for when we say, "Hallowed be thy name," although we have already been sanctified in baptism, so that we may persevere in that which we have begun to be.[203] But let those brothers, to whom as my admirers I ought not to be ungrateful, who profess, as you say, to embrace all my teachings except this one which has come into question[204]—let them see whether in the second part of the first of the two books which, at the beginning of my episcopate, before the Pelagian heresy appeared, I wrote to Simplicianus, the bishop of Milan, there remains anything which would provide grounds for calling into doubt that God's grace is not given according to our merits; and if I have not adequately established there that even the beginning of faith is a gift of God; and if from what is stated there it does not evidently follow

202. On De correptione et gratia, see Introduction to this and the preceding work. It was the failure of De corr. et gr. to convince his opponents that led Prosper to write to Augustine; see Ep. 225.2.

203. See above, 2.4.

204. Prosper, Ep. 225.9. Prosper here refers to Bishop Helladius (or Euladius) or perhaps to Hilary of Arles. On this question, see Introduction.

(even if it is not expressly said) that perseverance to the end is also given only by him who has predestined us to his kingdom and glory.[205] Besides, did I not publish some years ago that letter which I had already written to the holy Paulinus, the bishop of Nola, a letter which my opponents have recently begun to contradict?[206] Let them consider also the letter which I sent to Sixtus, priest of the Church at Rome, when I was engaged in the sharpest conflict against the Pelagians, and they will find that is like the letter to Paulinus.[207] From those they may realize that these things which now, amazingly enough, displease them, were said and written already a number of years ago against the Pelagian heresy. Nonetheless, I should not wish anyone to embrace all my views [1028] so as to follow me, except in those matters in which he has perceived that I have not erred. For at this moment I am writing a treatise in which I have begun to reconsider my works,[208] in order to show that I have not followed myself in all matters, but rather I think that, through the mercy of God, I have made progress in writing and did not begin at the point of perfection. For that matter, I would be speaking with more arrogance than truth if I were to say that even now, at my present age, I have arrived at perfection, in writing without any errors. But it makes a difference to what extent and in what matters one has erred, and how easily one corrects one's error, or with what obstinacy one attempts to defend it. Certainly there is high hope for a man, if the last day of this life finds him making such progress that whatever was lacking in his progress is supplied to him, and that he is judged as worthy to be perfected rather than punished.

(56) Therefore, if I do not wish to appear ungrateful to those men who have loved me because some profit came to them from my work before they loved me, how much more ought I to be unwilling to be ungrateful to God, whom we would not love unless he had first loved us and made us into lovers of him.

205. See *De praed. sanct.* 4.8.
206. This is *Ep.* 186, from Augustine and Alypius to Paulinus of Nola, written in 417.
207. *Ep.* 194, to Sixtus, written in 418.
208. The *Retractationes.*

For love is from him,[209] as have declared those whom he made, not only his great lovers, but also his great preachers. And what is more ungrateful than to deny the grace of God itself, by saying that it is given according to our merits? This is what the catholic faith was shocked at in the teaching of the Pelagians, and what it brought as a capital charge against Pelagius himself. But Pelagius condemned it, not indeed for love of the truth of God, but rather for fear of his own condemnation. And whoever, as a faithful catholic, is horrified to say that the grace of God is given according to our merits, ought not to withdraw that faith from the grace of God, by which he obtained the mercy to be faithful; and thus let him also attribute perseverance to the end to God's grace, by which one obtains the mercy which he asks for every day, that he should not be brought into temptation. But what mediate between the beginning of faith and the perfection of perseverance are those qualities by which we live rightly, which even my opponents agree are given by God and obtained through faith. But all these things, that is, the beginning of faith and the other gifts of God up to the end, God foreknew that he would grant to those whom he called. It is overly contentious, therefore, to deny predestination or to harbor doubts concerning it.

22.(57) However, predestination is not to be preached to the people in such a way as to give the impression, to the many who are ignorant or slow to comprehend, of being somehow in contradiction with the very preaching of it, just as also [belief in] the foreknowledge of God (which my opponents certainly cannot deny) seems to be undermined if it is said to men, "Whether you run or sleep, you will be what he who cannot be deceived has foreknown you to be." But it is the work of a deceitful or inexperienced physician to apply even a useful treatment in such a way that it either does no good or does harm. Instead it must be said, " 'So run that you may obtain [the prize],[210] and from your very running you will learn that you have been foreknown to be such as would run lawfully."[211]

---

209. Cf. 1 John 4.7.   210. 1 Cor 9.24.

211. An allusion to 2 Tim 2.5: "For he also who strives for the mastery is not crowned, unless he strive lawfully."

[1029] And the foreknowledge of God can be preached in any other way, so long as the slothfulness of men is warded off.

(58) It is quite true, then, that the set determination of God's will concerning predestination is such that some, who have received the will to obey, are converted from unbelief to faith or persevere in faith, while others, who remain attached to the delights of sins worthy of condemnation, even if they have been predestined, have not yet arisen, for the help of pitying grace has not yet raised them; for if any have not yet been called but have been predestined by God's grace to be elected, they will receive this grace, by virtue of which they may wish to be, and actually be, elected, but if any obey, yet have not been predestined to God's kingdom and glory, they obey only for a time, and will not remain in that obedience to the end. Now although these statements are true, they should not be presented to a multitude of listeners in such a way that they are applied directly to the listeners themselves and those words of our opponents, which you have included in your letters and I have inserted above, are said to them: "On predestination the set determination of the will of God is such that some of you, having received the will to obey, have passed from unbelief to faith."[212] What need is there to say, "Some of you"? For if we are speaking to the Church of God, if we are speaking to believers, why do we say that *some* of them have come to faith, and thus seem to do ill to the others, since we can more aptly say, "On predestination the set determination of the will of God is such that, having received the will to obey, you have passed from unbelief to faith and, having received perseverance, you remain in faith."

(59) Nor is what follows the above to be said at all, that is, "But others of you, who remain in the delights of sin, have not yet arisen, because the assistance of pitying grace has not yet raised you up," when one can and ought to say, well and fittingly, "But if any of you remain in the delights of sins worthy of condemnation, grasp the most wholesome discipline, but

212. Quoted above, 15.38. This passage does not appear in the letters of Prosper and Hilary that we possess.

when you have done this, do not be exalted as if by your own works, nor take glory as if you have not received this. 'For it is God who works in you, both to will and to accomplish, according to his good will.'[213] And your steps are directed by the Lord, so that you may choose his way.[214] But if you walk well and correctly, learn from this that you belong to the predestination of divine grace."

(60) Likewise, that which follows, "But if any of you have not yet been called, but God by his grace has predestined you to be elected, you will receive this grace whereby you will wish to be, and will be, elected," is said more harshly than it might be said, if we were to bear in mind that we are not speaking to men in general, but to the Church of Christ. For why is it not rather said thus: "And if any are not yet called, let us pray for them that they may be called"? For perhaps they have been so predestined that they will be granted to our prayers and will receive that grace, by which they will wish to be and will be made elect. For God, who has accomplished all that he predestined, has also willed that we pray for the enemies of the faith, so that we might understand from this that he gives even to unbelievers the grace to believe and makes those who were unwilling willing.

(61) Now, however, I would be amazed if any person in the Christian congregation who is weak in faith can in any way hear with patience the words which are joined to those just quoted, when it is said to them, "And from any of you who obey, if you have been predestined to be rejected, the strength to obey will be withdrawn, so that you will cease to obey." For to say this, what else does it appear to be than to curse, or in a certain sense to prophesy evil? But if it is desirable or necessary to say anything about those also who do not persevere, why should it not rather, at least, be stated as I did a short time ago,[215] in particular, so that this is said, not of those who listen in the congregation, but rather to them about others—that is, so that it is not said, "Any *of you* who obey, if you have been predestined to be

213. Phil 2.13.   214. Cf. Ps 36.23.
215. See above, 22.58.

rejected," but, "Any who obey," and so on, speaking in the third person and not the second? For something abominable, not something desirable, is said, and the audience is struck most harshly and hatefully, as if by a slap in the face, when one who speaks to them says, "And from any of you who obey, if you have been predestined to be rejected, the strength to obey will be withdrawn, so that you will cease to obey." What meaning does this lose, if it is stated thus: "But if any obey, yet have not been predestined to God's kingdom and glory, they obey only for a time, and will not remain in that obedience to the end"? Does this not express the same idea both more truly and more suitably, so that we do not seem as if we are wishing so great an evil upon them, but to be relating of others what our hearers hate and think does not pertain to themselves, hoping and praying for better things? But in that way in which our opponents think this must be said, the same statement, in virtually the same words, can also be declared of God's foreknowledge, which they are certainly unable to deny, so that it is said, "And any of you who obey, if you are foreknown to be rejected, you shall cease to obey." Beyond doubt this is most true; so it is, but also most outrageous, unsuitable, and unfitting, not because the language is false but because it is not healthfully applied to the well-being of human infirmity.

(62) But I do not think the manner which I have said should be used in the preaching of predestination should be sufficient for anyone who speaks before a congregation, unless he adds this or something like it, so as to say, "You, therefore, should also hope for this perseverance in obedience from the 'Father of lights,' from whom descends 'every best gift and every perfect gift,'[216] and ask for it every day in your prayers, and in so doing have confidence that you are not strangers to the predestination of God's people, for he himself grants even your doing of this. But far be it from you to despair of yourselves, since you are commanded to place your hope in him and not in yourselves. For 'Cursed be' everyone 'who places his hope [1031] in man.'[217] And 'It is good to have confidence in the Lord, rather

216. Jas 1.17.   217. Jer 17.5.

than to have confidence in man,'[218] for 'Blessed are all those that trust in him.'[219] Holding on to this hope, 'Serve the Lord with fear and rejoice unto him with trembling,'[220] for of life eternal, which God, who does not lie, has promised before all time to the children of promise, no one can be sure, until this life, which is a temptation upon earth,[221] is completed. But he will make us persevere in him to the end of this life, he to whom we say every day, 'Bring us not into temptation.' " When these and similar things are said, whether to small groups of Christians or to the multitude of the Church, why do we fear to preach the predestination of the saints and the true grace of God, that is, grace which is not given according to our merits, as the holy Scripture preaches it? Or indeed should we fear lest a man despair of himself, when it is shown that his hope must be placed in God, and not rather despair, if in an excess of pride and misery, he were to place that hope in himself?

23.(63) And would that those who are slow and weak in spirit, who cannot, or cannot yet, understand the Scriptures or the commentaries on them, would so listen, or fail to listen, to our discussions about this question, that they pay more attention to their prayers, which the Church has used and will always use, from its origins until the end of this world. For on this matter, which now against the new heretics I am compelled not only to mention but even to protect and defend, the Church in its prayers has never been silent, although at times in its discourses it has not thought it necessary to assert it explicitly, since it was under no pressure from an adversary.[222] For when was there not prayer in the Church for unbelievers and for its enemies, that they might believe? When has any one of the faithful had a friend, a neighbor, a spouse, who did not believe, and failed to ask on his behalf from the Lord for a mind obedient in the Christian faith? And who has ever failed to pray for himself,

218. Ps 117.8.   219. Ps 2.13.
220. Ps 2.11.   221. Cf. Job 7.1.

222. Augustine here articulates the theological principle of *lex orandi, lex credendi*, "the law of praying is the law of believing," the idea that the practice of the Church in prayer and liturgy is a norm of faith, a witness to the faith of the Church, perhaps not yet given expression in doctrine and theology. See Rahner-Vorgrimler, TD, art., "Lex Orandi, Lex Credendi."

that he might abide in the Lord? Or who, when the priest, in-
voking the Lord over the faithful,[223] says, "Give to them, O
Lord, to persevere in you to the end," has dared to criticize
him, not only in words but even in thought, and has not rather
responded to such a blessing of his, with believing heart and
confessing mouth, "Amen"? For in the Lord's Prayer itself, the
faithful pray for nothing else, especially when they say, "Bring
us not into temptation," but that they may persevere in holy
obedience. Just as, therefore, in these prayers, so also in this
faith was the Church born, does it grow, and has it grown, by
which faith it believes that the grace of God is not given according to the merits of those who receive it. For the Church
would not pray that faith be given to those who do not believe,
unless it believed that God converts to himself men's wills, both
those turned away from him and those turned against him. Nor
would the Church pray that it might persevere in the faith of
Christ, not deceived nor conquered by the temptations of the
world, if it did not believe that the Lord has our hearts in his
power in such a way that the good which we do not hold except
through our own will, we nevertheless do not hold unless he
works in us to will.[224] For if [1032] the Church indeed asks these
things from God, but thinks that these are given to it by itself,
then its prayers are not true prayers, but merely perfunctory—
and far be this from us. For who would truly lament, desiring
to receive what he prays for from the Lord, if he thinks that he
acquires it, not from the Lord but from himself?

(64) This is especially true, when we consider that, as the
Apostle says, "We know not what we should pray for as we
ought, but the Spirit himself pleads[225] for us with ineffable
groanings. For he that searches the hearts knows what is the

223. Augustine is referring to the "Prayer over the People," part of the dis-
missal rite in the ancient Roman liturgy, retained in the Lenten liturgy of the
Tridentine mass, and revived as the final blessing in the revised order of the
mass after the Second Vatican Council. See Jungmann, *The Mass of the Roman
Rite*, 2.427–32.
224. Cf. Phil 2.13.
225. Augustine's text here has *interpellat*, whereas the Vulgate reads *postulat*
(Douai: "asketh"). We follow Lesousky in translating, "pleads." The Gk is
ὑπερεντυγχάνει, a rare form translated in RSV and NAB as "intercedes."

mind of the Spirit, because he pleads for the saints according to God."[226] What does "the Spirit himself pleads" mean but "he makes to plead," "with ineffable groanings" but truthful ones, since the Spirit is truth? It is of this same Spirit that the Apostle in another place says, "God has sent the Spirit of his Son into our hearts, crying, 'Abba! Father!' "[227] And here, what does "crying" mean, if not "making to cry," by that figure of speech by which we call a day which makes people happy, a happy day? The Apostle shows this clearly elsewhere, when he says, "For you have not received the spirit of bondage again in fear, but you have received the Spirit of adoption of sons, in whom we cry, 'Abba! Father!' "[228] There he said "crying," but here, "in whom we cry," thus showing in what sense he said, "crying," that is, as I have explained above, "making to cry." By this we understand that this also is a gift of God, when with a sincere heart we cry spiritually to God. Therefore, let them be aware how mistaken they are, who think that it comes from us, and is not given to us, that we ask, seek, and knock; and who say that this is so, because grace is preceded by our merit, so that it follows after when, asking, we receive, and seeking, we find, and knocking, it is opened to us;[229] and who do not wish to understand that it also belongs to the divine gift that we pray, that is, that we ask, seek, and knock. For we have received "The Spirit of adoption of sons, in whom we cry, 'Abba! Father!' " And this the blessed Ambrose also saw. For he said, "And to pray to God pertains to spiritual grace, as it is written, 'No one says, "Lord Jesus," except in the Holy Spirit.' "[230]

(65) But all these gifts which the Church asks of the Lord and has always asked from the time of its origin, God so foreknew that he would grant to those whom he called, that he already gave them in predestination itself, as the Apostle declares without any ambiguity. For in writing to Timothy, he states, "Labor with the gospel according to the power of God who saves us

226. Rom 8.26–27.   227. Gal 4.6.
228. Rom 8.15.   229. Cf. Matt 7.7.
230. Augustine quotes these words also at *C. duas epp. Pel.* 4.11.30, where he identifies the source as Ambrose's *Commentary on Isaiah*. This commentary is lost. The passage quoted by Ambrose is from 1 Cor 12.3.

and calls us by his holy calling, not according to our works, but according to his own purpose and grace, which was given to us in Christ Jesus before eternal ages,[231] but is now made manifest by the coming of our savior Jesus Christ."[232] Therefore, let him say that the Church has at any time not maintained in its faith the truth of this predestination and grace, which now is defended with more painstaking care against the new heretics—let him say this, I say, who dares to say that at any time the Church has not prayed, or not prayed sincerely, either that unbelievers might believe or that believers might persevere. But if it has always prayed for these benefits, it has indeed always believed that they were gifts of God, [1033] nor was it ever right for it to deny that they were foreknown by him. And therefore the Church of Christ has never failed to hold the belief in this predestination, which belief is now being defended with new attentiveness against the new heretics.

Conclusion[233]

24.(66) But what more is there to say? I think I have sufficiently, or more than sufficiently, shown that both to begin to believe in the Lord and to remain in the Lord to the end are gifts of God. But the other good things which pertain to an upright life, by which God is rightly worshipped, even those on whose account I am writing this treatise concede to be gifts of God. Furthermore, they cannot deny that God has foreknown all his gifts and those upon whom he was going to bestow them. Therefore, just as other truths ought to be preached in such a way that he who preaches them may be heard with obedience, so predestination should be preached, that he who hears these things with obedience should glory, not in man, and consequently not in himself, but in the Lord. For this also is a precept of God, and to hear this precept with obedience, that is, "He

---

231. *Ante tempora eterna,* that is, "from all eternity." Vg reads, *ante tempora saecularia* (Douai: "before the times of the world").

232. 2 Tim 1.8–10.

233. This is a conclusion to this book and *De praed. sanct.* jointly.

that glories, let him glory in the Lord,"[234] is, like the rest, a gift of God. I do not hesitate to say that he who does not have this gift possesses in vain whatever other gifts he has. We wish that the Pelagians may have this gift, and that these brothers of ours may have it more fully. Therefore, let us not be quick in argument and slow in prayer. Let us pray, dear friends, let us pray that the God of grace may give even to our enemies, but especially to our brothers and admirers, to understand and confess that after the great and unspeakable catastrophe in which we all fell in one man, no one is delivered except by the grace of God, and that grace is not rendered according to the merits of those who receive it, as if it were something owed, but rather is freely given as true grace, with no merits preceding.

(67) There is no more outstanding example of predestination than Jesus himself, a subject concerning which I have already argued in the first book[235] and which, at the end of this book I have chosen to emphasize. There is, I say, no more outstanding example of predestination than the mediator himself. Let whatever believer who wishes to understand predestination well consider him, and in him he will also find himself. By "believer" I speak of one who believes and confesses that in Christ there is a true human nature, that is, our nature, but uniquely elevated, by its assumption by God the Word, into the one Son of God, in such a way that he who assumes and that which he assumes are one person in the Trinity. Nor was a quaternity made when the man was assumed, but the Trinity remained, for that assumption resulted, in an ineffable way, in the truth of one person in God and man. [1034] For we do not say that Christ was only God, as the Manichaean heretics say.[236] Nor do we say he was only man, as the Photinian heretics say.[237]

---

234. 1 Cor 1.31.   235. De praed. sanct. 15.30–31.

236. For the Manichaeans, Christ was a heavenly being (an "Aeon"), an offspring of the Father of Lights, who appeared in our time to set souls free, but did not have a body of real flesh, since flesh was essentially evil. See Augustine, De haer. 46, and Bonner, St Augustine, 161, 167–68.

237. Photinus (d. 376), a pupil of Marcellus of Ancyra, was bishop of Sirmium in Asia Minor from 344–351. His Christology appears, from the fragmentary references to it in ancient writers, including Augustine, to have resembled that of Paul of Samosata, bishop of Antioch, deposed in 268, who taught

Nor do we say he was a man in such a way that he lacked any of the characteristics which certainly belong to human nature, whether that he lacked a soul, or that in this soul he lacked a rational mind, or that his flesh was not taken from a woman, but made from the Word converted and changed into flesh—all three of which false and vacuous notions have constituted three separate and distinct groups of the Apollinarian heretics.[238] But we declare that Christ is true God, born of God the Father without any beginning in time, and that the same Christ is true man, born of a human mother at the determined fullness of time,[239] and that the humanity, by which he is less than the Father, does not diminish in any way his divinity, by which he is equal to the Father. But both of these are one Christ, who both as God most truly said, "I and the Father are one,"[240] and as man most truly said, "The Father is greater than I."[241] Therefore, he who created this man from the seed of David, in a state of justice, so that he never would be unjust, without any merit of his preceding will, he also makes just men out of unjust, with no merit of their preceding will, so that that man might be the head and these others his members. And he who brought it about that that man, with no preceding merits on his part, neither contracted from his origin nor committed by his will any sin which could be forgiven him, he also brings it about that,

that the Word of God abided in Jesus in such a way that there was no union of the human Jesus and the divine Word in one person, and Jesus was different from the Prophets only in degree. See *De haer.* 44–45, and the note by Chéné, BA 24, 835–36. In *Conf.* 7.19.25, Augustine says that he himself, as a catechumen and perhaps even later, held a view of Christ similar to that which he ascribes to Photinus.

238. Apollinaris (or Apollinarius) (c.310–c.390), bishop of Laodicea and friend of St. Athanasius, representing an extreme form of Alexandrian Christology, sought to safeguard the divinity of Jesus by holding that in him the Word of God replaced the spiritual part of his human soul. He held that a human person consisted of body, soul, and spirit, and in Christ the Word of God took the place of the spirit, or rational part of the soul (Quasten, *Patrology* 3.382). His opinion was condemned by the First Council of Constantinople in 381. The threefold division of Apollinarists found here is also found in *De haer.* 40 and more or less agrees with a text from the *Panarion* of Epiphanius (c. 315–403) which Augustine cites in *C. Iul. op. impf.* 4.17.

239. Cf. Gal 4.4.   240. John 10.30.
241. John 14.28.

without any preceding merits of their own, people believe in him, people for whom he forgives all sin. He who created that man such that he never had and never would have an evil will, he also makes in this man's members a good will out of an evil one. And therefore he predestined both him and us, because both in him, that he might be our head, and in us, that we might be his body, God foreknew not our merits which would precede, but his own works which were to be.

(68) Let those who read this work, if they understand it, give thanks to God, but let those who do not understand it pray that he, from whose face comes knowledge and understanding, will be their inner teacher.[242] But those who think I am in error, let them consider carefully again and again what I have said, lest perhaps they themselves be in error. But when through those who read my works I become not only wiser but also more accurate, I acknowledge God's favor to me, and this I look for especially from the teachers of the Church, if what I write comes into their hands and they deign to take notice of it.

242. Cf. Prov 2.6.

INDICES

GENERAL INDEX

Abel, 28–29, 52, 55–57, 134
Adam, 134, 136, 175; perseverance
of, 185, 193, 213; sin of, 15, 28,
99, 134–36, 171, 175, 188, 191,
201, 209, *see also* original sin
Altaner, B., 109
Alvarez, D., 188n
Alypius, 3, 11, 97, 326n
Ambrose, 12, 20, 25n, 79–81, 198,
236, 285–86, 301, 318–20, 333
Ambrosiaster, 10, 25n, 28n
angels, 281
apatheia, 17
apocatastasis, 119n
Apollinarians, 336
Apollinaris, 336n
Arbesmann, R., 72n
Arles, 186–87
Athanasius, 50n
Atticus, bp. of Constantinople, 103
Augustine: attitude toward Pelagius,
3, 6, 14–16, 26, 157–58, 160–62;
and controversy at Hadrumetum,
181–85; and controversy in
Provence, 185–99; developments
in theology of grace of, 10–11,
181–85, 223–28, 323–26; opposition to Caelestius, 12–14; opposition to Pelagius, 14–16, 92–99,
101, 182; relations with Orosius,
93; relations with Pelagius, 12, 97,
108, 157–62, 166–67
Augustine, works: *Ad Simpl.*, 10–11,
25n, 182, 194, 198, 222n, 226–27,
283n, 303n, 323, 325; *C. duas epp.
Pel.*, 112n, 293n, 296n, 333n; *C.
Iul.*, 53n, 111, 296n; *C. Iul. op.
impf.*, 53n, 187, 234n, 336n; *Conf.*
5n, 11, 198, 323–24, 336n; *De civitate Dei*, 43n; *De corr. et gr.*, 184–
86, 190, 198, 201, 213, 214n,

236n, 268n, 281n, 325; *De dono
pers.*, 11–12, 69n, 80n, 184, 186,
193, 199, 236n, 254n; *De dono
pers.*, date of, 186–87, relation to
De praed. sanct, 193, synopsis of,
195–99, text of, 271–337, title of,
193; *De Gen. ad litt.* 53n; *De gest.
Pel*, 3n, 5, 6, 7, 12n, 13, 14n, 15n,
27n, 93–110, 220n, 277n, 296n;
De gest. Pel., date of, 98–99, synopsis of, 103–9, text of, 111–77,
title of, 103; *De grat. Chr.*, 17, 99,
101n; *De grat. et lib. arb.*, 183–84,
216; *De haer.*, 187, 335n, 336n; *De
lib. arb.*, 16, 20, 84–87, 181n, 197,
214, 293–97; *De mor. eccl.*, 5; *De
nat. et gr.*, 3–21, 97, 105n, 108,
133, 134n, 157–59; *De nat. et gr.*,
synopsis of, 18–20, text of, 22–90;
De ord., 4n; *De pecc. mer.* 6, 14, 32,
50, 136; *De pecc. or.*, 9n, 13n, 99n,
103, 128n, 134n; *De perf. iust.
hom.*, 57n; *De praed. sanct.*, 186,
193, 199, 271n, 272n, 273n, 276n,
284n, 287n, 288n, 305n, 312n,
323n, 326n, 335n; *De praed. sanct.*,
date of, 186–87, relation to *De
dono pers.*, 193, synopsis of, 193–
95, text of, 218–70; *De sermone Domini in monte*, 69n; *De sp. et. litt.*,
14, 57n; *De Trin.*, 234; *Ep.* 102,
194, 210, 238–40, 288; *Ep.* 146,
14, 108, 160–62; *Ep.* 157, 12n,
15n, 94, 95, 105, 135; *Ep.* 166, 93;
Ep. 175, 97, 100; *Ep.* 176, 97, 100;
Ep. 177, 3n, 98, 100, 111n; *Ep.*
179, 3, 98, 111n; *Ep.* 186, 3, 98,
326; *Ep.* 191, 182n; *Ep.* 194, 181–
84, 326; *Ep.* 214, 183; *Ep.* 215,
183; *Ep.* 216A, 183; *Ep.* 4*, 98,
119n; *Ep.* 19*, 97, 111n, 189n;

Augustine, works: (cont.)
  Enchiridion, 254n; *Propp. ex Ep. ad Rom.*, 194, 210–11, 224–26; *Quaestiones in Heptateuchum*, 89n; *Retr.*, 14, 21, 85n, 103, 109–10, 184, 186, 194, 216, 224–27, 284n, 293–95, 326; *Sermo* 131, 101; *Sermo* 294, 14–15, 136–37; *Sermo* 315, 221n
Aurelius, bp. of Carthage, 13, 14, 97, 111, 135, 169
Avitus, 152n

Bañez, D., 188n
baptism, 9, 139; of infants, 9, 12–13, 15, 102, 295, 299, *see also* infants
basilica, 250n
Basilica Maiorum, 136
Bavel, T. van, 69n
believing, 222
Bonner, G., 13–14n, 15, 24n, 50n, 93, 95, 100n, 138n
Briccius (Brictius), bp. of Tours, 95
Brown, P., 4, 5, 6–7, 10, 16, 96
Bruyne, D. de, 69n
Burkitt, F., 69n
Burns, J. P., 182–84, 198–99n, 303n

Caelestius, 7, 12–14, 95–96, 97, 99–103, 105–8, 134–38, 140–43, 153–55, 157, 167–69, 171, 173–76, 247n
Cain, 55–56
call, of God, 195, 225; congruous, 11, 182, 303n; of the elect, 256–64; twofold, 256
Campagna, V., 21
Carthage, 14; Conference of 411 (with Donatists), 12, 136n, 138, 157; synod of 411 (Caelestius), 12–13, 94, 95, 105–6, 135–36, 157, 171; synod of 416, 97; Council of 418, 102–3, 247n
Cassian, John, 181, 185–91
Cassiciacum, 4, 10
Castro, T. de, 200
Celestinus, bp. of Rome, 103
Chadwick, H., 82n
Chadwick, O., 186–90, 191n
Chaeremon, Abbot, 190

charity, 34, 74, 89, 184, 225
Charus, 96, 98, 166
chastity, *see* continence
Chéné, J., 187n, 199
children, *see* infants
Christ, *see* Jesus Christ
church, 106, 138–40, 173
Clement VIII, Pope, 188n
commandments, 88–89, 106–7, 140–41, 173
Constantius, 102
continence, 306, 311–13
conversion, 182–84, 192, *see also* faith, beginning of
Cornelius, 232–33
Cresconius, 183
Ctesiphon, 16
Cyprian, 15, 112n, 137, 195, 196, 198, 223, 227, 231, 248, 251–52, 274–81, 305, 313, 318–19, 325
Cyril of Alexandria, 98

David, 214, 268
death, as consequence of sin, 41–42, 102, 134, 136, 175; timely, 195, 196, 248–53, 287, 290
deification, 50
Demetrias, 5, 16
devil, 69, 120, *see also* Satan
Diospolis, Synod of (416), 13n, 14, 15, 95–100, 103–110, 111–56, 163–76, 197, 220, 247n; verdict of, 156, 170, 298; *see also under* Pelagius
Divjak, J., 97–99
Domnus, 152n
Donatists, 4, 12n, 102, 106, 136, 138, 157
dualism, 192, 196, 285, 294–95, 297
Duval, Y.-M., 3n, 12n, 17n

eagles, 128–29
election, 182, 191, 201–8, 214, 224–25, 231–32, 256–64, *see also* call, predestination
Elizabeth, 53, 80
Eno, R., 97–98, 119n
Ephesus, Council of (431), 103
Erce Osaba, G., 109
Esau, 182, 283–84n

eucharist, 277, *see also* liturgy
Eugippus, 193
Euladius, *see* Helladius
Eulogius, bp. of Caesarea, 95, 97, 111n, 120
Eustochium, 100, 176n
Evagrius of Pontus, 17, 50n
Evans, R., 4, 7–10, 16, 17n, 82n, 112n, 127n
Evodius, bp. of Uzalis, 12n, 97, 181, 183
evil, 104, 122–23

faith, beginning of, 182, 192–95, 210, 220–23, 237, 264–70, 276, 324–25, *see also* conversion; as grace, 11, 147, 182–83, 193–95, 211–270 *passim*, 219–38, 244, 264–70, 276, 310, 315, 324; as merit, 147, 191, 205, 209–11, 225; and works, 147, 211, 225–26, 232–33, 242–44
fatalism, 192
fate, 296
Faustus of Riez, 188
Felix, companion of Florus, 181, 183
Felix, monk of Hadrumetum, 183
Ferguson, J., 4n, 12, 95, 100n, 101–3
flesh, and spirit, 19, 67–76
Florus, 181, 183–84
foreknowledge, God's, 191–92, 194–95, 197, 201–8, 210–12, 239–43, 260, 262, 264, 288–89, 302, 311; and preaching, 307–8, 327–28; and predestination, 316–19; *see also* predestination
free will, Augustine on, 10–11, 183, 227; Caelestius on, 155, 175; Massilians on, 203–4, 210; not sufficient for salvation, 57–58; Pelagius on, 8, 66, 104, 115–19, 172

Gennadius, 189
Goldbacher, A., 199
Good Thief, 190
grace, Augustine on, 11, 21, 24–26, 181–85, and *passim*; Caelestius on, 141–42, 175–76; Cassian on, 185–

91; of conversion, *see* conversion; of creation, 68–70; of faith, *see* faith; not free will, 142–43; not knowledge of law, 131–33, 141–43, 166, 172; not according to merit, 107, 146–54, 174, 182, 184, 197, 220–21, 223, 225, 244, 250, 253, 274, 283, 295–96, 297, 310, 324, 325, 327; and nature, 22–90 *passim*, 30, 61, 66, 131–34, 141–43, 157–58, 166, 230; operative, 183–85; of perseverance, *see* perseverance
graces, diversity of, 144–46, 173–74
Gregory of Nazianzus, 198, 320–21
Griffe, E., 95n, 187n, 189n

Hadrumetum, 181, 183–84, 274n
Hagar, 124–26
Hanson, R., 5, 6
Helladius (Euladius), bp. of Arles, 187–88, 208n, 325n
heresy, 128–30, 171, 324
Heros, bp. of Arles, 95, 97, 101, 112, 152, 172
Hilary of Arles, 186–87, 208, 325n
Hilary, of Marseille, 186–88, 190–93, 218; letter of, 209–17, Augustine's reply to, 218–337
Hilary of Poitiers, 20, 78–79
Hilary of Sicily, 15, 94, 95, 105, 135, 138n, 163
Holmes, P., 20, 109, 149n, 162n
Holy Spirit, 74, 80, 90, 116, 118, 182, 198, 198–99n, 211, 234, 254, 320–21n, 332–33
Honorius, Emperor, 102, 136n

ignorance, as effect of sin, 86–87, *see also* sin, effects of; sins of, 34–35, 85–86, 154–55, 175
immaculate conception, of Mary, 53n
infants, 115, 134–36, 175, 283–84, 286; baptism of, *see under* baptism; hypothetical merits of, 191–92, 194, 204–5, 245–53, 289, 298–300; salvation or damnation of, 28, 102–3, 184, 194, 196–97, 204–5, 214, 292, 295–300

Innocent, bp. of Rome, 94, 97–98, 100–101, 176–77n, 247n
Innocentius, priest, 97

Jacob, 182, 258, 283–84n
James, correspondent of Augustine, 3, 22, 133, 157–60
Januarianus, 183n
Jerome, 5–7, 13n, 16–17, 20, 50n, 82n, 83–84, 93, 95, 97, 98, 126n, 127n, 249n; attack on monastery of, 100, 109, 176–77
Jesus Christ, able to die, 41–42; divine and human natures, 253–55, 335–37; as physician, 18, 19, 38, 43–44, 51, 72, 210; predestination of, 195, 199, 253–56, 335–37; as savior, 37–38, 57; work of, Pelagius on, 9
Job, 78–79
John, bp. of Jerusalem, 16, 93–94, 95, 97, 98, 101, 111n, 150–52, 164–65, 177n
John Chrysostom, 20, 82, 109
Jovinian, 16
Julian of Eclanum, 7, 101, 103, 202, 247n
justice, 22

kingdom of heaven, 123–26, 172

Lactantius, 20, 77–78
La Tullaye, J. de, 20, 109
law, 13, 134, 136, 175; knowledge of, 104, 112–15, 172
Lazarus, bp. of Aix, 95, 97, 101, 112, 152, 172, 189n
lector, 250
Leontius, 200, 217
Lérins, 187
Lesousky, M. A., 188n, 199
Letter, P. de, 199
lex orandi, lex credendi, 331
limbo, 102, 247n
liturgy, eucharistic, 52, 301, 332
Livania, 126n
Lod, 95, see Diospolis
Lopez, E., 200
Lord's Prayer, 196, 273–81, 325, 332
Lucan, 129n

Lydda, 95, see Diospolis

Mani, 126
Manichaeans, Manichaeism, 4, 5, 7–8, 10, 123n, 186, 197, 293–97, 335
Marcellinus, 12n, 14, 32, 50, 136
Marcion, 123n, 126
Marseille, 185, 187, 189, 200, 209
Martin of Tours, 95
martyrdom, 196, 273
Mary, mother of Jesus, 19, 53–54; immaculate conception of, 53n; sinlessness of, 53–54
mass (massa), human race as, 11, 25, 182
mass, liturgy, see liturgy
Massilians, 189–93, 200–17, 218–20
Maxsein, A., 21
Melania, 5
Mercator, Marius, 5, 12n, 13n, 101, 126n
merit, see under faith, see under grace; merits, hypothetical, 287, 289, 291, 299, see also infants, hypothetical merits of
Molina, L. de, 188n
monastery, Augustine's, 308
monasticism, 4–5, 188
Monica, mother of Augustine, 11, 323–24
Morris, J., 5n
mortification, 243–44
Moses, law of, 8, 9
Myres, J., 5n

nature: human, 18, 22–25, 58–68, 72–76, 131–32, 212, 228–31; and grace, see under grace; see also sinlessness, possibility of
Neo-Platonism, 10
Nestorius, bp. of Constantinople, 103
New Testament, 124–26, 293
Ntedika, J., 119n

obedience, as gift, 305–6
Old Testament, 105, 123–26, 172–73, 293–94
Orange, Council of (529), 189n
Origen, 16, 17, 119–20, 249n

Origenism, 93, 104, 120
original sin, 12–13, 14, 28, 191, 201, 209, 212, 274, 289, 296, see also Adam, sin of; effects of, 24–26, 38–51, 188, 190, 246–48, 294, 297
Orosius, 6, 50n, 93–94, 95, 97, 127n, 150n, 152

Pagels, E., 13n
Palestine, 16–17, 93–101, 103
Parsons, W., 199
Passerio, 97, 152n
Paul, Apostle, 107, 144–54, 174, 190, 197
Paul of Samosata, 335–36n
Paula, 176n
Paulinus of Milan, 12–13
Paulinus of Nola, 3, 6, 12n, 98, 326
Pelagianism, Pelagians, 4, 7, 200, 201, 207, 244, 246–49, 253, 262, 274, 277, 293–99, 310, 323–24, 326–27; response to, summarized, 274; see also Pelagius
Pelagius, 3–10, 93–110, 188, 247n; after Diospolis, 96–97, 99–103, 108; character, 6; condemned by Innocent, 100; conflict with Jerome, 16–17; before John of Jerusalem, 94, 150–51, 165; as layman, 6; letters ascribed to, 96, 108, 126–28, 130–31, 163–66, 174–75; as monk, 5–6; as moralist, 7; in Palestine, 16–17, 93–103; paper (chartula), 96–97, 108, 111, 166–69; relations with Augustine, 3, 11–12, 14–16, 97, 157–62, 323; relations with Zosimus, 101–3; theology of, 7–10, 99; trial at Diospolis, 14, 95–97, 103–8, 111–56, 163–76, 220, 298–99, 310, 324, 327
Pelagius, works: Book of Testimonies (Liber capitulorum, Liber eclogarum, Liber testimoniorum), 95–96, 104, 112, 117, 127n, 163–64; commentaries on Paul, 10, 14, 138n, 151; De lege divina, 6; De libero arbitrio, 17, 99; De natura, 3–4, 15–16, 17, 22–90, 97–98, 100, 105, 133, 142,

154, 157–59; De vita christiana, 127
Pelikan, J., 53n
perfection, Christian, 4, 6
perseverance, defined, 271–72; grace of, 184–85, 192–93, 196–99, 271–302, 310, 324–25; and preaching, see predestination, and preaching
Photinus, 335, 335–36n
physician, see under Jesus Christ
Plinval, G. de, 10, 20, 98, 100n, 109, 127n, 151
Pliny, 129n
Porphyry, 210, 238
posse, velle, esse, 99
possibility, of not sinning, see sinlessness, possibility of; of sensing, 62–63
Possidius, bp. of Calama, 97
prayer, for faith, 331, 334; for perseverance, 282, 316, 331, 334, see also Lord's Prayer
Praylius, bp. of Jerusalem, 101
predestination 154, 174, 182, 185, 188, 190–95, 197–99, 200–208, 256, 260–64, 281–83, see also election, see also faith, as grace; as based on foreknown faith, 201–8, 210–12; defined, 302–3; and foreknowledge, 240–43, 316–19; and preaching, 197–98, 202, 206, 207, 209, 212–13, 302–34
pride, 19, 46–50
Priscillianism, 93
Proba, 5
Prosper of Aquitaine, 95n, 103, 185–88, 190–93, 199, 216, 218; letter of, 200–208; reply to, 218–337
Provence, 185–93
punishment, eternal, 98, 104, 119–22, 172
purgatory, 104, 119n

Quasten, J., 77n

rebuke, 184
Rees, B., 187n
rich people, 15, 135–36, 175
Rome, 12, 101–2

Rufinus, correspondent of Prosper, 185

Rufinus of Aquileia, 119n, 320–21n

Rufinus the Syrian, 7, 12–13

Sabinus, 183

Sallust, 22n

salvific will, God's, 190–91, 201, 203, 205, 214, 236

Sarah, 123–26

Satan, 45, *see also* devil

Saul, 214, 268

"Semi-Pelagians", 181, 188

Sentences of Sextus, 20, 21, 50n, 82

Sicilian Anonymous, 7, 15

Sidon, 196, 288–91, 303–4

Simplicianus, 10, 182, 226–27, 323, 325

sin, as effect of sin, 19, 38–43; effects of, on human nature, 19, 35–51, 86–87; nature of, Pelagius on, 18, 35–51; not a substance, 18, 36–37, 43, 82; *see also* Adam, sin of; *see also* original sin

sinlessness, actuality of, 51–58, 116, 127, 131, 134, 137–38, 173; possibility of, 8, 17, 18, 19, 27–35, 94, 105, 126–34, 135, 137, 150–51, 163–66, 173, 274, 277–78; possibility of, not based in human nature, 58–68, 72–76; possibility of, texts from Christian authors, 76–87; Scriptural examples of, 51–58, 116, 134, 137–38; through knowledge of law, 112–15

Sixtus, bp. of Rome, 181–82, 326

Thagaste, 10

Theodotus of Antioch, 103

Timasius, 3, 22, 133, 157–60

Trapè, A., 109

Trinity, 234

twins, 182, 196, 283–84, 292

Tyconius, 10

Tyre, 196, 288–91, 303–4

Urba, C. F., 20, 109

Valentinus, Abbot of Hadrumetum, 181, 183–84, 274n

Vandals, 189

Vergil, 218

Vincent of Lérins, 188

virginity, 106, 140–41, 173

Volpe, I., 109

Wallis, R., 199

Wermelinger, O., 13n, 100n, 102n

wisdom, 33–34; as grace, 312–15

Wisdom, Book of, 212, 248–53, 312

Xystus, bp. of Rome, 20, 21, 82–83

Zechariah, 80

Zosimus, bp. of Rome, 6, 95n, 101–3

Zumkeller, A., 200

Zycha, J., 20, 109

INDEX OF HOLY SCRIPTURE

Books of the Old Testament

Genesis
1.4: 257
3.5: 47
4.17: 56
5.4: 56
17.5: 241
21.10: 124
25.23: 256
32.25–33: 258

Exodus
20.17: 78

Leviticus
4.2–3: 35, 155
4.13–14: 155
4.22–23: 155
4.27–28: 155
19.2: 274

Deuteronomy
30.2: 89
30.14: 88–89

1 Samuel
8.57–58: 269
10.25–27: 268

1 Kings
8.46: 27
19.18: 317

1 Chronicles
12.18: 268

Job
7.1: 249, 300, 301
14.4 (LXX): 27

Psalms (Vulgate numbering)
2.1–2: 257–58
2.11: 331
2.11–13: 49
2.13: 331
8.3: 292
11.2: 65
13.1: 245
13.3: 27
16.4: 89
18.5: 23
22.6: 48
24.7: 154–55
24.10: 232, 292
24.17: 84
25.2: 280
27.9: 116
29.7–8: 42, 45
36.5–6: 47–48
36.23: 268–69, 329
40.5: 36, 65
43.19: 48
58.11: 48, 116, 147, 260
58.12: 118
65.9: 280
68.23: 231
70.5: 41
79.18–19: 282
83.6: 301
84.7: 221, 236, 280
84.8: 49
85.11: 49
91.2: 48
99.3: 147
100.1: 295, 304
101.5: 37

103.25: 216
106.20: 159
108.18: 117
117.8: 330–31
118.36: 268, 286, 301
118.73: 34–35
118.118: 79
118.133: 31, 143
126.1: 151, 233
138.10: 49
139.9: 118, 280
142.2: 59, 76

Proverbs
2.6: 312, 337
2.20: 89
8.35 (LXX): 80, 225, 231, 269, 320
20.9 (LXX): 122
20.24: 269
21.2 (LXX): 269
26.11: 308

Ecclesiastes
7.21: 27

Song of Songs (Canticle of Canticles)
4.8 (LXX): 147

Wisdom
1.11: 32
4.7: 249
4.11: 195, 212, 248–53, 291
7.1–7: 116–17
7.16: 306

347

8.21: 312
9.15: 64

Sirach (Ecclesiasticus)
3.22: 298
10.9: 65
10.14: 47
10.15: 46, 47
15.17–18: 117
18.30: 79
19.16: 115, 129
23.6: 118

Isaiah
6.9–10: 231
8.20 (LXX): 112, 172

9.2: 205
29.14: 58
45.11 (LXX): 241
54.13: 233, 235
57.16: 287
59.20–21: 257
65.2: 316

Jeremiah
9.23–24: 228
17.5: 219, 316, 330
32.40: 273, 282
38.31–32 (=31.31–32 Vg): 124

Baruch
2.31: 269, 306, 322

Ezekiel
11.19: 234, 269
18.24: 249
36.27: 244, 269

Daniel
7.18: 105, 123, 124, 172

Hosea
2.24: 205

Habakkuk
2.4: 242

Malachi
1.2–3: 224

Books of the New Testament

Matthew
1.21: 37, 38, 296
4.16: 205
5.8: 83
5.44: 236
6.8: 308
6.9–13: 274–81
6.10: 236
6.12: 52, 76, 85, 138, 139, 166
6.12–13: 35
6.13: 68–69, 75, 85, 131, 143, 278–81, 316
6.14: 52
7.7: 333
7.7–8: 203
8.22: 40
9.12: 23
9.12–13: 37, 38
9.13: 23
10.19–20: 143
10.20: 33
10.22: 272
10.29: 298–99
11.21–22: 288–91
11.30: 88
13.11: 267, 304, 306
13.13: 306
13.24–30: 138

19.10: 141
19.11: 141, 306
20.14–15: 284
20.16: 259
21.9: 54
22.11–13: 121
22.14: 121
23.35: 56
25.10–12: 121
25.33: 121
25.34: 201
25.46: 119, 172
26.41: 33

Mark
6.34: 116
10.46–52: 73
13.20: 225
14.38: 51, 75

Luke
1.3: 80, 319
1.6: 80
8.8: 306, 322
9.53: 320
10.30–35: 60, 67
11.9–10: 203
12.37: 49
13.25–27: 121
14.16–20: 256

16.22–26: 72
18.1: 304
19.20–24: 121
19.27: 121
22.32: 148

John
1.1: 309
1.12: 83, 286
1.14: 68
3.5: 28
5.14: 275
5.21: 27
6.28–29: 232
6.29: 233
6.36–37: 233
6.39: 259
6.43–45: 233–37
6.45: 259
6.54: 247
6.61–62: 237
6.64–66: 237
6.66: 267, 302, 306
10.30: 336
11.43–44: 27
12.37–40: 303–4
13.34: 89
14.1: 302, 304
14.6: 48
14.28: 336

14.30–31: 42
15.5: 48, 79
15.13: 89
15.16: 259–61, 265
16.12: 309
18.9: 302

Acts of the Apostles
1.2: 225
4.12: 57
4.24–28: 257–58
4.28: 268
9.1–19: 221
10.4: 232
13.48: 269
14.10: 144–45
16.14: 268
28.3: 144

Romans
1.1–4: 254–55
1.21–31: 39–40
1.24: 118
1.28: 241
2.11: 299
3.23: 25, 58
3.23–24: 23
3.24: 25
4.5: 23, 44
4.6: 146
4.12: 242
4.16: 241, 243
4.20–21: 222, 242
5.5: 34, 60, 74, 80, 82, 83, 84, 89–90, 225
5.12: 28, 57, 58, 297
5.12–16: 293
5.18: 58
6.12: 56, 74, 78
6.13: 56
6.14: 227
7.7: 132
7.7–8: 131
7.7–25: 227
7.12–13: 131–32
7.14: 227
7.14–16: 132
7.15: 65, 86, 133
7.18: 65, 66, 132, 133

7.19: 65, 86
7.20: 79
7.22–23: 73, 74
7.23: 43, 69, 81, 166
7.24: 173
7.24–25: 68, 69, 71–73, 131, 132, 172
7.25: 60–61, 75, 76, 78, 80, 83, 84, 88, 90, 114, 133, 171, 244, 298
8.7–8: 34
8.9: 186
8.13: 243
8.14: 116, 117, 244
8.15: 333
8.24–25: 64
8.26–27: 332–33
8.28: 264
8.28–29: 118, 256
8.29–30: 26
8.30: 260, 300, 311
9.8: 125, 225
9.10–29: 227, 283
9.11: 225
9.12: 256, 265
9.13: 224
9.14: 250, 290
9.14–21: 192, 202–3
9.16: 148, 151, 161, 225, 250, 291
9.18: 235, 292
9.19: 211, 235
9.20: 235, 238, 254, 284, 298, 307
9.21: 11, 25, 202, 206
9.22–23: 118, 235
9.23: 25, 234, 296
9.25: 205
10.1: 236
10.2–3: 22
10.2–4: 48
10.3: 58
10.4: 22, 58
10.8: 89
10.9: 209–10, 243
10.14: 23, 232, 304–5
10.17–18: 23

10.21: 316
11.2: 198, 316–17
11.4: 317
11.5: 224, 258
11.5–6: 231
11.5–7: 317
11.6: 146
11.7: 258
11.7–10: 231
11.17: 258
11.25–27: 256–57
11.28: 257–59
11.29: 256, 264, 265, 300, 305, 310, 311
11.33: 232, 238, 292, 298, 304
11.34: 250, 295, 307
11.35–36: 220
12.3: 147, 210, 223
12.10: 34
12.16: 300
13.8: 89
13.10: 89
14.4: 285
14.23: 147, 242

1 Corinthians
1.12: 228
1.17: 26, 29, 35–36, 57–58
1.18: 235–36
1.19: 58
1.21: 58
1.23: 256
1.24: 256
1.27–31: 228
1.31: 149, 229, 238, 250, 263, 292, 295, 305, 311, 334–35
2.2: 61
2.16: 117
3.1–2: 309
3.2–7: 228–29
3.5–7: 306
3.10: 306
3.10–15: 119
3.11–12: 119
3.15: 119, 120, 172
3.21: 229, 263

4.6–7: 229
4.7: 42, 147, 194,
    211–12, 223–24,
    227–28, 228–33,
    313
5.17: 24
7.7: 141, 306
7.25: 140, 221, 226
9.24: 327
10.12: 243, 285, 292,
    300
10.13: 287
11.19: 171
12.3: 333
12.6: 211, 225
12.9: 225
12.11: 244
12.17: 145
12.28: 107, 144–46,
    149
13.5: 122–23
14.18: 145
15.9: 149–50, 174
15.9–10: 152
15.10: 150, 151, 164
15.21: 171
15.54: 173
15.55: 166
15.57: 148
16.8–9: 266–67

2 Corinthians
2.12–16: 267
3.5: 221–22, 285,
    286, 300–301
3.6: 125, 131
4.13: 61, 225, 234
4.16: 83
5.10: 245–46
5.21: 31
6.1: 150
12.7–9: 44–45
13.3: 80, 319

Galatians
2.16: 232
2.21: 23, 24, 29, 58,
    131
3.5: 68
3.16: 258

3.23–24: 31
3.24: 23
4.6: 333
4.21–22: 124
4.23: 125
4.24–26: 124
4.26: 125
5.4: 58
5.6: 147, 286
5.11: 58
5.17: 65, 67, 68, 73,
    165
5.17–18: 74
6.7: 265, 273
6.17: 218

Ephesians
1.3–12: 261–63
1.4: 201, 240, 260,
    287, 291, 302, 317
1.4–11: 195, 196,
    282–83
1.5: 295
1.6: 264
1.11: 264–65, 281–
    82, 287
1.13–16: 265
1.23: 282
2.3: 81, 87
2.3–5: 24–25
2.8–9: 232
2.9–10: 241
3.19: 165
4.8: 84
5.14: 40
5.27: 106, 138–40,
    277
6.23: 223, 225, 315

Philippians
1.6: 302
1.19: 143
1.29: 196, 220, 272
2.8: 255
2.12–13: 45, 49, 300
2.13: 236, 263, 302,
    329, 332
3.1: 218
3.12: 154
3.15–16: 219

Colossians
1.13: 295
3.1–2: 301
3.25: 254, 299
4.2–4: 266
4.3: 267

1 Thessalonians
2.13: 266
3.2: 230
3.5: 280
5.21: 57

1 Timothy
1.5: 89
1.8: 88
1.15: 26, 38
1.20: 45
2.4: 159, 203–4, 236
2.5: 44, 61, 83, 245,
    253
2.7: 144
4.1: 144

2 Timothy
1.8–10: 334
1.12: 148
2.5: 327
2.13: 64
4.7–8: 147–48

Titus
1.12: 224
3.5: 25, 28

Hebrews
4.15: 31
5.14: 203
11.6: 242
12.2: 256

James
1.5: 35, 312
1.5–6: 34, 314
1.13: 280
1.14: 280
1.17: 314, 330
1.25: 74
2.5: 260
3.2: 34, 129

3.8: 18, 32–34
3.10: 33
3.13: 121
3.13–17: 33
3.14–16: 314
3.15: 26
3.17: 314
4.7: 75

1 Peter
  2.10: 205
  3.17: 272

2 Peter
  1.4: 108, 155, 175

1 John
  1.8: 32, 50–51, 54,
    79, 88, 138, 139
  2.19: 259, 285, 286–
    87
  3.2: 166
  3.5: 54
  3.9: 32
  4.7: 327
  4.18: 74
  5.3: 98

Lightning Source UK Ltd.
Milton Keynes UK
UKHW010047010323
417836UK00004B/47